# Political Parties in the European Community

Robert Charles
June 1991
Fletcher School.

Political and Economic Planning
*(now Policy Studies Institute)*

STATE ENTERPRISE: BUSINESS OR POLITICS?
*by David Coombes*

WOMEN IN TOP JOBS
Four Studies in Achievement
*by Michael Fogarty, A. J. Allen, Isobel Allen and Patricia Walters*

THE CONTAINMENT OF URBAN ENGLAND
Urban and Metropolitan Growth Processes or Megalopolis Denied — *Volume One*
The Planning System: Objectives, Operations, Impacts — *Volume Two*
*by Peter Hall, with Ray Thomas, Harry Gracey and Roy Drewett*
(Now available as a one-volume paperback)

PARLIAMENTARY SCRUTINY OF GOVERNMENT BILLS
*by J. A. G. Griffith*
(Jointly with the Study of Parliament Group)

THE LOCAL GOVERNMENT ACT 1972: PROBLEMS OF IMPLEMENTATION
*by Peter G. Richards*

THE POWER OF THE PURSE
The Role of European Parliaments in Budgetary Decisions
*by David Coombes et al.*

INNOVATION AND PRODUCTIVITY UNDER NATIONALISATION
The First Thirty Years
*by Chris Harlow*

PLANNING AND POLITICS
The British Experience 1960–76
*by Michael Shanks*

European Centre for Political Studies
European Cultural Foundation

# Political Parties in the European Community

*edited by*
Stanley Henig

GEORGE ALLEN & UNWIN
POLICY STUDIES INSTITUTE

First published in 1979

GEORGE ALLEN & UNWIN LTD
40 Museum Street, London WC1A 1LU

Policy Studies Institute
(formerly Political and Economic Planning and
Centre for Studies in Social Policy)
1–2 Castle Lane      ·eet
London SW1E 6DR


© George Allen & Unwin (Publishers) Ltd, 1979

**British Library Cataloguing in Publication Data**

Political parties in the European Community
  1. Political parties – European Economic Community
  countries
  I. Henig, Stanley   II. European Centre for Political
  Studies; European Cultural Foundation
  329'.02'094     JN94.A979     78–40902


ISBN 0–04–329024–8
ISBN 0–04–329025–6 Pbk

Typeset in 10 on 11 point Plantin by Northampton Phototypesetters Ltd
and printed in Great Britain
by Unwin Brothers Limited, Old Woking, Surrey

# Contents

# Acknowledgements

The research for this book was undertaken with the help of a grant from the Nuffield Foundation. It is published as part of the programme of the European Centre for Political Studies, a new research centre established in the Policy Studies Institute (formed through the merger of PEP and the Centre for Studies in Social Policy), with the sponsorship of the European Cultural Foundation. Editor and authors owe much to the great number of party officials, politicians, civil servants and academics who have given advice, information and assistance. The editor also owes a great deal to the unstinting help of the staff of the PSI.

S.H.
November 1978

# I
# Introduction

## STANLEY HENIG

During the ten years that have elapsed since the preparation of
the earlier PEP study,[1] academic interest in political parties has
continued to develop. In addition to work on national party
systems and individual parties, there have also been some significant contributions to the study of party in general.[2] Much
attention has been given in particular to examining sources of
electoral support[3] and the means by which parties mobilise
activists and voters. Such considerations have a special relevance
in the Western European context with the decision by member
governments of the Communities to proceed to direct election of
a European Parliament. Inevitably these elections and the Parliament which emerges from them will be dominated by parties.
Conceivably these will be emergent supranational parties drawing
support from all or many of the member countries. Even if this
turns out not to be the case, those living in the Community are
going to need to know a great deal more about the operation and
functions of parties in other member countries. This has helped
determine our decision to base this book, which can be considered
as both a second edition of, and a sequel to, the earlier work,
on just the nine member countries of the European Communities.
Economically these countries are increasingly integrated, with a
customs union, a common agricultural policy, common commercial policies, joint social and regional programmes and increasingly intertwined monetary arrangements. Internal and
external pressures are also combining to add a degree of political
integration of which the Political Co-operation Machinery and
the direct election of the European Parliament are the two most
visible symbols.

Parties stand in a special relationship towards movements for
European integration – they are subject as well as object – and
this will be explored later in this chapter. Compared to the earlier

book a relatively greater amount of space will be devoted to the European Parliament, the functioning of political groups therein and the European links of national parties – activity which may form the prehistory of Communitywide parties. The rest of the book is divided as before into national chapters containing analyses of party systems and assessment of the operation, structure and function of the major individual parties. Considerations of space preclude repetition of a great deal of the detailed historic material on the individual parties, for which reference to the earlier work is still necessary. In this respect our purpose has been to recount the party political history of the last decade and to update material on party membership, finance, electoral support and internal power structure. This shift in emphasis means that, more than before, the prime focus will be the operation of each party system, its interaction with the electoral system and its impact on government in the nine countries. Defining a framework for analysis is the purpose of the rest of this chapter which will examine the role of parties in democratic countries and the special tasks they are required to fulfil when societies are being integrated.

According to Walter Bagehot, the British Cabinet was 'a hyphen which joins, a buckle which fastens, the legislative part of the state to the executive part of the state'.[4] This serves as an apposite introduction to a consideration of the function of parties in democratic states and it may have even wider implications. A political party may be defined as *a group, however loosely organised, which seeks to gain political power through bringing about the election or appointment of governmental office holders under a given label.*[5] 'Governmental office holders' is a vague term covering a wide variety of roles – legislative, executive, administrative and even judicial – in respect of which there are major differences in party function. As far as political parties operating in democratic systems are concerned, the first two categories, legislative and executive, are critical. In all the European democracies considered in this book it is a function of parties to recruit members of national legislative assemblies or parliaments: indeed, it is normal for party membership to be a necessary condition for entry into these bodies.[6] Political parties are also the normal source of the executive. At the time the earlier study was being written the French presidential system seemed an obvious exception. President de Gaulle owed little to any party for his personal position and he paid only limited attention to party claims when appointing to other executive positions. Much of the frustration of the political parties during the Gaullist years arose from their being denied the opportunity of fulfilling a normal function.

There has been a gradual change under de Gaulle's successors and this seems likely to continue. However charismatic they may be, presidential candidates have some need of parties to help in their own campaigns whilst it is increasingly unlikely that non-political cabinets will be able to secure the necessary legislative acceptance of their programmes and policies. It is much less easy to discern a clear pattern when it comes to recruitment for posts in the administration. In some systems, such as the United Kingdom, considerable efforts are made to insulate the civil service from any party political pressures. Whilst no European country has imitated the United States in formally making high-level appointments the preserve of an incoming administration, political placing in the administration is an accepted part of the political process in Italy and France. Finally, in none of the nine countries are senior judicial appointments political in origin and any attempt to attach a party label would normally be considered improper. Again this contrasts with the position in the USA where the appointment system lends a great deal of importance to the general political stance of aspirants.

Parties are buckle and hyphen because they ensure that members of a government and their supporters in parliament are bound together by certain common theories and policies if not by a complete, coherent programme. Parties are central to the process of interest aggregation: the bringing about of sufficient consensus on major political, economic and social questions for stable government to· be possible. In one-party states interest aggregation takes place within and through the single mono-lithic, if heterogeneous, party. In democratic countries where by definition more than one party operates, a useful distinction can be made between those with two *majoritaire*[7] parties or groupings alternating in power and those operating a multi-party system where coalition between two or more groups is the norm. In the two-party system a great deal of interest aggregation takes place within each major group and alternation in power is brought about by the fact that both will be appealing to a very wide range of opinions and sectoral interests.[8] In multi-party systems individual parties may be more homogeneous in composition and outlook, whilst a great deal of interest aggregation takes place through the process of coalition. In both cases the parties serve as one channel of communication between government and governed.

There is a traditional view that one function of parties is to educate the public. Despite the development of the mass media they do still act as a forum and catalyst for political discussion, concentrating between and within themselves much of the public controversy about the desirable goals of government. Depending on the degree of politicisation, which varies among the nine countries, this process involves a large number of people in apparently helping to determine the course of public policy. Theoretically the parties making up the government should be able to ensure that policies reflect the wishes and needs of a large part of society and they may also be a useful adjunct in making executive and legislative decisions widely acceptable.

Modern technology has given governments other, more direct means of communication with the public, but party systems are still a useful indicator of the degree of consensus which it has been possible to establish in society. Obviously any system may distort in a variety of ways the expression of public opinion which is itself an abstraction. President de Gaulle argued that the multifarious parties of the Fourth Republic reflected France as in a cracked mirror: they emphasised the points of disunity. The purpose of the shift to a presidential system was to find a means of embodying through one person the essential unity of the nation. In the USA this object has been achieved historically through one office, the presidency, and two loosely articulated heterogeneous parties; in France direct presidential election and a multi-party system with many permanent minority parties coexist uneasily. The party function in bringing about that degree of consensus needed to make government acceptable is particularly important in federations. It may be significant that in the USA the Civil War was preceded by the breakdown of all the national political parties. Another more recent case concerns the incipient West Indies Federation. Failure to produce any federal parties may not have been the ultimate cause of the breakdown, but it reflected the lack of any political consensus for achieving a new governmental system. Switzerland is Western Europe's only country with a genuinely federal history and tradition and the existence of political parties which cut across cantonal, ethnic and religious boundaries is a crucial stabilising factor.

This is the additional dimension involved in a study of political parties in the nine member countries of the European Communities. Integration involves the assimilation of both sectoral policies and governmental procedures. Through the Communities the nine are already part of a neo-federal system in which government functions are divided by treaty between national and various central authorities. Parties can be considered as simply one more object in the integration process, but their role is necessarily more creative if that process is to be successful. Interest aggregation and the establishment of a degree of consensus on major political, economic and social issues are critical in the formation and preservation of any political community – national or supranational, centrist or federal. So long as Europe's parties operate solely within the national milieu there can be no kind of political community in Western Europe. Development of the Communities to date has already necessitated some working links between various parties on a transnational basis. These can take different forms and the first direct elections will be an initial test, for their nature will reflect attitudes towards integration and will also influence future progress.

Complementing and superseding our earlier study, this book has three functions. It aims to give up-to-date information on the operation of the party system and the functioning of the parties in the nine member countries of the European Communities. It sets out to supply the material necessary for comparative considerations relating to Western European political parties. Finally, it examines the ways in which these parties are gearing their activities to the ongoing process of European integration.

## NOTES

1 *European Political Parties*, a PEP study edited by Stanley Henig and John Pinder (London, Allen & Unwin, 1969).
2 For example, Giovanni Sartori, *Parties and Party Systems: A Framework for Analysis* (Cambridge, Cambridge University Press, 1976).
3 Particularly David Butler and Donald Stokes, *Political Change in Britain: The Evolution of Electoral Choice*, 2nd edn (London, Macmillan, 1974); and Ian Budge, Ivor Crewe and Denis Farlie (eds), *Party Identification and Beyond: Representations of Voting and Party Competition* (London, Wiley, 1976).
4 Walter Bagehot, *The English Constitution*, various edns.
5 Cf. Leon Epstein, *Political Parties in Western Democracies* (London, Pall Mall, 1967).
6 The only exception in the nine countries is the House of Lords in Britain where party label remains a minor source for recruitment.
7 A French term to signify parties which aspire to majority status: the logical opposite of minority parties.
8 There are two-party systems where each party tends to appeal to an exclusive demarcated group or series of groups. One result may be that one party always governs, the groups it represents being the larger. This is the case in Trinidad. Permanent exclusion of a large identifiable minority from access to political power may have implications for long-term political stability.

# 2
# Belgium

## XAVIER MABILLE AND
## VAL R. LORWIN

'Everything is mixed here, that which is old and that which is new. Red is the only colour which is lacking in the mixture,' wrote the exiled Prince Metternich to his daughter from Brussels.[1] A century and a quarter later, one may still recall the old reactionary's words about a very different Belgium. Every country's political life is indeed a mixture of the old and the new, but that of each country and each period of history is unique. The Tindemans government which took office in mid-1977 offers a good vantage point from which to look at the politics of a nation which is still an interesting mixture of the old and the new and of all colours.

One familiar element of the mid-1977 government was its multiparty character; since universal equal male suffrage was introduced in 1919, there have been only four years of one-party government (and those not very successful). Another was the presence of the two chief political forces of the country, the Social Christian (Catholic) Party and the Socialist Party. The former had been in almost every government of the century, and the latter more often in government than in opposition. The cabinet showed once again the numerical pre-eminence and the governmental vocation of the Christian Socialists, as well as the dominance of the Flemish wing within that party. But the cabinet's formation had also recalled the divergences between the Flemish and French-speaking wings of the party. Finally, the process of setting up the cabinet had illustrated the moderation and pragmatism of Belgian parties, and the habit of 'concertation' – round-table discussions by which political parties and socio-economic groups have produced solutions to pressing problems.

One new element in the government was the presence of all three of the new regional and linguistic parties, now known in

Belgium as the 'community parties'. Two of the three were in government for the first time. Another new element was a 'community pact', by which the five coalition partners agreed on general principles for the 'definitive' establishment of the new institutions of two cultural communities and three regions, as called for by the 1970 revision of the nation's constitution.

Since we cannot hope that generally informed English-language readers will have much acquaintance with the politics of the smaller European democracies, we first recall a few features of the political structure of Belgium. Then we discuss the political system, and the constellation of political parties and political issues, notably the language and regional issues which have dominated the last fifteen years of national politics. After a discussion of party coalitions and the electoral system, we consider each of the parties in turn, paying special attention to the social and regional bases of its support.

The cultural communities are the Flemish- and the French-speaking. (The correct speech of the Flemish population is Dutch, although local dialects persist.) There is also a very small German-speaking community. The regions are Flanders, the Dutch-speaking, northern provinces; Wallonia, the French-speaking, southern provinces; and Brussels, bilingual in public services because it is the nation's capital, but with an overwhelming majority of French speakers, and with some of its French speakers spilling over into suburban and ex-urban Flemish areas surrounding Brussels. Of nearly 10 million inhabitants (of whom well over half a million are foreigners), 56 per cent live in Flanders, 32 per cent in Wallonia and 11 per cent in Brussels. Since less than 1 per cent live in the German-speaking area of eastern Belgium, this must be their last appearance, except in one table, in this chapter.

THE POLITICAL SYSTEM

Since the early 1960s, Belgians have been gradually turning the unitary state created by the revolution of 1830 and the constitution of 1831 into a federal state. Exactly how, and even whether, the political system would succeed in this creation of a new Belgian state, to replace the original centralised institutions and a labyrinth of temporary new institutions, remains to be seen. Belgians have been speaking for two decades of a 'crisis of the regime'. If it is indeed a crisis – overt at times, latent at others – Belgians have lived through those years without more than occasional, marginal violence.

The monarchy is an element of continuity. Fierce controversy divided the country over the person of the wartime ruler, Leopold III. But the institution survived intact, with the support of the Socialists whose general strike in 1950 forced the king's abdication. Under Leopold's discreet and conscientious son, Baudouin, the monarchy is again playing its constitutional role, and even finding a new vocation in the state moving towards federalism. The king symbolises a certain national unity above – or amidst – the diversity of languages and regions. He exercises a mediating and arbitrating function in designating the *formateur* of each new government in the complexities of the multi-party system.

The cleavages and affinities of social and economic and religious life are directly reflected in a dense network of social organisation, and in the politcal system. That system is still to a considerable extent based on the organisation of much of voluntary association, education, press and politics around 'spiritual families' founded on religious and ideological affinities and antipathies, a system which in Belgium and Holland (and elsewhere) has been called by the Dutch name *verzuiling* (Huyse, 1970; Lorwin, 1966) or 'segmented pluralism' (Lorwin, 1971). We shall use the English-language term.

The two main 'spiritual families' are Catholics and Socialists, both still marked by a century of struggle between church and lay forces, Liberal and Socialist, over the control of education and of public life. While Catholicism remains the only organised faith of any numerical consequence (there are very few Protestants), probably fewer than half the population are practising Catholics. Until recently one could speak of a Liberal 'spiritual family', but in the 1960s the Liberal Party ostentatiously abandoned its historic anti-clericalism, to woo conservative Catholics. At the same time the Liberals' new party was rent by linguistic conflict. What remains of Liberalism is hardly a spiritual family, but the representation of a section of the middle and upper-middle class and of a conservative orientation in terms of 'freedom of enterprise' on most economic issues.

Religious practice and religious vocations have fallen off in the past two decades, and the party of Catholicism has lost in both votes and internal cohesion. The ideologies of Catholicism and Socialism, and even more that of Liberalism, have lost much of their intensity, and their bearers pursue strategies which are no longer exclusive and aggressive as they once were. The most crucial and longest-lasting conflict, that over the school systems, has been in principle resolved, and in practice left to a process of recurring negotiation and compromise, somewhat like the *modus vivendi* reached with regard to recurring issues between labour and management. Segmented pluralism has led from conflict to organisation and counter-organisation, and thence to a form of accommodation. That accommodation is in the method of resolution, not in the cessation of conflict or of competition for public office and power.

The structures of segmented pluralism still stand, however blurred the distinctiveness and force of the ideologies which originally gave them their reasons for existence. The Socialist unions, co-operatives and friendly societies remain powerful. Catholic social organisations – those of the working class paralleling the Socialists' organisations, while others represent the middle classes and farmers – all likewise remain strong. The Catholic unions are unique in Europe in surpassing the Socialist unions in numbers and equalling them in influence. Most of these Catholic social organisations – with the conspicuous exception of many Walloon Catholic union members – support the Social Christian Party and the Catholic school system. Socialist and Catholic and Liberal institutions have been invested with public functions like social insurance, whilst many, such as the cultural groups, receive substantial public subsidy.

The difference between the Catholics and 'the others' continues to affect party politics, the schools, and appointments to other state and para-statal institutions. They even play a role within a new party, the Francophone Democratic Front, founded on the rejection of the old religious-ideological basis of politics, but pragmatic enough to give some recognition to segmented pluralism in the distribution of power within its ranks. The heritage of segmented pluralism, therefore, continues to separate Belgians from each other. But it also binds Belgians, within each spiritual family, across the frontiers of language and region and, in the case of Catholic political action, also across the frontiers of social class.

The multi-party system reflects the crisscrossing of the fundamental religious-ideological and social cleavages of Belgian society, which created the original three 'national' parties, and the linguistic and regional cleavages which have created the community parties and given increasing autonomy to the linguistic or regional wings of the older parties. (For the relative importance of the regions, see Table 2.4.) The Social Christian Party has become, at the national level, only a tenuous working alliance of its Flemish- and French-speaking wings. The Liberals have split into three practically autonomous regional wings. The Socialists alone maintain a strong national organisation programme, but only by quasi-federal arrangements in both the party and the Socialist trade union movement.

PARTY COALITIONS

No party has had a majority in the two houses of parliament (Senate and House party balances do not differ greatly) since the installation of equal male suffrage in 1919, with the exception of the 1950-4 legislature. Parliamentary arithmetic imposes coalition government, since the alternatives of minority government or extraparliamentary cabinets have found no favour in Belgium, except for two brief minority Social Christian cabinets, of a transitional nature, after elections in 1958 and 1974. The moderate and pragmatic nature of the political parties, and their capacity for compromise *à la belge*, as they like to say, have meant that since the war any party might be a coalition partner of any others. This quality we might refer to by a short and breezy term coined from the German, *Allgemeinkoalitions-fähigkeit.*

Compromise in coalition formation – though not necessarily in coalition accomplishment – is encouraged by the close relationship between the important arena of municipal politics and that of national politics. Municipal office is the usual training ground for national ambitions, and municipal political machines and preference votes are often the foundation of parliamentary and even ministerial careers. In many large communes (municipalities) and in the provinces, coalition government – fostered by proportional representation – prevails. Members of all parties have had the experience of being in local alliances with parties they opposed in parliament. Such experiences tend to foster a certain tolerance of the role of opposition, as well as the appetite for, and expectation of, office.

The traditional stability of electoral behaviour was shaken by the national elections of 1965 and 1968, which inaugurated the period with which we are specially concerned. These elections marked a rupture with the overwhelming domination of the national parties. They established the community parties as recognised features of the political landscape, as sources of competitive pressure upon the three national political formations, as contributors to policy formation, and soon as candidates for coalition posts. Despite many alarmed commentaries by Belgian and foreign observers, these parties were not 'extremist' in programmes or tactics; they played the parliamentary game. The first one to be invited to join a government did so in 1974, and the others did so as well in 1977.

Electoral changes since 1965 may be summarised in terms of four groupings of the parties: the three traditional political forces; the two main political forces of Belgium, Social Christians and Socialists; the community parties; and finally the socioeconomic

Left (or presumed Left), Socialists and Communists. (For election results, see Tables 2.1 and 2.2.)

The Social Christian, Socialist and Liberal Parties together received over 90 per cent of the vote in the 1950s and 1961. In 1965 and the following elections, they fell to less than 75 per cent, with a slight recovery to 78 per cent in 1977. During the 1950s, up to and including the election of 1961, the Social Christians and the Socialists together had the support of over 78 per cent of the electorate. Since 1965, their support has been in the neighbourhood of 60 per cent.

The rise of the community parties is of course the counterpart of the decline of the traditional parties. Along with the general reasons for the rise of regional and linguistic particularism in Europe in the past two decades, there are specifically Belgian reasons. The settlement of the traditional school quarrel, through mutual recognition of the legitimacy of both the Catholic and the official school systems, removed the chief argument for the political unity and separateness of Catholics, and left them more open to regional and linguistic political appeals. It also removed much of the ideological basis not only of Liberalism but also of Belgian Socialism, rooted as they were in anti-clericalism. Regional demands reflected a great postwar shift in the centres of economic dynamism and power. Flemish economic development made the elites of that region more self-confident and assertive; Walloon stagnation led to demands for regional autonomy as against a centre which was not sufficiently attentive to Walloon needs, and as against a Flemish majority whose numbers were now equalled by both its economic power and its self-organisation. For the first time now there were mass movements both in Flanders and in Wallonia, acting as pressure groups on the old parties as well as stimulating the organisation of new parties.

In 1961 the Flemish People's Party was still the only community party, winning just 3.5 per cent of the national vote. In 1965 it almost doubled that vote, while for the first time there appeared a Brussels Francophone list and two small Walloon lists prefiguring the Walloon Party. From 1968 on, the Flemish People's Party, the Francophone Democratic Front and the Walloon Party together won over 15 per cent of the national vote, reaching 22 per cent in the early 1970s but falling to 17 per cent in 1977.

The electoral break of 1965 indicated a diminished radicalisation on social and economic issues among the voters. Socialists and Communists together (the latter very weak since the immediate postwar period) drew about 40 per cent of the vote up to and including 1961. Since 1965, they have drawn about 30 per cent. These numbers, of course, cannot reveal anything about changing degrees of radicalism in the parties' programmes or behaviour. But there has been no great intensification of radicalism, despite some increased militancy of Socialist programme and language during the years of Socialist opposition between 1974 and 1977. The Communists have continued to be the tepid critics of both the Socialist Party and the social system.

Characteristic of the party system is the pre-eminence of a different party in each region, although none has a hegemony. The strongest, the Social Christians, lost their majority in Flanders in the landmark election of 1965, and have not come near to regaining it, although hovering around 40 per cent and reaching 44 per cent in 1977. In Wallonia, the Socialists lost their near-majority position in 1965, and have hovered around 36 per cent, with 39 per cent in 1977. In Brussels, the Francophone Democratic Front has taken the leading position since 1971, but with only 35 per cent that year, as in 1977.

THE ELECTORAL SYSTEM

The proportional representation characteristic of most Continental democracies prevails in Belgian elections at all levels. In national elections, Belgium uses the D'Hondt system (Hill, 1974; Senelle, 1974). The constituency is the electoral *arrondissement*, but parties may combine their results at the provincial level of the province for better utilisation of their remainders from the *arrondissement* level. Each of the nine provinces contains between two and five electoral *arrondissements*; the number of seats at stake in House elections varies from two in the smallest constituency to thirty-five in Brussels. With the number of House seats now fixed at 212, the constitution has since 1971 provided for redistribution of the number of seats to correspond to changes in population as shown by each decennial census.

The gap between proportions of votes and of seats is small. In 1968, for example, the largest party (the Social Christian) received 31·3 per cent of the votes and 32·6 per cent of the seats in the House. The smallest, the Communist Party, received 3·3 per cent of the votes and 2·6 per cent of the seats. The system does not encourage fragmentation to the same degree as the Dutch, but it has permitted the community parties to move rapidly from small beginnings to significant representation.

The Senate may be entirely altered in composition and functions by reforms now under consideration. At present its functions are the same as those of the House, but it is chosen by a combination of direct and indirect election, all on a PR basis. One hundred and six members are elected directly; fifty members are elected by the councils of the nine provinces, and twenty-five are co-opted by the other one hundred and fifty-six senators. All are chosen at the same time as, or immediately after, the House elections. The least-populated provinces have a slight over-representation because there is a minimum of three provincial senators per province. The co-opted senators were originally to be an elite which would, hopefully, raise the intellectual level of the Upper House. In practice, many are party worthies who failed direct election.

In national elections the voter may not split his vote between parties. He may either vote the 'head of the ticket', that is, the straight party ticket in the order to which the party presents its candidates, and in which the seats it wins will be assigned, or he may cast a vote of preference for some candidate placed below the head of the ticket. In recent years preference votes have taken on greatly increased importance. Party discipline to vote the 'head of the ticket' has weakened, even among the Socialists, once the most disciplined voters. In expensive personalised campaigns, many candidates, among both the 'bourgeois parties' and the Socialist Party, have sought preference votes by smug photographs and slogans of a banality hardly exceeded even in American elections.

Each election produces many new and unlikely slates, some serious single-issue slates and others mere fantasy. In the 1977 campaign these ranged from the Unified Feminist Party (2,481 votes in two House constituencies) to the Snow White and the Seven Dwarfs slate (495 votes in a single constituency). The extreme Right and extreme Left usually produce a number of minuscule parties. So far all have been ephemeral.

Primary elections, run by the parties and not by the state, used to be a significant feature of candidate selection by the three main parties in all the larger constituencies. In areas where Catholic socioeconomic groups were well integrated with the party, that is to say in Flanders, the slates were often simply the product of agreement among the leaders of farmers, labour and middle-class groups. In other areas, Social Christian slates emerged from hotly contested primaries. In large constituencies, as a study of Brussels Socialist primaries shows, the number of candidates was so large, and the state of political information so low, as to make it impossible for the average party member to make an informed choice. In all parties, the national organs or individual leaders intervene to issue general directives, to approve or modify local slates, or to resolve conflicts of personalities or groups.

In recent years there have been fewer primaries, partly because the campaign period has been shortened. The institution retains importance in the Walloon federations of the Socialist Party, where anti-establishment tendencies are strong. In other areas, tickets are made up mostly by sub-regional units of the parties or committees of 'wise men', subject as before to intervention by national party authorities. Voting is obligatory.

The penalties for non-voting are mild, however, and the high participation rate (95 per cent of registered voters in 1977) is the result of habit rather than constraint, although the latter may have helped determine the former. The protesting citizen, the careless and the utterly indifferent may still cast spoiled or blank ballots. In 1977 these amounted to 431,000, or 7 per cent of the total cast.

## THE SOCIAL CHRISTIAN PARTY

The Social Christian Party constitutes the largest political force of the country. Founded in 1945 it is heir to the old Catholic Party. The founders of the Social Christian Party affirmed their intention of 'deconfessionalising' political action, but the party has remained that of Catholic candidates and of the Catholic electorate. Despite the recent political mobility of that electorate, it is still its principal representative. The conclusion of the 'school pact' among the Social Christian, Socialist and Liberal parties in 1958 led to a considerable deconfessionalisation of political life. This coincided with – and was partly responsible for – the rise of the 'community problem', that of the relations among the language communities and the regions. The Catholic/non-Catholic cleavage did not disappear, but it remained for the most part latent.

The regional distribution of each party's strength is important in understanding its behaviour, its relations with other parties, and coalition politics. The Social Christians are the largest political force in Flanders, while in Wallonia they are second to the Socialists (and in the elections of 1965, 1968 and 1971 were only third). In 1977, 70 per cent of Social Christian voters were Flemish (see Tables 2.3, 2.4 and 2.5).

Strained relations between Flemish and Francophones in the party led to a decision of its 1965 convention to concede extensive autonomy to its two wings. Autonomy was carried further when in 1968 the Flemish Social Christian members of parliament insisted on the separation of the Flemish and French sections of the international Catholic University of Louvain. The demand expressed in the popular slogan 'Walloons, get out!' made a profoundly disagreeable impression on Francophone Catholic opinion. Not only was the university a great international institution, but it had been the training ground for most of the Catholic elites of Belgium. The Flemish Social Christians' insistence on the French section's moving to Francophone territory brought down the Catholic–Liberal coalition government, and the principle of separation won the day. Both the government and the Belgian episcopate, which administered the university, had to yield. (The French section was moved from Leuven to a new site at Louvain-la-Neuve, the new Louvain, not far from Brussels.)

Since 1968, the two wings of the once-national party have taken such a distance from each other on many issues as to constitute essentially two different parties. They have several organs in common, such as a research centre, a national treasurer and a general president; the last office has, however, remained vacant for years. The Flemish and Francophone Social Christians appeal as separate parties to the voters of each region, and they even have separate lists in the bilingual constituency of Brussels. But they manifest some solidarity and at least present themselves as one party when they negotiate with other parties and claim posts in government, for example in the election of co-opted senators and, most important, to claim the prime minister's post in the formation of a new cabinet.

The two wings of the Social Christian Party appeal to all sections of the population, from workers and farmers to storekeepers and industrialists, as do most religiously based parties elsewhere. This implies internal tensions and necessitates compromise as well as the need to give representation to different social groups in the designation of party officials, candidates for office and representatives in government.

The situation, however, differs between the two regions. The Flemish Social Christian Party is the representative of three clearly defined social milieux. One is that of Catholic workers, in the unions and other organisations, whose political activity is co-ordinated by the Flemish wing of the Christian Workers' Movement. Another is what the Belgians call the 'middle classes', mostly small businessmen and self-employed, whose organisation is the National Union of the Christian Middle Classes. The third is that of Catholic farmers, represented by the powerful Belgian Farmers' Union (Boeronbond). There is a strong articulation between these three groups and the party. Although the three groups are strongly differentiated, the tensions among them are only intermittent and generally surmountable. A certain number of party figures, moreover, are not identified with any one of these groups.

In Wallonia, tensions between an identifiable Right and Left are kept alive by greater social distance among different groups, and by the minority position of the Social Christian Party. In many electoral districts, it cannot hope to carry off more than a single seat in national elections. This makes it impossible to give different social groups a place on the electoral slate which will ensure each the election of an MP. The social groups are less well structured in Wallonia, and their integration with the Social Christian Party is weaker than in Flanders. For several years there has been something of a polarisation in the party between Christian Democracy, an alignment close to the Catholic labour organisations affiliated with the Francophone Christian Workers' Movement, and the Political Centre of Self-Employed and Cadres, which has loomed more and more as the organised right wing of the party. Yet a number of party leaders, including the two most recent presidents, refuse to be classed as members of any wing of the party.

Many Catholic workers do not identify with the party. Christian Democracy represents only a part of the Catholic working class in Wallonia and Brussels. Some of those Catholic workers refuse to recognise any political party as an adequate political representative; some are active in federalist parties; yet others are interested in a dialogue with the Socialists or even in co-operation with the Communists. At the upper end of the social scale, part of the right-wing Catholic electorate in Wallonia and Brussels has been attracted by the wings of the old Liberal Party, which have elected some Catholic personalities on their slates. In the Brussels agglomeration, the two Social Christian parties coexist in very different local situations in the various municipalities. Their relations there vary from co-operation to undisguised antagonism.

Since 1958 the Social Christians have been members of every government, as no other party has been. Even their setback in the important election of 1965, confirmed in the elections of 1968 and 1971, did not greatly erode their negotiating position; they kept their lead over the Socialists, the only other candidates for coalition leadership.

THE SOCIALIST PARTY

The relative strength of Socialist bases is the reverse of that of the Social Christians: second force in the country as a whole and in Flanders, but first in Wallonia. Socialist strength in Wallonia reflects a tradition based on early industrialisation and 'dechristianisation' of that area. The oldest modern industrial areas, especially the 'industrial furrow' from the coal-mining area of the Borinage to the coal and steel and heavy-metal fabricating areas around

Liege, are the most solid Socialist bastions. Victims, like the Social Christians, of the 1965 break in electoral continuity, the Socialists, unlike their chief rivals, have not improved their situation since, and have lost ground particularly in the Brussels area. The chief base of membership and voting support of the Socialist Party is among manual labourers and among white-collar workers of both private and public sectors. This is of course also the base of the Socialist-led trade union movement, the General Federation of Labour of Belgium, as well as the co-operative movement and Socialist friendly societies. The General Federation of Labour's recruitment is broader than that of the party since it includes Communists, supporters of the community parties, members of Trotskyite and Maoist groups, and some workers who are anxious to maintain the independence of the unions *vis-à-vis* all political parties. The unions alternate between close co-operation with, and criticism of, the Socialist Party, often depending on whether the latter is in the government or in the opposition: the latter role usually encourages union co-operation with the party.

Outside the milieu to which it has traditionally appealed – until the last war it was called the Workers' Party – the party has sought to get the hearing of the middle classes. There is even a Socialist organisation for the self-employed, but it has enjoyed little success. Like other parties, the Socialist Party has experienced the pressures of community problems. Its structure has resisted rather well, however. It has found in its vocation of representing workers of both language groups, and in the willingness of its Flemish sections to admit some federalist demands of its Walloon sections, factors of unity which have so far prevailed over those of division. The price of unity has included the recognition of two rival Socialist federations, one primarily Francophone and the other Flemish, in the Brussels electoral district.

Since the Second World War, the Socialist Party has been second to the Social Christian Party in the frequency and duration of its participation in national governing coalitions. Until the school pact, the Socialist Party allied either with the Social Christian Party, whose Christian Democratic wing was close to it on social and economic policy, or the Liberal Party, whose concern to defend the official school system against the Catholic schools it shared. After the school pact, however, in 1961, the Liberals transformed their party into one which was no longer anti-clerical but was anti-socialist. The Socialists could thereafter join with the Social Christians in an alliance all the more logical as many felt that only an alliance of the two principal political forces could carry out the necessary reform of institutions, and as others felt that the best guarantee of social peace was an alliance of the two parties associated with the two powerful trade union movements. But with the Social Christians alone, the Socialists were in a *tête-à-tête* with a stronger partner. To avoid this, they could join in a tripartite government, as they did in 1973 (with a very unsuccessful single year's duration), or demand the inclusion of the community parties without the Liberals, as they did in 1977.

The Socialist Party programme is one which stresses social change. None the less it is the Belgian party which has itself changed least, despite a recent rejuvenation of ageing leadership. The party would like to be the political expression of the whole working class. But the existence of the powerful Catholic unions, friendly societies, and co-operatives, closely integrated with the Social Christian Party in Flanders and in a relationship still fairly strong even with the Walloon Social Christian Party, denies that role to the Socialist Party, which has retained much of its tone of hostility to the church and even to religion. The party is therefore the prisoner of contradictory attractions and requirements. On the one hand, coalition practice would require it to respect the existing structure of its chief partner, the Social Christian Party. On the other hand, its hope of a redistribution of political forces, to achieve what its ideology declares to be its historic mission, cannot be realised except by the dissociation of the labour or Christian Democratic wing from the body of Catholic political action.

An appeal for the 'regrouping of progressives' has, since May 1969, been a recurrent theme in the public declarations of the Walloon Socialist leaders. In fact this appeal, addressed chiefly to the Christian Democrats, but also to Communists, progressive federalists and the independent Left, has met with little response. A climate of mutual suspicion continues to cloud relations between Catholics and Socialists. They have dense networks of competing socioeconomic organisations. The very different balance of power in the chief regions of the country makes regrouping on a national level difficult.

### THE LIBERAL PARTIES

Oldest of the Belgian political parties, the Liberal Party underwent a profound change in 1961, when it took the name of Party of Liberty and Progress. (Its followers continue to be called 'Liberals', however.) It repudiated its anti-clericalism, and opened its membership and even leadership to traditionally aloof or hostile elements, particularly right-wing Catholics alienated from the Social Christian Party by its collaboration with the Socialists.

In 1965 this strategy received a handsome electoral pay-off, with the Party of Liberty and Progress moving from twenty seats in the House to forty-eight. This was also a period in which the party stressed its attachment to the unitary concept of national institutions. However, failure to progress electorally in 1968, and differences of opinion about parliament's revision of the constitution in a federalist direction in 1970, created a malaise in the party. The result was a moving apart of the Flemish and Walloon wings. Each sought to meet the sentiment of their voters by taking up federalist positions. A further mutation occurred when, at the close of 1976, the Walloon Liberals joined with elements from the right wing of the Walloon Party to form the Party of Reforms and Liberty in Wallonia. (In our tables of election results, we have combined national results for all members of the 'Liberal family'.)

Liberal family members, however much they differ, generally share the desire to be in office. Curiously, the extent of the Liberal success in 1965 seemed to weaken the negotiating position of the Liberals in coalition formation thereafter. They participated in governments only between 1966 and 1969, and between 1973 and 1977. They had taken positions which meant that they had to be allied with the Social Christians, and could join with the Socialists only in a broad coalition, such as the 1973–4 tripartite government. In any case, parliamentary arithmetic no longer permitted a Socialist–Liberal coalition to govern as in 1954–8.

The structures of the Liberal world became rather fluid after 1968, but by 1977 there seemed to be a certain stabilisation, even in Brussels. The great majority of Brussels liberals were in the Liberal Party, which had in its ancient stronghold returned to the original name. The Francophone Liberals hostile to it no longer had any special representation of their own, and Brussels Flemish Liberals were in the party's Flemish sub-party. The three Liberal parties have a research centre in common and seem to have achieved a rapprochement. One of the remaining differences is in relation to what the Belgians call 'ethical problems'. Only the Flemish Liberals support liberalisation of laws on contraception and abortion, which have recently become political issues.

COMMUNITY PARTIES

The Flemish People's Party is the heir to the old tradition of Flemish nationalism, which has taken different forms since Belgian independence and which became party-forming between the wars. The party grew in electoral strength from 1958 to 1971, and since 1968 has had about 10 per cent of the votes nationally, and over 16 per cent in Flanders. Its chief demand has been for a federalism of two partners, the two language communities, in which Brussels would not be an independent third partner, thus avoiding a Belgium composed of two Francophone regions and Flanders. The party has also been the bearer of Flemish economic demands, and the still emotional issue of amnesty for those convicted of acts of collaboration with the enemy in time of war. It has at times been pulled between right-wing Flemish nationalism and a more socially progressive federalism. Another tension, not along the same lines, has been that between those elements in the party favouring participation in national government and those opposing it; at least temporarily, the former won out in 1977.

The Flemish People's Party has participated in pressure-group activities; joining with non-party elements of the Flemish movement, which include a wide variety of associations ranging from the cultural to single-issue associations and to *ad hoc* demonstration organisers. In such action, the party is quite different from the Flemish wings of the older parties. Unlike the Social Christians and Socialists, the Flemish People's Party does not have firmly structured social bases. By the time it appeared on the scene, the trade unions and middle-class and peasant groups of other political tendencies had already pre-empted most of the ground of social and economic organisation.

Liberal leaders have made a number of suggestions since 1974 as to the desirability of a 'centre regrouping' – around them, of course. Given the centrist nature of the main body of all six Belgian party formations, one wonders about the need or possibility of such a centre regrouping.

The Francophone Democratic Front was created in 1964 in the Brussels region at first essentially on a single-issue programme: the abrogation of the language laws of 1962–3. Passed by a Social Christian–Socialist government, these sought to meet Flemish criticism of 1930s legislation which had first recognised the equality of the Flemish language in the life of the nation and its capital. Specifically, the 1962–3 laws sought to assure Flemish speakers greater rights in education and in administration in the communes of the Brussels area, in ways which militant Francophones regarded as damaging their career opportunities in administration. Soon the party went on to develop a wide-ranging programme, and since 1970 it has formally advocated federalism. In every election since its creation, except for 1974, it has made gains. Drawing support from each of the three old spiritual families, the Francophone Democratic Front has recognised the value of balance among them within its own ranks.

Unlike the two other community parties, the Francophone

Democratic Front has solid local political bases. After the communal elections of 1970, it became the strongest party in Brussels, and it has been a member of a number of local governing coalitions since then. At the next communal elections in 1976 it won an absolute majority in half a dozen communes of the agglomeration, including several of the largest. It has become the party of a substantial number of burgomasters and aldermen, with the political base and experience those offices bring. The party's electoral following and its hold on municipal offices make it more than a passing phenomenon, and give it rather the quality of a structural element of the Belgian political scene.

The Walloon Party appeared in the national election of 1968, following on some smaller groupings which had elected two deputies in 1965. It won 10 per cent of the votes of the Walloon area in 1968 and almost twice as many in 1971. In communal elections, however, it had much less success, and it failed to develop important local bases. In 1974 the Walloon Party joined what had been a brief minority government created by the Social Christians and the Liberals. It was a marginal member, but with the Francophone Democratic Front outside the government, the ties which the two parties had created a few years earlier were severely strained. Government participation generated severe internal tensions in the Walloon Party. After its lack of success in the 1976 communal elections, the crisis broke into the open. Considering that some new initiatives of the party president and his followers were far too much to the left, three of its four leaders in the government and several MPs left the party and helped set up the new Liberal party, the Party of Reforms and Liberty of Wallonia. The party which went into the elections of 1977 was therefore very different from the party of the previous elections. Somewhat shopworn after its brief government experience and suffering heavy losses to the new Walloon Liberal party, it emerged, numerically, below its level of 1968.

THE COMMUNIST PARTY

The Communist Party represents a permanent minority current, which had its brief moment of popular following only in the immediate aftermath of the Second World War. Almost non-existent in Flanders, it has a significant following in some areas of Wallonia. It has tried to escape from political isolation in recent years in many ways. It has concluded some local electoral alliances with left-wing Catholics and independents of the Left. Except in a few localities, these electoral cartels have not paid off. Related to their concern to escape from political isolation, is the

Communists' care to play the parliamentary game according to the rules. They have also participated in a number of interparty efforts characteristic of the political system, for example, the 'community dialogue' of 1976–7.

Political leaders have for years spoken of the virtues of having a single government for the period of one parliament, and letting that parliament run out its full four years before it is dissolved. Between 1950 and 1965, three of the four parliaments had sat for four years. But between 1965 and 1977, all four parliaments were dissolved after only three years. Numerous have been the *formateurs* of governments who called for a coalition of the three major political families as essential to necessary changes in institutions. The broad coalition set up in 1977 omitted the Liberals. For the first time, however, it included the three parties dominant in each one of the three regions – the Flemish Social Christians, the Walloon Socialists and the Francophone Democratic Front. The complex of national solidarities and antipathies, and the equilibria required among regional parties and subparties, had called forth a 'pentapartite' majority. A coalition far larger than that needed for a parliamentary majority had been created to induce the minimum effective majority to combine. Such an 'excess majority' carried obvious dangers of congestion, incessant negotiation and renegotiation, and dislocation, even if local intransigences did not thwart the national statesmanship.

Coalitions are common practice, not only at the national level but also at provincial and, more important, communal level. Provincial coalitions, formed after elections held at the same time as the parliamentary elections, are often in tune with national situations. Communal elections held at fixed six-year intervals tend to be influenced by different factors. With a government (in 1977) which affirmed the will to achieve a definitive regionalisation, a new problem appeared. How much would party pressures from the national level weigh upon the formation of regional coalitions? The very spirit of regionalisation seems to call for such coalitions to emerge from the play of regional forces. For the coalition formula to appear imposed upon the region from the highest levels of politics and government could aggravate one of the difficulties of the multi-party system, namely, that the voter at the moment of deciding his vote does not know which coalition his decision will help put into power. The question is part of the broader one of the quality and value of the citizen's participation in Belgian political life. It is a life which seems to abound in barriers to public information and in closed circuits in the taking of decisions. The profound and original meaning of the demands which led to a partial regionalisation in the structures of the nation and the parties was the will to bring the centres of decision closer to the citizen.

The political system has been rich in compromise. The parties which have been the expression of cleavages have also been the agencies of many compromises. These have enabled a country of religious division and language diversity, of conspicuous social stratification and economic inequality, to avoid violence and continue discussion while achieving much gradual change. It has not been a politics of great vision and boldness (how often do we find these in our democracies?), but neither has there been any great alienation of large groups of the people, at least in the last generation. The tone and the outcome of political life have had the quality the Flemish call *middelmattig*, that is, inbetween very good and bad, 'average', and at times, of course, mediocre. That is often the quality, or appearance, of compromise: only the alternatives are worse.

Compromise has the costs of its benefits, and some costs mount with the years. The continuing implementation of the school pact has required vast sums to match facilities and services of the Catholic and the official networks of education, as they compete with each other out of public funds. Similarly, the structures of segmented pluralism which furnish the health services of this welfare state duplicate expensive facilities, while Socialist and Catholic networks of medical care, hospitals and sanatoria compete to attract and retain members.

A second cost is that of immobilism. One form of compromise arrangement is a mutual veto by each recognised group over proposals for experiment or change by another group, when the proposals require an extension of equipment or plant which is too costly to be duplicated. The third sort of cost is that of complexity upon complexity. The institutions and understandings of political and religious, linguistic and regional diversity are so complex, in public and quasi-public and mixed institutions, ranging from regional and cultural community organs to the many systems of social insurance, that only the specialist can understand them. Even the most serious-minded citizen is at a loss in trying to share in political decisions on these issues. Simplification of institutions may be the price of their and the country's democratic functioning.

Thoughtful party leaders and members recognise the need for reforms. With all the parties' faults – and the litany of their faults is the commonplace of discourse in all our countries – they remain the essential channels of national choice, and they will no doubt be channels, if not the only ones, of regional and cultural community choice as well. Among existing institutions of voluntary action, they come most often to the citizen with proposals related to concepts of the general interest (along with many special-interest proposals). Other ideas and other, perhaps more viable or more exhilarating, projects must come from other types of private and public institutions: from trade unions and employer associations, from religious groups and humanists, from the centres of intellectual inquiry and training, even from public servants who can escape the servitudes of short-run crises, as well as from the myriad of human associations.

Belgium used to be known as an 'associationist' country, because of its dense network of voluntary associations. Perhaps from some of the newest, as from the older, associations of today will come part of the stimulus and the strength for the political parties to meet the challenges of an old society whose complexity is almost in inverse relation to the nation's relative size.

## STATISTICAL APPENDIX

Table 2.1    *Votes for House of Representatives, by Party, 1965–1977 (as percentages of total numbers of valid votes)*

|      | Chr. | Soc. | Lib. | Com. | VU | FDF | RW | Misc. |
|------|------|------|------|------|------|------|------|------|
| 1965 | 34·4 | 28·3 | 21·6 | 4·6 | 6·7 | 1·3 | (1·0)[1] | 2·1 |
| 1968 | 31·7 | 28·0 | 20·9 | 3·3 | 9·8 | 2·5 | 3·4 | 0·4 |
| 1971 | 30·0 | 27·3 | 16·4 | 3·1 | 11·1 | 11·3[2] | | 0·8 |
| 1974 | 32·3 | 26·7 | 15·2 | 3·2 | 10·2 | 10·9[2] | | 1·4 |
| 1977 | 35·9 | 26·8 | 15·6 | 2·7 | 9·8 | 7·3[2] | | 1·6 |

*Notes:*
Chr.  – Christian Social Party
Soc.  – Socialist Party
Lib.  – Party of Liberty and Progress (formerly Liberal Party) and various members of 'Liberal family'
Com. – Communist Party
VU    – Flemish People's Party
FDF   – Francophone Democratic Front (Brussels)
RW    – Walloon Party
Misc. – Miscellaneous lists
For full names of parties, including Flemish and French names, see Glossary.

[1] Miscellaneous Walloon lists, prefiguring RW.
[2] FDF–RW cartel.

*Sources:* Various *Courriers Hebdomadaires* of CRISP (Centre de Recherche et d'Information Socio-Politiques), based upon official returns to Ministry of Interior.

Table 2.2 *Distribution of Seats in House of Representatives, by Party, immediately after Election, 1965–1977*

|      | Chr. | Soc. | Lib. | Com. | VU | FDF | RW | Total |
|------|------|------|------|------|-----|-----|-----|-------|
| 1965 | 77 | 64 | 48 | 6 | 12 | 3 | 2 | 212 |
| 1968 | 69 | 59 | 47 | 5 | 20 | 5 | 7 | 212 |
| 1971 | 67 | 61 | 34 | 5 | 21 | 10 | 14 | 212 |
| 1974 | 72 | 59 | 33 | 4 | 22 | 9 | 13 | 212 |
| 1977 | 80 | 62 | 33 | 2 | 20 | 10 | 5 | 212 |

*Note:*
For full names of parties, see Glossary.

Table 2.3 *Votes for House of Representatives, by Party, 1977[1] (as percentages of total valid vote of region)*

|  | Chr. | Soc. | Lib. | Com. | VU | RW | FDF | Misc. | Region |
|---|------|------|------|------|-----|-----|-----|-------|--------|
| Flanders | 43·9 | 22·4 | 14·4 | 1·3 | 16·3 | — | — | 1·7 | 100 |
| Wallonia | 25·2 | 39·5 | 18·8 | 5·5 | — | 9·5 | — | 1·5 | 100 |
| Brussels | 23·5 | 17·1 | 11·8 | 2·8 | 6·2 | — | 34·9 | 3·7 | 100 |
| 'Eastern Cantons'[2] | 43·0 | 12·7 | 22·3 | 0·8 | — | 1·8 | — | 19·4[3] | 100 |

*Notes:*
[1] For full names of parties, see Glossary.
[2] The 'cantons de l'Est', on the German frontier, are the seat of the German-speaking minority, with 0·7 per cent of the national electorate.
[3] Includes 19·2 per cent for party of German-speaking Belgians.

Table 2.4 *Distribution of Major Party Electorates, by Region, 1977 (as percentages of national electorate of each party, legislative elections of 17 April 1977)*

|  | Flanders | Wallonia | Brussels |
|---|----------|----------|----------|
| Christian Socials (CVP–PSC) | 70 | 22 | 8 |
| Socialists (BSP–PSB) | 48 | 45 | 7 |
| Liberals (PVV–PRLW–PL) | 53 | 37 | 9 |
| National electorate | 57 | 31 | 12 |

*Notes:*
For full names of parties, see Glossary.
Electorates exclude German-speaking cantons.

*Source:* CRISP, *Courrier Hebdomadaire*, no. 763, 21 April 1977, pp. 18–19.

Table 2.5   A.   *Membership of Political Parties, Selected Years, 1966–1973 (to nearest thousand)*

|      | CVP | PSC | PSB–BSP | PLP–PVV | PCB–KPB | VU |
|------|------|------|------|------|------|------|
| 1966 | 110,000 | 38,000 | 204,000 | 90,000 | 13,000 | 17,000 |
| 1970 | 108,000 | 39,000 | 225,000 | 78,000 | 13,000 | 36,000 |
| 1973 | 102,000 | 38,000 | 250,000 | 70,000 | 15,000 | 50,000 |

B.   *Membership of Political Parties by Region, 1972*

|      | CVP | PSC | PSB–BSP | PLP–PVV | PCB–KPB | VU |
|------|------|------|------|------|------|------|
| Flanders | 86,000 | — | 107,000 | 31,000 | 3,000 | 40,000 |
| Wallonia | — | 41,000 | 112,000 | 28,000 | 10,000 | — |
| Brussels | 14,000 | 4,000 | 23,000 | 5,000 | 1,000 | 6,000 |
| Belgium | 101,000 | 45,000 | 241,000 | 65,000 | 14,000 | 46,000 |

*Note:*
Some totals slightly off because of rounding.

*Source:* CRISP, *Les Partis Politiques en Belgique*, 1975, p. 14.

## GLOSSARY

Names of Political Parties used in Text
(French and Flemish names, and Brussels name for Liberals)

Social Christian Party:   Parti Social Chretien
                          Christelijke Volkspartij
Communist Party:   Parti Communiste de Belgique
                   Kommunistische Partij van België
Flemish People's Party:   Volksunie
Francophone Democratic Front:   Front Democratique des Francophones
Liberals:   Parti des Reformes et de la Liberte de Wallonie
            Partij voor Vrijheid en Vooruitgang
            Parti Liberal (Brussels)
Socialist Party:   Parti Socialiste Belge
                   Belgische Socialistische Partij
Walloon Party:   Rassemblement Wallon

## NOTES

The authors thank Peter Jackson and Professor Martin O. Heivler for helpful critical reading of the manuscript.

1 Clemens Lothar Wenzel, Prince von Metternich, 13 May 1850, in A. de Klinkowstraem (ed.), *Mémoires, documents et écrits divers . . . publiés par son fils le Prince Richard de Metternich* (Paris: Plon, 8 vols, 1880–4, Vol. 8, 1884), p. 267.

# FURTHER READING

CRISP, Centre de Recherche et d'Information Sociopolitiques, Brussels, current analyses of political, economic and social forces and events, and special numbers before and after municipal and national elections.

CRISP (1974) *Les Institutions de la Belgique régionalisée.*

CRISP (1975) *Les Partis politiques en Belgique*, by Luc Rowies.

Debuyst, Frédéric (1967) *La Fonction parlementaire: Mécanismes d'accès et images* (CRISP).

Delruelle, Nicole, Evalenko, René, and Fraeys, William (1970) *Le Comportement politique des électeurs belges* (Université Libre de Bruxelles).

Hill, Keith (1974) 'Belgium: political change in a segmented society', in R. Rose (ed.), *Electoral Behaviour* (New York, Free Press), pp. 29–107.

Huyse, Luc (1970) *Passiviteit, pacificatie en verzuiling in de Belgische politiek* (Antwerp, Standaard).

Ladrière, Jean (1970) 'Le système politique belge: situation 1970', in *Courrier Hebdomadaire*, no. 500 (Brussels, CRISP).

Lorwin, V. R. (1966) 'Belgium: religion, class and language in national politics', in R. A. Dahl (ed.), *Political Oppositions in Western Democracies* (New Haven and London, Yale University Press), pp. 147–87, 409–16 and 444–5.

Lorwin, V. R. (1971) 'Segmented pluralism: ideological cleavages and political cohesion in the smaller european democracies', *Comparative Politics*, vol. III, pp. 141–75.

Lorwin, V. R. (1975) 'Labor unions and political parties in Belgium', *Industrial and Labor Relations Review*, vol. 28, pp. 243–63.

Luykx, Theo (1969) *Politieke Geschiedenis van België*, 2nd edn (Brussels, Elzevier).

Mabille, X. (1976) 'Adaptation ou éclatement du système de décision en Belgique', *Recherches Sociologiques*, vol. VII, pp. 111–49.

Mabille, X., and Lorwin, V. R. (1977) 'The Belgian Socialist Party', in W. E. Paterson and A. H. Thomas (eds), *The Social Democratic Parties of Western Europe* (London, Croom Helm), pp. 389–407.

Meynaud, Jean, Ladrière, J., and Perin, François (eds) (1965) *La Décision Politique en Belgique* (Paris, Colin; Brussels, CRISP).

Molitor, André (1974) *L'Administration de la Belgique: Essai*, (Brussels, CRISP and Institut Belge de Science Politique).

*Res Publica*, review of the Belgian Institute of Political Science, frequent issues and some whole numbers devoted to parties and elections.

Senelle, Robert (1974) *La Constitution Belge Commentée* (Brussels, Ministry of Foreign Affairs).

Urwin, D. W. (1970) 'Social cleavages and political parties in Belgium: problems of institutionalisation', *Political Studies*, vol. XVIII, pp. 320–40.

Van den Brande, A. (1963) 'Mogelijkheden van een sociologie der belgische conflicten na de Tweede Wereldoorlog, 1944–1961', *Sociologische Gids*, vol. X, pp. 2–29.

# 3
# Denmark

## JOHN FITZMAURICE

### HISTORY AND CONSTITUTIONAL DEVELOPMENT

Denmark is a geographical and cultural bridge between continental Europe and Scandinavia and even the North Atlantic area. The country has a homogeneous population of 5·1 million and with the exception of the German minority in Slesvig and the North Atlantic territories of Greenland and the Faeroes, no regional or minority problems exist. The economic life of the country has, until relatively recently, been dominated by agriculture. Even now, 9·8 per cent of the working population are engaged in agriculture, fisheries or the food industry and 35·3 per cent of exports come from these industries. Economic facts together with geographical position have done much to shape both the foreign policy options and the domestic political environment of the country.[1]

Denmark avoided entanglement in the First World War by an astute policy of neutrality, regained the northern part of Slesvig in 1920 and was relatively untouched by the traumatic economic and political events of the late 1920s and 1930s. There was little right- or left-wing radicalism and the moderate reformist Social Democrat–Radical government under Thorvald Stauning ensured political and economic stability. In foreign policy, she placed her faith in collective security and the League of Nations and in neutrality in conflicts between the great powers. As the storm clouds of war gathered over Europe, she hoped, as before, to remain neutral and avoid involvement in the coming struggle. On 9 April 1940 these hopes were cruelly dashed by the German invasion and five bitter years of Nazi occupation were to follow. The experience of occupation temporarily radicalised politics and the Social Democrats fought the 1945 election on a left-wing manifesto and the Communists won eighteen seats in the

Folketing. From then on, in one form or another, there would always be an organised political force to the left of the Social Democrats. The experience of the war led Denmark to abandon her neutrality and in 1949, after attempts to form a Scandinavian military alliance had failed, she joined NATO, together with Norway and Iceland, but without Sweden or Finland. In 1973, after considerable and bitter controversy, she joined the European Community.

THE SYSTEM OF GOVERNMENT[2]

Denmark is a constitutional monarchy. The Crown has no political role. Executive power is in the hands of a cabinet of about fifteen members formally appointed by the monarch and responsible to the Folketing.

The central focus of political life is the Folketing (legislative). This body has 179 members (175 from metropolitan Denmark, 2 from the Faeroes and 2 from Greenland), elected for a maximum term of four years, but the Crown can dissolve the Folketing and provoke new elections at any time. The electoral system is a strongly mathematical system of PR: 135 MFs are elected in 17 multi-member seats (2–15 seats); the remaining 40 seats are allotted as topping-up seats to ensure proportional representation to parties having obtained at least 2 per cent of the national vote. To be eligible to contest an election a party must produce about 17,000 signatures of bona fide electors.

The government must enjoy the confidence of parliament or at least must be safe from a motion of no confidence. Parliament not only sustains and controls the government, but legislates, passes appropriations and exercises powers of control in the field of foreign and market policy. Since 1941 the Folketing has had a number of seventeen member specialised committees dealing with legislation and control functions in various areas of policy. Parties with a minimum of seventeen members can be represented and smaller parties can make pacts with other small parties to gain a seat. The Finance Committee, the Foreign Affairs Committee and the Market Relations Committee are the most important. The role of these Folketing committees and interparty negotiation is central. Governments mostly are minority governments which have to cobble together package deals on measures and negotiate their way forward from issue to issue, perhaps basing themselves on a core of allies, but always being ready to drop off or add some parties according to circumstance.

THE PARTIES[3]

*The Left*
Collectively called the Socialist parties, the Left is now represented in parliament by four parties, for which the Danish abbreviations will be used: the Social Democrats (s), the Communist Party (DKP), the Socialist People's Party (SF) and the Left Socialists (VS). The Left now has about 42 per cent of the vote. It has rarely obtained an overall majority, although for two short periods from 1966 to 1968 and again from 1971 to 1973 S and SF obtained a slender majority. In the late 1950s and early 1960s either S and DKP or S and SF came very close to an overall majority, but for political reasons this potential was ignored. Earlier, S (with 42·1 per cent in 1960 and 46·1 per cent in 1935) and the combined Left (S and DKP in 1935 and in 1945) obtained a higher percentage than now. As for the parties to the left of the Social Democrats (SF, DKP, VS), these have never obtained more than 12·5 per cent.

*The Social Democrats (S).* s was organised by Louis Pio in 1871 as a Danish section of the First International. After initial repression, the movement grew, largely through the trade unions of which there were over 100 sections by 1875. The first congress was held in 1876, with seventy-five delegates representing fifty-six organisations (forty-one unions and fifteen political associations) with 6,000 members. Here the 'Gimle' programme was adopted and a party organisation under the chairmanship of Pio was formed. The programme, closely modelled on the SPD 'Gotha' programme, showed clear Marxist influences in that it declared for wide common ownership, albeit by legal means. There were also calls for immediate reforms: full political democracy, the repeal of indirect taxes, regulation of working hours and welfare measures. The subsequent programme of 1913 was in tone more moderate and added demands for measures in support of small farmers. In its 1919 policy statement, the party adopted wide-ranging proposals for public ownership of insurance companies, the shipping industry and coal and food importing companies. The 1945 manifesto adopted after the liberation, entitled 'The Future Denmark', was radical, in the belief that a decisive move to the left had occurred. This manifesto condemned monopoly capitalism and proposed wide government intervention and nationalisation. The programme was an electoral liability both in that votes were lost to the Communists and co-operation with the Radicals was made difficult; it was soon implicitly in cold storage. The party's third programme, adopted in 1961, is rather general and emphasises democratisation more than socialisation. It proposes a '. . . democratisation of society as a whole so that the possibilities of free choice, economically and culturally are brought within the grasp of each individual'. It was supplemented, in 1969, by a working programme entitled 'The New Society – Policies for the 1970s'. In this document emphasis was placed on industrial democracy and progressive co-ownership. The 1973 congress called for a new programme to be prepared for the 1977 congress. The drafting committee set up by the national executive in September 1974 completed its work in the autumn of 1976 and the programme was adopted in September 1977. This new programme declares the aim of democratic socialism to be '. . . the liberation of man, to ensure his security and give him the possibility of full development, in society and responsible to society', and 'it builds on respect for the individual and equal opportunity for all'. It equally condemns both capitalism and state capitalism and seeks to further equality, freedom and solidarity. The programme recognises the vast improvements in living standards and of freedom for the working class, but emphasises the steady concentration of economic power in few hands to which the party must respond. Here it places the main emphasis on economic democracy, the quality of life and of economic growth and the new economic context of the new relationship with the Third World and Denmark's membership of the EEC.

The social basis of the party is clear: 85 per cent of its voters are from the working class. It is marginally stronger in Copenhagen and the other large cities, but its support is remarkably even throughout the country. Even in such rural areas as Lolland/Falster and the north of Jutland the party's vote is only about 3 per cent below the national vote. Only in mid-Jutland, where the Right has its main traditional strongholds, does the party's vote fall more than 5 per cent below the national vote.

The party gained representation in the Folketing for the first time in 1884 with two seats, which had risen to twelve by 1898. In 1909 it helped the Radical Party to office, thus inaugurating a political partnership which was to dominate Danish politics for the next fifty years. During the First World War, when the country's delicate neutrality policy required broad support, s first entered the government. s emerged as the largest party after the 1924 election and Thorvald Stauning formed an s minority government which was unable to achieve major reform, but lasted two and a half years and proved that the party was *salonfähig*. In 1929 Stauning was able to form a majority coalition with the Radicals, which was to last until the occupation and put through major social reforms.

After the war, the party lost support to the Communists and had to go into opposition until 1947. From then until 1966 it governed first as a minority government, and later with the Radicals or with the Radicals and the Justice Party, except for the short three-year period of Liberal–Conservative government, 1950–3. In 1960 the DKP had been replaced on the far left by the SF under the popular Aksel Larsen, which obtained 6·1 per cent and eleven seats. This new party could less easily be contained in a ghetto as a political 'untouchable' and in 1966, for the first time, S and SF gained a Socialist majority, slender though it was. Aksel Larsen refused a formal coalition which would have committed SF to supporting NATO and Danish EEC membership. However, the two parties did form a 'contact committee' and co-operate on domestic issues for fourteen months until the split in SF broke the majority. This led to a polarisation and threw the Radical Party into the arms of the 'bourgeois' parties and led to the creation of a VKR government under Hilmar Baunsgaard (R), which lost its majority after the 1971 election which saw Mr Krag return to power in an S minority government supported by SF. He resigned immediately after the EEC referendum and was replaced by the more left-wing former union leader Anker Jørgensen. A number of factors – the leftward movement in the Social Democratic Party, the growing revolt against high taxation, the bitter aftermath of the EEC referendum campaign – contributed to the dramatic 1973 election, provoked by Erhard Jacobsen leaving the Social Democrats. This colourful and energetic character left S as a protest against the leftward trend to found the Centre Democrats.

At this election all the previously represented parties lost ground, even SF. However, the result was worse for S which fell back to 25·7 per cent, its lowest percentage since before 1914, and furthermore it now found two (and after 1975 three) parties to its left. It lost power to the Liberals until the 1975 election when it made a partial recovery to 29·9 per cent and again formed a precarious minority government which had to call an election in February 1977 since it could not obtain a long-term agreement on certain aspects of economic policy, which would have provided at least a minimum of political stability. The 1977 election saw *stabilisation*, but no dramatic return to the position of the 1960s.

Membership is individual and based on the local branch. Each branch elects its executive and chooses delegates to the constituency and county organisations. The annual conference composed of about 500 delegates (two from each constituency, officers of various tiers of the party organisation) discusses matters of policy and administration. Between annual meetings, party business is carried on by the forty-eight-member national executive and its executive committee. The national executive committee is composed of a representative from each of the fourteen county organisations, twenty representatives of the party branches, representatives of the trade unions, co-operatives, youth movement and the parliamentary group, as well as party officers such as the chairman, vice-chairman and secretary. These diverse groups are also represented on the executive committee. The parliamentary group has an autonomous status and elects its own officers. Over long periods the parliamentary leader and the chairman have been one and the same person, which has evidently avoided conflict. The parliamentary leader must normally consult the national executive, as well as the parliamentary group, before agreeing to enter government.

*The Communist Party (DKP)*. The party was founded in 1919 from a number of splinter groups from s and other socialist societies. It contested its first election in 1920 and first won representation in the Folketing in 1932 (two seats) and obtained modest representation throughout the 1930s. With its role in the resistance, immediate postwar admiration for Russia and the general shift to the left, the election of 1945 saw an explosion with the party gaining 12·5 per cent of the vote and eighteen seats (out of the then 149).

With the onset of the cold war and the cold-shoulder tactics of s, which refused to co-operate with the Communists, this ground could not be held and support was halved at the next election and by 1957 had fallen to 3·1 per cent and six seats.

Meanwhile, rumbling dissent and internal contradictions had set in, fueled by the general secretary Aksel Larsen who returned from the 20th congress of the Soviet Party to issue a denunciation of DKP's blind loyalty to Moscow. In his report he stated: '. . . the party should free itself from the tradition that we automatically support everything that comes from the Socialist countries'. He was to continue in this manner, criticising the Soviet invasion of Hungary and supporting the Yugoslav position against the Soviet Union, as well as proposing a specific Danish road to socialism. In November 1958 the central committee expelled him from the party. He was to found the Socialist People's Party (SF) which led to the DKP losing all its seats in the Folketing in 1960. From then until the 1973 election it was not represented in the Folketing and concentrated on maintaining party discipline, organising in factories and campaigning on issues such as opposition to NATO and particularly opposition to Danish EEC membership, which could bring it support from outside the ranks of normal DKP voters. It was returned to the Folketing in 1973 and improved its position slightly in both 1975 and 1977. The political situation did not permit the far left parties to play a major role in this period. Furthermore, the presence of three Marxist parties to the left of the Social Democrats has led to strong ideological conflict between these parties, which has tended to limit their individual and collective impact on politics as a whole. The main goal of the DKP, particularly in the February 1977 election, has been to attempt to bring the Social Democrats to co-operate with the parties of the Left rather than with the Centre-Right.

*Socialist People's Party (SF)*. Aksel Larsen founded SF as '. . . a real mass party . . . and not a steel hard militant sect'. It was to be a party 'which builds on working people, but which is able to stimulate Danish politics and co-operate with all democratic and socialist forces'. The main policies of the party, as set out in its 1963 programme, and in subsequent policy statements, are anticapitalist, emphasising public control and intervention in the economy, workers' participation in industry and strong social services. In foreign policy, the party seeks closer ties with the Socialist states and the Third World. SF opposes NATO and Danish EEC membership. At the time of EEC membership the party was the only anti-EEC party in the Folketing. Since 1973, its members (Per Dich and from 1974 Jens Maigaard) have been active in the European Parliament and the Folketing's Market Relations Committee, following the line that the referendum of October 1972 gave only a limited 'mandate' for entry to the Community as it then was and not for further institutional development. The first congress was held in February 1959 and the party obtained eleven seats at its first election in 1960, thus becoming larger than the Radicals. Stability was maintained at the 1964 election. At the 1966 election the party almost doubled its number of seats to twenty, a spectacular leap forward, which created with s the first 'labour' majority in the Folketing. For the next fourteen months the Social Democrats, in a reversal of their earlier cold-shoulder policy, co-operated closely with them and they even offered SF seats in the cabinet. A joint SF–S committee was formed, the so-called 'Red Cabinet', to determine the outline of the policy to be followed, except for foreign affairs, defence and EC questions where the government co-operated with the 'bourgeois' parties. There was growing tension within SF over this moderate line and the issue of an incomes policy which arose in December 1967 after devaluation was only an immediate pretext for six MFs to rebel against the 'Larsenist' line and defeat the government. The SF lost in the ensuing election and was reduced to fourteen seats. The 1971 election saw a return to S minority government after the bourgeois VKR coalition had been defeated. At the 1973 election SF lost votes like all the established parties, in spite of its association with opposition to the EEC. Since 1973 SF has found itself considerably squeezed between S on the one hand and DKP and VS on the other. In this situation its support has been constantly eroded and the 'generation' shift after the death of Aksel Larsen in 1971 has not been easy; there has been constant tension between the Folketing group and the mass party, culminating in a purge of five MFs before the 1977 election. Attacks on the S-government incomes policy were counter-productive and SF reached its lowest ebb at the 1977 election with seven seats and no evident political role.

*The Left Socialists (VS).* The VS was formed in December 1967 by the six SF rebels, led by Erik Sigsgaard. Four of them secured election, but the small group was plagued by factionalism and political impotence, with two of its more talented and popular members, Hanne Reintoft and Pia Dam, leaving the group to sit as independents. As a result the party lost its seats in 1971, and remained out in 1973 (1·5 per cent), but returned in 1975 with just 2·0 per cent and four seats, increasing to five in 1977. The party is strongly anti-EEC and anti-NATO, but opposes state capitalism. Sceptical about parliamentary institutions, it believes in active work among trade unionists, women's rights groups, tenants associations, etc. It believes that such activity can heighten political consciousness and create a 'revolutionary situation' in which the institutions of capitalism will ineluctably and irreversibly melt away. As a parliamentary force VS is relatively ineffective, but has tabled interesting proposals on energy saving and alternative energy sources.

*The Centre and Centre-Right*
These terms do not exist as such in Danish usage. All non-socialist parties are classified as 'bourgeois' parties. This designation referred historically to Venstre and the Conservatives, but since the polarisation of 1968 has come to include unequivocally the Radical Party. There is now a tendency to identify three groups of 'bourgeois' parties:

the moderate parties (Radicals, Centre Democrats, Christian People's Party)

the traditional bourgeois parties
others (Progress Party, the Independents 1953–66, Justice)

Except for two very short periods (1966–8 and 1971–3) the
bourgeois parties taken as a whole have always represented a
majority in the Folketing. Taking the period before 1973, their
high point was the early 1920s where Venstre and the Conservatives
often came close to a majority and in more recent times in 1968
when the VKR triangle obtained ninety-eight seats. Before 1973 the
bourgeois parties were essentially Venstre and the Conservatives.
Venstre have shown an organic decline from 34 per cent in 1920
to their present 13 per cent. In this light, the 1975 result must
seem an aberration. The Conservatives were until 1968 always
the smaller of the two leading bourgeois parties; their share of
the vote, until 1973, remained remarkably stable. The Radicals
have been in an ambiguous position. Until 1968 they did not act
as a bourgeois party, but rather as a 'bridge' across the centre.
In fact, they have only joined one bourgeois coalition (1968–71)
whereas they have very frequently supported s governments. It
seems, too, that their period as a bourgeois party is now over.
The party seems to desire to revert to a bridging role.

*The Liberals* (Venstre – v). The party came into being in the
period after 1848 in the struggle for democratic parliamentary
government. In 1872 the various Liberal factions joined in the
United Left (Venstre means Left) and issued the first modern
party programme. In the 1880s local branches were formed. The
party was, however, beset by factionalism, as it has been ever
since. One section compromised with the Right. In 1901, with the
*systemskift* (system change), the Liberals formed their first government. The party began as the Farmers' Party, but now subtitles
itself 'Denmark's Liberal Party'. Its main support is to be found
in rural areas such as northern and central Jutland, but the 1975
gains also resulted in an inflow of urban voters, largely from other
bourgeois parties. The party has traditionally sought balance and
moderation. It supported and indeed fought for the parliamentary
system, but in the 1930s and early 1940s opposed too-radical
reforms of the constitution. At first it opposed the abolition of
the Landsting and only came to accept it when the principle of
the abrogative referendum was accepted by the other parties. It
believes in 'Freedom under Responsibility'. Economic freedom
cannot be total and social solidarity must be expressed through a
system of social security, which, however, has in recent years
become too extensive. The party supports a limited incomes policy
and limited forms of industrial democracy. It strongly supports
tax reductions and savings in public expenditure, but as a govern-

ment party from 1968 to 1971 and from 1973 to 1975 became acutely aware of the very real practical obstacles in the way of such a policy. As was seen in the recent election campaign, v now gives absolute priority to measures of economic stabilisation. These are the main themes of the 1970 programme 'Towards the Year 2000', which also presents v as a forward-looking modern party, as well as resting on its traditions. Its future is uncertain. The aggressive tactics of its leader Poul Hartling in the period after 1973 have produced mixed results. His insistence on forming a government with a mere twenty-two seats and then surviving for a year before going to the country with a coherent economic programme enabled him to almost double v's representation from twenty-two to forty-two in 1975. However, this was a Pyrrhic victory, since v lost power to s. His refusal to adopt a constructive attitude to the minority s government has been heavily sanctioned by the electorate, with v dropping back to twenty-one seats, less than in 1973 and indeed less than at any time in this century. This result may bring Hartling's leadership and certainly his strategy into question.

The organisation is similar to that of s. Congress is the supreme authority. It is made up largely of delegates from the local branches, with some *ex officio* delegates. The national executive has fifty to sixty members of which only three are chosen by the congress, the rest being *ex officio* members. There was no central party organisation until 1929 and it remains weaker than in some other Danish parties.

The party has suffered from at least three significant splits. The first was that of the Radicals in 1905 (small-holders, pacifists and urban intellectuals). The second was from the Right. Led by former leader and prime minister Knud Kristensen, a group left in opposition to the constitutional reform of 1953, to form the right-wing Independent Party, which was represented in the Folketing from 1960 to 1966. Thirdly, in the early 1960s a group called Liberal Debate was formed to combat moves to the right and more specifically a mooted fusion or close alliance with the Conservatives. This group which was mainly centred in Copenhagen broke away *en bloc* with two MFs (Westerby and Diderichsen) to form the Liberal Centre in 1965.

*The Conservatives (KF).* The Conservative People's Party was formed in 1915 by the more progressive elements in the old Right. KF is mainly an urban and suburban party, especially in Copenhagen. The Conservatives have rarely been in government (1950–3 and 1968–71). Like Venstre, KF emphasises freedom and economic initiative and incentive, but it is not neo-liberal. It supports the welfare state as necessary. KF has a strong national tradition. It strongly supports NATO and the defence effort. It has been the most pro-EEC of all the Danish parties.

Participation in the 1968–71 VKR government, where Poul Møller was finance minister (he introduced the PAYE tax system) and Knud Thestrup was justice minister (he abolished censorship and obscenity laws), lost the party considerable support and led eventually to the debacle of the 1973 election. KF lost heavily to both the Christian People's Party (KrF) and to the Progress Party (FrP). At the same time it lost representation in the European Parliament. The policy of the party's new chairman, Pour Schlüter, has paid off. Co-operation with the S minority government in a number of 'package deals' seems to have led to the party's quite considerable gains in the February 1977 general election. At present, as has been the case at other periods in Danish history, the KF appears a more likely partner for S than does V.

The party executive has about sixty to sixty-five members and a representative assembly of 300–500 members. The supreme organ is the national council (900–1,100 members), representing largely the local party districts in proportion to Conservative votes at the last election. The Folketing group has a separate chairman and it is the group which does most of the preparatory work on policy matters, subject to the final ratification of the national council.

*The Radical Left (RV)*. The RV is a centre-left party which broke away from Venstre in 1905 and rapidly gained influence on the political scene, forming its first government under Zahle as early as 1909. In 1913 RV began its co-operation with the Social Democrats which was to dominate Danish political life for the next fifty years. The party represented the urban left, intellectuals and small-holders, as well as pacifists. These various strains remain important in the party even today. In its heyday, RV obtained 21·1 per cent of the vote in 1918, but in 1929–68 its vote never rose above 10 per cent. It reached 15·0 per cent in the landslide of 1968, when it gained many floating voters in the general polarisation of that election, a figure it virtually held in 1971. In successive elections in 1973, 1975 and 1977, its vote declined to a low of 3·6 per cent. However, Radical influence has always been greatly disproportionate to its moderate size, on account of its strategic position in the political spectrum, to the immediate right of the Social Democrats in often evenly balanced parliaments. The main aim of RV is to promote co-operation on a broad basis, across the middle in Danish politics.

The party has always acted as a bridge, moderating both Socialist and bourgeois blocs. Votes flow to and from the party from both left and right. The large gains of 1968 were a clear recognition of this bridging function. RV clearly said 'Yes' to a bourgeois government, but also 'Yes, but . . .'. Today the party is mostly a middle-class white-collar party, but it still retains elements of its original voter clientèle, in that about 8 per cent of its electorate still come from small farmers.

These origins are reflected in the party's policy concerns: measures to assist small farmers and the initial opposition of the party to NATO and opposition of a minority to EEC membership (in 1971 21·3 per cent of the party's voters were in some degree hostile to NATO and in the same year 18·7 per cent were opposed to EEC membership).

The structure and organisation of RV is similar to that of other 'Old' parties. The national conference elects members of the executive and approves programmes. The executive follows the familiar pattern of a few representatives of the national conference and a majority of *ex officio* members from the Folketing group, Radical Youth, the Radical Press and the local and regional party organisations.

In recent years RV has suffered from identity problems and resulting internal tensions. Was it a bourgeois party? If so, should it, as in the 1968–71 period, commit itself to an alliance with the bourgeois parties? Or was it a centre-left party, closer to the Social Democrats? Its unclear position and therefore its un-reliability both to any potential bourgeois bloc centred around Venstre and to the Social Democrats has cost the party support and now leaves it in serious difficulties.

*The Centre-Democrats (CD).* This party was formed just before the 1973 election by Mr Erhard Jacobsen, then a Social Democrat MF and the well-known and popular mayor of Gladsaxe, a Copen-hagen suburb. He left s and formed the new party in protest against the move to the left by Anker Jørgensen after 1972. He criticised the party's over-close identification with the trade unions and alliance with SF, as well as the general increase in left-wing influence in cultural life and the media.

CD is avowedly a centre party, opposing ideological con-frontation and bloc politics. It opposed growing left-wing in-fluence and in the European Parliament (after 1975) joined the Conservative group, but at the same time sought to prevent the formation of a minority bourgeois government which would have been dependent on the Progress Party. It is loosely organised and decentralised, depending for its impact largely upon the charismatic personality of Erhard Jacobsen and a few other leaders.

CD unequivocally favours the mixed economy, but seeks to spread wealth and economic power more widely. It opposes special interests such as trade unions gaining what it considers excessive influence in government. Enterprise and initiative should be rewarded, but the welfare state should not be dismantled. CD has strongly attacked modern methods in education and left-wing influence in state-subsidised culture and in radio and television. In foreign affairs, the party is strongly pro NATO and the EEC. The 1973 election result gave CD an excellent result, with fourteen seats, but in 1975 it only just retained its representation with a mere four seats, some of its votes going to Venstre and some perhaps back to the Social Democrats. In 1977 it gained seven seats, to reach eleven. This would seem to indicate that CD has become a relatively permanent feature of the political landscape.

*The Christian People's Party (KrF).* KrF was founded in April 1970, during the VKR bourgeois coalition, largely as a protest against the legalisation of pornography and the easing of the abortion laws, measures proposed by the Conservative justice minister Thestrup and supported by all five parties then represented in the Folketing. More widely, KrF was, as were other new-old parties such as the CD, Progress Party and the Justice Party, a protest against the failure of the bourgeois coalition to pursue a bourgeois policy and against 'moral permissiveness'. The first party programme, filling out the statement issued by the founders, was adopted in 1971. The KrF is ecumenical with representatives of both the high and low church wings of the Lutheran Church, the Catholics and the free churches in its leadership. The party sought to bring a Christian moral *Weltanschauung* into politics and in the words of the programme supports '. . . the pillars of society: the home, church and school'. Many Danish church leaders did not react favourably to the formation of a specifically Christian party, with the clear implication that the other parties were not, could not be and even need not be Christian in outlook. KrF replies to this criticism by referring to the successful sister party in Norway and to the existence of Christian Democratic Parties in many other European countries. At the same time, the party proposes to act as core, or catalyst to a Christian outlook in Danish politics, exercising in this way a pressure on the other parties.

KrF was soon to suffer from considerable internal dissensions on these and other issues, which probably contributed in large measure to the failure of the party to gain representation in

1971. The central issue was the attitude to the bourgeois VKR government then in power: should KrF support its continuation in office, or propose an alternative formed by S, V and KrF? How 'purist' should the party be? These tensions and the defeat of 1971 provoked a leadership change and in March 1973 Jens Møller became chairman. KrF profited, as did all the 'out' parties, from the public mood of disenchantment, at the 1973 election. Modest gains were made in 1975 and lost in 1977. KrF has been a full participant in the numerous pacts made by both the Hartling and Jørgensen governments.

The position of KrF can be summarised by the slogan: 'To the right in cultural matters and to the left in social matters.' KrF is pro NATO and EEC and supports increased aid to the Third World. More recently, the moral and cultural issues which were at the origins of the party have tended to recede into the background and the party has operated more as a classic centre party.

*The Progress Party (FrP).* The Progress Party was founded by tax lawyer Mogens Glistrup in August 1972. He had already become a public figure through his appearances on television attacking the tax system. He has now been indicted on twenty-three counts of tax fraud, but maintains that he has done no more than exploit the idiocies of the tax system in a perfectly legal manner.

The party's name and records were purchased for about 800 kroner from its former leader, who had been attempting to form a pensioners' party. The FrP developed rapidly through the formation of local branches following mass meetings. Soon the party had over 40,000 members and a newspaper, *Fremskridten*, founded in October 1973. It was above all the speaking and publicity talents of Mogens Glistrup which caught the public imagination and brought in the support. By the summer of 1973 when an election was looming, the FrP reached over 20 per cent in opinion polls. The party's appeal was avowedly populist; its main targets were high income tax, government expenditure and bureaucratic interference in economic life. At the 1973 election the party obtained 15·9 per cent of the vote and twenty-eight seats at its first attempt, thus becoming the second largest party in the Folketing. At the 1975 election, after some internal splits, it fell back to twenty-four seats, but in 1977 obtained twenty-six seats.

Party organisation both inside and outside the Folketing remains loose. Group meetings are held in public and party discipline only applies to the most fundamental points in the party programme. On other issues each MF and indeed party member is free. The somewhat anarchic manner in which the party was founded and developed and the uneven character of its vote over the whole country brought a somewhat unbalanced group into the Folketing in 1973. The attempt of the far Left and the FrP to topple the Hartling government in September 1974 was torpedoed by four dissident members of the group. The style of the party is unique; it depends on the personality of its leader. Mr Glistrup has a talent for political theatre. He has coined phrases of his own, attacking 'paper pushers' and 'desk-popes' (bureaucrats). Initially, FrP proposed as its defence policy to replace the armed forces by an automatic reply system in the ministry, saying 'we surrender' in Russian. Mr Glistrup has also attacked state subsidies to the arts, all foreign aid, nordic co-operation and even Danish diplomatic representation.

The basis of the party is its offensive against taxation and bureaucracy. It proposes to abolish income tax gradually over five years and to abolish all wealth and capital gains taxes. Such a programme would be made possible by massive and radical cuts in public spending and in the level of state activities. All state subsidies would be phased out, as would state intervention in economic activity. There would be major savings in military expenditure and in foreign policy activities. All foreign aid would be abolished. These savings would add up to 30 milliard kroner. The sole area in which expenditure would actually be increased would be that of control of environmental pollution, where more severe standards would be applied.

The party also emphasises the fight against bureaucracy. Social services would be reduced, restructured and decentralised. The number of members of the Folketing would be reduced to forty and the cabinet to eight. Local authorities would be given greater autonomy. There would be numerous reductions in the staffing of the public services (by about 150,000 jobs). Pensions would be simplified by giving equal pensions to all. In foreign policy, FrP is pro-EEC, but vigilant against excessive bureaucracy. A large current in FrP is opposed to NATO and desires very large cuts in military expenditure.

For the future, the FrP faces tough choices. It has become more structured and disciplined. In spite of virulent attacks from all quarters and ridicule from experts, it has maintained its apparently naive and slogan-like policies on income tax and its populist appeal. However, its vote seems to have settled down at about 14 per cent and its dynamism seems to have lost its steam. At the same time, it has not won acceptance as a valid partner from other parties, who, however, will now view the party as less of a threat. As a result, it must attempt the delicate task for a protest party, of transforming itself just enough to enter the mainstream of the political process so as to obtain influence on policy, without losing its cutting edge. It it does not succeed in this operation, it may see its vote gradually seep away.

*The Justice Party (DR)*. The Justice Party is unique in the world and a permanent survivor on the Danish political scene. DR was founded in 1919 from a number of smaller movements which had adopted the economic theories of the American Henry George ('Poverty and Progress') and the theories on moral justice of Danish philosophers such as Severin Christensen and Aksel Dam. It first gained representation in the Folketing in 1926 and was thereafter continuously represented until 1960. It was in the late 1940s and early 1950s that DR reached its peak, with 8·2 per cent and twelve seats in 1950. It gained nine seats in 1953, fell back to six at the second election of that year, and rose to nine seats in 1957. It owed these results probably more to an incipient protest vote and to the personality of its leader Viggo Starcke. In 1957 it entered a coalition government with S and RV. This strange coalition which some considered 'against nature' arose from the purely negative desire of the three parties to keep the Liberals and Conservatives out of power. The coalition was fairly successful, but proved disastrous for DR which lost all its seats in 1960. It was then to remain in the wilderness until 1973, to drop out again in 1975, no doubt considered to have supported Hartling too closely, and then to return in 1977.

DR is a liberal party in the nineteenth-century sense. It opposes *all* intervention in economic life by the state and interference in collective bargaining and industrial democracy. Its central policy plank is the single tax theory of Henry George. This single tax on land values would replace all other taxes and would be adequate to cover a pared-down level of government expenditure. DR's liberalism leads it, as an unconditional free-trade party, logically to oppose the EEC. It has undoubtedly gained support from outside its normal adherents on this issue, as the only non-socialist anti-EEC party. Also the party opposes the normal system of party government; it desires to see governments composed of all parties represented in the Folketing.

PARTY INTERACTION

The situation can be broadly divided into three periods, but each period exhibits many common features.

*Pre-1966*
The Folketing was dominated by the four 'old' parties: S, R, V, K,

which in the period 1920–66 never fell below 85 per cent of the vote.[4] Smaller parties which appeared, such as the DR, DKP, SF, U, were ignored and to a considerable extent allowed to wither away from the indifference of the 'old parties' who did not wish to co-operate with them. Danish democracy is co-operative; a party excluded from co-operation with others will achieve nothing. In this period government was either based on the S–R formula or on the V–K formula. These were perceived as the rival combinations around which calculation revolved. The 1957–60 'triangular' government was formed precisely to permit a basic SR government and prevent a VK government.

### 1966–73
This was a short but interesting period which saw a fundamental change and indeed polarisation in Danish politics. The SF gained twenty seats in 1966 and forced its way on to the scene. There was now an S–SF majority. SF could be no longer ignored. The Social Democrats, therefore, took SF as a serious partner. This provoked a reaction from the Radicals who joined the bourgeois VKR bloc which emerged as an alternative government in 1968. When it in turn was defeated in 1971, it was replaced by a Social Democrat minority government relying on SF (1971–3). Denmark was moving towards, if not a two-party system, a two-bloc system on a classic Right–Left alignment.

### Post–1973
The 1973 election saw five new or 'new-old' parties returned and all (even SF) existing parties lost ground. This shock has not completely ceased to reverberate through the system. All the new parties have proved more durable then past experience would have suggested. The relative return to normality heralded by the 1977 election has not brought the old parties their prominence back. The system, if there is any 'system', could be likened to that found in a number of multi-party chambers in periods of political instability – the French Fourth Republic, the Weimar Republic's Reichstag and the present Italian Parliament before the PCI proposed the *compromesso storico*. Here certain parties, often both of the far Right and Left, were not considered *salonfähig* – they were not part of the normal political process. This left political interaction concentrated in a narrow band of the political spectrum – usually the broad centre. Since 1973 neither the Progress Party nor the far Left (DKP and VS) have been considered part of the political mainstream. Within the centre there have been two 'poles of attraction': the Venstre (1973–5) and

s (1975–8). The issue has been, within a given centre bloc, which party would exercise leadership? Would government be centre right or centre left? In this process the votes of the far Left and even of the FrP have been counted as a *mass de manoeuvre* without there being any thought of giving those parties any equivalent influence. This was demonstrated again in 1978 when the complications of an eleven party Folketing led to an s–v government. The reinforcement of some of the parties in a stabilized centre suggests that unlike some comparable systems Denmark seems to be back on a path to greater stability.

These dynamics are the essence of Danish co-operative democracy. Parties must cultivate a co-operative image; even at election time they must behave in a constructive manner which will minimise rather than maximise political distance from potential allies. Even the far Left and FrP must accept this basic truth. A party which cannot enter into package deals with others will have little or no influence on public affairs and in the longer term will lose the esteem of the public. Ideological purity and extreme isolation rarely pay, for no party can ever expect a majority alone.

Parties must master the delicate art of interparty negotiation: participating in package deals, accepting compromise, without losing essential party identity or abandoning key issues for which the party stands. The losses of both Venstre and R and the gains of K and s in the 1977 election are but the most recent illustrations of the penalties of refusing reasonable co-operation and the gains from promoting it. A survey of the 1977 election by Mr Glans of Aarhus Institute of Government published in *Information* of 25 April 1977 provides some interesting and up-to-date information on both voter movement and volatility and on the occupational composition of the electorates of the various parties, showing changes between the 1975 and 1977 elections.

The Social Democrat gains of 1977 mean that the party has once again become the majority party among workers (55 as against 47 per cent in 1975), but the proportion of workers in the electorate of the party declined from 59 to 52 per cent. There were also strong gains among students and senior white-collar workers and officials. On the far Left, the claims of these three parties to be 'workers' parties' were mildly weakened. The whole far Left only obtained 12 per cent of workers' votes in 1977, as against 17 per cent in 1975. These figures were made up of 6 per cent for DKP as against 8 per cent in 1975, 2 per cent (2 per cent) for vs and 4 per cent (7 per cent) for SF. At the same time, the proportion of these parties' electorates made up of workers also

Table 3.1 Distribution of Votes and Seats in Elections, 1968–77

| Party[1] | Leading Figure | 1968 % | 1968 Seats | 1971 % | 1971 Seats | 1973 % | 1973 Seats | 1975 % | 1975 Seats | 1977 % | 1977 Seats | Electorate | Characteristic Policies Position in Spectrum | Years in Govt since 1918 |
|---|---|---|---|---|---|---|---|---|---|---|---|---|---|---|
| S | Jørgensen | 34·2 | 62 | 37·3 | 70 | 25·6 | 46 | 29·9 | 54 | 37·0 | 65 | urban workers, office workers | centre left/left | 38 |
| RV | Haugaard | 15·0 | 27 | 14·4 | 27 | 11·2 | 20 | 7·9 | 13 | 3·6 | 6 | suburban, middle class, intellectuals | centre left | 28 |
| KF | Schlüter | 20·4 | 37 | 16·7 | 31 | 9·1 | 16 | 5·5 | 10 | 8·5 | 15 | suburban, upper-middle class | centre right | 14 |
| DR | Christensen | 0·7 | 0 | 1·7 | 0 | 2·8 | 5 | 1·8 | 0 | 3·3 | 6 | middle class, anti-EEC, non-socialists | centre right/liberals | 3 |
| SF | Petersen | 6·1 | 11 | 9·1 | 17 | 6·1 | 11 | 4·9 | 9 | 3·9 | 7 | intellectuals, urban workers | moderate left | (2)[3] |
| DKP | Jespersen | 1·0 | 0 | 1·4 | 0 | 3·6 | 6 | 4·2 | 7 | 3·7 | 7 | urban working class | left | (1/2)[4] |
| LC | Westerby | 1·3 | 0 | — | — | — | — | — | — | — | — | urban liberals | centre | |
| CD | Jacobsen | — | | — | — | 7·8 | 14 | 2·1 | 4 | 6·4 | 11 | urban | centre | |
| P | | — | | — | | — | | — | | 1·2 | 0 | pensioners | special interest | |
| KrF | Møller | — | | 1·9 | 0 | 4·0 | 7 | 5·3 | 9 | 3·4 | 6 | rural, suburban middle class | centre | |

| Code | Leader | | | | | | | | | | | | Description | |
|---|---|---|---|---|---|---|---|---|---|---|---|---|---|---|
| v | Hartling | 18·6 | 34 | 15·6 | 30 | 12·2 | 22 | 23·3 | 42 | 12·0 | 21 | 14 | rural electorate | right |
| U | Poulsen | 0·5 | 0 | — | — | — | — | — | — | — | — | | rural, conservative farmers, middle class | right |
| VS | Sigsgaard | 2·0 | 4 | 1·6 | 0 | 1·5 | 0 | 2·0 | 4 | 2·7 | 5 | | urban intellectuals | left |
| FrP | Glistrup | — | — | 15·9 | 28 | 13·6 | 24 | 14·6 | 26 | | | | middle and lower-middle class | anti tax/bureaucracy |

¹ S  = Social Democrats
RV = Radical Liberals
KF = Conservatives
DR = Justice Party
SF = Social People's Party
DKP = Communists
LC = Liberal Centre
CD = Centre Democrats
P  = Pensioners' Party
KRF = Christian People's Party
V  = Venstre (Liberals)
U  = Independents
VS = Left Socialists
FrP = Progress Party

² The figures concern only the 175 seats elected in metropolitan Denmark. Four seats are elected in Greenland (two) and the Faeroes (two).
³ SF was the formal 'support party' for the s government in 1966–8 without having any seats in the cabinet.
⁴ The Communist Party participated in the liberation government (1945).

declined, quite catastrophically for SF (down from 40 to 29 per cent).

Venstre resumed its traditional position as a rural-based, farmers' party, with farmers now representing 47 per cent of its electorate, as against 30 per cent in 1975. The Centre Democrats and Conservatives reinforced their position among clerical workers and self-employed. The CD share of workers votes actually fell by 2 per cent, underlining the party's shift to the right. The Progress Party became strongly rural, with 65 per cent of its electorate now being rural; it lost support among urban workers, largely to S (8 per cent of its 1975 vote).

VOTER SHIFTS

Only S was totally successful in holding its 1975 electorate to the tune of 93 per cent. The two bridging parties SF and RV showed extreme volatility, holding only 48 and 41 per cent respectively of their 1975 electorate in 1977. The RV had the lowest 'loyalty' score, which underlines again the 'pipeline' role of the party on which we have already commented. Looking at its performance in more detail, we see that it lost a 4·19 per cent share of the vote to other parties and made a small gain of 0·65 per cent to give a net loss of 3·4 per cent.

Even those parties which made net gains showed considerable volatility. Indeed, only 50 per cent of the 1975 CD voters voted for that party in 1977. The best scores were obtained by the most clearly defined and ideological parties: S (93 per cent), FRP (79 per cent), DR (77 per cent), VS (71 per cent) and DKP (71 per cent).

Parties gained or lost votes to or from the parties perceived as most immediately next to them in the ideological spectrum. SF lost support mainly to S (31 per cent) and to DKP or VS (6 and 7 per cent). RV lost support to S (27 per cent) and to CD (9 per cent of its 1975 electorate). S, KF and CD also gained from their ideological neighbours, but not so much from each other. The gainers, who were in fact the *de facto* majority, not only helped each other politically, but poached relatively few voters from each other. (See Table 3.1 for a summary of the history and character of the parties.)

NOTES

1  For a history of Denmark, see P. Lauring, *A History of the Kingdom of Denmark* (Copenhagen: Høst, 1960).
2  See Kenneth E. Miller, *Government and Politics in Denmark* (Boston: Houghton Mifflin, 1968).

3 Information based on:
  Miller, op. cit., ch. 3, pp. 57–94.
  P. Møller (ed.), *De Politiske Partier* (Copenhagen: Det Danske Folag, 1974).
  T. Krogh and M. Sorensen, *De Politiske Partier og deres Programmer* (Copenhagen: Gyldendal, 1972).
  A. H. Thomas, 'Danish social democracy and the European Community', *JCMS*, vol. 13, no. 4
4 Erik Damgaard, 'Stability and change of the Danish party system over half a century', *Scandinavian Political Studies*, vol. 9, 1974.

# BIBLIOGRAPHY

## THE POLITICAL SYSTEM

Borre, O. (1975) 'The general election in Denmark 1975', *Scandinavian Political Studies*, vol. 10.

Damgaard, E. (1976) 'The functions of Parliament in the Danish political system', in European Parliamentary Symposium, *European Integration and the Future of Parliaments in Europe* (Luxembourg).

Finer, S. E. (ed.) (1975) *Adversary Politics and Electoral Reform* (see esp. section on the Scandinavian states by N. C. M. Elder) (London, Anthony Wigram).

Hurwitz, S. (1960) *The Ombudsman* (Copenhagen, Det Dansk Selskab).

Jones, W. G. (1970) *Denmark* (London, Ernest Benn).

Lauring, P. (1960) *A History of the Kingdom of Denmark* (Copenhagen, Høst).

Laux, W. E. (1963) *Interest Groups in Danish Politics* (Ann Arbor, Mich., Ann Arbor).

Miller, K. E. (1968) *Politics and Government in Denmark* (Boston, Houghton Mifflin).

Pedersen, M. N. (1967) 'Consensus and conflict in the Danish Folketing 1945–65', *Scandinavian Political Studies*, vol. 2.

## DENMARK AND THE EEC

Eklit, J., and Pedersen, M. N. (1973) 'Denmark enters EEC', *Scandinavian Political Studies*, vol. 3.

Fitzmaurice, J. (1973) 'Scandinavian referenda and EEC entry', *European Review* (Spring).

Fitzmaurice, J. (1976) 'The national parliaments and European policy making: the case of Denmark', *Parliamentary Affairs*, vol. XXIX, no. 3, pp. 282–91.

Thomas, A. H. (1975) 'Danish Social Democracy and the European Community', *Journal of Common Market Studies*, vol. 13, no. 4, pp. 454–68.

## THE PARTIES

Bille, L. (1974) S-SF: *Kilder til belysning af Forholdet mellem Socialidemokratiet og Socialistisk Folkeparti 1959–73* (Copenhagen, Gyldendal).

Jørgensen, A. (1975) *Til Venstre for Midten* (Copenhagen, Fremad).

Kaarsted, T. (1964) *Regeringskrisen 1957: Trekantregerings tilblivelsen* (Aarhus, Aarhus Universitetsforlag).

Kolding, K. (1958) *Danmarks Retsforbundet* (Copenhagen, Det Danske Forlag).

Krogh, T., and Sørensen, M. (1972) *De Politiske Partier og deres Programmer* (Copenhagen, Gyldendal).

Maddeley, J. T. S. (1977) 'Scandinavian Christian Democracy: throwback or protest', *European Journal of Political Research*, no. 5, pp. 267–86.

Møller, P. (ed.) (1974) *De Politiske Partier* (Copenhagen, Det Danske Forlag).

Nielsen, H. J. (1977) *The Uncivic Culture: Attitudes towards the Political System and Votes for the Progress Party 1973–75* (Copenhagen, Institute for Political Studies, Research Paper 2).

Thomas, A. H. (1973) *Parliamentary Parties in Denmark 1945–65* (University of Strathclyde Survey Research Centre, Occasional Paper No. 13).

Thomas, A. H. (1977) 'Social Democracy in Denmark', in W. E. Paterson and A. H. Thomas (eds), *Social Democratic Parties in Western Europe* (London, Croom Helm).

Upton, A. F. (1973) *Communism in Scandinavia and Finland* (New York, Doubleday).

# 4
# France

## MICHAEL STEED

France was the home of one of the first manifestations of the form of political organisation which we now recognise as the political party. In the flux of the French Revolution men with similar political purposes found it useful to meet together regularly to discuss, to act in consort and to be identified as such: the names of some of these clubs, such as the Girondins or the Jacobins, are still remembered. In due course, with a legislative assembly and periodic elections by universal suffrage, the Third Republic developed other types of party: that based essentially on the assembly group and that structured around local committees of leading citizens. Whilst these various primitive forms of party have largely given way to the modern, all-embracing mass party in most of Western Europe, in France they survive and indeed flourish. Alongside them are the larger, more modern parties and it is these which tend to dominate French politics. The bewildering number of smaller groups, changing labels, pseudo-parties and organisations linking parties reflects the very uneven development of the French party system. Most of the names and some of the substance have changed greatly during the last decade. Yet the very frequency of changing labels and shifting electoral fortunes reflects the persistence of traditional behaviour. Disentangling the lasting from the ephemeral is itself a permanent problem in analysing French politics.

In the late seventies there are three well-established, large parties. The Parti communiste français (PCF)* has the most secure electoral base with a fifth of the total vote and a fully developed and structured organisation claiming half a million members. It has been out of office for over thirty years. By 1978 Parti socialiste (PS) was electorally the leading party of France. Yet as recently as 1969 its presidential candidate was a very poor

* For a complete list of abbreviations see glossary at end of chapter.

fourth, with barely 5 per cent of the total vote. Gaullism, the latest emanation of which is the Rassemblement pour la République (RPR), has been electorally the most successful party during the Fifth Republic, establishing for itself a dominating position without precedent in French political history. Yet the precariousness of its position was illustrated in the 1974 presidential election when its candidate was a poor third with less than 15 per cent of the vote.

However, not one of the leading offices of the Republic in early 1978 was in the hands of any of these parties. The presidency of the Republic was captured in 1974 by the leader of what by most measures would be accounted the fourth party, renamed the Parti républicain (PR) in May 1977 but then the Fédération nationale des Républicains indépendants (FNRI). Yet that party had polled only 7 per cent at the 1973 legislative elections. The prime minister since 1976 had been a non-party man. The presidency of the Senate was in the hands of a product of the Christian Democrat tradition, represented since May 1976 by the Centre des Démocrates sociaux (CDS). His predecessor had been Radical, joining the Mouvement des Radicaux de Gauche (MRG) when the party split. The president of the 1973–8 National Assembly, though he has flirted with Gaullism, spent most of his political career with the Radicals, rejoining the other wing of the party, the Parti radicale-socialiste (PRS) in April 1977. His successor was a Gaullist, elected against the wishes of the RPR.

The party system thus provides a generous role for smaller parties and for personalities, operating through alliances and electoral cartels. No party stands apart from this system, though from time to time a party tries to. For periods the system of alliances assumes a settled form, although links reflecting previous alliances are generally retained through inertia and in the expectation that a·change of partners may come at any time.

This means that for certain, limited purposes it is blocs of parties which perform the functions that in other multi-party European states are performed by individual parties. One consequence of this is that electoral statistics in France have different, and questionable, significance. It is not possible to assess the true electoral support of most smaller parties. Thus the 7 per cent figure quoted earlier for the Independent Republicans in 1973 is the number of votes cast for RI candidates where they were standing expressed as a percentage of all votes cast. Many of the 28·5 per cent of the votes cast for candidates standing under the label Union des Républicains de progrès (URP) in other constituencies were in some sense RI votes since the RIs, the Gaullists and some Centrists had combined to form the URP cartel at the first round of that election. Only the figures for the Communist vote are truly comparable with election statistics in countries with more typical party and electoral systems.

The thesis of this chapter is that the French party system can be understood only in terms of three different groupings, one of which – the simple dualism of Left and Right – has become increasingly dominant, though not necessarily permanently. Table 4.4 on page 85 sets out these groupings – and some actual electoral and parliamentary alignments. It is evident that there is no simple, or enduring, pattern.

On the left of Table 4.4, parties are identified by six traditional political families, or strands of political ideas. Five have been present in French politics for more than half a century, and the other, Gaullism, although only existing as such for the last thirty years has some links with ideas of heroic leadership, plebiscitory democracy and socially progressive authoritarian rule which were characteristic of mid-nineteenth-century Bonapartism and revived briefly later in that century as Boulangism. For all the kaleidoscope of names and big shifts in voting, since the Second World War there have rarely been votes of more than 2 per cent for parties or presidential candidates not clearly belonging to one of these six political families.[1] The variation is otherwise around splits inside, and alliances between, these six enduring forces.

Three – Christian Democrat, Socialist and Communist – are immediately recognisable as parts of wider European movements with coherent ideologies. The French parties came closest to a simplification resembling other Continental party systems immediately after the Second World War when three well-organised mass parties representing these forces totalled 75 per cent of the votes cast. This reflected a temporary eclipse for the older Conservative and Radical forces, both representing particular attitudes together with a tradition of pragmatism rather than a developed ideology and neither having ever found the form of a modern mass party. Although peculiarly French in their loose organisation and political language, they have similar traditions to the Conservative and Liberal parties of Britain and Scandinavia. Gaullism, of course, is an essentially one-country political phenomenon, though it has certain resemblances to other parties with charismatic leaders and which have developed out of a constitutional crisis, notably Fianna Fáil with which it is linked in the European Parliament.

These six groups are used for the part of this chapter on individual parties, arranged in approximate order of electoral success. However no elections, parliamentary, presidential or local, have been fought simply on this sixfold basis since 1947. One of two other alignments, or a mixture between them, have dominated all electoral battles.

One is a simple Left–Right dualism, although the Right in France never admits to that title. Historically, this dualism reflected the old battle between secular and clerical forces or between those who identified with the French Revolutionary tradition and those who did not. It grouped, therefore, the Communists, Socialists and Radicals as the Left and the other three as the Right. This was the line-up at the popular front election of 1936 and again in the affiliations of lists in 1956.[2] It reappeared in the second round presidential contests in 1965 and 1974 and increasingly at parliamentary elections during the Fifth Republic. Dualism between the Left and what calls itself the Presidential Majority has steadily entrenched itself in French politics in the seventies and with it the notions of alternative government inherent in a two-party system and a trend towards class rather than church attendance (the measure of the secular versus clerical battle) as the basis of voting.

None the less, an alternative alignment has stubbornly refused to disappear. This is that of the four Centre families against both the Gaullists and the Communists. That was the basis of most Fourth Republic governments, and of affiliations in the 1951 election. It reappeared as the Cartel des Non at the 1962 referendum and elections and carried Alain Poher to the presidency of the Senate in 1968. Poher tried, with partial success, to make the combination an electoral force at the 1969 presidential elections; the dualism of 1965 temporarily broke down. The combination has represented common policies on defence and European integration, and a common support for French parliamentary democratic traditions and a certain style of politics. It was no coincidence that the issue of direct elections to the European Parliament in the summer of 1977 threatened to cut off both Gaullists and Communists from their current allies and resurrect the centre bloc.

It is a profound characteristic of the French party system over a long period that whenever one of these alignments threatens to become permanent, questions arise which pull the parties towards the other one. The 1951 centre bloc electoral alliance gave way to a rapprochement between the Gaullists and the Conservatives in 1953 whilst the Communists backed the Mendès-France premiership of 1954, thus opening up the dualist fissure. The Cartel des Non was already breaking down at the second round of the 1962 elections; but no sooner had the dualist alignment dominated the run-up to and the results of 1967 elections than the parties of the Left started squabbling and only hastily patched up a temporary alliance for 1968. Broadly, whenever the dominant pattern is dualist, tensions between the Gaullists and the non-Gaullist Right, and between the Communists and the non-Communist Left, sooner or later set in; and whenever the centre bloc is in operation, storms begin to develop at the Left–Right fissure. Since Christian Democrats and Radicals dislike having to align themselves according to this fissure (which tends to split particularly the Radicals) they frequently seek to revive the centre bloc.

It is possible to interpret developments in the French party system in the 1970s in two very different fashions. One is that the inherent potential of the two alternative alignments is still present and that, when the right circumstances arise, the present dualism will give way to a restored centre bloc, such as a Giscard–Mitterrand alliance which is much whispered of by all parties in France. The other is that we have been witnessing a fundamental change in the system, whereby dualism is now so entrenched in French politics that a return of the centre bloc is no longer the option that the account given above suggests. The most recent British account of French party politics published before this chapter went to press (*Political Parties and Elections in the French Fifth Republic* by J. R. Frears, published December 1977) is strongly committed to this latter interpretation, and certainly most of the evidence in the eight years following May 1969 (when Pompidou succeeded in enlarging the Presidential Majority despite the counter-attraction of Poher's candidature and the Socialists decided that, with Poher's failure, their path to power definitely lay in an alliance with the Communists), supports it.

During this period yet another would-be centre pole, the Mouvement Réformateur (MR) linking some Radicals with the Centre Démocrate (CD) at the 1973 elections, won fewer votes than its component parties had ever won before. In 1974 the attempt to keep an organised grouping independent of the two larger blocs was abandoned as the MR's leaders opted for Giscard d'Estaing, while its voters seem to have split very roughly two to one in his favour in the second-round duel between him and Mitterrand. At the 1976 cantonal and 1977 municipal elections dualism was extended to all parts of France. Socialist councillors who had previously been elected in local centre bloc alliances were obliged to break off such links.[3] In one notorious case, Nantes, rebel Socialist councillors who had thought their chances were much better sticking to the traditional alliance and who had therefore left their party, lost their seats.[4] The PS celebrated this victory and its commitment to the dualist approach by moving its June 1977 congress to Nantes.

Nantes seemed to symbolise both the end of electoral support for personality-based centrism and the desire of a large majority of the electorate for a simple choice between Left and Right. As the 1978 parliamentary elections loomed, the two blocs appeared both united and entrenched. The Radicals had split and were cemented into their respective sides. The Christian Democrat formations had opted for the Right, but many individual Catholics had chosen to join the Socialists.

However, during the twelve months between the 1977 municipal elections and the 1978 parliamentary elections, the behaviour of all parties began to fit much better the first, more traditional interpretation. The RPR leader, Chirac, who had been steadily distancing himself from the rest of the presidential majority since August 1976, sabotaged efforts to establish a common majority position under the leadership of the prime minister (which is how the majority, with the Gaullists dominant, had been co-ordinated in previous elections). In response the three smaller majority parties, the PR, CDS and PRS, came together as the Union pour la Démocratie française (UDF) so that the presidential majority in March 1978 consisted of two rival blocks, one Gaullist and the other flying more specifically Giscardien colours but in reality representing the successors of the Fourth Republic parties. In contrast to 1973, when there had been a single URP candidate in most constituencies, most voters in 1978 could choose between a Gaullist and a UDF candidate. In further contrast, the 1973 choice between the MR and the non-Gaullists part of the URP had disappeared in many constituencies. The RPR and UDF united in condemning the common programme, and in distancing themselves from what they termed collectivism, so the Left–Right fissure remained. But within the Right bloc, the Gaullists had made themselves more distinct from the other parties than at any time during the Fifth Republic.

A parallel split developed inside the Left bloc. Quarrels about costing the common programme, which had stood as the cornerstone of the unity of the PS, PCF and MRG since 1972, broke out in May 1977. After sulky exchanges between the party leaders, meetings in early autumn ended in dramatic disagreement. Demands made by the Communists seemed mainly responsible for the breach, but the PS and more especially the MRG appeared not unwilling to differentiate themselves from the PCF. The Left went to the polls without any firm agreement about how they would co-operate in the second ballot or, in the event of victory, after the election; but between the two ballots, a hasty agreement was reached.

The March 1978 elections were fought by four fairly evenly

matched party-formations, working in two pairs, which exactly
reflected the alternative groupings of Left/Right and of the centre
bloc against the Gaullists and Communists. *Plus ça change, plus
c'est la meme chose.*

## SOME CHARACTERISTICS OF FRENCH POLITICAL PARTIES

By general European standards, French parties have few members;
the French people are not avid payers of regular subscriptions to
organisations, whether political or occupational. Only the three
largest parties have memberships in six figures. Some of the other,
smaller parties claim figures of 25,000, 50,000 or more; but for
none of them is the number of members particularly relevant to
their electoral or political strength. In France a personality, a
handful of followers and a shred of political ideology can still
acquire credible status as a party.

Another measure of support and penetration used to be the
readership of the parties' own newspapers, but these have
declined greatly in significance. Both the Gaullists *(La Nation)*
and the SFIO *(Le Populaire)* once thought a daily newspaper was
essential to a party's means of communication; but the new PS
and RPR have gained strength without one. The Communists still
circulate daily a couple of hundred thousand copies of *L'Humanité*.
That circulation, and the fact that the PCF probably has more
paid-up members than all the other parties added together,
demonstrate how far it is a different sort of party, still strongly
entrenched in its own section of the community but thereby less
capable of communicating with society at large.

The finance of French parties has always been secretive, and
the little stickers 'PAID FOR OUT OF TAXES' which PSU
militants stuck all over the lavish Gaullist posters at one election
reflected a popular belief. Parties charge high membership rates
by British, though not by other Continental, standards. All parties
receive money from business. These are either (for most of them)
contributions from privately owned enterprises or (especially in
the case of the Communist Party) through controlling enterprises
themselves. The PCF uses its control of many municipalities to
provide its own enterprises, such as wholesale book distribution,
with monopoly outlets. Private business has, as in all similar
countries, always given support to non-Socialist parties; but in
France the importance of boosting the non-Communist part of the
Union of the Left is reputed to have led to a considerable in-
jection of business funds into the PS and MRG.

There is no direct public financing of parties, though certain
election expenses are reimbursed. However, the widespread

practice of allowing state-paid employees to devote much or all of their time to party activities constitutes a major indirect subsidy. The practice is linked to the system of ministerial *cabinets*, whereby members of the government bring personal political assistants on to their department payroll, and to a more general blurring of the roles of neutral bureaucrat and political partisan which has long characterised the French political system. It is not only government parties which benefit from publicly paid personnel; in a country where the norms of public life value pluralist democracy, opposition parties have also been able to use civil servants. Furthermore, all deputies have recently been allocated a political assistant, many of whom are partly engaged in party work. Mayors of larger towns also have their staffs, and the PCF in particular has been able to draw on resources through its municipal strength.

It follows that the real resources of French political parties are greater than the expenditure of their financial income, although the latter may be considerable. One journalist estimated from the total output and distribution of publicity material that two rival candidates of the Right for the mayoralty of Paris in March 1977 together spent 15 million francs, while the Left (which had no expectation of winning) spent a further 1·3 million francs – making a total of nearly 2 million pounds sterling on that campaign alone (Véronique Maurus in *Le Monde*, 10 March 1977).

The parties differ very greatly in structure but a common feature is the importance of the department as the level of local organisation. Despite the use of a single-member constituency system since 1958, and the growing if limited importance of the planning regions, the departmental party officials or committee remain the key point between the party national organs and Paris headquarters on the one hand and the local section or individual member on the other.

French parliamentary life, in both the National Assembly and the Senate, is organised around groups. These only roughly correspond to the parties outside parliament. In the assembly the rule that the minimum size for a group is thirty means that members of smaller parties must join together; but the confusion of labels and alliances by which some groups relate to parties owes more to the style of French politics, the carry-over of electoral alliances imposed by the two-ballot system and the uncertainties as to whether some of the smaller political groupings are really parties anyway. Sometimes realignments between parliamentary groups precede changes in the parties outside parliament; sometimes earlier party relationships are preserved, fossil-like, in parliament. The creation of the Pompidolian Centrist party, CDP, in 1969 had been clearly presaged after both 1967 and 1968 elections by the character and leadership of the Assembly group, Progrès et Démocratie moderne (see below, p. 75). In the Senate, by way of contrast, the seven groupings have preserved an alignment of parties which corresponds better with the Fourth Republic party system than that of the Fifth – reflecting the continuing presence of both Conservatives and Radicals in local government (from which the Senate is elected). One irritating consequence of this is that it is not easy to reconcile the political composition of the French parliamentary bodies with election results.

A more important result is that the relationship between the parliamentary and extra-parliamentary wings of parties is complex and variable – both between parties and over time within certain parties. This is further complicated by the quasi-separation of the executive from parliament and the role of personalities in French politics. Only the Communists have a straightforward relationship: their parliamentary groups are homogeneously composed of deputies who are members of the PCF and elected with a Communist label; and their party has a strict policy of controlling the action of its parliamentary representatives. This relationship has never been put to the test of a sustained period in government.

There is one form of organisation in French parties which is notable by its absence. In a country where the major elective post is now the presidency, there is no established machinery whereby parties perform the key function of selecting candidates; one could not imagine a clearer contrast with the USA, where parties can be said to be organised at national level mainly around the presidential nomination process. The failure of the Fifth Republic parties to reorganise themselves around a presidential system may yet prove to be a factor undermining the stability of that system.

## THE GAULLIST PARTY

Gaullism as an organised party was launched by General de Gaulle in 1947 as the Rassemblement du Peuple français (RPF); in December 1976, Jacques Chirac launched its latest emanation as the evocatively similar RPR (Rassemblement pour la République). In between, Gaullism had used roughly six other names – roughly, because there is ambiguity between the party titles and those umbrella labels given to Gaullist-led electoral alliances. These terminological problems pinpoint both the party's essential continuity, the more pronounced with Chirac's leadership, and the uncertainty of its role and impermanence of its organisational structure.

Prior to the resignation of President de Gaulle in 1969, Gaullism had had at least five quite distinct phases, politically and organisationally. Before 1947, there were individuals close to the general, plus a small political group calling for his leadership but without his direct involvement. After 1947 the RPF, a structured mass party, centralised and autocratically led by de Gaulle himself, was organised as a challenge to the system of the Fourth Republic. Later, towards the end of the Fourth Republic, a clutch of Gaullist parliamentarians maintained a small party mainly to further their own careers inside that very system. In the early years of the Fifth Republic during the trauma of the Algerian War a more normal party emerged, divided internally over the Algerian question, and with the president deliberately keeping his distance. Until 1962 de Gaulle's position rested on the willingness of other parties to let him govern (and solve the Algerian conundrum), and the Gaullist party was not a key part of his government's parliamentary position.

With the November 1962 parliamentary elections, the Gaullist party's role changed; henceforward, it became crucial to the political stability of the Fifth Republic, providing a parliamentary majority committed to upholding the government that the president nominated and almost incidentally also committed to its policies. The extra-parliamentary organisation of the party languished, although following a rather narrow victory in the March 1967 parliamentary elections, a renamed party was launched in November 1967 with a more articulated and member-based structure. The electoral landslide of the following year, however, was achieved through a simple appeal to voters to rally to the government and the Republic; not because a more firmly based party had been built.

Thus the party, by then called the Union des Démocrates pour la République (UDR) which carried President Pompidou to office in 1969, and ensured him continued power through a parliamentary majority in 1973, reflected strikingly different formative influences, posing many questions as to its real nature. The core of its leadership throughout, though by 1969 this was beginning to change, consisted of the faithful followers of de Gaulle, usually dating right back to June 1940. With them went a core of attitudes and political language, reflecting de Gaulle's own emphasis on the French nation, on leadership and on the institutional achievements of the Fifth Republic. Although they could make it sound a distinctive ideology, the success of Gaullism depended in reality on a large measure of pragmatism and willingness to adjust to the changing roles of both France and of the party within French politics. Particularly from 1962 onwards, the UDR had been recruiting new militants, deputies and in due course leaders simply as the party of government: new generations too young to have been in the resistance, or even to have supported the RPF, were moving up the party hierarchy. Because the age cohort of 'Gaullists from the first hour' had been providing a steadily ageing leadership, some marked change, affecting the role of the party, was bound to occur in the 1970s.

Broadly there were two theories at this stage as to the nature and future of the UDR. Among its enemies, it was often assumed that it was so much a product of the charismatic appeal of de Gaulle that it could not long survive his departure. A view more common among political scientists was that 'personal Gaullism' had been replaced by 'party Gaullism', and that the UDR which Pompidou took over should be seen as a 'modern conservative party' (Charlot, 1971; Frears, 1977). The party had consolidated itself, with a clear, right-wing electoral base and a majoritarian vocation. France seemed to have acquired a party less like the earlier Gaullist formations and more akin to the British Conservatives, the German Christian Democrats or the US Republicans.

Yet there were at least three respects in which the UDR did not resemble any of these three. First, it simply had not spent the necessary time for the habits and attitudes of a long-established majoritarian party to sink in. Most Gaullist leaders in the early 1970s had entered the party when its role had been different, and old attitudes die hard. Secondly, its leadership group, in practice, was an oligarchy inherited from the past whose role was legitimised through personal contact with de Gaulle – the Gaullist barons, as they came to be known. The party had not established a set procedure in which leadership could be renewed – whether through open competition within known rules (e.g. the US Republicans) or through a clear and permanent focus of power (e.g. the parliamentary front bench in the British Conservative Party). Authority over the UDR flowed from the president and through his nominee, the prime minister; without these offices, where would the party have been? Thirdly, the party had not swallowed its allies as had the Christian Democrats across the Rhine during the 1950s. Had the UDR insisted after 1962 that all who wanted to wear the Gaullist ticket at elections must be members of the party, it is possible that a single broad party of the Right would have emerged. But Pompidou's strategy was to maximise his chances of electoral success (in 1962, 1967, 1968 and again in 1969) by engaging sections of other parties to work under a looser Gaullist umbrella, and so first the FNRI and then the CDP were born. As the presidential majority was enlarged, so the distinctively Gaullian character of the Gaullist party was emphasised – both by the Gaullists themselves, and by their quasi-Gaullist allies who wished to retain a *raison d'être* for their separate existence. It is likely that the two-ballot system facilitated this process, thus confirming Duverger's thesis about its tendency to lead to multi-partism (Duverger, 1951, p. 269).

During Pompidou's five presidential years, the UDR's continuing dominant role seemed to confirm Charlot's thesis. None the less, there were indications, both in the disputation between the UDR and its smaller allies and in internal debate, that the party's role and *modus operandi* were highly uncertain. At the November 1973 Nantes conference, two historic Gaullists, Jacques Chaban-Delmas (Pompidou's first prime minister, and the evangelist of the socially progressive side of Gaullism) and Michel Debré (de Gaulle's first prime minister, and keeper of the party's nationalist conscience) 'gained control of the movement' (*Le Monde*, 20 November 1973) in a conflict with more pragmatic Gaullists then in government, including Jacques Chirac, minister of agriculture.

There is an inherent contradiction involved in a party whose essential purpose is support of the head of state and his government coming under the control of those contesting the direction of that government. The crisis came with Pompidou's death, when Chaban-Delmas was nominated with little support outside the ranks of the party (and indeed without the backing of some within it, such as Chirac) and fought a campaign on quintessentially Gaullist themes. He polled under 15 per cent, and that overstates the hard-core Gaullist vote since he had considerable personal support in Aquitaine.[5] After Giscard d'Estaing's victory and Chirac's appointment as prime minister, Gaullist morale sank, the party's rating in opinion polls began to drop towards the Chaban-Delmas presidential vote and the future of the UDR looked problematical. Then, in December 1974, Chirac staged an extra-ordinary coup (with the connivance of Alexandre Sanguinetti, secretary-general) whereby he himself was elected secretary-general and thus took control of the party apparatus. At the time, it looked like both a reversion to normal (with authority over the Gaullist party flowing through the prime minister – however he had been appointed) and a new departure (as a non-Gaullist president appeared indirectly to have brought the party to heel). It was to prove to be neither; as Chirac's views diverged from those of the president, he used the Gaullist party as his personal political base. Following his resignation in August 1976, he at once set out to transform the UDR into a Chiracien party.

The RPR was born in December 1976 with rapturous support for the new leader. Chirac's pugnacious electioneering style and use of historic Gaullist language symbols rekindled some of the enthusiasm and loyalty which de Gaulle had once inspired. In many respects the RPR is closer to the RPF than any of the intervening forms that the party had taken – in spirit, role and structure. Once again it has a heroic leader who is at the same time directly in charge. The secretary-general, first Jerôme Monod and then in April 1978 Alain Devaquet, is the leader's appointee – with no pretence, as the UDR had preferred, at election by the membership. The organs of the party reflect the same practice of centralised direction. The UDR had not exactly been the most democratic of parties, as demonstrated by the ease of Chirac's takeover, but it had a structure based on the elective principle which could have permitted a transition to a more normally organised type of party. The RPR is unique among major Western parties in the dictatorial role it gives its president. Since Chirac has followed de Gaulle's precedent of making a solitary claim to the mantle, he is not surrounded by a collective leadership out of which he has emerged.

Yet while the RPR, like the RPF, is the vehicle of a leader instead of the support of a government, it is operating within the Gaullist Republic. It cannot too openly contest the authority of a president elected by the means, and using the *de facto* powers, for which Gaullists fought. Like the RPF it will find it difficult to survive for long unless electoral success comes its way; yet, given its style and the cumbrous institutions of the Fifth Republic, outright electoral success will not prove a simple goal. The battle for the mayoralty of Paris, which Chirac won in March 1977, showed that the new formula had a real appeal; the RPR claimed a flood of new members over and above the quarter of a million or so which the UDR claimed.[6]

Chirac has renewed the roots of Gaullism, and tapped a very particular strand of French politics which goes back to Bonaparte. He has made the Gaullist party more aggressively different from the others, and thereby reinforced the multi-party element within the party system. Yet his own background and career is that of a technocrat and a pragmatic man of government, for whom leadership of a broad, modern Conservative party would be more appropriate. His capture of the Gaullist party raises more questions about its future than it answers.

## THE SOCIALIST PARTY

Like the RPR, the Parti socialiste has undergone a transformation, although its story is very much simpler. From 1920 France's Socialist Party, then called the SFIO, has fought a battle with the Communist Party for pre-eminence on the Left. At its peak (24 per cent of the votes, and over a third of a million members in 1945) the SFIO was still second to the PCF, and from that point its support steadily declined – and aged – for a quarter of a century. At the last election where the SFIO's support can be measured separately from Radical and other allies, it was down to 12·7 per cent (1962); and throughout the 1960s its membership hovered around a claimed 80,000. It had strong regional bases in the Marseilles area, in the two northernmost industrial departments, and in an area of declining rural population in the southwest. But in most of France, it was a minor party. By the 1969 presidential election when Gaston Deferre, mayor of Marseilles, polled a mere 5·1 per cent, compared with 21·5 per cent for a Communist and 4·8 per cent for two more left-wing Socialists, the sexagenarian SFIO seemed to be on its death-bed.

Meanwhile, there were plenty of signs of life on the non-Communist Left. The 1960s saw a growth of clubs and movements which, whilst they temporarily accentuated the division and therefore the weakness of the Left, were to make a key contribution to strengthening and diversifying it in the 1970s. The major movement of clubs was the Convention des Institutions républicains (CIR) led by François Mitterrand. The CIR included both Catholic groups (though one of the main clubs attracting progressive Catholics, the Club Jean Moulin, remained outside the CIR) and a strand inherited from the Mendesist Radicals, notably the Clubs des Jacobins, animated by Charles Hernu. Several other clubs grouped former SFIO members, who had left in disgust at the party's compromises and often spent a period in the Parti socialiste unifié (PSU); a number of these came together in the Union des Clubs pour le Renouveau de la Gauche (UCRG), led by Alain Savary; a further recognisable grouping was of former Communists (often of the generation of revulsion against the Soviet invasion of Hungary), most notably in the Union des Groupes et Clubs socialistes (UGCS) animated by Jean Poperen who had also spent a period in the PSU. The move of the left wing of what had been the Christian Democratic movement in the Fourth Republic towards a socialist identification was still more important in the trade union world; the former Christian trade union organisation renamed itself 'Democratic' in 1962 and under the leadership of Edmond Maire began to make contact with socialist thinkers and organisations. There were also stirrings which had no connection with particular political traditions and which were looking towards a new socialism freed from the hang-ups of the past – the element of those who were sometimes called technicians. Hubert Dubedout, for instance, won the mayorality of the fast-growing city of Grenoble in 1965 on a reform platform and became one of the leaders of a movement of municipal action groups.

All the groups and personalities named in the preceding paragraph have since come together in the new PS. It was founded in 1969, just after that disastrous presidential election, out of the SFIO and UCRG; and Alain Savary took over from that archetypal man of the SFIO's past, Guy Mollet. During the following two years there was an enormous rejuvenation of the local base of the party, which was probably the true turning-point. In 1971 a congress of unification was held at Epinay; Mitterrand and the CIR merged into the PS and Mitterrand himself became its new leader. Most of the clubs disappeared, and their educational policy and research activities were channelled into the new party. The PSU, which had shown signs of becoming a significant rival to the SFIO in the early years of the Fifth Republic and again in the maelstrom of revolutionary ideas following the events of May 1968, barely survived; the bulk of its former leading members found a new home in the PS and most of its voters followed suit.

The result has been an extraordinarily successful integration of old and new, so much so that the current division inside the new party cuts right across its various sources. Within a couple of years, party debate had crystallised around a Mitterrandist majority (to whom were attached the principal SFIO survivors such as Deferre, and Pierre Mauroy; Michel Rocard (PSU Presidential candidate in 1969) who joined the PS in 1974; together with Mitterrand's own key supporters from the CIR) against a surviving club which had originated inside the SFIO – the Centre d'Etudes, de Recherches et d'Education Socialiste.

CERES, whose leading member is Jean-Pierre Chevènement, has attracted particularly the younger, often more Catholic members of the party so that the secularist position, once the hallmark of militant socialism, has become attached to the more traditional and therefore right-wing members. CERES sees itself as more committed to the strategy of the Communist–Socialist alliance (and therefore more predisposed to take account of the Communist position on questions such as European integration) and as the apostle of the worker self-management form of Socialism. However, Mitterrand's consistent strategy for nearly two decades has been the route to power via a Communist alliance (in contrast to the tergiversations of the SFIO), and the PS as a whole, plus its trade union allies, is now well committed to the self-management approach. The dispute is perhaps more one of style and party-generation; the Mitterrandist leadership is a judicious mixture of politicians of varying experiences, whilst the rapid success of the PS since Mitterrand became leader has attracted many newer, more impatient members who (especially in departments where long-serving deputies are still entrenched) prefer to send representatives more in tune with their own background and ideas to party congresses. Paradoxically, CERES has probably helped to unite the party, providing a dialogue between itself and the Mitterrandists which cut across and submerged the divisions of the fissiparous 1960s. CERES is particularly critical of the personal concentration of power in Mitterrand's hands and, should his leadership cease to be associated with success, the new division could become more dangerous. On the basis of voting at the last two congresses, CERES represents a quarter to a third of the party membership; but it is much stronger where the party used to be weaker – in Paris and in the Catholic west.

On the other wing of the party, there is a continuing element of centre incliners, but they seem to prefer to lie low and wait on the fate of the alliance with the PCF. A few SFIO personalities refused to accept that alliance, and two small splinter parties emerged, the Mouvement démocrate socialiste de France (MDSF) and the Parti socialiste démocrate (PSD). The MDSF came under the MR umbrella in 1973 and was part of the presidential majority from 1974; the PSD tried to find a role as an independent grouping. Although there were ten ex-SFIO deputies who had attached themselves to the MDSF or PSD by the end of the 1973 Assembly, they failed to find any popular support. One, Emile Muller, stood at the 1974 presidential election and polled a mere 0.7 per cent.

The new PS has been able to accommodate CERES as a sort of party within the party more easily because it altered the majoritarian voting system of the SFIO to one of proportional representation for any tendency with the support of at least 5 per cent of the votes at its biennial congress. The preparation of that congress is an elaborate process. Motions are exchanged between the departmental federations and the central steering committee, which attempts to composite. The federations' delegations vote in proportion to local support for resolutions. Thus the party engages in a continuous and formalised debate about its ideology and strategy, and the congress elects the main governing body of the party, its steering committee, to reflect the weight of views in that debate. In turn the steering committee elects by a proportional system a twenty-seven-member executive bureau, which in turn appoints part of itself as the national secretariat. Although the secretariat too was chosen on proportional lines in 1973, it became homogeneously Mitterrandist after the 1975 congress.

Mitterrand's formal position as leader rests on being the first secretary within this secretariat, which normally meets weekly at the party headquarters – though his real personal power is far greater than this status implies. The secretariat combines administrative functions and political leadership; its members are a mixture of leading political figures and long-serving party organisers. The work of the PS headquarters is divided into fifteen sections, each of which is directed by a member of the secretariat. Mitterrand himself took the portfolio of training *(formation)*, indicative of the importance which the PS attaches to the education of its militants in its ideology and political methods.

At the Epinay congress in 1971, the PS claimed 80,300 members inherited from the SFIO. In the following five years it doubled this figure. This is higher than the SFIO at any time after 1948, but much less than the PCF, and probably less than the RPR. Despite its striking renovation, the PS has not succeeded in creating a mass party comparable in size with most other West European Socialist parties.

THE COMMUNIST PARTY

Compared with the Gaullists and Socialists, the Parti communiste français is a rock of stability on the French political and electoral scene. Yet it has been going through a steady change of heart about its role in a multi-party system which, if genuine, has profound consequences for the future of French politics.

Throughout the Fourth Republic the PCF was polling regularly just over a quarter of the total vote; in 1958 a slice of that vote deserted, and it has since polled a steady fifth. PCF dominance in the trade union world, its local bastions, especially in the working-class suburban municipalities around Paris, its monolithic structure and heavy, ideological style of politics have remained constant features since the Second World War. The strength of Communism in France goes back to 1920, when a majority of the SFIO congress voted to affiliate to Lenin's Third International, so splitting the politically mobilised working class. The variegated geography of that split, with some areas (e.g. the Paris region) strongly Communist, others strongly Socialist (e.g. the south-west) and others (e.g. the northern industrial area or the Mediterranean coast) the scene of continuous rivalry between two strong forces, has remained much the same ever since. The fact that the Bolsheviks so inspired a segment of Socialist support as to capture it for the Third International reflected in turn earlier revolutionary and anti-state traditions in French Socialism. Although French Communism was strongly rooted in native soil, it was to earn a reputation as the tool of Moscow, exemplified by the thoroughly Leninist character it rapidly adopted, by slavish adherence to the twists and turns in Soviet foreign policy and by its extreme intolerance of dissent. Relations with Socialism in France developed very differently from those in Italy. During the period that Italy's leading Communists and Socialists shared Mussolini's jails or exile, the PCF vacillated between denunciation of the SFIO as traitors and the popular front alignment. The PCF's move into intransigent isolation with the onset of the Cold War in 1947 meant a complete breach with the SFIO – in contrast to the position in Italy.

From the early sixties, when it became clear that the Fifth Republic had lasting qualities, up to late 1977, the PCF's domestic strategy was simple: to forge an alliance with the Socialist Party as a route to power. To this end, it consistently attacked Socialists whenever they made centre-bloc alliances, and sought a common candidate from the first round of presidential elections, joint lists at municipal elections and second-round pacts in parliamentary elections. Increasingly the PCF demanded that this co-operation be dependent on a common programme of government. This proposal was completely rejected at first, though an increasing number of municipal popular fronts and a single presidential candidate for the Left had been achieved by 1965. Between December 1966 and January 1968 there were a number of common declarations by the PCF and the FGDS (which had its own common programme) pinpointing both agreements and disagreements. Finally the common programme of the Left emerged in June 1972.

Parallel with this achievement, the PCF has somewhat distanced itself from Soviet Communism. From a tentative stretching of independent muscles in 1964, when it sent a delegation to Moscow to inquire why Krushchev had been dismissed, to open attacks on the treatment of dissenters in the USSR in recent years, this has gone a long way. Periodically, PCF equivocation over what happens in other countries has disturbed relations with the PS – particularly Soviet repression in Czechoslovakia in 1968–9 and events in Portugal in 1975–6. These developments apart, *détente* between East and West has eased the PCF's strategy and is probably a condition for its further pursuit. Similarly, the PCF has altered its ideological stance. At its 22nd congress, in February 1976, the doctrine of the 'dictatorship of the proletariat' was formally abandoned with great show. The notion of several roads towards Socialism, depending on national circumstances, has become part of the teaching of a party once totally committed to the Russian model. Although its ideological evolution has been slower than those of the Italian and Spanish Communist parties, the PCF has deliberately associated itself with the others: the association which has earned the title 'Eurocommunism'.

Striking as these changes are, they have been made from above in the classic fashion of democratic centralism. The 1976 congress displayed an unbelievable unanimity, similar to that of the PCF's most Stalinist period. Structure and internal style remain little altered.

The base of the party is the cell, into which members are gathered, immured and activated; the cell is the most characteristic form of Communist organisation, and a leading authority on West European Communist parties has argued that 'if and when [Communist parties] lose their specific nature and become more like other western political parties, the process will begin with the decline of the cell' (McInnes, p. 100). At the 1976 congress, the PCF proudly proclaimed that it had increased its cells from 19,518 in 1972 to 23,178. Of these, the greatest increase was in the most classic form, the workplace cell (from 5,376 to 8,072); in 1976 35 per cent of cells were at the workplace, 42 per cent were local and 23 per cent were rural (i.e. villages). Within the cell, democratic centralism allows critical discussion; above it in the hierarchy of sections, departmental federations and the periodic grand congress which 'elect' the ruling central committee (which in turn 'elects' the political bureau), unanimity and obedience to the party's line are the rule.

The party also claims an increase in its membership, and more especially a steady inflow of new, younger members. At a special national conference in January 1978, it announced that 58 per cent of delegates had joined the party in the last ten years, and 29 per cent since 1972. It does seem to have made a net gain in membership during the Fifth Republic, though its vote has remained stable; in contrast the higher level of electoral support in the Fourth coincided with a dramatic drop in membership. The PCF's own statistics reveal a big turnover in membership, both gaining and losing about 40,000 members in an average year – or nearly a tenth of its claimed half a million members. Despite this rejuvenation and turnover, the PCF core consists of long-standing loyalists, most of them carefully trained in party schools. The party possesses a large central bureaucracy, based on a newly built headquarters in eastern Paris. It also has many activists working in party-owned enterprises, and further tends to regard its parliamentarians and local councillors in the same light. Communist deputies hand over their salaries to the PCF, and receive in return the party's own skilled manual worker-based wage. Much of the work of the massive party staff is internally directed, in propaganda or even in organising festivities to provide dedicated members with a social life.

How genuine is the conversion of this party, so unlike other French parties, to the democratic norms which the other parties accept? Since the only valid test can be if the PCF wins power, an evaluation based on its record and character must be tentative. It has been noted that French Communism grew out of French Socialism. It has attracted support from the 1920s until the mid-1970s as the major vehicle of political emancipation available to the French working class. The positions which the PCF is now taking are wholly consistent with this history; the maturation of a once-revolutionary party is approximately half a century behind that of the other wing of French Socialism which remained in the SFIO after 1920. Furthermore, the changes of the last two decades are a fairly natural response to the environment of an increasingly affluent working class in a mixed economy; it would have been even more surprising if the PCF had not developed its analysis of the route to power. At the same time, just as the potential for these changes was always present, so the party now retains the potential to move back to a more Stalinist approach.

The development of a large bureaucracy in charge of the movement, so well entrenched in power in many local councils and in the trade union movement and so versed in electoral and parliamentary tactics, has made the party a very different creature from the Leninist concept of a revolutionary cadre. For that bureaucracy, the natural response and the way to an easy life has been to defend the positions already gained by the PCF and seek more in the same manner. Such an interpretation is a much better explanation of the actual behaviour of the PCF during the 1947–65 period than any theory of preparing for revolution. It defended vociferously, and after 1958 demanded the return of, proportional representation; a system which is certainly in its interest so long as it has a fifth or a quarter of the vote, but could prove not to be if it advanced to 40 per cent or so. The May 1968 events provided some test of the PCF's true orientation. The collapse of authority and the general strike took it by surprise. It responded by successfully exploiting the opportunity to achieve material advances for its working-class clientèle, and denounced those, such as the PSU and the non-PCF trade unionists (let alone committed revolutionary groups) who saw the potential of a true revolutionary situation: in effect, the PCF contributed to the survival of the political system.

Why, then, did the PCF demand revisions in the common programme in the summer and autumn of 1977 which it must have known that the PS and MRG could not meet and which caused disunity on the Left in the critical run-up to the 1978 elections? Puzzled observers speculated over internal pressures within the PCF for a return to a harder line, or even that the PCF was acting on behalf of a Soviet preference for the existing French government. There is a fairly simple answer, fully consistent with the analysis of the defensive psychology of the PCF given above. In by-elections in 1975–6 and in certain key contests in the March 1977 local elections where the PCF and PS presented rival lists (e.g. Villeurbanne – a major industrial suburb of Lyons), the PCF had been overtaken as the major party of the Left; its own support was stagnating or declining whilst the PS made all the electoral gains out of the co-operation between the two parties. When the PCF had pursued and signed the common programme, it had been electorally strong enough to hope to be the larger partner in a government of the Left; by 1977 all the evidence pointed to the PS having become stronger. In the election campaign, the PCF leader Georges Marchais stressed the importance to the party of its percentage vote – its target was 25 per cent, and 21 per cent (its 1973 poll) was the essential minimum if the Union of the Left was to survive. Curiously, the PCF's move away from the tactic of unity of the Left may only reflect just how preoccupied with electoral politics it has become.

THE CONSERVATIVES

Like Gaullists, French Conservatives (or Moderates, as they are called in French) have a habit of changing names every few years. The Parti républicain (PR) was the title taken in May 1977 by what had for eleven years been the Fédération nationale des Républicains indépendants; the latter in turn had emerged out of a split in the Fourth Republic Conservative party, the Centre national des Indépendants et Paysans (CNIP) in 1962.

The rump CNIP contained those Conservatives who were opposed to co-operation with de Gaulle, whether because they disagreed with his policies over Algeria or Europe or his disregard for the constitution (the actual precipitant of the breach), or because they had less electoral need for Gaullist votes. It remained strong at local government level (and therefore in the Senate), where its local personalities could still count, but was almost wiped out of the National Assembly, for which it had no distinctive electoral appeal. For fifteen years after the split two Senate groups, one mainly urban and the other agrarian, contained both CNIP and FNRI supporters; but in October 1977, two homogeneous party groups were formed in the Senate. During the preparations for the 1978 elections, CNIP was still considered distinct and significant enough to be treated as a partner within the presidential majority by the larger parties, and it kept apart from the UDF. Of the nine deputies elected who belonged to CNIP, two attached themselves to the RPR group, two joined the UDF and two more attached themselves to it and three decided to sit in the National Assembly as *non-inscrit*. CNIP seems to survive as a useful vehicle for Conservative personalities who wish to avoid being associated too closely with Gaullism or Giscardienism; but it is difficult to see that it stands for anything positive.

The FNRI was difficult to categorise or pin down as a party. For many purposes – the bulk of its parliamentarians, its voting strongholds, its loose structure (the word 'independent' in its title is an indication of the party's attitude towards discipline) and its pragmatism in policy – it was a clear continuation of the CNIP of the 1950s, and with it the inheritor of a tradition and practice of French Conservatism dating back to the first parliamentary groupings of the nineteenth century. A recent study of the surviving role of the aristocracy in French politics showed that nearly a fifth of the RI deputies were of noble descent (*Revue Française de Science Politique*, 1973, pp. 990–1). If a conservative party is characterised by the recruitment of both voters and parliamentarians from socially privileged sections of society, the FNRI clearly remained one.

Yet the FNRI was also the Giscardien party. Valéry Giscard d'Estaing effectively created its national organisation in 1966, to back up the already existing RI parliamentary group. He controlled that organisation until he became president, and the leader who succeeded him, Michel Poniatowski, was his close ally, and indeed had been his *chef-de-cabinet*. CNIP, and then the RI group, had not sought to project an ideology, preferring to rest on the standing of its deputies and its reputation for defence of business and agricultural interests. Giscard through the FNRI, on the other hand, set out to project a modern, innovating and reformist image, as well as to distance himself from Gaullism. The FNRI became the vehicle of his presidential ambitions and, as a party, closely identified with him. The ideas he has sought to project, expressed by his objective of an 'advanced liberal society', are clearly not the most natural for the successor party to CNIP. So what sort of party did the FNRI, and now the PR, become?

If the party be judged by its parliamentary group, it is very clearly Conservative rather than Giscardien. In 1969, when Giscard d'Estaing committed his ultimate act of rebellion against de Gaulle by campaigning for the 'No' vote in the referendum, four-fifths of the RI deputies supported the 'Yes' vote. Again in 1974, when the abortion law, one of Giscard's most controversial liberal reforms, passed the National Assembly, the RI group voted against it by a greater majority than any other political group. This reflects the RI electoral base. Its deputies mostly represent areas which have long tended to vote Conservative, and owe their election to a mixture of that tradition, their own personal standing and the Gaullist vote. Prior to 1978, most were endorsed by the Gaullist umbrella at the first ballot, and it was impossible to distinguish the Républicain indépendant vote.

Since the 1974 presidential election, there may be a potential Giscardien vote. The relaunching of the party under its new label is certainly designed to mobilise it. Many PR members have been attracted by the style and policies of the president. These are most notable in two associated groups – Perspectives et Réalités and Génération sociale et liberale. The first is a network of clubs, designed to attract pro-Giscardien individuals and to provide the forum for political discussion which is lacking within the party itself. The latter is the name taken after 1974 by the RI youth section, which sets out to project a liberal Giscardien image. None the less at international level it is associated with the British and Scandinavian Conservatives and with the German Christian Democrats in the European Democratic Students organisation.

The structure of the party is very loose. The RI groups in the National Assembly and Senate act as if they were caucus parties, and are not subjected to any attempt to decide policy by an outside organ of the party. But the party's headquarters are under the firm control of Giscard d'Estaing and his chosen successors. No party congress was held until 1971, and the party's statutes have no provision to decide how it is composed; since it is not seen as a decision-making body, any member can turn up. When the decision was taken to relaunch the party in early 1977, following Chirac's launch of the RPR, Jean-Pierre Soisson (one of Giscard's ministers) was persuaded to take over as leader, summoned a rally in Fréjus and proclaimed the new party. In accordance with the president's policy, he then ceased to be a minister. On re-entering the government in April 1978, Soisson announced that an outgoing minister, Jacques Blanc, would succeed him as secretary general of the PR.

The PR took over the FNRI's parliamentarians, ambiguities and, such as it was, organisation. During the remainder of 1977, it had some success in projecting a Giscardien image. However, when the UDF was formed (with the PR the bigggest partner, and Soisson taking a leading role), the presidential reformist appeal became attached to the larger umbrella body and the UDF rather than simply the PR was projected as the way people could vote Giscardien. After the success of the UDF, relative to the RPR, there was much post-election talk of bringing the constituent parts of the UDF together as a single party. It will probably not happen, but if the UDF survives as an alliance, the electorally elusive phenomenon of Giscardienism will be attached to it, while the PR becomes more clearly the Conservative partner within that alliance.

### THE CHRISTIAN DEMOCRATS

The Centre des Démocrates sociaux (CDS) was founded at a congress in May 1976, symbolically meeting in the western Catholic stronghold of Rennes – which paradoxically was to fall to the Left in the 1977 municipal elections. The congress united two smaller parties, the Centre démocrate (CD) (launched in 1966 by Jean Lecanuet), and the Centre pour Démocratie et Progrès (CDP) (formed in 1969 as a vehicle for those centrists who wanted to support Pompidou). Both the CD and CDP had attracted local personalities from various backgrounds; and the CD had claimed an influx of new supporters following Lecanuet's presidential campaign. There is also some evidence that in the 1973 elections, when the CD fought in the MR cartel with the Radical Party, it was tapping a genuinely centre-inclined vote which sought an alternative to both large blocs.

The core of the party remains the Christian Democratic tradition, which produced a strong party – the Mouvement républicain populaire (MRP) – immediately after the Second World War. Lecanuet himself had been president of the MRP before 1965 when he sought election as president of the Republic, and continued as the president of the new CDS in 1976. The secretary general of the new party, Jacques Barrot, came from the CDP; he was also deputy for the same department as his father had been for twenty years under the MRP label.

As well as leaders, the Christian Democratic tradition provides the CDS with a loyal (but probably steadily dwindling) Catholic vote in certain areas, with militants and with a philosophy. The new 'social democrat' label is wholly misleading. The party, proudly recalling Robert Schuman as former leader of the MRP, is the most pro-European of the French parties. Since it has kept the postion as representative in France of a Christian Democratic movement that is stronger in most other Community countries, it has something to gain from political integration. Its continuing problem has been to find a meaningful role in the domestic politics of Fifth Republic France. Centrism as a political vocation is defined by what the other sides stand for and as first Pompidou and then Giscard d'Estaing have enlarged their side, they attracted first part and then all of the CD. During the 1960s, the CD saw itself as the focus of a new, large centrist regrouping; under the Giscardien presidency it has found ministerial office but as a minor partner. It is not too unhappy in this role, since many of the proclaimed reforming and pro-European sentiments of the president are close to its heart. Indeed, CDS comes closer to embodying much of what he stands for than the PR.

Though a small party, the CDS has a fully articulated structure of committees from its biennial congress (which elects both president and secretary general) to its political bureau. The upper echelons of the party are dominated by parliamentarians; when Lecanuet was leader but out of parliament, the leader of the Assembly group Progrès et Démocratie moderne, Jacques Duhamel, emerged as a rival leader and this division presaged the split into CD and CDP in 1969. The CDP never became any more than a club of personalities, based on parliamentarians. After Giscard d'Estaing's election, the two elements came together again in the National Assembly as a single group two years before a unifying congress.

## THE RADICALS

Two parties, the Mouvement des Radicaux de Gauche and the Parti radical-socialiste, compete for the title of the inheritor of the oldest party in France; when the split occurred, the latter kept the party headquarters in Place de Valois and so are often known as Valoisiens, the epithet of legitimacy used in the successive splits which the Radicals have suffered. The split reflected the Radicals' political history, the nature of their surviving vote and the French electoral system. The party derives from the defenders of the achievements of the French Revolution, although it was not formally founded until 1901. During the Third and Fourth Republics, it played a highly pragmatic and often conservative role in government – and split frequently over doing so; but it never lost the sense of being on the Left. During the first ten years of the Fifth Republic the Radicals co-operated closely with the SFIO, forming the Fédération de la Gauche démocrate et socialiste for the 1965 presidential and 1967 and 1968 parliamentary elections. In 1969 the party backed the centre candidature of Poher. His failure and the creation of a Socialist Party determined to seek power in close alliance with the Communists left the Radicals uncertain over their future.

Out of the dilemma emerged the MRG, under the leadership of Robert Fabre, which formed another electoral alliance with the

Socialists in 1973, the Union de la Gauche socialiste et démocrate (UGSD, a significant reversal of the adjectives, reflecting the ascendancy of the socialist over the radical element), and the Valoisiens who, under the leadership of Jean-Jacques Servan-Schreiber, attempted a centrist alliance with the CD under the MR label. In 1974, Servan-Schreiber supported Giscard d'Estaing, and the two sections of the old party found themselves entrenched into the opposing blocs of Left and Right.

Given the split, and the fact that most Radicals seek election in a first-ballot alliance and consequently contest only a limited number of constituencies, it is difficult to estimate the national Radical vote. There is probably a small core vote, mainly professional middle class, which is progressive on value issues but more centrist on economic questions. There is a regional Radical vote in the more rural areas of the south-west, where the regional newspaper, *La Dépêche du Midi,* is closely associated with Radicalism; and there are pockets of support elsewhere, mainly in eastern France and in Corsica. The south-west vote has traditionally allied with the Left in the two-ballot system, and the logic of that fact means that the MRG draws its principal strength from this region. The PRS is more a club of personalities, and has attracted several ministers in Giscard d'Estaing's governments; what vote it has is scattered and usually associated with local personalities.

Radicalism remains stronger at the local government level; even with the polarisation at the 1977 municipal elections, most lists, whether of Left or Right, included the odd Radical. Consequently it has kept some of its past strength in the Senate, where a single group, the Gauche démocratique still keeps together senators from the MRG and the PRS together with a few who have tried to keep some links with both.

Curiously the two-bloc system has given each wing of the old party a role which it had failed to find when united in opposition. The MRG cunningly exploited its position as a brake on the Union of the Left, and attracted support on that account. Fabre staged a dramatic walk-out during the renegotiation of the common programme in September 1977 to publicise disagreement over the Communist demand for more nationalisation. At the same time Servan-Schreiber was boycotting talks between the RPR, PR, CDS and CNIP designed to agree on joint candidates because he demanded that there should be a non-Gaullist in every constituency at the first ballot. Although the two small Radical parties thus appeared as focal points of opposition to the Communists and Gaullists, they also assisted the tactics of those two large parties in their respective manoeuvres *vis-à-vis* their allies.

Both at the beginning of the Fourth Republic and again at the inception of the Fifth, the shattered remnants of the Radical Party were widely written off as having no future; and following the divisions of the early seventies, observers have repeated the verdict (Frears, 1977, p. 126). But the party survived to play a key pivotal role in the Fourth Republic, and its two successors are manoeuvring themselves to repeat the performance as the political system of the Fifth develops.

## THE FRINGE

The far Left is the most prolific producer of small parties. With the decline of the PSU, the largest group now is the Trotskyist Lutte ouvrière. Its 1974 presidential candidate, Arlette Laguiller, polled 2·4 per cent on a platform which mixed socialism and feminism; in 1978, it confirmed its espousal of women's liberation by putting forward nearly half of all the women candidates standing. Other groups include Ligue communiste revolution- naire (Trotskyist), Front autogestionnaire (an alliance of the PSU with worker-control, ecological and regionalist groups at the 1978 elections) and Union ouvrière et paysanne pour la démocratie prolétarienne (Maoist).

The other prolific source of political labels are the Gaullistes de Gauche. There have always been some who were attracted by de Gaulle's personality, his institutional ideas or his foreign policy and who longed to link that with a renewed Left. Despite several efforts, they never found a distinctive electoral base and have been unable even to form a single organisation to represent their thinking. Two groups, each led by a former minister, claim in an unclear way to represent a Gaullism unsullied by Giscardien ideas or Chirac's compromises – the Mouvement des Démocrates (Michel Jobert), and the Fédération des Républicains de Progrès (Jean Charbonnel). The Union des Gaullistes de Progrès repre- sents those who have thrown in their lot with the Union of the Left.

The far Right also persistently tries to revive or maintain old causes, and monarchist candidates still appear at French elections. Two small parties fought the 1978 elections on a wide scale – the Front national (led by Jean-Marie Le Pen, who was once a Poujadist deputy) and the Parti des Forces nouvelles – but won little support.

The fringe group which has gained most ground in recent elections represents a new idea – ecology. An ecological candidate, René Dumont, polled 1·3 per cent in the 1974 presidential elections and in the 1976 cantonal elections some local ecological groups sponsored candidates in areas of Alsace threatened by nuclear power stations, and polled well. At the 1977 municipal elections, local ecological lists took 10 per cent of the vote in Paris and similar shares in some other cities; they probably attracted some centrist votes, but evidentally also tapped a strong current among younger, better-educated voters which reflected wider criticisms of materialistic society and the functioning of political institutions as well as strictly environmental concerns. In September 1977 a number of local groups formed Collectif Ecologie-78 for the purpose of contesting the parliamentary elections. The organisation of this grouping reflected the decentralist ideas current in the ecological movement, and its distrust of traditional political structures. It placed its national headquarters in Lyons, not in the capital city, and elected an eight-member co-ordination committee instead of a leader, president or secretary general. It made it a point of principle that none of its candidates would take part in any alliance formation between the two rounds of the March 1978 elections, a behaviour wholly uncharacteristic of French parties. But not all ecological groups accepted the label Ecologie-78, and some did form alliances with the far Left. The ecologists have yet to decide whether they wish to form a new party or are simply a pressure group exploiting the electoral process.

In the 1978 elections, there were ecological candidates in over two-fifths of the constituencies, sometimes more than one; the total vote would probably have been near to 4 per cent if all constituencies had been fought. Their regional support (see p. 84) reflected the patchiness of their effort. They fielded most candidates and received the highest votes in areas such as the Rhine and Rhône valleys and certain coastal sites, where there is opposition to nuclear power stations. The ecologists outpolled the PCF in the Alsace constituencies they fought, and in the neighbourhood of one proposed station, Pèlerin in Loire-Atlantique, they polled 19·5 and 35 per cent in the two communes affected.

The other movement hovering between pressure group and political party are the autonomist groups. Principally in Corsica and Brittany, but also to a lesser extent in the Basque area and throughout the south of France (known to its autonomists as *Occitanie*), various organisations have used dramatic direct action methods (and sometimes violence) to forward claims of cultural oppression and economic neglect by the centralised French state. Although France has always been culturally more diverse than La République française liked to acknowledge, such movements have only awakened any popular interest in the last dozen or so years –

at just the same period as the electoral advances of nationalist parties in Great Britain and language parties in Belgium. However, in France these movements have generally eschewed the party form of political action. As yet there is not much evidence that they would get electoral support if they tried; the Strolladar vro-Parti fédéraliste européen fought twenty-six of the thirty Breton constituencies in 1973 but took only 1·9 per cent of the Breton vote. In 1978 fewer candidates stood; a scatter of autonomists in Alsace, Brittany, Corsica, Catalan-speaking Roussillon and parts of Occitanie all failed to win more than a handful of votes.

## MARCH 1978

The second round of the sixth parliamentary elections of the Fifth Republic on 19 March 1978 saw the polarisation between Left and Right carried a stage further. Apart from those constituencies where the newly introduced rule that no candidate who had not received a vote equivalent to at least 12·5 per cent of the electoral register could stand at the second round meant that either Left or Right was not represented, there was only one single constituency in the whole of France on that day where the contest was not a duel between Left and Right.

In those terms the result was a small but clear victory for the presidential majority, in both votes and seats. The column 'Final Votes' in Table 4.5 shows how, when the votes which were effective for deciding who won each seat are considered, there was a lead for the Right of 2·8 per cent, and a corresponding majority in seats of seventy-eight. It was widely believed that the very unevenly sized constituencies would give the Right an advantage; in the event this factor did not affect the result, since there were thirty-nine constituencies won by the Right with majorities of less than 2·8 per cent. This means that, if an evenly distributed 1·4 per cent had voted Left instead of Right that day, both the seats and votes in metropolitan France would have been exactly evenly divided. The deputies elected in the overseas departments and territories did, however, assist the presidential majority, dividing fourteen to three in its favour.

The swing to the Right between the two rounds was probably affected by the increased participation and perhaps by the preferences of those who voted for the also-rans of the first round. But the key factor was the unwillingness of a critical proportion of Socialist and MRG voters to obey the discipline of the Left where its standard-bearer was a Communist. This is strikingly clear if we compare the 404 Left–Right duels of 1978 with the split of votes between Giscard d'Estaing and Mitterrand in 1974 (50·7 to 49·3 per cent). Table 4.1 shows the average change in the constituencies concerned according to the candidate in 1978:

Table 4.1   *Party Performance in Straight Left/Right Fights in 1978*

|  |  | Performance Compared with | |
| --- | --- | --- | --- |
| *1978 Candidate* | *No. of Cases* | *Mitterrand (%)* | *Giscard d'Estaing (%)* |
| PCF | 143 | −3·3 | |
| PS | 240 | +0·4 | |
| MRG | 20 | +1·2 | |
| PRS | 17 | | +1·3 |
| CDS | 48 | | +1·7 |
| PR | 95 | | +0·3 |
| RPR | 220 | | +0·7 |
| All | 404 | −0·9 | +0·9 |

Not only does the failure of Communist candidates to attract as many votes as Socialists stand out; the ability of Radical and CDS candidates to improve on their bloc's vote is also clear. Interestingly, the PR was not so successful. In the minds of the voters it had a parallel attractiveness to the RPR, showing that for marginal centrist voters the PR is still a Conservative party, and that the critical distinction lay between candidates from the Christian Democratic and Radical traditions on the one hand and Conservatives and Gaullists on the other – not between the UDF and the RPR.

Thus, in a sense, the most polarised of all French parliamentary elections still showed up the importance of a centrist vote, and of the political forces which appeal to it. It is difficult to estimate the real strength of these forces since they mostly fought in alliances with other parties. On actual votes cast Christian Democracy attracted just over 5 per cent and the two wings of Radicalism just over 4 per cent – voting levels perilously close to the 5 per cent threshold to be introduced for the proportional allocation of seats in the European parliamentary elections in France in 1979. The table of regional voting shows that the CDS has largely retreated to certain areas of traditional Catholic voting; Alsace and Brittany (from which a third of CDS deputies now come) were the bases of the late Third Republic progressive Catholic Parti démocrate populaire. As for the Radicals, most of the variation in the Valoisien vote reflects local personalities (e.g. in Auvergne, Gabriel Perronet, president of the party 1975–7); the MRG has clearly taken over more traditionally Radical voting areas in Burgundy, Corsica and the south-west. However, in the south-west, its strongest region with seven of its ten deputies, its vote is well below the Radical vote of fifteen years ago. Although they together represent at least a tenth of French voters, these parties are dependent for parliamentary representation on peripheral regional support and alliances with other parties.

The Conservative PR and CNIP represent a further 12 per cent. The very uneven distribution of their vote demonstrates the influence of political tradition. The PR's weakness in Alsace (historically a Catholic and Gaullist stronghold), Aquitaine (Socialist and Gaullist) and Limousin (the most left-wing of the regions) shows very clearly that its audience is not a national presidential one but is more an inheritance of the moderate tradition. Competing with the Gaullists on a big scale for the first time since the Républicains indépendants emerged, it advanced its vote compared with previous measures of its support. The traditional pattern of the vote suggests that this was a Conservative vote absorbed into the Gaullist alliance in 1962 which has only had a fuller opportunity of voting separately from the UDR/RPR in 1978. The PR emerged as strongest in South-East France, from which a third of its deputies are elected. All the pockets of CNIP support lie in the Northern half of France.

The Communist vote also shows the continuation of its traditional pattern. Indeed, whilst losing 2·7 per cent in the Paris region (which still contributes nearly a third of all Communist deputies) the PCF held its 1973 vote in its other six strongest regions lying in the industrial north, Limousin and the Mediterranean coast, whilst losing ground slightly elsewhere. Locally it made some progress in areas with structural economic problems; but in general it is striking that the past pattern persists so strongly. Although the party lost ground in votes, and indeed polled its lowest vote since the war apart from the very special elections of 1958 and 1968, it won twelve extra parliamentary seats.

The Socialist vote is a total contrast. On mainland France, the PS was able to poll nearly a fifth of the vote in every region, and rarely advanced beyond a quarter. This nearly uniform vote is a quite new feature for French Socialism, and reflects the sharp gains that the party has made in the Paris area, where the PCF has clearly now lost its near monopoly of the Left vote, and in the traditional Catholic or Conservative regions. The advance in its national vote in the last two elections has been overwhelmingly concentrated in these previous areas of weaknesses, and the party's vote was actually falling in certain traditionally left-wing constituencies where Socialists compete with Communists. Consequently, its voting advance gave it fewer additional seats than the PCF; in a constituency voting system, the even distribution of its vote works against it. Failure to anticipate this factor contributed to disappointment at the small advance towards parliamentary victory. Yet the even distribution of the PS's support reflects its success in establishing a national audience and in breaking out of the restricted base of the SFIO's support – achievements which were critical for it to overtake the PCF in popular support.

The Gaullist vote, which with the RPR's competition at the first round with its erstwhile allies was a truer measure of purely Gaullist support than we have had since 1958, is less evenly distributed than the PS's but much more so than that of any other party (save Lutte ouvrière). It, too, has a national audience. Although the vote for Gaullist-based alliances such as the URP, and for President de Gaulle himself in 1965, had tended to be concentrated in the more traditionally right-wing areas and especially in the north of France, the RPR is as strong in more left-wing regions, notably Limousin (Chirac's own region) and Aquitaine. In that respect too, its vote is more like the support which rallied to the first Gaullist party of the Fifth Republic, the Union pour la nouvelle République, in 1958. Indeed, except for the advance of the Socialists and the decline of the parties comprising the UDF, the 1978 distribution of votes between the political forces is strikingly similar to that of 1958.

This assumes that the significant distribution of the vote in 1978 is between the traditional political forces. The UDF was formed hastily just before the election, and was initially no more than a machinery for distributing the UDF label to candidates of the three component parties and certain personalities. But as the alliance enabled the PR, CDS and PRS each to gain seats, the three party leaders sought to project a united image; a single group was formed in the National Assembly, and it was agreed to set up a permanent national organisation. In so far as the election was a success for President Giscard d'Estaing and for the prime minister, Raymond Barre (who stood with the UDF label at the election), it appeared to be a success for the united action of the three parties. Chirac's behaviour, in drawing the RPR into a state of semi-opposition within the presidential majority following the election, re-emphasised the common ground of the UDF in supporting the president. If the UDF were to survive and become a permanent force, it could profoundly alter the French party system into one of four equal-sized parties.

The likelihood is that the UDF will prove as short-lived as the URP, FGDS, MR and many others. The analysis of regional support above shows how each partner is dependent on a traditional voting base and the different leaning of these voters is clearly shown in Table 4.2 in the following appendix.

# STATISTICAL APPENDIX

## Election Results

Election statistics in France differ according to source and, given the ambiguity of the party labels that many candidates carry, are subject to many real problems of interpretation. The following tables have been adapted by the author from established sources.

*Party Alignments 1967–78* shows the shares of the votes won as recorded by R. Rose and T. McKie *The International Almanac of Electoral History* for 1967 and 1968; *Le Monde*, 1973.

*The March 1978 Legislative Elections* is a combination of author's calculations and the Ministry of the Interior official figures, which have been used for the UDF, Presidential Majority, and extreme-left categories. The 'final vote' column combines the first-ballot votes in constituencies where it was decisive and second-ballot votes in the remainder.

Table 4.2    *Perceptions of UDF Voters, February 1978*

|  | PRS % | CDS % | PR % | RPR % |
|---|---|---|---|---|
| Proportion placing themselves centre or left rather than right | 69 | 54 | 31 | 25 |
| Preferring as a governing alliance: | | | | |
| RPR–UDF | 13 | 19 | 39 | 57 |
| UDF–PS | 46 | 27 | 13 | 5 |
| RPR–UDF–PS | 25 | 43 | 39 | 33 |

*Note:*
In identification and perception of natural allies, the Conservative PR voter remains closer to Gaullism and the Radical to Socialism, whilst CDS response mirrors the dilemma of the MRP throughout its history. The UDF only looks like a single party in the voting statistics of the French Ministry of the Interior.

*Source:* Le Monde, 11 March 1978.

Table 4.3   *Regional Variation in Party Support (March 1978)*

|                   | RPR  | PR   | CDS  | PRS  | MRG  | PS   | PCF  | Ecologist |
|-------------------|------|------|------|------|------|------|------|-----------|
| Alsace            | 33·6 | 3·7  | 15·9 | —    | 0·8  | 19·2 | 6·6  | 6·1       |
| Aquitaine         | 28·7 | 2·8  | 5·5  | 3·4  | 3·1  | 28·2 | 18·7 | 1·8       |
| Auvergne          | 16·3 | 17·2 | 5·0  | 7·1  | 0·5  | 26·5 | 19·2 | 1·0       |
| Brittany          | 24·4 | 13·6 | 12·6 | 0·8  | 0·4  | 24·5 | 14·8 | 0·7       |
| Burgundy          | 27·9 | 9·7  | 1·6  | 1·0  | 5·3  | 24·0 | 18·0 | 0·9       |
| Centre            | 22·8 | 13·8 | 4·2  | 0·4  | 2·3  | 21·7 | 20·7 | 0·6       |
| Champagne         | 26·4 | 11·9 | 7·0  | 2·7  | 0·9  | 22·0 | 22·8 | 1·6       |
| Corsica           | 33·3 | 12·9 | —    | —    | 24·6 | 4·4  | 16·0 | 0·9       |
| Franche-Comté     | 22·5 | 13·3 | 5·6  | 5·6  | 3·0  | 27·9 | 14·9 | 1·4       |
| Languedoc         | 15·8 | 12·0 | 8·5  | 0·5  | 1·7  | 24·1 | 27·8 | 1·1       |
| Limousin          | 30·8 | 2·0  | 1·7  | 0·7  | —    | 24·5 | 30·4 | 0·3       |
| Lorraine          | 18·3 | 16·2 | 3·3  | 6·0  | 0·4  | 25·4 | 16·6 | 0·6       |
| Midi-Pyrénées     | 21·6 | 10·3 | 3·6  | 2·0  | 8·8  | 25·5 | 18·0 | 2·3       |
| Normandy, Lower   | 19·0 | 19·2 | 5·6  | 5·7  | 0·3  | 22·5 | 10·7 | 3·6       |
| Normandy, Upper   | 22·6 | 10·8 | 4·7  | 1·4  | 2·9  | 19·4 | 26·0 | 1·4       |
| North             | 20·1 | 5·0  | 4·0  | 1·5  | 0·7  | 27·4 | 27·7 | 1·3       |
| Paris règion      | 24·2 | 9·5  | 3·6  | 1·8  | 1·8  | 18·9 | 24·4 | 3·7       |
| Pays de la Loire  | 30·5 | 12·0 | 4·7  | 0·8  | 0·8  | 23·6 | 12·2 | 0·7       |
| Picardy           | 23·0 | 6·1  | 3·0  | 4·3  | 1·2  | 20·6 | 27·7 | 0·7       |
| Poitou-Charentes  | 22·6 | 9·8  | 5·9  | 2·8  | 5·7  | 23·2 | 17·1 | 0·5       |
| Provence          | 19·4 | 14·8 | 5·0  | 1·6  | 1·6  | 20·4 | 26·9 | 3·0       |
| Rhone-Alpes       | 16·7 | 16·9 | 4·7  | 1·7  | 1·8  | 23·3 | 18·8 | 4·1       |

*Note:*
The figures in this table are the parties' share of the total first-ballot vote in each of the twenty-two planning regions. They reflect, therefore, both the parties' level of popular support and, especially for the smaller parties, the proportion of seats contested. In some regions there were also significant votes for candidates of the presidential majority not identified with any particular party within it. For tables of regional distribution of party support for 1965–73 see Frears (1977, p. 78 'Opposition Centrism', p. 122, Socialist, p. 152, Communist).

| Political families | Current parties | Senate groups | 1969 presidential line-up | 1974 presidential line-up | 1967 elections % votes | 1967 elections assembly groups | 1968 elections % votes | 1968 elections assembly groups | 1973 elections % votes | 1973 elections assembly groups | 1978 elections % votes | 1978 elections assembly groups |
|---|---|---|---|---|---|---|---|---|---|---|---|---|
| Gaullist | RPR | 30 | Pompidou 44·0% | Chaban-Delmas 14·6% | 37·7 | 200 | UDR 45·1 | UDR 293 | URP 34·6 | UDR 183 | 22·8 | 145 |
| Conservative | PR | 57 | | Giscard d'Estaing 32·9% | (3·7)[2] | RI 42 | (1·9)[1] | RI 61 | | RI 55 | 11·0 | UDF 120 |
| | CNIP | 15 (see p.71) | CDP | | | | | | | | 1·2 | |
| Christian Democrat | CDS | 57 | CD · Poher 23·4% | | 12·6 | 41 | 10·3 | 33 | MR 12·6 | 30[2] | 5·2 | |
| Radical | PRS · MRG | 38 | | | | | | | | 34 | 2·1 · 2·1 | |
| Socialist | PS | 52 | Deferre 5·1% · (Rocard 3·7%) | Mitterand 43·4% | FGDS 19·0 · PSU 2·2 | 121 | FGDS 16·5 · PSU 3·9 | 57 | UGSD 19·2 · PSU 3·3 | 102 | 22·9 | 112 |
| Communist | PCF | 20 | Duclos 21·5% | [3] | 22·5 | 73 | 20·0 | 34 | 21·4 | 73 | 20·6 | 86 |

*Notes:*

[1] Unattached moderates.

[2] *Union centriste*, a short-lived parliamentary group representing pro-Pompidou centrists (CDP).

[3] Remaining votes divided between nine other candidates.

Table 4.5   *The March 1978 Legislative Elections (Metropolitan France only)*[1]

|  | First-ballot votes | | Final votes | | Seats won | Assembly groups[3] |
|---|---|---|---|---|---|---|
|  | '000s | % | '000s | % |  |  |
| RPR | 6,400 | 22·8 |  |  | 142 | 145 |
| PR | 3,100 | 11·0 |  |  | 69 |  |
| CDS | 1,450 | 5·2 |  |  | 33 |  |
| PRS | 600 | 2·1 |  |  | 9 |  |
| CNIP | 325 | 1·2 |  |  | 9 |  |
| Soc. Dem.[2] | 300 | 1·0 |  |  | 2 |  |
| UDF | (6,025) | (21·4) |  |  |  | 120 |
| Majority personalities |  |  |  |  | 12 |  |
| Presidential majority | 13,000 | 46·3 | 14,516 | 51·1 | 276 |  |
| PS | 6,425 | 22·9 |  |  | 102 | 112 |
| PCF | 5,800 | 20·6 |  |  | 86 | 86 |
| MRG | 600 | 2·1 |  |  | 10 |  |
| Lutte ouvrière | 475 | 1·7 |  |  | — |  |
| Other Extreme Left | 450 | 1·6 |  |  | — |  |
| The Left | 13,750 | 48·9 | 13,732 | 48·3 | 198 |  |
| Ecologists | 600 | 2·1 } | 156 | 0·6 | — |  |
| Others | 750 | 2·7 } |  |  | — |  |
| Non-inscrit |  |  |  |  |  | 11 |

*Notes:*
[1] The seventeen overseas deputies sit as follows: nine RPR, four UDF, one PS, two non-inscrit (opposition), one non-inscrit (government).
[2] MDSF and PSD; some PSD votes are included with the majority, others are not.
[3] One PR deputy decided to sit non-inscrit and one CDS deputy attached himself to the RPR group; otherwise the PR, CDS, PRS, MDSF and PSD members formed the UDF group. The majority personalities went five to the UDF and seven non-inscrit; the MRG attached itself to the PS; for CNIP see p. 77.

## GLOSSARY

### List of Parties, etc., Referred to by their Initials; Dates of Foundation given in Brackets

CD:   Centre démocrate (1966; merged with CDP in 1976 as CDS)
CDP:   Centre Démocratie et Progrès (1969–76)
CDS:   Centre des Démocrates sociaux (1976)
CERES:   Centre d'Etudes, de Recherches et d'Education Socialiste

CNIP: Centre national des Indépendants et Paysans (1948; Paysans added in 1951; ceased to be a major party in 1962 when RIS split off)

CR: Centre républicain (1957; returned to PRS 1977)

CIR: Convention des Institutions républicains (1964–71; joined PS)

FGDS: Fédération de la Gauche démocratique et socialiste (1967 and 1968 election cartel for SFIO, PRS and CIR)

FNRI: Fédération nationale des Républicains indépendants (1966; became PR in 1977)

MDSF: Mouvement démocrate socialiste de France (1973)

MRG: Mouvement des Radicaux de Gauche (1973)

MR: Mouvement réformateur (1973 election cartel for CD, PRS, CNIP, CR and MDSF)

MRP: Mouvement républicain populaire (1944, faded away after 1966 when CD launched)

PCF: Parti communiste français (1920)

PRS: Parti radicale-socialiste (1901; a short title used by PRS – full title Parti républicain, radicale et radicale-socialiste)

PR: Parti républicain (1977)

PS: Parti socialiste (1969)

PSD: Parti socialiste démocrate (1973)

PSU: Parti socialiste unifié (1960)

RI: Républicains indépendants (name used by one of the CNIP Senate groups and by the pro-Gaullist ex-CNIP group in the Assembly after 1962, attached to FNRI from 1966)

RPF: Rassemblement du Peuple français (1947–53)

RPR: Rassemblement pour la République (1976)

SFIO: Section française de l'Internationale ouvrière (1905–69; joined PS)

UCRG: Union des Clubs pour le Renouveau de la Gauche (1963–9; joined PS)

UDF: Union pour la Démocratie française (1978 election cartel for PR, CDS and PRS)

UDR: Union des Démocrates pour la République (1968–76; became RPR)

UGCS: Union des Groupes et Clubs Socialistes (1967–9; joined PS)

UGSD: Union de la Gauche socialiste et démocrate (1973 election cartel for PS and MRG)

URP: Union des Républicains de Progrès (1973 election cartel for UDR, FNRI and CDP)

## NOTES

1 The extreme Right has twice polled a substantial vote: 12 per cent for the Poujadists in 1956 and 5 per cent for Jean-Louis Tixier-Vignancourt at the 1965 presidential elections.

2 At the 1951 and 1956 elections a list system of voting with only partly proportional allocation of seats encouraged parties to affiliate their lists with each other. Since 1958 a two-ballot system of election in single-member seats has

encouraged parties to engage in agreements for mutual desistment at the second ballot.

3 In most larger French towns, local councils consist of the list which wins a majority at the first or second round; consequently parties readily form alliances to secure an overall majority for the combination of which they wish to form part and elections are only rarely contested by purely single-party lists.

4 In Nantes at the 1971 elections the mayor, leader of a Radical splinter group called the Centre républicain, led a list composed of Socialists, anti-Gaullist Conservatives (CNIP) and his own CR group to win with 58 per cent of the vote at the first ballot against 26 per cent for a presidential majority (UDR, FNRI and CDP) list and 16 per cent for the Communists. Sixteen of the seventeen outgoing Socialist councillors stuck with that alliance, but at the second round in March 1977 a PS–PCF–MRG list won with just 50·3 per cent of the votes in a duel with the new, enlarged presidential majority including the socialist rebels.

5 In seven departments around his personal bastion of Bordeaux, Chaban-Delmas polled 28·4 per cent; in the rest of the country he polled 13·5 per cent.

6 In the June 1975 conference report the UDR stated that it had 255,467 members but that only 144,736 were up to date with subscriptions; 83·5 per cent were over 30, compared with 70 per cent of the population over 16. See Charlot, 1967, p. 116, and 1971, p. 131, for the uncertainties of Gaullist party membership.

# BIBLIOGRAPHY

### GENERAL

Many books on current French politics date rapidly. The two most recent in English are:

Frears, J. R. (1977) *Political Parties and Elections in the French Fifth Republic* (London, C. Hurst).

Wright, Vincent (1978) *The Government and Politics of France* (London, Hutchinson University Library).

Two classic works remain invaluable:

Thomson, David (1958) *Democracy in France since 1870* (London, Oxford University Press).

Williams, Philip M. (1964) *Crisis and Compromise : Politics in the Fourth Republic* (London, Longmans).

Other useful books include:

Ardagh, John (3rd edn, 1977) *The New France* (Harmondsworth, Penguin).

Hayward, Jack (1973) *The One and Indivisible French Republic* (London, Weidenfeld & Nicolson).

Campbell, Peter (1958) *French Electoral Systems and Elections since 1789* (London, Faber).

Pickles, Dorothy (1972, 1973) *The Government and Politics of France,* Vol. 1 *Institutions and Parties,* Vol. 2 *Politics* (London, Methuen).

### POLITICAL PARTIES (grouped in order of coverage in this chapter)

Charlot, Jean (1967) *L'UDR : Etude du pouvoir au sein d'un parti politique* (Paris, Armand Colin).

Charlot, Jean (1971) *The Gaullist Phenomenon* (London, Allen & Unwin).

Hartley, Anthony (1972) *Gaullism – the Rise and Fall of a Political Movement* (London, Routledge & Kegan Paul).

Barrillon, Raymond (1967) *La Gauche française en mouvement* (Paris, Plon).

Poperen, Jean, *La Gauche française*, Vol. 1 *Le nouvel âge 1958–65*, Vol. 2 *L'Unité de la Gauche* (Paris, Fayard).

Wilson, Frank L. (1971) *The French Democratic Left 1963–69* (Stanford, Calif., Stanford University Press).

Hauss, Charles (1978), *The New Left in France: Unified Socialist Party* (Westport, Greenwood Press).

Fauvet, Jacques (1965) *Histoire du Parti Communiste français*, 2 vols (Paris, Fayard).

Kriegel, Annie (1972) *The French Communists* (Chicago, University of Chicago Press).

Tiersky, R. (1974) *French Communism 1920–1972* (New York, Columbia University Press).

Anderson, Malcolm (1973) *Conservative Politics in France* (London, Allen & Unwin).

Colliard, Jean-Claude (1971) *Les Républicains Indépendants* (Paris, PUF).

Remond, Rene (1966) *The Right Wing in France from 1815 to de Gaulle* (Philadelphia, University of Philadelphia Press).

Bosworth, W. (1962) *Catholicism and Crisis in Modern France* (Princeton, NJ, Princeton University Press).

Irving, R. E. M. (1973) *Christian Democracy in France* (London, Allen & Unwin).

Irving, R. E. M. (1979) *The Christian Democratic Parties of Western Europe* (London, George Allen & Unwin/RIIA).

de Tarr, Francis (1961) *The French Radical Party from Herriot to Mendès-France* (London, Oxford University Press).

Nordmann, Jean-Thomas (1974) *Histoire des Radicaux 1820–1973* (Paris, Table Ronde).

OTHER BOOKS CITED

Duverger, Maurice (1951) *Les Partis politiques* (Paris, Armand Colin).

McInnes, Neil (1975) *The Communist Parties of Western Europe* (London, Oxford University Press).

# 5
# The Federal Republic of Germany

## TONY BURKETT

Almost thirty years have passed since the Federal Republic of Germany was established and its constitution, the Basic Law, adopted. The second German Liberal democratic state has enjoyed over twice the life-span of its Weimar predecessor whose collapse ended in the dictatorship of Adolf Hitler. Since 1949 the Bonn Republic has evolved to become the most politically stable as well as the most prosperous of the EEC states, although the auguries of the immediate postwar period suggested that it might be otherwise. The stability and efficacy of the Republic's political institutions and the widespread support for them shown by consistently high turn-outs at elections suggest that the West Germans learned from the mistakes made during the thirteen years of Weimar. If those mistakes have been avoided since 1949, it is in large part due to the parties and their leaders themselves, for both have abandoned most of those very orientations and ideologies which made party politics so divisive in Weimar.[1] Here perhaps is the most important difference between the two systems and it is a psychological rather than a constitutional one. In Bonn party conflict has been less fundamental and less bitter and the consensus consequently much stronger. This almost universal commitment to constitutional norms and procedures owes more to changes in attitudes and behaviour than to changes in the framework of the political system. Indeed, the major features of that system owe much to the Bismarckian constitution of 1871 as well as to that of Weimar, although some crucial adaptations were made in 1949.

## THE POLITICAL STRUCTURES

The experience of the Weimar Republic led to a sharp reduction in the political powers of the head of state and a consequent strengthening of the position of the head of the federal executive. The role of the federal president is now largely ceremonial – save in carefully defined circumstances – and its incumbents no longer enjoy the right to appoint or dismiss federal chancellors. Elected for five year terms by the federal convention (Bundesversammlung) consisting of members of the Bundestag and an equal number of members from provincial parliaments, presidents have for the most part kept their office out of involvement in party controversy. Gustav Heinemann who held the position from 1969 to 1974 saw it as important in the educational sense, and earned wide respect for the way he sought to encourage a national commitment to democratic values.

West Germany is unique amongst Community members in having a federal structure. German federalism differs from the US model in a number of particulars. There are parliamentary executives at both levels of governments, those at the provincial level are led by minister presidents. The federal executive is headed by the federal chancellor who does not have to seek approval of his cabinet from the Bundestag. German federalism takes its uniqueness, however, from the way that powers are divided between the two spheres of government – the Bund (federation) and Laender (provinces). Few powers are directly assigned to either sphere although the Bund enjoys legislative and executive rights over foreign affairs, defence, citizenship, currency, railroads, air transport and posts (Basic Law, art. 73). The Laender have competence over police, education and local government. The principle of 'vertical' division, so crucial in the US constitution, is far less important in the Federal Republic than another principle of division, namely, the 'horizontal' one in which the federal government and parliament have the bulk of the legislative powers either exclusively or concurrently with the provinces, whilst the latter are responsible for the greater part of administration. The Basic Law contains (art. 74) a list of these 'concurrent powers' over which the Laender may only legislate if the Bund does not so choose. Generally the Bund has exercised that right. Article 83 gives the Laender the right to administer federal laws 'as their own affair'. Thus there are few federal administrative agencies within West Germany even though most law is federal law only a small part of which may have been amended by the provincial diets to adapt it to local conditions.[2]

It is the provincial governments and their bureaucracies which are most concerned with public administration in the Federal Republic and it is this form of federalism which accounts for the composition of the other legislative chamber, the Bundesrat

(Federal Council) – often referred to erroneously as the Upper House. The Bundesrat consists of forty-one members, all of whom are ministers in the provincial governments. The powers of the Bundesrat are considerable. It has the right to pass, amend or reject the federal budget, any federal bill which affects Laender interests, and delegated legislation affecting provincial administration which the federal cabinet may issue. The recent tendency has been for the Bundesrat to claim more rights over federal legislation than hitherto.[3] Political partisanship has been less evident than the stress the federal council has always placed on provincial rights. Nevertheless there have been more signs of party conflict since their control of most Laender governments has given the CDU/CSU a majority in the Bundesrat whilst the SPD/FDP have controlled the Bundestag. A Mediation Committee exists to settle disputes between the two houses and most issues have been resolved amicably. Increasingly federal laws are emerging from Bundestag and Bundesrat in a more detailed and comprehensive form, leaving the provincial parliaments (Landtage) with less opportunities to fill local provisions into federal law.[4] This is but one example of the centralising tendencies manifesting themselves in the federal system and which have led to Landtage exercising little control over the decisions their governments make within the Bundesrat. At the same time the establishment of inter-Land bodies to co-ordinate and co-operate in some fields of activity, as well as federal intervention in some Laender responsibilities like higher education and police services, have tended further to reduce the role of Landtage. Although these centralising tendencies have not totally removed Laender autonomy, some disquiet was expressed in 1977 by a Commission of Inquiry on the Constitution at the growth in the power of the Bund at the expense of the Laender.[5] These tendencies aside, the system of 'co-operative' federalism has worked smoothly because both spheres of government have generally respected the rights of the other. Tensions which exist have not led to many cases of attempted federal interference in Laender affairs like those which marked Hindenburg's presidency in Weimar. Federal presidents too have usually accepted the limitation of their constitutional role made by the Basic Law.

The power of appointment and dismissal of the chancellor are now firmly vested in the Bundestag (BL art. 63) which in practice means he must be the candidate of the party – or more often, parties – holding an overall majority in the house. At the same time, the Bundestag is prevented from capriciously dismissing a chancellor by the Constructive Vote of No Confidence (BL art. 67) which prevents him from being dismissed unless at the same time a successor is elected. Thus a majority of members can only combine to force a chancellor's resignation if it agrees to support a new head of government. This device has been resorted to on only one occasion – in 1972 – when it failed. In practice its success depends upon agreement amongst parliamentary parties to form a new coalition to succeed that led by the outgoing chancellor. For the most part however coalitions formed immediately after an election have lasted for the entire length of the ensuing parliament and coalition agreements at Laender level too have usually survived a full term. A broad but flexible convention has been established that if parties form coalitions at the federal level they do so too at Land level if none has an overall majority.[6] All federal and most Laender governments have been coalitions and this successful tradition owes much to the first chancellor, Konrad Adenauer, who also did much to shape the office, accruing to it more power and prestige than envisaged by the framers of the Basic Law. Adenauer's success in building stable conditions was made possible because he put dogma far below maintaining his governments and principally himself in office. The same pragmatic approach typified the part he played in the establishment of his party, the CDU. Adenauer's success here was crucial, for it was also to be a major contribution to the eventual development of the present party system which contrasts strongly with that of Weimar and for whose eventual emergence, in 1949 at least, the auguries were not good. It is no exaggeration to say that political parties were anathema to the Germans in the immediate postwar period, a legacy of the divisions and interparty warfare of Weimar and of the Nazi totalitarian state. The framers of the Basic Law must be credited with some courage, therefore, for resisting the public mood. By accepting that political parties had to play a crucial part in the re-establishment of German democracy and by recognising the part they should play in the political system, the Basic Law was to begin the process by which those parties achieved the status of constitutional organs of the state.[7]

## THE WEST GERMAN PARTY SYSTEM

Article 21 of the Basic Law lays down the principle of the free establishment of political parties to 'participate in the forming of the political will of the people'. It also provides that 'parties who by their aims or behaviour seek to impair or abolish the free democratic order or threaten the existence of the Republic shall be declared unconstitutional by the Federal Constitutional Court'. It was under these provisions that the Socialist Reich

Party (SRP) was dissolved in 1952 and the German Communist Party (KPD) in 1956. Subsequently, these parties – or at least their members – regrouped to form new parties where constitutions and behaviour carefully avoided the risk of suffering the fate which had overtaken their predecessors. Some observers have questioned the democratic validity of Article 21 and even more its applicability in these two cases; still others have claimed that the decision to ban the KPD after the SRP was a *quid pro quo* arrangement to placate national opinion.[8] No other party has been referred to the Court since 1956, and the ensuing low level of support for all minor parties may have been responsible for government's reluctance to invoke Article 21 against potentially subversive parties. More succinctly, the device now used is the *Radikalerlass* – the weeding out of potentially subversive individuals from the public service, as 'constitutionally unreliable', on the grounds of their membership of 'radical' parties which curiously are still allowed to organise and operate freely and openly. Thus, though Article 21 has not been invoked against these groups their members run the risk of being investigated by Laender authorities to test their loyalty to the state and its ideals. Those found to hold beliefs unacceptable to the authorities face the prospect of being banned from any of the professions and trades included in the wide nomenclature of 'civil servant' used in West Germany. The outlawing of 'unconstitutional' elements and groups is not a new feature in German political life where the fundamentals of 'opposition of principle' and those of 'loyal opposition' have not always been clearly understood or differentiated by political elites or their electorates.[9]

Federal legislation has more fully defined the role of political parties in the democratic processes, laying upon them responsibilities for the political education of citizens and the encouragement of active participation in the conduct of public affairs. The Party Law of 1967 which codifies these responsibilities is not only detailed and specific in laying down the role expected of parties; it also accepts too that the state itself has a duty to assist them in carrying out their functions. Generous provision of state aid to the parties was made possible under the Act. Subventions are given to the parties at parliamentary, federal and land level. Parliamentary parties *(Fraktionen)* receive money for their Bundestag activities. In 1972 the amounts given were:

|          | DM       |
|----------|----------|
|          | DM       |
| CDU/CSU  | 8·7m.    |
| SPD      | 8·2m.    |
| FDP      | 2·6m.    |

It is the amounts awarded to the parties outside parliament how-ever that are largest. In 1958 the Federal Constitutional Court ruled that contributions to parties by individuals and companies previously held to be tax-deductible, were in fact subject to tax, a decision which threatened an important source of revenue especially that of the CDU/CSU and the Free Democrats (FDP). The Court subsequently ruled that the law passed in 1959 granting subsidies to parties must be extended beyond those represented in the Bundestag.[10] Now any party which receives at least 0·5 per cent of the vote at a Bundestag election is entitled to receive 3·50 DM for each vote gained. Payment of these sums is spread out over the four years following an election and they must only be used for election expenses, not day-to-day administration which must be paid for from party membership dues or donations. Payment is authorised by the president of the Bundestag. The amounts due to each party after the election of 1972 were:

|      | DM     |
|------|--------|
| SPD  | 114m.  |
| CDU  | 114m.  |
| FDP  | 24m.   |
| CSU  | 23m.   |

Thus by most European standards West German parties are able to mount costly – and some would say profligate – election cam-paigns to mobilise support. A similar lavish expenditure is made possible at the Land level where parties receive subsidies too – at the rate of 2·50 DM per vote. Dues from memberships are also quite considerable. Each major party operates a sliding scale by which a member pays a subscription fixed according to his income. Parties need these monies for day-to-day administration and they have organised periodic recruiting drives to increase membership which nevertheless has recently been declining (see Appendix). By law parties must publish accounts and declare all donations exceeding 20,000 DM given by individuals and those exceeding 200,000 DM given by companies.

Constitutional status and state patronage alone could not guarantee the increasing legitimacy of the parties nor indeed the reduction in the number of political parties from the eleven repre-sented in the Bundestag in 1949 to the four[11] which have survived to monopolise every seat in the federal parliament and most in provincial ones since 1961. This too was a departure from the party traditions of Weimar where particularisms – regional, religious and economic and opposition of principle – encouraged by the electoral system led to a multiplicity of mutually antagonistic parties and a consequent weakness in executives. The years in which the Bonn Republic emerged were years of allied tutelage, of the Cold War and of an almost obsessive activity to rebuild and expand the national economy. Conscious of these pressures, German leaders abandoned the indulgences of Weimar, skilfully playing on the growing reliance of the Western allies on their loyalty and good will. Coalition agreements were generally honoured and the initially bitter rhetoric between the CDU and SDP was gradually toned down. In the meantime the electorate, though generally prepared to support their new leaders with high turn-outs, eschewed most other political activities, showing more concern for, and placing more faith in, the nation's economic performance than in the political system. It was against this background that some nimble footwork by the leaders of the CDU led to increasing electoral support for their party. Originally committed to a large degree of state intervention in the economy by its Ahlen programme 1948 – a misreading of public mood – the CDU virtually abandoned it in favour of Erhard's concept of the social market economy. This flexibility is the hallmark of the 'Volkspartei' formula which the CDU developed. The 'catch-all' formula[12] eschews ideology except where necessary as rhetoric for mobilising electoral support; it also places an emphasis on holding power and maintaining the social and economic *status quo*. The development of this formula was to be Adenauer's major lesson for his new party, one its precursors and rival had hitherto not achieved. Placing such importance on winning widespread electoral support and thus political power affected both Adenauer's party and the political orientations of the state they built. Essentially it meant accommodating as wide a group of social and economic interests as possible, reconciling their claims and providing them with access to the growing wealth provided by the expanding economy. Successfully answering these demands led to growing electoral support for the CDU by these groups which became increasingly reliant on Adenauer and his party as their hold on the Bonn system tightened. Thus the CDU became much more than Germany's first party of the Centre Right which straddled the hitherto unbridgeable gulf between Catholic and Protestant. It became the party of the state.

## THE CHRISTIAN DEMOCRATIC UNION (CDU)

Like his contemporary De Gaulle, Adenauer had fashioned his party to be a 'vote-gathering' machine which garnered electoral support to legitimise his chancellorship.[13] A loose confederation of Laender parties adapting to the local conditions, interests and traditions present in the postwar reconstruction era, the CDU's supra-confessional stance brought Catholic and Protestant conservatives, business men and some labour leaders together in an alliance which Adenauer held together by the force of his personality and by the adhesives of rising living standards and his pro-Western foreign policy. In spite of the supra-confessional formula the CDU heartlands were the Catholic regions of the south (save for Bavaria where the CDU did not establish an organisation – see below, p. 101). Dominance in the heavily populated industrial state of North-Rhine Westphalia and eventually in the northern agricultural and largely Protestant Schleswig Holstein led to the CDU's overwhelming electoral superiority. Although the CDU benefited from the success of its economic policies there was widespread support too for Adenauer's foreign policy which was to found the Republic's roots firmly in the Western Alliance, winning acceptability for his country with its former enemies. By the time of his retirement West Germany had been fully accepted into the Western camp. The Republic had been allowed to rearm, was a member of NATO and had been instrumental in founding the EEC – a further success in Adenauer's policy of seeking friendship with France.

Domestically there had been opposition to many of these moves but by the beginning of the sixties Adenauer had the satisfaction of seeing his principal opponents accept all his international commitments.[14] It seemed that the formula which Adenauer and his party had evolved to win and hold power in the Republic was to lead to permanent CDU dominance. As he dominated his governments, so 'Der Alte' dominated his party, exploiting its confederal structures and manipulating its machinery often in a high-handed manner which betrayed his authoritarian upbringing. Rivals were ruthlessly isolated, conflicting interests appeased. As Kurt Sontheimer observes: 'At its heart [the CDU] was a collection of dignitaries from more or less conservative groups in which the democratic forming of political will within the party was unimportant. Having succeeded early with the German electorate, the CDU concentrated keeping in power.'[15] Adenauer concentrated on this objective with the generally enthusiastic acquiescence of his party's rank and file. Until 1968 party conferences were rallies for acclaiming party leaders rather than determining policy. Some unrest amongst the other leaders of the CDU had brought reforms against Adenauer's wishes in the party organisation in 1956, seeking to strengthen the party's federal executive committee by increasing the size of its presidium. The changes proved unsuccessful since Adenauer as party chairman flagrantly refused to convene either the executive committee or the larger federal committee. This high-handedness, demonstrated also in attempts to block Erhard's succession, was not confined to party affairs. As early as 1959 Adenauer had considered taking over the office of federal presidency, elevating its status to that enjoyed by De Gaulle in France. These autocratic tendencies showed even more clearly during the debates on the Spiegel affair in which Adenauer's contempt for concern at breaches in civil liberties suggested a predilection for the effectiveness of government rather than its answerability.[16] Nothing more clearly demonstrated Adenauer's love affair with political power than the graceless way in which he relinquished it. Largely due to growing public disenchantment with him the CDU had lost ground in 1961, but in 1965 with Erhard as its new chancellor the party won back some support both with the electorate and its coalition partners the Free Democrats who had latterly been amongst Adenauer's most bitter critics.

It was the legacy of the later years of Adenauer's dominance of his party whose chairmanship he did not relinquish until 1966 which was to bring its problems to the CDU in the sixties and seventies. The success of the Volkspartei formula places high demands on effective leadership. Adenauer's success in welding disparate and conflicting interests into an electoral alliance also meant the party was composed of 'centrifugal forces which threaten to destroy it'.[17] As with Tory leaders in Britain, 'Adenauer's success . . . and his alternative appeasement policy within the party helped him to keep the CDU together, because for all the interests represented in the party there was always the superior common interest in remaining in power'.[18] Always a 'voters' party' rather than a 'members' party', the CDU since Adenauer's time has been unable to find a leader to match his stature or ability to hold the electoral combination of business, Catholics, farmers, the middle classes and the old together. Changes in social attitudes, religious values and above all the decline in the economy contributed to the events which eventually left the CDU in opposition, a role it was unable to adapt to because it had been constructed as a party of power.

The confederal structure of the CDU and its emergence under Adenauer left the party with a system of internal government which has proved to be unwieldly largely because his successors have never enjoyed the same personal prestige and dominance. Between conferences the party is directed theoretically by the federal committee (Bundesauschuss), a large body consisting of the smaller and more important federal executive committee (Bundesvorstand) plus delegates from the Land parties and other affiliated organisations like the women's group and the youth section (Junge Union), the leaders of CDU Landtage *Fraktions*, full-time secretaries of Land parties and chairmen of the party's policy groups. The executive committee consists of presidium (federal chairman, managing chairman, their deputies and four further members), together with representatives of the Land organisations, the party's Bundestag Fraktion, federal treasurer and general secretary. It is this body which has effective control of the party, and although not so dominated by its leader as in Adenauer's day it has never asserted the same control of the party as the equivalent body in its major rival the SPD.

## THE SOCIAL DEMOCRATIC PARTY (SPD)

The early years of the Republic were lean ones for the SPD. Neck and neck with their rivals in 1949, they watched the CDU forge ahead leaving them with opportunities to participate in government only at the Land level in traditional SPD provinces like Hesse, Hamburg and Bremen. Other areas of strong SPD support in Weimar had been lost to the East German regime. The SPD's Marxist origins did not help its electoral image in the era of the Cold War either although its first postwar leader Kurt Schumacher was a fierce opponent of the KPD and Stalinism. It was largely he who resisted any accommodation with the KPD, which through a merger forced on the SPD in the east had produced the Socialist Unity Party (SED) in the Democratic Republic. It was at the Bad Godesberg conference of 1959 that the SPD broke its links with its Marxist past, adopting a new programme which meant in effect that the party had decided to follow its great rival along the road to become a Volkspartei, coming to terms with the state and the economic system built by Adenauer and Erhard. The new programme committed the party to acceptance of the profit motive and to social reform measures, whilst also renouncing the party's traditional opposition to the church.[19] More important perhaps was the SPD's renunciation of its Marxist rhetoric which had always been more evident than its Marxist policies.

Even more crucial than these new domestic orientations was the party's acceptance of a bipartisan foreign policy and of membership of the EEC. The new men who had forged the Bad Godesberg programme like Brandt, Schmidt and Wehner were to figure large in the SPD's eventual elevation into government at the federal level. How far the formal adoption of the programme benefited the SPD in the sixties is difficult to say. The slow but steady rise in the party's votes in the elections of 1957, 1961 and 1965 earned the label 'Genosse (Comrade) Trend' which nevertheless relied on some disenchantment with the CDU as much as the willingness of important social groups to indicate to their members the acceptability of the SPD as a party of government. Although the SPD always found its major support amongst industrial workers it has never had the same formal ties with the trade union movement upon which the British Labour Party has always depended. Furthermore, even after Bad Godesburg the traditional antagonism between the SPD and the Catholic Church – fuelled by Schumacher in the fifties – lingered on. One feature of the Republic's political system – its federal structure – did however give the SPD some opportunities to gain experience in government. Brandt in Berlin and Schmidt in Hamburg used their posts in Land governments to win a national reputation.

By origin a mass party, the SPD has always had a larger membership than its rival and its income from dues (calculated on a sliding scale) has always been greater than those of the CDU, although it has never been able to rely as heavily on donations from interest groups and individuals. Organisationally the SPD has always been more centralised than the CDU and as in mass parties the influence of the party conference in the formulation of policy is more a token of inner party democracy than a reality. Although the federal structures of the state allow for some variation in policies between parties at the Land level, the determination of national policy is very much in the hands of the central party executive. The need to make policy accommodation with the FDP has meant too that the coalition-bargaining process limits the influence of both leaders and the rank and file over legislative proposals. The parliamentary group *(Fraktion)* is an important instrument in determining policy, and its executive committee's chairman, presently Herbert Wehner, holds a position of great potential influence.

The Party Executive *(Vorstand)*, statutorily charged with the responsibility for the leadership of the party, consists of over thirty members and is dominated by its nine-member presidium. Because the party relies more heavily on membership dues for day-to-day running of its affairs than on gifts from individuals or organisations, control by the rank and file tends to be too loose to be effective. Thus the party *Fraktion,* the executive and powerful Land-based politicians wield most influence in the SPD, which are usually able to stifle agitation for more left-wing policies, especially those voiced by its youth section. The Young Socialists (Junge Sozialisten) are an almost permanent source of trouble to the leaders of the party who, anxious to emphasise the pragmatic orientations the SPD now stands for, are subject to frequent embarrassing demands for more socialism. Distancing themselves from 'socialism' has had to be a principal objective for the SPD leaders and for reasons which are not just connected with the electorate's belief in the sanctity of the free market economy which has produced such widespread affluence. 'Socialism' is the creed of the other Germany and the spectre of the Democratic Republic is a strong, albeit negative, symbol in the political culture of West Germany, the antithesis of the social, political and economic values of the Federal Republic. The threat posed to affluence by a 'socialist' state control of the economy is reinforced by the more recent Marxist/anarchist terror groups, the presence of spies and the radicalisation of the young. Evocations of what socialism leads to can be seen in the example of the other Germany and this is a powerful weapon for the Union Parties. The SPD with its Marxist origins is thus sensitive to the charges that its domestic policies are 'socialist' and its foreign and defence policies lead to weakness in relations with the Soviet bloc and the GDR in particular. Risking such charges when it pursued Ostpolitik so courageously, the SPD has nevertheless adopted cautious and orthodox policies in the control of the economy. In this its leaders have been able to resist the demands of their left-wingers for radical social and economic reforms, claiming that their Liberal coalition partners would never accept such policies. Thus for the dominant right wing of the SPD, the FDP is not only a necessary ally in government but a welcome justification for the party's centrist image so vital in winning support amongst moderate, unaligned voters of the middle and skilled working classes.

## THE CHRISTIAN SOCIAL UNION

Bavaria has always been prone to the separatist and religious cleavages so manifest in earlier German states. Even in Weimar, there was an autonomous Bavarian People's Party (BVP) which operated independently of the otherwise nationwide Zentrum. The same relationship has survived in the period since 1949. The CDU and the CSU are indeed separate parties which have reached an accommodation by which neither has attempted to establish an organisation within the other's territory and yet which have always combined into a common parliamentary group. The co-operation between the two Union parties was cemented by their mutual reliance in holding and achieving power but it is fair to say that the unfamiliar role of opposition has increased tensions between them. Even before the Republic was constitutionally established the CSU often took an independent line – the Bavarian Landtag was the only one not to endorse the Basic

Law – and this tendency to independence has often led to disagreements between the two party groups within the *Fraktion*. The influence of the CSU within federal politics as a conservative ginger group and its survival as the last of Germany's regionally based parties are interconnected.[20] The CSU enjoys a permanently secure power-base within Bavaria, a predominantly rural, agricultural province in which 70 per cent of the population is Catholic. Bavarian Catholicism has always been more conservative than that of those areas of the Republic where industrialisation has been heavy and where the church has shown itself to be more liberal.[21] The secularisation processes of the fifties and sixties which eventually caused a weakening of the hold of the CDU over some Catholic voters did not manifest itself so markedly in Bavaria where the CSU has increased its support amongst the rural electorate. At the same time the Catholic hierarchy in Bavaria has continued to encourage its communicants to support the party. The CSU has inherited the traditions and benefits of Bavaria's interlocked regional and religious interests and is able as a result to dominate the provincial Landtag and the region's representation in Bonn. Save for the brief upsurge of another rural (and separatist) party, the BP, in the early years of the Republic the CSU's hold on the province has never been broken or indeed shaken.

It is the secureness of its power-base and the traditional particularisms of Bavarian society which has always made the CSU an important factor in federal politics and which has always affected the electoral strategy of the CDU. Dominated by Catholic conservatives, the CSU has always been much more homogeneous than its sister party. Liberal influence has always been weaker in the CSU than that exercised by the 'social' wing of the CDU. With a fierce and unrelenting antagonism to the Communist bloc, marked resistance to social reform in areas like education, strong emphasis on provincial rights and the agricultural interests of its economy, the CSU's stance as a party of the populist right has meant it has become one of the pillars of modern German nationalism. At the same time the CSU poses a threat to its ally should it ever decide to spread out of Bavaria and attempt to establish itself as a national party based on the electoral support of the CSU's right-wing voters. In this respect the leader of the CSU, Franz Josef Strauss, has seemed to personify both the strength and weaknesses of his party and its ally. For Strauss is not only a considerable electorate asset in mobilising the nationalist conservative vote for both parties, but also anathema to many independent liberal-minded voters. Strauss's record in the Spiegel affair caused grave doubts about his commitment to

civil rights – and led eventually to his resignation at FDP insistence.[22] His subsequent leadership of the anti-*détente* lobby in
the Republic, the violence of his language, his uncompromising
opposition to Ostpolitik and his antagonism to social and political
reform cause him and thus his party to be regarded with suspicion amongst liberal middle-class voters, especially in the
north.

### THE FREE DEMOCRATIC PARTY (FDP)

Liberalism in Germany has had a chequered career, largely
because of its tendency to divide and form two parties as it did in
both Weimar and the Second Reich. National liberalism and
progressive liberalism based on the two conflicting impulses of
entrepreneurial freedom and of state restraint on that freedom to
ensure personal liberties could not reach an accommodation.
Catholic liberalism too went its own way in the formation of the
Zentrum. Once the Christian Democrats had evolved a formula
which straddled the religious division and once they had accepted
the implications of the social market economy evolved by the
former Liberal Ludwig Erhard, there appeared to be little chance
for the FDP's electoral survival. Nevertheless the party has
survived, although its policy orientations of the fifties and early
sixties have changed from those of economic and nationalist
conservatism to those of a party of reform and a preparedness to
advance *détente*.[23] At the same time as the party has changed
its outlook – and its leaders for that matter – it has managed to
avoid the electoral oblivion which has overtaken all other minor
parties in the lifetime of the Republic.

Initially the FDP survived absorption and eclipse by the CDU
through ability to differentiate itself from Adenauer's party, and
by winning a variable measure of support from sections of the
electorate which withheld their votes from the two main party
blocs. Thus in 1961 the FDP gained substantially from public
disenchantment with Adenauer and it has always placed an
emphasis on maintaining its own integrity, stressing separateness
from coalition partners and portraying itself as a moderating
influence on them. This has been a largely successful formula,
for the FDP have enjoyed more periods in government at the
federal level than either of the two major parties.

The FDP has always suffered from the lack of a firm base of
electoral support amongst the influential pressure groups which
dominate the pluralist society of West Germany and whose
involvement formally and informally with government, parliament and the parties gives them a crucial involvement in public

policy making. Thus the FDP became an important element in the power-structure of the CDU state built by Adenauer. Small businessmen prospered from the Erhard economic policies and the secularisation processes of the sixties reduced the importance of religion as a political value affecting voting choice. Originally heavily dependent on Protestant votes amongst farmers as well as businessmen, the FDP saw these being eroded without any compensatory support rising amongst Catholics. This was to lead to a sharp and swift reorientation of the party's policy positions as it sought out electoral support in new areas, not least among young voters, which was made possible by a change of leadership in which the 'left wing' tradition of German liberalism was better represented than in the years of coalition with the CDU.

Because the traditions of liberalism vary from Land to Land the FDP's organisational structure has more closely resembled that of the CDU than that of the SPD. It comprises a congress, a national committee and a federal executive, but governmental responsibilities have generally ensured that the leadership of the party has controlled its machinery and its policy orientations. Membership of the FDP has always been small and its reliance on state subsidies is very heavy. Perhaps even more than the CDU the party was affected by the Constitutional Court's ruling on the taxing of payments to parties (see above, p. 95), and the subsequent granting of state aid under federal law was introduced in part because of liberal pressure. Nevertheless, as a nationally based party the FDP is very much the pauper of the four major parties. Its total federal vote, below that of the CSU, means it has smaller state funds for campaigning nationwide than the CSU has at its disposal for electioneering in Bavaria alone.

German liberals have generally held the balance of power in both Bundestag and most Landtage and have been consistently wooed as coalition partners. Thus they have wielded a disproportionate influence on government at both levels. They also have a vested interest in the continuation of the present electoral system which the two major parties have occasionally threatened to transform into one of first-past-the-post.[24] Such a system would destroy the FDP's chances of any representation. It was this weapon which both major parties have raised in the past, usually as a threat against liberal recalcitrance. That the issue is now virtually dead because of the reliance of both the SPD and the CDU on liberal support in forming governments, is perhaps the most important indication of the strength of the FDP's pivotal position in West German politics.

## THE ELECTORAL SYSTEM

Both single member constituencies and proportional representation with party lists are used in federal and provincial elections in the Federal Republic. It should be emphasised however that the constituency seats are included in the overall distribution of seats due to each party. Each voter has two votes, the first of which he gives to a named candidate he wishes to support as his constituency member. Constituencies have – on average – 160,000 voters. The candidate with a simple majority of votes is elected. The second vote may only be cast for a party. These second votes are totalled for the whole of the country and the 496 seats in the Bundestag are divided in proportion to the percentage vote won by each party. The number of constituency seats already won by the party are then deducted and the remainder are filled from the party's list in each Land. Parties which fail to win 5 per cent of the national vote or which win less than three constituencies are excluded. This system has operated in every federal election since 1957 when some minor amendments adopted in 1953 and 1956 finally shaped it as it is today.

The electoral law gives formal recognition to the existence of parties and its rules regulating the allocation of seats nationally as well as the method of dividing votes cast tend to favour larger parties. Technically the parties fight on a Land basis, but they are allowed to combine all their second votes into one national vote for the apportionment of seats. Regionally based parties are thus at a disadvantage because their totals are too small to beat the 5 per cent hurdle since it applies to national total votes and only parties with a national organisation and manifesto are allowed to combine their Land votes nationally. Only the CSU survives because its massive Bavarian vote – usually over 55 per cent of the province's turnout – is equal to about 10 per cent of the national vote. Each party's national vote is then divided by the D'Hondt (greatest average) system – that is by 1, 2, 3 4 and so forth. The resulting quotients are then arranged in rank order until 496 seats have been allocated. Thus after the election of 1976 the system worked as shown in Table 5.1. Thus of the first twelve seats, the SPD has six, the CDU, four, the CSU, one, and the FDP, one. The process is continued until all 496 seats are allocated nationally, whereupon each party's vote is then redivided into each of its Land totals and the D'Hondt formula reapplied. Thus one party's Land list competes against its other nine (except in the case of the CSU whose seats have already been allocated because it fights in only one Land). When the number of the party's seats in each Land has been determined the constituency seats it has won are subtracted and the remainder filled from the

Table 5.1    *Distribution of Seats between Parties, 1976 Election*

| | Parties | Second votes won |
|---|---|---|
| | SPD | 16,099,000 |
| | CDU | 14,367,000 |
| | CSU | 4,028,000 |
| | FDP | 2,995,000 |

*Calculation of quotients*

| Divisor | SPD | CDU | CSU | FDP |
|---|---|---|---|---|
| I | 16,099,000 | 14,367,000 | 4,028,000 | 2,995,000 |
| 2 | 8,049,000 | 7,183,000 | 2,014,000 | 1,497,000 |
| 3 | 5,366,000 | 4,789,000 | 1,342,000 | 998,000 |
| 4 | 4,024,000 | 3,591,000 | 1,007,000 | 748,000 |
| 5 | 3,219,000 | 2,273,000 | 805,000 | 599,000 |
| 6 | 2,683,000 | 2,394,000 | 671,000 | 499,000 |

*Rank – ordering of quotients*

| Quotient | Party | No. of Seats |
|---|---|---|
| 16,099,000 | SPD | 1st |
| 14,367,000 | CDU | 2nd |
| 8,049,000 | SPD | 3rd |
| 7,183,000 | CDU | 4th |
| 5,366,000 | SPD | 5th |
| 4,789,000 | CDU | 6th |
| 4,028,000 | CSU | 7th |
| 4,024,000 | SPD | 8th |
| 3,591,000 | CDU | 9th |
| 3,219,000 | SPD | 10th |
| 2,995,000 | FDP | 11th |
| 2,683,000 | SPD | 12th |

party's Land list. Thus in 1976 the total seats were divided as shown in Table 5.2. The FDP has not won a constituency since 1957 but has always cleared the 5 per cent hurdle. There are no by-elections; vacant seats are filled by taking the next candidate on the Land list of the party concerned. The electoral system proposed for the European Assembly elections, 1978, by the SPD/FDP will be based on the present system, but with a national

Table 5.2    *Division of Total Seats, 1976*

| Party | Seats allocated | Constituency seats | List seats |
|---|---|---|---|
| SPD | 214 | 113 | 101 |
| CDU | 190 | 95 | 95 |
| CSU | 53 | 40 | 13 |
| FDP | 39 | — | 39 |

list. The opposition would have preferred a regional list system, especially the CSU which might suffer considerably under a national list system.

## POLITICAL DEVELOPMENTS, 1965–77

Although Erhard's succession to the chancellorship and the recovery of the CDU in the 1965 election suggested that his party had re-established its control of the political system, economic recession helped to destroy both Erhard and his government. The outcome was the formation in 1966 of the grand coalition of the CDU/CSU and SPD under Kurt Kiesinger. This proved to be a watershed in the development of West German party politics.[25] For the Social Democrats it was an opportunity to kill the often-repeated charge that they were untried or, worse, incapable of holding power, and although the coalition succeeded in overcoming the recession, opposition to the pact within the party seemed to be vindicated by SPD losses in Laender elections.

Reactions to the grand coalition outside the two major party blocs were equally strong. Left-wing opposition evinced itself in the formation of the Extra Parliamentary Opposition (APO) which led eventually to the foundation of a 'Moscow' Communist Party (DKP) as well as a Maoist one (KPD). The street protests of APO as well as the recession brought increasing support for the National Democratic Party (NPD) an amalgam of right-wing parties founded on the bones of the banned SRP in 1964.[26] Land elections during the period 1966–8 showed a rise in the NPD's support rather than that for the Liberals who were swamped in the Bundestag where the coalition held 447 seats.

It was developments within the FDP at this time which were to have the most far-reaching effects upon party politics in the period following the formation of the grand coalition. The Liberals had lost over a third of their vote in the 1965 Bundestag election, and Land elections since then had not seen an improvement in the party's position. However the FDP was undertaking a change in orientation alongside a change in leadership. The conservative Erich Mende was replaced by the middle-of-the-road Walter Scheel who with his deputy, Hans-Dietrich Genscher, and the sociologist Rolf Dahrendorf presided over a distinct move to the left by the FDP. Though deeply divided, the Liberals began to move towards a position in foreign affairs which was to lead to the rejection of the Hallstein doctrine and its replacement by what became known as the Ostpolitik, an accommodation with the Soviet Union and the GDR, one which accepted the realities of divided Germany. Social reform in education and justice were the domestic planks which the Liberals hoped would help them with their somewhat adventurous strategy of seeking support amongst the young and especially new voters. In the meantime the Liberals could only hope that the coalition would not agree to amend the electoral system on the lines of that used in Britain, which would surely have meant their extinction.

Frequent squabbles between the partners suggested that a re-establishment of the grand coalition after the election of 1969 was not certain. In any case the likelihood of the SPD and FDP forming a government was increased when, earlier in the year, the Liberals had supported the Social Democrat candidate for the federal presidency, Gustav Heinemann.[27] Although the Liberals lost support, the two parties enjoyed a majority of twelve seats in the Bundestag and subsequently formed a government.

The SPD had every reason to feel satisified with its 1969 performance. 'Genosse Trend' had carried it out of its 30 per cent 'ghetto' after twenty years and the party had won support in a number of important areas and amongst key groups in society. The party had had above average gains in middle-class areas where services, administration and new technological industries predominated.[28] Especially important were advances in Catholic cities, particularly in the populous Cologne–Bonn area. Indeed, it was the SPD's advance in the Land of North-Rhine Westphalia (see Table 5.3), the most heavily populated of all the Republic's regions, which accounts for the rise of the SPD to overall parity with the Union. A similar decline in CDU fortunes can also be attributed to its fallback in the region. The decline of the CDU in

Table 5.3   *SPD and CDU Percentage Votes – North-Rhine Westphalia 1949–72*

|     | 1949 | 1953 | 1957 | 1961 | 1965 | 1969 | 1972 |
|-----|------|------|------|------|------|------|------|
| SPD | 31·4 | 31·9 | 33·5 | 37·3 | 42·6 | 46·8 | 50·4 |
| CDU | 36·9 | 48·9 | 54·4 | 47·6 | 47·1 | 43·6 | 41·0 |

this province was accompanied by one in northern Germany as a whole. Generally the party has not suffered such a sharp decline in the south – Saarland being an exception. However, Union losses have generally been those inflicted on the CDU, while the CSU's vote has remained remarkably stable. The relative electoral performance of the two groups thus joined the growing list of contentious matters between the Union parties and gave weight to Strauss's arguments that the CDU should adopt the hard-line policies on which the CSU has always fought. The Union parties have always denied that the election of 1969 indicated a desire for a real change of power in Bonn but rather insist that the electorate had given them a moral claim as the largest parliamentary group to form a government.[29] Ironically, it was the device of nimble coalition building – a legacy of the departed Adenauer – which removed power from his party's hands. Twenty years' domination of federal government had left the Union eminently incapable of performing its new role as opposition.[30] There seemed few reasons why it should try. The smallness of the new coalition's majority plus the fact that some FDP deputies had refused to vote for Brandt as chancellor encouraged the Union to believe that the coalition could and would break up. Thus the CDU/CSU began to play a game of guerilla warfare in the Bundestag whilst its only attempt to restore its electoral fortunes was to replace Kiesinger as quickly as possible. The choice of its young but experienced *Fraktion* leader Rainer Barzel was to prove an unhappy one.

Party conflict sharpened over Brandt's Ostpolitik and the resulting parliamentary manocuvrings showed West German politicians at their worst. Defections from the coalition to the CDU/CSU left government and opposition equal in Bundestag seats and the government failed to get its budget passed. So restrictive are the provisions of the Basic Law on dissolving the Bundestag that Brandt had to engineer his own defeat in order to call an election in 1972. The coalition's triumph then was aided by the manoeuvrings over Ostpolitik which the unfortunate Barzel had performed because of splits in the Union's ranks.[31] In the struggle for the German centre the CDU found they had lost that crucial area to the coalition, for the Union's postures over Ostpolitik and its graceless performance in opposition alienated an important section of the electorate, the independent, moderate middle classes who were prepared to relegate any doubts about the coalition's conduct of the economy to giving approval to Ostpolitik. In a 91 per cent turn-out the SPD won 17 million votes – an increase of 3·1 per cent – and the Liberals over 3 million – an increase of 2·6 per cent. Although the Union increased its votes – by mopping up the remnants of the now defunct NPD's electorate, it trailed behind the coalition which now had an overall majority of forty-six seats.

The euphoria was shortlived. By early 1974 Brandt had resigned after his personal assistant Guenther Guillaume was arrested and charged with spying for the GDR. Scheel became federal president shortly after. The new leaders of the coalition were Helmut Schmidt, former economics minister, and Hans-Dietrich Genscher, the new leader of the FDP, and under their leadership the coalition was to suffer the impact of the international recession following the oil crisis of 1973–4. Both parties underwent repeated setbacks at Land elections – especially the Social Democrats – even though the coalition could claim with some justice that West Germany's economy suffered less than all its Western partners from the effects of the recession. The liberal mood of the late sixties and early seventies changed sharply with strong waves of public reaction to terrorist activity by the Baader Meinhof gang and the '2nd of June' movement, to 'radicalist tendencies' by some teachers, to a general decline in law and order and to the fall in economic expectations. These were all inter-related themes which Strauss and the new leader of the CDU Helmut Kohl could play upon and they did so skilfully in the 1976 election campaign. Their central theme was that 'Socialism' had and would continue to debilitate the Republic economically and politically.[32]

It is in the issues and conflicts revealed at an election campaign that the different and opposing strands of party politics are most dramatically focused. To the outside observer the areas of contention between the major parties in the Federal Republic appear to be so small that the British phenomenon of 'Butskellism' seems to be the most appropriate analogy. Perhaps an even better analogy to the West German party system would be an American one, however. The abundance of public funds permits the parties to mount elaborate and expensive campaigns in which the techniques of mass-advertising take precedence over debates on policies and issues. Policy differences – where they exist – are often subordinated to the promotion of leaders, especially the chancellor candidates of the major parties. Alongside the hard-selling of rival leaders the differences between the parties are blurred into emotional portmanteau slogans – 'Freedom', 'Progress' and 'Model Germany' – which are promoted with the intensity of a commercial advertising campaign. As in the USA, ideology has little part to play in the formation of public policy. Both countries engage in the politics of the pork barrel, a form of activity encouraged both by the federal nature of their political systems and by the existence within each of strong, well-organised pressure groups which have developed the lobbying system and use it to their maximum advantage.[33] In the case of West Germany it is not only the nature of the political system or that of her pluralistic society which has led to the decline of ideology in the party battle. The orientation of the West German voter, whether as an individual or as a member of one or another interest group, is largely determined by his orientations towards the economic system. The existence of the other Germany, with its economic collectivism and its perceived restrictions on personal freedom in the political and economic fields, produces public pressure on West German leaders to nurture and protect the free enterprise system developed by Erhard. The nature of the social market economy is thereby excluded from major reform or amendment, more so perhaps than anything in the Basic Law. To achieve sufficient electoral support the SPD has abandoned any extension of state ownership and, harnessed as it is to its Liberal coalition partners, it is forced to moderate its proposals for state economic intervention to make them acceptable to the FDP. This was true, for instance, over plans for extending workers' participation in industrial management (*Mitbestimmung*) in 1976. The sanctity of the free enterprise system is one which the Union defends fiercely, arousing latent fears that the SPD might be trying to resurrect 'Socialism' by stealth thus threatening not only the free enterprise system but the abundance it provides.

At the same time the experience of Weimar, strengthened by the perceived threat from the East, has produced pressure to establish consensus not only in constitutional arrangements but in policy areas too. An avoidance of conflict to which West German leaders are prone is evinced in attempts to produce once-and-for-all solutions to political problems, all-party agreements which are permanent and total, and this tendency is further strengthened by the dominant role played in legislation by 'experts' and the specialist committees of the Bundestag as well as by the influence of pressure groups in the law-making process. Areas of party conflict like foreign policy are also diminished because of the Federal Republic's position as a front-line nation of the West. The bipartisan foreign policy forged between the major parties after Schumacher's death has not been fundamentally abandoned, the disagreements over Ostpolitik notwithstanding.

One issue which appears to be becoming more important in the Federal Republic is that of law and order, an area which is likely to benefit the Union as it might any other conservative party in Western Europe. Here the desire of all politicians to adopt a supra-party formula for dealing with terrorist activity may be a case where public pressure for an even stronger line – such as the restoration of the death penalty – will lead the parties to engage in a dutch auction in toughness in dealing with those who for whatever reason have contracted out of the political system and turned to criminality and violence. Social reform – an area in which Brandt hoped to have some successes and where he failed – might be further relegated to take second place to cracking down on all forms of dissent. Already important matters concerned with the public weal like the building of nuclear power stations and the reform of education – especially higher education – have become muddled with the law and order issue because of the involvement of radicals in them. In responding to these demands from vocal minorities West German politicians have yielded to the temptation of suggesting that all dissent, all opposition is 'opposition of principle', opposition to the form of the state. In responding to widespread demands for handling dissent with firmness, German political parties may fall too easily into the trap of neglecting individual liberty, a posture other generations of political leaders adopted too eagerly and with dire consequences.

Certainly if the law and order issue is about to become a major one in the party arena in the Federal Republic it seems likely to be one which will benefit the Union. Even without it the present coalition faces a very insecure future and may have been replaced by a CDU/CSU/FDP government before the end of the present Bundestag. Perhaps the West German political system is about to enter another watershed out of which new alignments may appear. A period in opposition might be as necessary for the SPD as Herbert Wehner believes it to be, an opportunity for the party to rethink its approach to wielding power in this the most stable and yet most enigmatic of EEC member-states.

Table 5.4  Federal Republic of Germany Bundestag Election Results, 1965–1976 (second votes)

| | 1965 | % | seats | 1969 | % | seats | 1972 | % | seats | 1976 | % | seats |
|---|---|---|---|---|---|---|---|---|---|---|---|---|
| Number of registered voters | 38,510,000 | | | 38,677,000 | | | 41,446,000 | | | 41,957,000 | | |
| Number of votes cast | 33,416,000 | 86·8 | | 33,548,000 | 86·7 | | 37,762,000 | 91·1 | | 38,176,000 | 90·7 | |
| Number of valid votes | 32,620,000 | | | 32,966,000 | | | 37,460,000 | | | 37,824,000 | | |
| SPD | 12,813,000 | 39·3 | 202 | 14,066,000 | 42·7 | 224 | 17,175,000 | 45·8 | 230 | 16,099,000 | 42·6 | 214 |
| CDU | 12,387,000 | 38·1 | 196 | 12,079,000 | 36·6 | 193 | 13,191,000 | 35·2 | 177 | 14,367,000 | 38·0 | 190 |
| CSU | 3,136,000 | 9·6 | 49 | 3,115,000 | 9·5 | 49 | 3,615,000 | 9·7 | 48 | 4,028,000 | 10·6 | 53 |
| FDP | 3,097,000 | 9·5 | 49 | 1,903,000 | 5·8 | 30 | 3,130,000 | 8·4 | 41 | 2,995,000 | 7·9 | 39 |
| NPD | 664,000 | 2·0 | — | 1,422,000 | 4·3 | — | 207,000 | 0·6 | — | 122,000 | 0·3 | — |
| DKP | [1] | | — | [1] | | — | 114,000 | 0·3 | — | 118,000 | 0·3 | — |
| Other parties | 522,000 | 1·6 | — | 380,000 | 1·1 | — | 28,000 | 0·0 | — | 92,551 | 0·1 | — |

Note:
[1] The DKP had not been formed and consequently did not contest the elections of 1965 and 1969.

Sources: H Kaack, Geschichte und Struktur des deutschen Parteiensystems, Obladen, Westdeutscher Verlag, 1971, pp. 295, 356–9.
Das Parlament, 19 yr, no. 40, 4 October 1969; 22 yr, no. 48, 25 November 1972; 26 yr, no. 41, 9 October 1976.
Die Zeit, no. 42, 8 October 1976.

Table 5.5  *Federal Republic of Germany Party Strengths by Laender, 1965–1976 (%)*

| | SPD | | | | + or –<br>1965–76 | CDU/CSU | | | | + or –<br>1965–76 | FDP | | | | + or –<br>1965–76 |
|---|---|---|---|---|---|---|---|---|---|---|---|---|---|---|---|
| | 1965 | 1969 | 1972 | 1976 | | 1965 | 1969 | 1972 | 1976 | | 1965 | 1969 | 1972 | 1976 | |
| Schleswig Holstein | 38·8 | 43·5 | 48·6 | 46·4 | +7·6 | 48·2 | 46·2 | 42·0 | 44·1 | –4·1 | 9·4 | 5·2 | 8·6 | 8·8 | –0·6 |
| Hamburg | 48·3 | 54·6 | 54·5 | 52·6 | +4·3 | 37·6 | 34·0 | 33·3 | 35·9 | –1·7 | 9·4 | 6·3 | 11·2 | 10·2 | +0·8 |
| Lower Saxony | 39·8 | 43·8 | 48·1 | 45·7 | +5·9 | 45·8 | 45·2 | 42·7 | 45·7 | –0·1 | 10·9 | 5·6 | 8·5 | 7·9 | –3·0 |
| Bremen | 48·5 | 52·0 | 58·1 | 54·0 | +5·5 | 34·0 | 32·3 | 29·5 | 32·5 | –1·5 | 11·7 | 9·3 | 11·1 | 11·8 | +0·1 |
| North-Rhine Westphalia | 42·6 | 46·8 | 50·4 | 46·9 | +4·3 | 47·1 | 43·6 | 41·0 | 44·5 | –2·6 | 7·6 | 5·4 | 7·8 | 7·8 | +0·2 |
| Hesse | 45·7 | 48·2 | 48·5 | 45·7 | ±0·0 | 37·8 | 38·4 | 40·3 | 44·8 | +7·0 | 12·0 | 6·7 | 10·2 | 8·5 | –3·5 |
| Rhineland Palatinate | 36·7 | 40·1 | 44·9 | 41·7 | +5·0 | 49·3 | 47·8 | 45·8 | 49·9 | +0·6 | 10·2 | 6·3 | 8·1 | 7·6 | –2·6 |
| Baden Württemberg | 33·0 | 36·5 | 38·9 | 36·6 | +3·3 | 49·9 | 50·7 | 49·8 | 53·3 | +3·4 | 13·1 | 7·5 | 10·2 | 9·1 | +4·0 |
| Bavaria | 33·1 | 34·6 | 37·8 | 32·8 | –0·3 | 55·6[1] | 54·4 | 55·1 | 60·0 | +4·4 | 7·3 | 4·1 | 6·1 | 6·2 | –1·1 |
| Saarland | 39·8 | 39·9 | 47·8 | 46·1 | +6·3 | 46·8 | 46·1 | 43·4 | 46·2 | –0·6 | 8·6 | 6·7 | 7·1 | 6·6 | –2·0 |
| National Result | 39·3 | 42·7 | 45·8 | 47·6 | +3·3 | 49·4 | 46·1 | 44·9 | 48·6 | –0·8 | 9·5 | 5·8 | 8·4 | 7·9 | –1·6 |

*Note:*
[1] Figures for Bavaria are for CSU.

*Sources:* Tony Burkett, *Parties and Elections in West Germany*, London and St Martins, New York, Hurst, pp. 106, 117, 124. *Das Parlament*, 26 yr, no. 41, 9 October 1976.

Table 5.6    *Bundestag Election, 1972 – Percentage Support for Parties amongst Men, Women and Age Groups*

| Group | SPD | FDP | CDU/CSU |
|-------|-----|-----|---------|
| Men | 47 | 9 | 43 |
| Women | 46 | 8 | 46 |
| 18–24 yrs | 55 | 9 | 35 |
| 25–34 yrs | 48 | 10 | 41 |
| 35–44 yrs | 48 | 9 | 43 |
| 45–59 yrs | 44 | 8 | 46 |
| 60+ yrs | 42 | 6 | 51 |

*Source:* Manfred Berger *et al., Bundestagswahl 1976: Politik und Sozialstruktur, Zeitschrift for Parlamentsfragen,* 8 yr, no. 2, July 1977 (reproduced by courtesy of the editor).

## APPENDIX

*Party Membership (thousands) 1960–1976*

| | 1960 | 1965 | 1970 | 1972 | 1976 (est.) |
|-----|------|------|------|------|-------------|
| SPD | 650 | 710 | 820 | 850 | 820 |
| CDU | 300 | 285 | 300 | 380 | 340 |
| CSU | 52 | 100 | 109 | 112 | 104 |
| FDP | 85 | 85 | 85 | 60 | 52 |

*Source: Bericht der Bundesregierung, 1972.*

## NOTES AND REFERENCES

1 For a more detailed analysis of the development of German political parties both in Weimar and the period 1949–68, as well as the distribution of power in the parties, see R. Morgan, 'The Federal Republic of Germany', in S. Henig and J. Pinder (eds), *European Political Parties* (London, PEP/Allen & Unwin, 1969), ch. 2, pp. 21–67.
2 For a detailed examination of German federalism and the relations between the Bund and Laender see Nevil Johnson, *Government in the Federal Republic of Germany: The Executive at Work* (Oxford, Pergamon, 1973).
3 Heinz Laufer, *Der Foederalismus der Bundesrepublik Deutschland* (Stuttgart, Kohlhammer, 1974), p. 63.
4 Manfred Friedrich, *Landesparlamente in der Bundesrepublik* (Opladen, Westdeutscher Verlag, 1975), pp. 51–69.
5 Friedrich, op cit., pp. 25–35.
6 Although the FDP entered coalitions with the CDU in two provinces after the re-election of the SPD/FDP coalition in Bonn in late 1976.
7 The development of the West German party system is traced in detail in Heino Kaack, *Geschichte und Struktur des deutschen Parteiensystems* (Opladen, Westdeutscher Verlag, 1971), pp. 155 and 362.

8  Alfred Grosser, *Germany in Our Time* (London, Pall Mall, 1971), pp. 139–40.

9  Otto Kirchheimer, 'The waning of opposition in parliamentary regimes', *Social Research,* Summer 1957, pp. 127–57.

10 Nevil Johnson, 'State finance for political parties in Western Germany', *Parliamentary Affairs,* vol. 18, no. 3, Summer 1965, pp. 279–92.

11 The four being: the SPD, the FDP, the CDU and the CSU; the last is a Bavarian party which has always formed a common parliamentary party with the CDU but which is in fact a separate party with its own organisational structure, programme and indeed style. The CDU and CSU are often referred to as 'the Union'.

12 Otto Kirchheimer, 'The transformation of the West European party systems', in J. La Palombara and M. Weiner (eds), *Political Parties and Political Development* (Princeton, NJ, Princeton University Press, 1966).

13 See Arnold J. Heidenheimer, *Adenauer and the CDU* (The Hague, Nijhoff, 1960), for an account of the rise of the CDU.

14 For an account of the process within the SPD, see William J. Paterson, *The SPD and European Integration* (Saxon House, Farnborough, 1974).

15 Kurt Sontheimer, *The Government and Politics of West Germany* (London, Hutchinson, 1972), p. 87.

16 Ronald F. Bunn, 'West Germany: The Spiegel affair', in R. F. Bunn and G. F. Andrews (eds), *Politics and Civil Liberties in Europe* (Princeton, NJ, Princeton University Press, 1967).

17 Lewis J. Edinger, 'Political change in Germany', *Comparative Politics,* vol. 2, no. 4, July 1970, p. 578.

18 Sontheimer, op. cit.

19 See Hans K. Schellenger, *The SPD in the Bonn Republic, A Socialist Party Modernises* (The Hague, Nijhof, 1968).

20 Alf Minzel, *Die CSU* (Opladen, Westdeutscher Verlag, 1976), pp. 182–201.

21 Carl Amery, 'Bayern – oder Das Aergernis der Ungleichzeitigkeit', in C. Amery and J. Koelsch, *'Bayern – ein Rechts-Staat?'* (Hamburg, Rowohlt, 1974), pp. 9–18.

22 Bunn, op. cit. pp. 148–52.

23 The FDP's policy reorientations are contained in Karl-Herman Flach, Werner Maihofer and Walter Scheel, *Die Freiburger Thesen der Liberalen* (Hamburg, Rowohlt, 1972).

24 David P. Conradt, 'Electoral-law politics in West Germany', *Political Studies,* vol. XVIII, no. 3, September 1970, pp. 341–56.

25 John M. Herz, 'The formation of the grand coalition', in J. B. Christoph and B. E. Brown (eds), *Cases in Comparative Politics,* 2nd edn (Boston, Mass., Little Brown, 1969), pp. 207–39.

26 Reinhard Kuehnl, Rainer Billing and Christine Sager, *Die NPD, Struktur, Ideologie und Funktion einer Neofaschisten Partei* (Cologne, Pahl-Rungstein, 1969).

27 For the importance of this on the subsequent election see Hans D. Klingemann and Franz Urban Pappi, 'The 1969 Bundestag election in the Federal Republic of Germany: an analysis of voting behaviour', *Comparative Politics,* vol. 2, no. 4, July 1970, pp. 523–48.

28 ibid.

29 Werner Kaltefleiter, 'The impact of the election of 1969 and the formation of the new government on the German party system', *Comparative Politics,* vol. 2, no. 4, July 1970, pp. 593–604.

30 See Dierk-Eckhard Becker and Elmar Wiesenthal, *Ohne Programme nach Bonn oder die Union als Kanzlerwahl-Verein* (Hamburg, Rowohlt, 1972).

31 William E. Laux, 'West German political parties and the 1972 Bundestag election', *Western Political Quarterly,* vol. 26, no. 3, September 1973, p. 512.

32  Tony Burkett, 'Freedom or socialism? Reflections on the West German elections 1976', *New Europe*, vol. 5, no. 1, Winter 1977, pp. 60–7.
33  Thomas Ellwein, *Das Regierungssystem der Bundesrepublik Deutschland*, 2nd edn (Cologne, Westdeutscher Verlag, 1965), pp. 97–120.

# BIBLIOGRAPHY

## GENERAL WORKS ON THE POLITICAL SYSTEM OF THE GERMAN FEDERAL REPUBLIC

Dahrendorf, R., *Society and Democracy in Germany* (London, Weidenfeld & Nicolson, 1968).
Ellwein, T., *Das Regierungssystem der Bundesrepublik Deutschland* 3rd edn (Opladen, Westdeutscher Verlag, 1973).
Grosser, A. *Germany in Our Time* (London, Pall Mall, 1971).
Heidenheimer, A. J., *The Governments of Germany*, 3rd edn (London, Methuen, 1974).
Herz, J. M., *The Government of Germany*, 2nd edn (New York, Holt, Rinehart & Winston, 1972).
Irving, R. E. M. *The Christian Democratic Parties of Western Europe* (London, George Allen & Unwin/RIIA, 1979).
Johnson, N., *Government in the Federal Republic of Germany : The Executive at Work* (London, Pergamon, 1973).
Kloss, G. *West Germany : An Introduction* (London, Macmillan, 1976).
Roberts, G. K. *West German Politics* (London, Macmillan, 1972).
Sontheimer, K., *The Governments and Politics of West Germany* (London, Hutchinson, 1972).

## FEDERALISM AND THE PARLIAMENTARY SYSTEM

Bermbach, U. (ed.), *Hamburger Bibliographie Parlamentarische System der Bundesrepublik Deutschland 1945–1970* (Opladen, Westdeutscher Verlag, 1973).
Friedrich, M. *Landesparlamente in der Bundesrepublik* (Opladen, Westdeutscher Verlag, 1975).
Laufer, H. *Der Foederalismus der Bundesrepublik Deutschland* (Stuttgart, Kohlhammer, 1974).
Rausch, M. *Bundestag und Bundesregierung* (Munich, Beck Verlag, 1976).
Schaefer, F. *Der Bundestag*, 2nd edn, (Opladen, Westdeutscher Verlag, 1975).
Thaysen, U. *Parlamentsreform in Theorie und Praxis* (Opladen, Westdeutscher Verlag, 1972).
Thaysen, U. *Parlamentarisches Regierungssystem in der Bundesrepublik Deutschland* (Opladen, UTB, 1976).

# 6
# Ireland

## B. CHUBB

I

Many of the political institutions of the Republic of Ireland resemble in their general form and working those of the United
Kingdom from which they were copied. The successful transplant
of British forms and practices was due largely to the fact that
Ireland as an integral part of the United Kingdom had experienced
the same social and educational development as Great Britain in
the half-century up to the First World War, and had absorbed
willynilly much of the culture of her larger imperial neighbour.
Although Ireland was part of the least well-developed western
periphery of the British Isles, it was at independence a compara-
tively advanced country whose people had educational standards
comparable to those of Britain; with a GNP per head lower
certainly, but not all that much lower, than Britain's; with a
developed administration; with a political culture markedly influenced by British ideas and practice; with some experience of
democratic politics; and with leaders who, while they had little
direct experience of participation in British politics, accepted
British liberal-democratic standards and practices and were un-
acquainted with any other political system. Because the split of
Sinn Féin (the independence movement) over the terms of the
treaty with the United Kingdom precipitated a civil war in 1922
and created a major political division, the party system, though
never two party, was markedly bi-polar as was the British, and
parties from the beginning adopted strictly competitive as opposed
to coalition strategies.

The result of this combination of circumstances was that
Ireland developed and has retained a cabinet government and
cabinet–parliament relationships similar to those in the United
Kingdom. One-party governments have held office for forty-
four out of the fifty-five years from 1922 to 1977 and there has

always been a 'government' and opposing it an 'opposition' that was recognisable, though sometimes rather dimly, as an alternative government. Although 'government' and 'opposition' did not alternate in fact with any great frequency because of the dominance of one particular party, at least the possibility was always there and was occasionally realised (see Table 6.1).

In this situation, voters have always seen general elections as occasions on which they chose governments and elections have been the decisive party battle-sites. To win is for the victorious leaders to acquire the right to a virtual monopoly of initiating legislative proposals in the Oireachtas (parliament) and to govern its timetable and its legislative output, besides managing the central government and controlling the administration of services. The Oireachtas, like the British Parliament, appraises, amends and approves the government's proposals and monitors its performance in a rather inefficient and ineffective way: its positive contribution to the content of legislation is small.

Although at independence there was a considerable combination of circumstances that led to Irish political parties resembling the British in many ways, allowances being made for differences of scale, their origins lay in Irish affairs, and their social bases were, and are, very different. Given the considerable ethnic, demographic, social structural and religious differences between the two countries, important differences were to be expected.

The British mass parties which developed from the 1860s onwards, being the product of British social structure and divisions, were never relevant to Ireland or Irish conditions and acquired no real basis of mass support in the country, except in the case of the Ulster Unionists. While Great Britain rapidly became an industrialised, urbanised and class-polarised society, Ireland remained largely rural and agricultural and, with land reform from the end of the century, became increasingly dominated by small-holders, owning and working tiny family farms. In the countryside, and particularly in the west, the remnants of a peasant, pre-industrial culture lingered on to an extent that depended on distance from Dublin and from town influences generally.

As a consequence, the party system that developed in the Irish Free State had little continuity with the British system or, because of the debacle of the Irish Parliamentary Party at the 1918 general election, with Irish party life before independence. Only the Labour Party, founded in 1912, continued to exist; and even it had been much changed by the events of 1916 and after. Moreover, since Great Britain so effectively screened Ireland from Continental Europe and because Ireland was, and is, a Catholic

Table 6.1  *Irish Governments, September 1922–June 1977*

| Date of appointment | Government[1] | Nature of Government and Duration | | |
| --- | --- | --- | --- | --- |
| | | One party with majority of own supporters | One party without majority of own supporters | Coalitions |
| September 1922 | Pro-Treaty[1] | 1 year 0 months[2] | | |
| September 1923 | Cumann na nGaedheal | 3 years 9 months[2] | | |
| June 1927 | Cumann na nGaedheal | | 4 months | |
| October 1927 | Cumann na nGaedheal | | 4 years 5 months[3] | |
| March 1932 | Fianna Fáil | | 11 months | |
| February 1933 | Fianna Fáil | 4 years 5 months | | |
| July 1937 | Fianna Fáil | 5 years 0 months | | |
| June 1938 | Fianna Fáil | | 11 months | |
| July 1943 | Fianna Fáil | | 11 months | |
| June 1944 | Fianna Fáil | 3 years 8 months | | |
| February 1948 | Inter-party[4] | | | 3 years 4 months |
| June 1951 | Fianna Fáil | | 3 years 0 months | |
| June 1954 | Inter-party[5] | | | 2 years 10 months |
| March 1957 | Fianna Fáil | 4 years 7 months | | |
| October 1961 | Fianna Fáil | | 3 years 6 months | |
| April 1965 | Fianna Fáil[6] | 4 years 3 months | | |
| July 1969 | Fianna Fáil | 3 years 8 months | | |
| March 1973 | National Coalition[7] | | | 4 years 3 months |
| June 1977– | Fianna Fáil | | | |
| | | 30 years 4 months | 14 years 0 months | 10 years 5 months |

*Notes:*

[1] From Spring 1923 called Cumann na nGaedheal.

[2] Government majority due to the fact that Fianna Fáil, the biggest opposition party, did not take their seats.

[3] The government had the support of the Farmers' Party which, however, ceased to operate as a party and its members for all intents and purposes became members of Cumann na nGaedheal.

[4] A coalition of all parties except Fianna Fáil. It also included Independents.

[5] A coalition of Fine Gael, the Labour Party and Clann na Talmhan.

[6] Fianna Fáil won exactly half the seats.

[7] A coalition of Fine Gael and the Labour Party.

country whose Catholicism is of a rather home-grown, conservative kind, Marxist or other Continental influences were few and made no impact. A study of Irish parties need, therefore, look no further back than independence or much beyond the borders of Ireland itself.

II

Throughout the history of the state, party politics have been dominated by the same three parties – Cumann na nGaedheal (which became Fine Gael in 1933), Fianna Fáil and the Labour Party. Other parties have held seats in the Dáil (House of Commons), and two such persisted to contest and win seats for over a decade.

Up to the mid-fifties Independents regularly won from 5 to 10 per cent of the seats. However, after a decade or so from the Second World War when small groups and individuals flourished, the dominance of the three major parties has increased in the last quarter of a century and has been overwhelming since 1965 (see Table 6.2 and Appendix).

Once the two major parties, Cumannn na nGaedheal (Fine Gael) and Fianna Fáil, had emerged to reflect the major division in Irish life and politics, they took and have held their places as permanent rivals in the electoral and parliamentary arenas with

Table 6.2    *Combined Strength of Major Parties, 1932–1977*

| Election | Fianna Fáil, Fine Gael and Labour | | Fianna Fáil and Fine Gael | |
|---|---|---|---|---|
| | First prefs (%) | Seats (%) | First prefs (%) | Seats (%) |
| 1932 | 88 | 89 | 80 | 84 |
| 1933 | 86 | 87 | 80 | 82 |
| 1937 | 90 | 94 | 80 | 85 |
| 1938 | 95 | 95 | 85 | 88 |
| 1943 | 81 | 84 | 65 | 72 |
| 1944 | 78 | 83 | 70 | 77 |
| 1948 | 70 | 77 | 62 | 67 |
| 1951 | 84 | 85 | 72 | 74 |
| 1954 | 88 | 91 | 75 | 78 |
| 1957 | 84 | 88 | 75 | 80 |
| 1961 | 88 | 92 | 76 | 81 |
| 1965 | 97 | 98 | 82 | 83 |
| 1969 | 97 | 99 | 80 | 87 |
| 1973 | 95 | 99 | 81 | 85 |
| 1977 | 93 | 97 | 81 | 86 |

a combined share of the vote that was, except for a period in the forties, always more than three-quarters. Each, then, has been able to recruit its increment or something like it of the new voters with consistent regularity. Only during the forties did Fine Gael sag for a while.

The Labour Party never quite fitted into the dominant pattern of Irish politics. Established by trade union leaders and intended to be the same sort of alliance of socialism and trade unionism as had been established in Great Britain, it found itself cut off by partition from its greatest single source of strength, the industrial north-east. Operating in a predominantly rural country of small-holders in which a trade union-based party was largely irrelevant, it at first stood aside to allow Sinn Féin a clear run at the 1918 general election and, when that movement split, it argued – wrongly – that the national issue was not the most important one for Irish people. Nevertheless, it had established itself by the early twenties in the rural areas of the east and south, based on the support of agricultural labourers' organisations. Until 1927, when Fianna Fáil chose to enter the Dáil, it was the major opposition party and played its part in the establishment of constitutional and parliamentary politics. Thereafter it became and remained a third party.

This domination of the political scene by the parties that were present or which emerged at the foundation of the state means that Ireland conforms to the pattern identified as typical of Western countries by Lipset and Rokkan (1967, p. 52):

'The most important of the party alternatives got set for each national citizenry during the phases of mobilisation just before or just after the final extension of the suffrage and have remained roughly the same through subsequent changes in the structural conditions of partisan choice.'

As Garvin has pointed out, it looks as though the considerable stability of the Irish system stems from the coincidence in time of 'the last phase of political mobilisation in Irish society between 1923 and 1932' and the emergence of the state from a civil war that produced at that very moment a deep division so that 'the national question dominated domestic politics' (Garvin, 1974, p. 310).

III

The party configuration described above places Ireland in Sartori's category of *moderate pluralism,* a political form in which 'competition remains centripetal', which is 'conducive to moderate politics and which in its operation is essentially bi-polar'.[1] We may go further with Sartori. For thirty-five out of the last forty-five years from 1932, when Fianna Fáil was for the first time fast approaching its full potential, Ireland could best be described as having a *predominant party system*. This is defined by Sartori as

'a type of party pluralism in which – even though no alternation in office actually occurs – alternation is not ruled out and the political system provides ample opportunities for open and effective dissent, that is, for opposing the predominance of the governing party.'[2]

Such alternation did in fact occur, first, in the decade 1948–57 after an unbroken spell of sixteen years of Fianna Fáil govern-ments; and, secondly, after another sixteen years of Fianna Fáil, 1973–7. It was brought about by the coalition of the other two major parties (boosted in 1948 by the addition of minor parties and independent deputies). This alternative – Fine Gael plus Labour – has so far been the only possibility, given the electoral strengths of the parties and, arising therefrom, Fianna Fáil's refusal to contemplate coalition.

With the three permanently established parties able to retain their positions for more than forty years, each in a different league in respect of the size of its support, Ireland has been locked into a rigid framework that has brought great stability; some would say stagnation.[3] Above all, the fact that Fianna Fáil has always been able to hope for, and often obtain, an overall majority of seats in the Dáil has been the salient feature of Irish electoral history and thus of party politics.

Table 6.3  *Strength of the Major Parties, 1932–77*

| | First-preference votes (%) | | Seats (%) | |
| --- | --- | --- | --- | --- |
| | min. | max. | min. | max. |
| Fianna Fáil | 42 | 52 | 44 | 57 |
| Fine Gael | 20 | 35 | 21 | 38 |
| Labour | 8 | 17 | 5 | 15 |

A party placed as Fianna Fáil has been, particularly one that has seen itself, because of its origins, as more of a national movement than a party, is, in Maurice Duverger's term, a *parti a vocation majoritaire*, that is a party that has a parliamentary majority or which thinks and acts as if it is likely to be able to command a majority (Duverger, 1951, p. 315). It will not contemplate coalition and when it takes office without a majority of its own supporters will chafe, as de Valera did in 1932–3, 1937–8 and 1943–4 while he waited for an opportunity to dissolve parliament and mend his hand. If it has in addition a messianic leader as Fianna Fáil had in the person of de Valera from its inception right up to 1959, coalition is even less thinkable. Such a stance, as Table 6.4 shows, was in any case rational.

Table 6.4　*Percentage of First-Preference Votes and Seats won by Fianna Fáil at General Elections, 1932–1977*

| Election | FPs (%) | Seats won (%) | Into Office/ Opposition |
|---|---|---|---|
| 1932 | 44·5 | 47·1 | Office |
| 1933 | 49·7 | 50·3 | Office |
| 1937 | 45·2 | 50·0 | Office |
| 1938 | 51·9 | 55·8 | Office |
| 1943 | 41·9 | 48·6 | Office |
| 1944 | 48·9 | 55·1 | Office |
| 1948 | 41·9 | 46·3 | Opposition |
| 1951 | 46·3 | 46·9 | Office |
| 1954 | 43·4 | 44·2 | Opposition |
| 1957 | 48·3 | 53·1 | Office |
| 1961 | 43·8 | 48·9 | Office |
| 1965 | 47·8 | 50·0 | Office |
| 1969 | 45·7 | 52·0 | Office |
| 1973 | 46·2 | 47·9 | Opposition |
| 1977 | 50·6 | 56·8 | Office |

What Table 6.4 also shows is the knife-edge situation in which the party often found itself. The additional support sometimes needed to win or retain power was forthcoming from independent deputies, who were often in effect camp-followers. It is no wonder that the party attempted to alter the electoral system to the 'first-past-the-post' system, once in 1959 and again in 1968, both times without success.

If it was natural for Fianna Fáil to be strictly competitive, coalition might seem to have been appropriate for the other two parties. Given the pattern of electoral support, such a strategy would lead to a one-party versus two-party type of bipolarism and, if persisted in over a long period, eventually perhaps to permanent alliance – not merely coalition but coalescence (Sartori, 1976, pp. 187–8). For Fine Gael and Labour to pursue strictly competitive strategies was to allow Fianna Fáil to retain power and to keep the centre of the party stage. Coalitions were formed and held office 1948–51, 1954–7 and in 1973–7, but in the sixteen years 1932–48 and a further sixteen 1957–73, considerations other than of maximising electoral chances and winning at least a share of power prevailed in Fine Gael and Labour. In contrast to the natural-ruling-party stance that characterised Fianna Fáil, their demeanour was ambivalent for long periods from 1932 onwards. On the one hand, they behaved in the Dáil as responsible oppositions, and both there and before the pulic they presented themselves as alternative governments; on the other, they failed to pursue the only strategy that could possibly bring them to power.

That they were unwilling to contemplate coalition during the first sixteen-year period of Fianna Fáil domination was perhaps inevitable, for both were ideological parties. Fine Gael embodied one side of the major political divide: it had its origins in the pro-treaty position and constitutionality: it stood for the legitimacy of the state and the constitution against the anti-treaty Fianna Fáil which was, in the words of one of its leaders, Seán Lemass, only a 'slightly constitutional' party. As an outgoing government party it, too, thought of itself as a party *à vocation majoritaire*. For its part, Labour was a working-class party set up to be the antithesis of the parties of the bourgeois Right. Although it was on European standards the palest of pinks, coalition with the middle-class Fine Gael was for long unthinkable. In fact, the apparently more radical Fianna Fáil was more palatable, but, after a brief flirtation in 1932, such a coalition was not an offer and, in any case, Fianna Fáil in power showed itself to be increasingly conservative and as unattractive to Labour as Fine Gael was.

The coalitions of 1948 and 1954 whose *raison d'être* was simply and solely to provide an alternative to Fianna Fáil, heralded the end of an era and to some extent the end of ideology. Yet, after a decade, both parties returned to competitive politics with audible sighs of relief. Fine Gael's fortunes had changed for the better and it resumed its *vocation majoritaire*, though such a stance was as yet scarcely credible. The Labour Party, on the other hand, had lost seats during this decade and its more left-wing elements ascribed this to coalition leading to the party losing its credibility as the proletarian alternative.

It was another sixteen years before they came together again. By this time each of them – as also Fianna Fáil – had experienced considerable strains as they painfully sought to adjust to rapid industrialisation and modernisation, and to the consequent replacement of constitutional by economic issues in an era of welfare and consumer politics. To a great extent they were all drained of ideology; they overlapped considerably in the policies they proposed; and they competed for the votes of a public that was increasingly 'single-peaked' in its attitudes. A temporary move to the left by Labour at the 1969 election, when it put forward a programme for a 'New Republic', was soon corrected by a fresh generation of office-hungry young deputies as it became obvious that the seventies were not going to be socialist, least of all in Ireland. Coalition was clearly on the cards. Since one thing had *not* changed, namely, the critical size of Fianna Fáil support, that party saw no need to alter its attitude to coalition. Thus, coalition could only be once again between Fine Gail and Labour, and once again it succeeded in 1973. If this had been a winning combination over two or more elections, a new era in Irish politics might have been ushered in in 1973. However it was not; in June 1977, Fianna Fáil swept back to power with the biggest majority it had ever had and the dominant pattern of Irish politics repeated itself yet again.

It is only in recent years that systematic studies have been made of the social bases of party support and of the social structure of Irish politics. There are no explorations of the sources of party support based on poll data before 1969 and few since then. Whyte's analysis of the 1969 data is the most important study in this area so far (Whyte, 1974). For the earlier period, resort has been had to ecological analysis (Rumpf, 1959, 1977; Pyne, 1968; Gallagher, 1976; Garvin, 1977). The two major facts to emerge are, first, as Whyte concluded, 'Irish electoral behaviour is exceptionally unstructured', i.e. it is not possible to explain partisanship satisfactorily by social characteristics or influences such as occupation, class, religion, or region, (1974, p. 645); and, secondly, that this was not always so.

Fianna Fáil is truly a national party in that it draws its support from all classes, from both town and country, and from all over the country. It has more of most categories among its adherents than either of the other parties and notably far more of the urban working class (and of trade unionists) than the Labour Party. Until recently it was only among the large farmers that it was markedly less popular than Fine Gael (Manning, 1972, p. 114, Table 1; Irish Marketing Surveys, 1976, p. 15), but the most recent survey, made during the 1977 election campaign, suggests that even this is no longer so (see Table 6.5).

Fianna Fáil's long domination of Irish politics arises from its success in effecting a transformation from being a radical party, with what Garvin (1977, p. 176) described as a 'populist, autarkic and anti-urban programme' to a 'catch-all' party as described by Kirchheimer (1966, p. 186):

'If the party cannot hope to catch all categories of voters, it may have a reasonable expectation of catching more voters in all those categories whose interests do not adamantly conflict . . . Even more important is the heavy concentration on issues which are scarcely liable to meet resistance in the community. National societal goals transcending group interests offer the best sales prospect for a party intent on establishing or enlarging an appeal previously limited to specific sections of the population.'

Support in its early days came mainly from among the small farmers – at the 1933 general election 60 per cent of the voters of the western counties (overwhelmingly small farm country) voted

Table 6.5    *Social Bases of Party Support, 1977*

|  | Fianna Fáil | Fine Gael | Labour | Coalition[1] | Other | Don't Know[2] |
|---|---|---|---|---|---|---|
| *All* | 47 | 21 | 11 | 8 | 4 | 11 |
| *Occupational category*[3] |  |  |  |  |  |  |
| AB | 40 | 28 | 4 | 5 | 8 | 17 |
| C1 | 40 | 27 | 8 | 7 | 5 | 15 |
| C2 | 51 | 14 | 14 | 9 | 5 | 9 |
| DE | 52 | 12 | 20 | 5 | 3 | 10 |
| F1 | 40 | 32 | 2 | 11 | 4 | 14 |
| F2 | 48 | 31 | 1 | 11 | 2 | 7 |
| *Area type* |  |  |  |  |  |  |
| Cities | 42 | 18 | 16 | 6 | 6 | 14 |
| Towns | 44 | 19 | 15 | 10 | 2 | 9 |
| Rural | 51 | 24 | 6 | 8 | 3 | 10 |
| *Region* |  |  |  |  |  |  |
| Dublin | 38 | 18 | 17 | 6 | 6 | 15 |
| Rest of Leinster | 47 | 23 | 9 | 10 | 4 | 9 |
| Munster | 56 | 16 | 12 | 5 | 2 | 11 |
| Connacht and Ulster | 45 | 31 | 2 | 11 | 3 | 8 |

*Notes:*

[1] Respondents who indicated support for the national coalition without specifying which party.

[2] Includes respondents whose replies were categorised as 'would not vote', 'undecided' and 'don't know' as well as those who refused to answer.

[3] Categories are as follows: AB – upper-middle class and middle class; C1 – lower-middle class; C2 – skilled working class; DE – semi- and unskilled working classes and other low-income households; F1 – farmers or farm managers of holdings of 50 acres or more; F2 – farmers with holdings less than 50 acres and farm workers.

*Source:* Irish Marketing Surveys Ltd, Omnibus Report, *Political Opinion*, June 1977.

Fianna Fáil – from former countrymen turned urban workers, and from some of the middle class who had risen from small farmer backgrounds. Its moderation and growing conservatism in office, once constitutional matters were settled to de Valera's satisfaction, and its pro-business policies, brought it support from other sections of the community, particularly in the midlands and east and particularly an increasing number of the commercial and industrial middle class.

Conversely, as Gallagher has shown, after a few years in office, it lost some support in its former strongholds, the most agricultural constituencies, i.e. those with the highest proportion of people in employment in agriculture (Gallagher, 1976). Eventually it settled down with its present pattern of support, again somewhat stronger in the most agricultural constituencies than in the least; but in most areas, as in most categories of voters, stronger than the other parties. (See Table 6.6 and also Table 6.5 above). Inevitably, it had its difficulties reconciling its rural and nationalistic origins and its core supporters with its wider national and more modern image. These came to a head over policy towards Northern Ireland and culminated in 1970 in the 'arms scandal' crisis and the dismissal of two ministers and resignation of two others. It survived them with no loss of electoral support. Always better-organised and more professional than its opponents, it was well placed to reap the harvest of discontent with the national coalition government, as the results of the 1977 election showed.

As the party of the Treaty and Commonwealth status, Fine Gael (originally called Cumann na nGaedheal) at first attracted more of the business community, shopkeepers and professional people than Fianna Fáil, together with the middle-sized and large farmers, especially those who, though supporting independence, had had their economic ambitions satisfied by land redistribution. Conversely, it attracted fewer of the small farmers and the urban

Table 6.6    *Pattern of Fianna Fáil Support, 1938–73*

| Voters in | 1938 | 1943 | 1965 | 1969 | 1973 |
|---|---|---|---|---|---|
| Most agricultural constituencies | 60% | 42% | 48% | 52% | 53% |
| Intermediate constituencies | 50% | 41% | 48% | 45% | 46% |
| Least agricultural constituencies | 49% | 43% | 48% | 43% | 43% |
| All constituencies | 52% | 42% | 48% | 46% | 46% |

Note:
Percentages rounded to nearest whole numbers.
Source: Michael Gallagher, *Electoral Support for Irish Political Parties, 1927–1973* (London and Beverly Hills, Sage, 1976), Table 2 (p. 24) and Table 3 (p. 28).

working class. As Fianna Fáil advanced to the status of a dominant party, Fine Gael declined and, with little positive to offer, reached its nadir in the forties. Its willingness to grasp the opportunity offered in 1948 to combine with other parties to oust Fianna Fáil and to lead a coalition government marked a turning point and it slowly increased its support to reach its strongest position ever in 1973. However, it suffered a reverse in 1977 and its hopes of realising its *vocation majoritaire* have once again receded.

Although it too is a national party in the sense that it has significant support in every part of the country, Fine Gael always was, and still is, somewhat more class-based in its support than Fianna Fáil. It is stronger among the farmers, from whom it derived about two-fifths of its support in 1977, and among the middle class (one third of its support in 1977) than it is among working-class groups (Irish Marketing Surveys, 1977, and see also Table 6.5 above). An effort by some of its younger leaders to widen their party's appeal with a social democratic 'Just Society' programme in the mid-sixties was resisted by their conservative colleagues who undoubtedly reflected the attitudes of their solid urban and rural middle-class supporters. However, differences between Fianna Fáil and Fine Gael should not be exaggerated, as Whyte's correlations of party support and a number of class-related variables such as home ownership, trade union membership, subjective social class, etc., showed (1974, pp. 632*ff*.). The parties differ most perhaps where they always did, in the attitudes of their supporters to some basic nationalist issues. Gallagher noted that the proportion of Irish speakers in constituencies has always been the most significant predictor of Fianna Fáil support, and sometimes negatively of Fine Gael's (1976, p. 25 and Table 1). Similarly, Whyte showed that in all classes Fianna Fáil supporters were more likely to support the idea of an Irish-speaking Ireland than Fine Gael's (1974, p. 642). He concluded that Fianna Fáil supporters 'are more nationalistic in outlook than Fine Gael ones', though he warned that 'this conclusion cannot be pressed too far'. Clearly, though, the fact that these two parties cannot satisfactorily be assigned markedly distinctive social bases does not mean that differences are not present.

More obvious differences in patterns of support lie between the Labour Party and the other two. Labour is a working-class party but not *the* party of the working class: Fianna Fáil attracts far more urban-worker support. Because of its ability to attract and hold the votes of rural labourers in the twenties, when it failed to establish itself among the urban workers, Labour became stronger outside Dublin than within, its main strength lying in the south and east. Gallagher's analysis confirms 'the widely held

Table 6.7    *Pattern of Labour Party Support, 1961–73*

| Voters in | 1961 % | 1965 % | 1969 % | 1973 % |
|---|---|---|---|---|
| Dublin city | 8 | 20 | 31 | 24 |
| Other constituencies | 12 | 15 | 14 | 12 |
| All constituencies | 12 | 15 | 17 | 14 |

*Source:*  Gallagher, op. cit., p. 45.

view that the backbone of Labour's support over the years has been agricultural labourers' (1974, p. 42). After 1961, however, its position in Dublin improved markedly (see Table 6.7). By 1969, it had overtaken Fine Gael in the city, though it fell back somewhat at the 1973 and 1977 elections. With this pattern of support, the endemic difficulties of any labour party, namely, how to satisfy both its moderate and its leftist supporters, are exacerbated because its rural adherents are very moderate indeed. Nevertheless, with four-fifths of its supporters among the working class, over half of them from the semi-skilled and unskilled (DE) categories, Labour is essentially a class-based party (Irish Marketing Surveys, 1977).

Certainly the Irish public see a distinct difference between the Labour Party and the other two, despite the fact that its mainstream leaders and the less conservative of the leaders of Fianna Fáil and Fine Gael differ little in their attitudes to social and economic problems. An inquiry by Irish Marketing Surveys Ltd in 1976 into the concept of Left and Right in politics found that Fianna Fáil and Fine Gael were 'perceived to be positioned remarkably close to one another', with the bulk of electors placing them in the centre or slightly to the right of centre. However, 'the distribution of replies was very wide which suggests that many voters . . . find it difficult to apply this dimension to Fianna Fáil and Fine Gael'. The Labour Party was 'generally ascribed a left-wing stance' (1976, p. 6). It should be noticed, however, that nearly one-third of respondents opted out of answering the question, presumably finding the concept either difficult to comprehend or to apply. Young people, too, it seems, have the same picture. Studying the attitudes of Irish secondary school students to politics, Borock and Pfretzschner found that many of them 'failed to make sharp or clear distinctions amongst parties, but that in so far as such distinctions are drawn, Labour is more precisely identified than the other two parties'. Overwhelmingly, students believed that labourers and the unemployed would favour the Labour Party (1976, pp. 7 and 10–12).

Unstructured by European standards as Irish voting behaviour is today, originally, i.e. at the beginning of the state's history, there seems to have been a much more marked structural pattern as Rumpf (1959, 1977), Pyne (1968), Gallagher (1976) and Garvin (1977) have demonstrated. To a very limited extent the pattern is still discernible, though now overlaid by changes from the late thirties onwards. It is possible, as Whyte concluded, that 'the extension of support for Fianna Fáil in the 1930s and the erosion of support for Fine Gael at the same period blurred class lines that had originally been more visible' (1974, p. 646). Perhaps the persistence of the remnants of a pre-industrial culture in the countryside and the continued movement of rural people into Dublin, bringing their political culture with them, has retarded the development of patterns such as are seen in other Western European countries: Ireland had and still has the highest proportion of farmers and rural inhabitants of all EEC countries.

Figure 6.1    *Right, Left and Centre in Irish Politics, 1976*

(*Question asked:* As you know, politicians and political parties are often referred to as tending to be *right* or *left* in their policies, and to talk about right of *centre* and left of *centre*. Using this card I would like you to rate each of the three main political parties [etc]. . . )

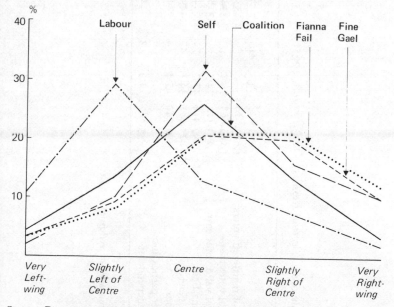

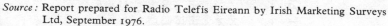

*Source:* Report prepared for Radio Telefís Eireann by Irish Marketing Surveys Ltd, September 1976.

Table 6.8  *Election Results: Dáil Éireann, 1965–77*

| | 1965 | % | seats | 1969 | % | seats | 1973 | % | seats | 1977 | % | seats |
|---|---|---|---|---|---|---|---|---|---|---|---|---|
| No. of registered voters | 1,683,019 | | | 1,735,388 | | | 1,783,604 | | | 2,118,606[1] | | |
| No. of votes cast | 1,264,666 | 75·1 | | 1,334,963 | 76·9 | | 1,366,474 | 76·6 | | 1,616,770 | 76·3 | |
| No. of valid votes cast | 1,253,122 | 74·5 | | 1,318,953 | 76·0 | | 1,350,537 | 75·7 | | 1,603,027 | 75·7 | |
| Fianna Fáil | 597,414 | 47·7 | 72 | 602,234 | 45·7 | 75 | 624,538 | 46·2 | 69 | 811,615 | 50·6 | 84 |
| Fine Gael | 427,081 | 34·1 | 47 | 449,749 | 34·1 | 50 | 473,781 | 35·1 | 54 | 488,767 | 30·5 | 43 |
| Labour | 192,740 | 15·4 | 22 | 224,498 | 17·0 | 18 | 184,656 | 13·7 | 19 | 186,410 | 11·6 | 17 |
| Other parties and Independents | 35,887 | 2·9 | 3 | 42,472 | 3·2 | 1 | 67,572 | 5·0 | 2 | 116,235 | 7·2 | 4 |

*Note:*
[1] Voting age lowered from 21 to 18.

Certainly, recent research has demonstrated the effects of rural cultural values on the working of the political system and in particular on the role of party 'actives' in the constituencies (Chubb, 1963; Garvin, 1974; Bax, 1976; Sacks, 1976). Garvin had argued, indeed, that Irish politics should be seen as a case of a 'periphery-dominated centre' (1974).

The emergence of parties with more distinctive social bases might not be too far away. The rural culture which has so much influenced politics with the consequential persistence of elements of personalism and clientèlism and which is inherently very conservative is being inexorably eroded by the increasing pressures of industrialisation and urbanisation. Already the strains of accommodating to these pressures have been visible in all three parties. Each of them experienced pressure for change and underwent crises in recent years. Each of these crises — Fianna Fáil's Northern Ireland arms scandal, Fine Gael's abortive 'Just Society' movement and Labour's short-lived lurch to the left with its 'New Republic' programme — was in its way a crisis of modernization: and none of them was unequivocally resolved in the first round. There are signs that all three of the parties might be approaching the bell for round two.

## NOTES

1 Sartori, 1976, pp. 178–9.
2 ibid., p. 200.
3 See Table 6.3.

## REFERENCES AND FURTHER READING

Bax, M. (1976) *Harpstrings and Confessions* (Van Garcum, Assen).

Borock, D. M., and Pfretzschner, P. A. (1976) 'Irish students and the political parties', paper delivered at South-Western Political Science Association meeting in Dallas, Texas, April.

Carty, R. K. (1976) 'Social cleavages and party systems: a reconsideration of the Irish case', *European Journal of Political Research,* vol. 4, pp. 195–203.

Chubb, B. (1963) ' "Going about persecuting civil servants": the role of the Irish parliamentary representative', *Political Studies,* vol. xi, pp. 272–86.

Duverger, M. (1951) *Les Partis Politiques* (Paris, Armand Colin).

Gallagher, M. (1976) *Electoral Support for Irish Political Parties 1927–1973* (London and Beverly Hills, Sage).

Garvin, T. (1974) 'Political cleavages, party politics and urbanisation in Ireland: the case of the periphery-dominated centre', *European Journal of Political Research,* vol. 2, pp. 307–26.

Garvin, T. (1977) 'Nationalist elites, Irish voters and Irish political development: a comparative perspective', *Economic and Social Review*, vol. 8, pp. 161–86.

Irish Marketing Surveys Ltd (1976, 1977) *Report* prepared for Radio Telefís Éireann, September (not published); Omnibus Report, *Political Opinion*, June (not published).

Kirchheimer, O. (1966) 'The transformation of the Western European party systems', in J. La Palombara and M. Weiner (eds), *Political Parties and Political Development* (Princeton, NJ, Princeton University Press).

Lagoni, R. (1973) *Die Politischen Parteien im Verfassungssystem der Republik Irland* (Frankfurt am Main, Athenäum Verlag).

Lipset, S. M., and Rokkan, S. (eds) (1967) *Party Systems and Voter Alignments* (New York, The Free Press).

Manning, M. (1972) *Irish Political Parties, an Introduction* (Dublin, Gill/Macmillan).

Pyne, P. (1969–70) 'The third Sinn Féin Party: 1923–1926', *Economic and Social Review*, vol. 1, pp. 29–50 and 229–257.

Rumpf, E. (1959, 1977) *Nationalismus and Sozialismus in Irland* (Meisenheim am Glan, Verlag Antontlian K( 2nd edn by E. Rumpf and A. C. Hepburn, *Nationalism and Socialism in Twentieth Century Ireland* (Liverpool, Liverpool University Press).

Sacks, P. (1976) *The Donegal Mafia, an Irish Political Machine* (New Haven and London, Yale University Press).

Sartori, G. (1976) *Parties and Party Systems, a Framework for Analysis*, Vol. 1 (Cambridge, Cambridge University Press).

Schmitt, D. E. (1973) *The Irony of Irish Democracy* (Lexington, Mass., D. C. Heath).

Whyte, J. (1974) 'Ireland: politics without social bases', in R. Rose (ed.), *Comparative Electoral Behavior* (New York, The Free Press).

# 7
# Italy

## P. A. ALLUM

INTRODUCTION

The fundamental feature of the Italian political system since the expulsion of the Communist Party from the tripartite national government by De Gasperi in May 1947 has been the almost total control of state and para-state institutions by the Catholic Christian Democrat Party. Christian Democrat domination in a parliamentary system based on proportional representation has been possible because the party has received the largest share of the vote (between 35 and 42 per cent, except in 1948 when it won 48 per cent) of a stable electorate in all general elections since the war. This domination has been strengthened by the fact that the Communist Party has been the largest opposition party with votes rising from 18 per cent in 1946 to 27 per cent in 1972. Moreover, it was natural that in the Cold War period, the formative period of the postwar party system, the Christian Democrats, with American support, should regard the Communist Party as a totalitarian Trojan horse (because of the latter's ties with the Soviet Union and the fact that its own appeal was largely anti-communism) and hence shun it as a prospective coalition partner.

The political system organised on the basis of this anti-communism can best be defined as an 'imperfect one-party regime' in contrast to Giorgio Galli's well-known definition of it as an 'imperfect two-party system'.[1] In any event, the Christian Democrat domination of the political system has been theorised by Catholic party leaders from De Gasperi to Andreotti in this way:[2] Italy is a special type of democracy which cannot afford the luxury of alternating governments because the arrival of the opposition led by the Communist Party in power would, by definition, destroy it. Hence, the Christian Democrat Party has no option but to remain in power, with the Communist Party confined to permanent opposition. In fact, Aldo Moro, former prime minister, and one of the left-wing leaders of the Catholic Party, went even further in an interview in August 1972.[3] Not only did he claim that the Christian Democrats' permanence in office was the primary characteristic of Italian democracy (and he regretted that sincere Italian democrats did not understand such an obvious fact) but added that the function of the Communist Party in the Italian political system was to help the Christian Democrats by accepting this opposition role.

The Cold War enabled the Christian Democrats and their centrist allies, Social Democrats, Republicans and Liberals, to mobilise the support of all sections of society, except the hard core of the working class organised by the Communist Party and its trade union confederation, the CGIL, on the basis of market individualism and consumerism. Thus forged into a solid power bloc, the middle classes were strong enough to offset the electoral power of organised labour. The government dispensed subsidies and payoffs to tie large numbers of people to the state institutions by means of the government party machine. Jobs, houses, schools, hospitals, everything, were often dependent on the patronage of local Christian Democrats. For its success, this strategy required almost continued economic expansion to satisfy an ever-increasing number of clients.

The result of the Christian Democrats' immovability from office for more than thirty years has been political immobility which has led to the progressive degradation of the political system. The coalitions of the Christian Democrats and some minor lay parties, sometimes called 'centrist', 'centre-right', 'centre-left' or even 'converging parallels', has led to the politics of Tweedledum and Tweedledee. A hundred years ago the Risorgimento poet Giosue Carducci described the politics of the Depretis era in verses of striking topicality: 'And thus from year to year/And from Ministry to Ministry I/ shift from Centre-Right to Centre-Left And/Live from hand to mouth.' More recently, the chairman of Fiat, Gianni Agnelli, was more prosaic, but more illuminating, in his description of the basis of Christian Democrat power: 'With 40 per cent of the votes, the DC controls 80 per cent of the power.'

Safe in the knowledge of their political supremacy, the Christian Democrats have been afraid for much of the postwar period to promote dynamic policies for fear of dividing and alienating their own support. The marginalisation of their only serious rivals, the Communist Party, has meant an absolute domination of Italian life and so they have administered rather than governed the country from one cabinet crisis to another in the manner of the French Third and Fourth Republics. The consequences of this type of government were a spontaneous and uncontrolled economic development which culminated in the economic miracle of the early sixties. Inability to master economic development meant that once the favourable factors were exhausted, Italy has fallen back into a prolonged economic crisis. The irony of this situation, as far as the Christian Democrats have been concerned, is that their fears have been realised spontaneously. Social and economic forces that they did not attempt to control began to undermine their support and that of their allies. The divorce referendum of 12 May 1974 demonstrated that the Catholic Church is no longer able to mobilise the majority of the Italian people. The regional elections of June 1975, followed by the general elections of June 1976, confirmed that a new electoral realignment had taken place.

The Christian Democrats remained the largest single party in the 1976 elections with 38 per cent of the vote, but the Communist Party shot up to 34 per cent, cutting the difference between the two parties to 4 per cent instead of double figures. Moreover, the Christian Democrats' retention of a relative majority was largely at the expense of the small lay parties (their usual government allies) and the Right. As a result, the Christian Democrat party can no longer govern as it has done for the previous twenty-nine years, without the active assistance of the Communist Party. In 1976, the minority Andreotti government was formed with the Communist Party's abstention on votes of confidence and its support on legislative measures. The further increase in political violence in the winter of 1976–7 led to the opening of negotiations between Christian Democrats, Communists, Socialists, Republicans and Social Democrats to see if agreement could be reached on a government programme with wide parliamentary support. On the consequences would seem to depend the crisis or survival of the present political system in Italy.

PARTY ORGANISATION

All Italian national parties claim to represent an exclusive ideological position and so not surprisingly the full spectrum of modern ideologies is represented in parliament. Communism is represented by Democrazia Proletaria (an alliance of minor Marxist revolutionary parties) and the PCI, which claims to be a Marxist working-class party that believes in the revolutionary transformation of society to socialism by democratic means (the parliamentary road to socialism). Socialism is represented by the

PSI which represents the radical non-Marxist constitutional Left. Social Democracy still elects a number of MPs more on the basis of a conservative rather than truly socialist appeal. Republicanism and Monarchism are still represented by parties of those names despite the fact that the constitutional form of the political system was decided by referendum some thirty years ago. In fact, the PRI has become, with the passing of time, more of a progressive conservative party while the various Monarchist parties have virtually disappeared as autonomous bodies after having been the vehicles for the defence of precise personal interests.

The PLI and MSI use liberalism and fascism as ideologies to defend conservative and reactionary interests: the former among big business and the latter small business and the petty bourgeois. In the early 1970s the MSI had some success in broadening its support with the onset of the economic crisis. Finally, catholicism is represented by Christian Democracy, a party which readily accepts the spiritual guidance of the church and its hierarchy, but none the less claims to be non-confessional and so politically independent of church control. The party combines the two ideological tendencies of the Catholic movement in the last century: liberal Catholicism and social Catholicism. This means that it often exhibits two political minds in its activity. In fact, the party is prey to endemic conflict between ultra-conservatives and the liberal Catholic Right (normally a majority), and a progressive, reforming, and generally minority social Catholic Left. Anti-communism and obedience to spiritual direction form the cement which have bound the two wings together and ensured Catholic dominance of postwar Italian political life.

Organisationally, all the national parties sooner or later copied the Communist Party model of a mass party, even if they lacked mass membership, and gave themselves a branch-like structure. They are organised at three levels: at the local level in the commune, the party section (or the cell in the workplace as well in the case of the Communist Party) was part of the provincial federation, the intermediate unit, which was part, in turn, of the national unit, the national executive or central committee. The executive committees at all levels (i.e. sections, federations and national executive) are elected at periodically held congresses of delegates representing the paid-up members at that level, which debates policy and elects delegates to the congresses at the superior level. The supreme party body is the national congress which elects the national executive or central committee and secretariat which controls the party in the periods between congresses. Congresses also ratify party policy; they are held at irregular intervals, usually every other year, for most parties.

At the same time, all parties promote collateral para-political organisations, such as unions, co-operatives, women's and youth movements, and even professional associations and sports clubs. Thus the three mass parties were initially flanked by the General Confederation of Italian Labour (CGIL) as a result of the Pact of Rome of June 1944 on united union policy. After the union split of July 1948 the Catholics set up the Italian Confederation of Free Trade Unions (CISL) and the Social Democrats and Republicans the Union of Italian Labour (UIL). In the late sixties and early seventies with the movement towards unity, which was achieved for the engineering workers (FLM), the ties between parties and unions became weaker, although they did not disappear altogether. At certain moments the unions demonstrated considerable autonomy from the parties.[4] In 1948, the Neofascists founded the CISNAL.

In the commercial field the Communist Party promoted the League of Co-operatives; and in the agricultural field the Christian Democrats organised the National Federation of Small Farmers *(Coldiretti)*, and the Communist Party first the *Federterra* (for agricultural labourers) and later the Peasants' Alliance. In addition, most parties publish their own daily papers: *L'Unità* (Communist), *L'Avanti!* (Socialist), *Il Popolo* (Christian Democrat), *La Voce Repubblicana* (Republican), *Il Secolo d'Italia* (Neofascist), *Il Manifesto* (Proletarian Communist), etc. Some parties have founded their own publishing houses: *Editori Riuniti* (Communist), *Cinque Lune* (Christian Democrat), *Edizioni dell'Avanti* (Socialist), *Edizioni della Voce* (Republican), etc.; and where possible patronise cultural associations and clubs oriented ideologically in their direction: *Istituti Gramsci* (Communist), *Club Turati* (Socialist) etc. The object of this many-sided activity is to ensure the party a permanent political presence in civil society.

Most party organisations are stronger in the north than in the south and islands. Thus the Communist Party sections and cells are more numerous in the industrial centres of the north and centre than elsewhere. The Socialist Party is best organised in Lombardy, Emilia, Tuscany and Sicily and worst organised in Piedmont, the Venetias and the mainland south. On the other hand, the Christian Democrats have as many sections in the south as in the north and centre, but congress discussion over the years reveals that many of the southern sections exist on paper only. In the south the party still depends to some extent on the parish as much as the formal section organisation for the continued penetration that has ensured the Christian Democrat vote in rural areas in successive elections, although now less successful than it once was. The Neofascist Party is also stronger in the south than in the north, but its formal organisation is fairly weak.

Italian parties are parties of direct membership. Membership is an individual act and there are no arrangements for block affiliations by, say, trade unions. Most parties fix the minimum age at 18 years, although it is 14 in the case of the Neofascists. Moreover, most parties require that members accept, and even profess, their goals and ideals. In addition, the Christian Democrat statute requires that its members have 'an irreproachable moral and political behaviour', while the Communist Party statute contains special provisions for dealing with applicants who have held important posts in other parties, or are seeking readmission to the party after having been expelled.

Membership is high, particularly in comparison with other countries with direct membership parties, such as France and West Germany. Three parties claim to be mass parties with over half a million members: the Communist and Christian Democrat Parties with between $1\frac{1}{2}$ and 2 million members, and the Socialist Party with around 500,000. Figures for the other parties are uncertain, but approximations have been suggested as follows: Social Democrats 200,000, Republicans 100,000, Communist Proletarians (PDVP) and Radicals, 50,000 each, and around half a million for the various right-wing groups (Liberals 100,000, Neofascist and National Right 400,000, etc).[5] Distribution of party membership reflects the location of party sections fairly closely. Thus over a third of Communist Party members are found in the two regions of central Italy (Emilia and Tuscany) and the remainder are unevenly distributed over the country. In general, there are still more members in the north than in the south; northern members are concentrated in the large and medium-sized towns and southern members are dispersed in the countryside and agro-towns. The geographical distribution of the Socialist Party is more uneven than that of the Communist Party: strong and weak federations nestle side by side in different parts of the country. In general, the Socialist Party membership strength in the north and centre is tied to socialist traditions: in the south it is linked to the political positions of national and local leaders, like that of Mancini in Calabria. This contrast has become more marked since the Socialists entered the coalitions in 1964, because while it expanded in the south, it lost support in the north and the Red Belt.

The territorial distribution of the Christian Democrat membership does not follow any expected pattern. Southern membership levels now exceed the so-called 'white Catholic' provinces of the

north-east (Venetias). This Christian Democrat penetration of the
south reverses the immediate postwar situation, and is due to the
important positions that local leaders have been able to build up
thanks to years of continuous office. If all southern regions have
their bosses – Moro in Apulia, Colombo in Basilicata, De Mita
and Gava in Campania – they have laid the foundations for a
system that has become generalised throughout the country as
the examples of Rumor and Bisaglia in the Veneto, Piccoli in
Trento and Andreotti in Latium testify.

In addition, the high annual turnover of southern Christian
Democrat membership confirms the artificial nature of many
southern 'congressional' membership figures. Membership of the
minor lay parties conforms to this overall pattern: either they
have a stronger northern membership like the Republicans and
Liberals, or they have a higher southern membership which is
largely bogus, as is often the case of the Neofascist and former
Monarchist Right.

The social composition of party membership (see Table 7.1)
reflects the different groups to which the parties appeal. About
60 per cent of the members of the Communist Party come from
the working classes. However, if in the early postwar years the
backbone of the party was formed by the industrial working
class it has subsequently become changed to one of working-class

Table 7.1 *Social Composition of Communist and Christian
Democrat Party Members in 1971 (percentages)*

|  |  | PCI | DC |
| --- | --- | --- | --- |
| I | Bourgeoisie[1] | 1·0 | 3·7 |
| II | Middle classes | 21·9 | 40·4 |
| IIa | New middle class | 4·5 | 21·7 |
| IIb | Old middle class | 17·4 | 18·7 |
| III | Working class | 47·5 | 20·9 |
| IIIa | Industrial workers | 39·5 | 17·4 |
| IIIb | Agricultural labourers | 8·0 | 3·5 |
| IV | Inactive population | 29·6 | 35·0 |
| Total |  | 100·0 | 100·0 |
| Total membership |  | 1,521,631 | 1,740,000 |

*Note:*
[1] This is here used in the strict sociological sense.

*Source:* Adapted from M. and P. Pallante (eds), *Dal Centro-Sinistra all'Autunno
Caldo* (Bologna, Zanichelli, 1975), pp. 160–5.

families. This is because many industrial workers have quit, but the family members of those who have remained have joined where they did not previously. Also there has been a large influx in the seventies of young people of all classes. Regional differences are still strong: in the north, the industrial working-class component is strong, while in the centre there are many middle-class groups (small businessmen, artisans and share-croppers) and in the south it is the peasantry who form the bulwark of the party. The various Socialist parties are not basically working-class in composition. Before the reunification between the Socialists and Social Democrats in 1966, only about a third of the Socialist Party members were workers and another third peasants (mainly small farmers). Since 1966 this proportion of workers and peasants has tended to diminish while middle-class members have increased in both Socialist Parties, particularly after the split of 1969, although the extent is difficult to assess because of lack of data. The principal reason for party membership of many socialists appears to be family tradition, of son following father; and the chief motive for going to the party section is recreation, i.e. to play cards or watch television rather than talk politics, although this too is changing.

The Christian Democrat Party is composed of all classes with one-fifth of members coming from the working classes. Another two-fifths come from the middle classes almost equally divided between the old and the new middle classes; and the final two-fifths, significantly, from the non-active population. Membership from the new middle classes has been continuously on the increase in the postwar period, which shows that the Christian Democrats now recruit the professional intelligentsia. Finally, over a third of party members are women, generally housewives, which acccounts for the large proportion of the inactive population (the rest are pensioners and students) among Christian Democrat party membership. This proportion of women is the largest for any Italian party.

The middle and upper classes furnish the majority of members of the other parties: professional and businessmen in the Republican and Liberal Parties, etc. The Neofascist and Monarchist Right recruit most of their members from nostalgic aristocrats, petty bourgeois on the make, and, at certain moments, the urban poor of the big southern cities.

Party personnel *(quadri)* fall into four grades: at the lowest level are found the party activists who are ready to be mobilised for party proselytism and propaganda; at the next level come the party officials who man, generally without pay, the local sections; at the third level are the provincial federation officials, many of whom are permanently employed by the party, and all of whom are prospective recruits to the Italian political class; finally, at the top level are the national party leaders and MPs who control the party. It is difficult to give precise figures for each grade of party personnel. Activists in the Communist and Christian Democrat parties are a veritable army of some 100,000 strong each (i.e. between 5 and 10 per cent of the membership);[6] a figure of 15,000 was advanced for the Socialist Party some years ago. The other parties certainly cannot match the Communists' and Christian Democrats' number of activists. Local officials of the Communist and Christian Democrat parties number about 50,000 each, with a proportionally smaller number for the other parties. The provincial officials provide a hard core of between 1,000 and 2,000 people, dedicated to politics according to party; and finally a figure of between 100 and 500 depending on the size of the party represents the national party leadership and MPs. Top leadership in any party, at any one given moment, rarely exceeds some twenty to thirty carefully selected individuals. Moreover, influence in party leadership is never static: a man who is important in today's conjuncture may well not be tomorrow.

The important point about party personnel is that there is a qualitative jump between the local and provincial level: in all parties the activists and the local officials mirror the party membership in their social composition, but the provincial and national party leaders do not (see Table 7.2), being predominantly middle class in all parties. For example, roughly half the Communist Party local officials are workers and peasants, but only one-eighth of the party's provincial and national leaders belong to the working classes. Similarly, over 90 per cent of the Christian Democrat provincial and national party leaders come from the middle and upper classes and only 2·5 per cent are working class, whereas some 15 per cent of its local officials are

Table 7.2  *Social Composition of Parties' National and Provincial Leaders in 1967 (percentages)*

|     |                | PCI   | PSI   | PRI  | DC    | PLI   | MSI  |
| --- | -------------- | ----- | ----- | ---- | ----- | ----- | ---- |
| I   | Bourgeoisie    | 1·7   | 3·5   | 4·4  | 3·4   | 8·2   | 2·0  |
| II  | Middle classes | 85·8  | 87·8  | 89·7 | 94·2  | 89·0  | 95·2 |
| III | Working class  | 12·5  | 9·7   | 5·7  | 2·5   | 2·8   | 2·8  |
| Numbers |            | 1,057 | 2,195 | 435  | 1,873 | 1,080 | 246  |

*Source*: Adapted from G. Sani, 'Profilo dei dirigenti di partito', *Rassegna Italiana di Sociologia*, vol. XIII, no. 1, January 1972, p. 129.

workers. Thus if the Communist Party is, as has often been claimed,[7] a vehicle of social promotion at the local level because of the wide access to positions of public responsibility that it offers people of humble origins, the avenue it opens is much narrower at the higher echelons and seems to be getting less. None the less, the avenue is still sufficiently wide to provide a model for aspiring party workers and local officials. Indeed, Sani in his study of party leadership notes that all parties' leadership is characterised by a 'high rate of upward social mobility'.[8] In the Christian Democrat party, the road to power is by way of the professions: teachers in the north and lawyers in the south, and all are extensively recruited from Catholic organisations. Over two-thirds of party leaders began their careers in this way a decade ago, but it has certainly declined since. A similar pattern, without the emphasis on Catholic organisations, prevails in the other parties.

### ELECTIONS AND THE ELECTORATE

The list system of PR is in force for both houses, but while the pure form is used for the Lower House, a modified version is in use in the Upper House. For the Chamber the country is divided into thirty-two constituencies which are composed of two or three adjoining provinces. Each party presents a list of candidates (not greater than the number of seats allocated to the constituency on a population basis) separately in each constituency, or it may combine with one or other parties to present a joint list. The number of candidates of each list elected is proportional to the number of votes which it receives in each constituency using the method of distribution of the corrected quotient $N+2$. Fractional remainders are gathered in a national pool and divided on a proportional basis depending on the national vote, no party participating in the distribution of fractional remainders if it has not elected at least one candidate outright in at least one constituency.

The voter also has the opportunity of indicating (either by name or list number) his preference among candidates. The number of preference votes that can be given, usually three or four, varies according to the size of the constituency. In addition, the voter has the right to strike out the names of any candidates on the list to which he is opposed. The candidates elected in each list are those who receive the highest number of preference votes (after subtracting the strikings out) in proportion to the number of seats allocated to that list in the constituency.

For the Senate, each region is divided into a number of single-member constituencies equal to the number of seats allotted to the region on the basis of the population. Each party presents a candidate in all or some of the constituencies. Since seats are assigned on a regional basis (i.e. there are no fractional remainders gathered together in a national pool), joint lists are more frequent than for the Chamber. A candidate who receives more than 65 per cent of the poll is automatically declared elected; the remainder of seats are distributed on a proportional basis within the region. The successful candidates in each list are those for the constituencies in which each party polls its highest proportion of the vote according to the number of seats allocated to it.

Proportional representation is the most stable of all electoral systems, because it accurately relates seats to votes won and lost. This contrasts with the simple-majority, single-ballot system which accentuates mobility in representation because it turns small changes in votes into larger turnovers in seats. Similarly, the former encourages minor party representation which is discouraged by the latter. These simple propositions can be verified by comparing British and Italian electoral results in the period between 1945 and 1970. In British elections, swings of around 2 per cent in the votes for the two major parties provoked changes in seats in the House of Commons of around 8 per cent. In Italy, much larger swings have given smaller changes in seats; in 1968 the swing was 3·1 per cent and less than twenty seats (i.e. 3 per cent) changed party affiliation. Indeed, with the growth of electoral stability in Italy in this period more seats changed party affiliation in the life of a parliament than at a general election. For instance, in the 1963–8 parliament between twenty-five and thirty members of the Chamber of Deputies changed political affiliation. Moreover, the twenty-three socialist MPs who split away from the Socialist Party to form the left-wing Proletarian Socialist Party in 1964 were returned at the 1968 elections. On strictly mathematical PR half of them would have been returned in 1972 but for the rule that a party list must elect at least one candidate in a constituency, which deprived their party of any representation in the Chamber. None the less, the electoral advance of the Communist Party in the regional and general elections of 1975 and 1976, following on the failure of the Catholics to win the divorce referendum of 1974, suggests that a radical realignment of the electorate is taking place in Italy as well, which we shall have to consider below.

For the moment, it is worth noting that, if the electoral system accentuates stability of representation, this process has been powerfully abetted by the remarkable growth in the partisan stability of the electorate in the period between 1946 and 1972.

Vote movement between parties in Chamber of Deputies' elections declined from 21·4 per cent in 1946–8 to 3·1 per cent in 1963–8; and a similar phenomenon occurred in Senate elections. This, as we have hinted, is a general and not a specifically Italian phenomenon. All electorates are basically stable, as the example of most Western European countries testifies, except when a traumatic political event causes a fundamental electoral realignment. The Cold War and the manner of its presentation to the Italian electorate in 1948 – the stark choice between civilisation and barbarism, Christ and Anti-Christ, God and the Devil, Good and Evil, etc. – was such a traumatic political event, and it was responsible for a fundamental alignment which lasted a quarter of a century in Italy. Arguably the divorce referendum following on the post-'hot autumn' social struggles and the manner in which Fanfani presented the choice facing the Italian people was another that has forged a new alignment in which the Communists are placed as leaders of an alternative majority, *in nuce*.

Be this as it may, a number of indices illustrate the nature of the electoral stability which Italy has known for the greater part of the postwar period. First, electoral turn-out is, and has remained, high. In contrast to the pre-fascist period, when turn-out rarely reached 60 per cent of the restricted electorate, it has never dropped below 92 per cent since 1948. Moreover, the same regions have been consistently the highest – the 'red' provinces of Emilia-Romagna and Tuscany. Secondly, the degree of voting stability can be measured by examining the electoral returns at the communal level on a countrywide basis. The Cattaneo Institute of Bologna did this for 7,144 of the 8,000 Italian communes for the elections of 1946 and 1963, and Galli and Prandi commented on the results as follows: 'the figures confirm the general conclusion that Italian party voting is relatively stable. Although there are considerable fluctuations within some communes between elections, the fluctuations within a zone are fairly modest.'[9] Both Communist and Christian Democrat votes were more stable in those regions – 'red' and 'white' – where their vote is backed by an institutionalised subculture; and less stable in those regions – mainland south and islands – which are dominated by the southern clientèle system.

A third index is the fierceness of the fight for the so-called preference vote.[10] This is the vote for individual candidates that the elector can give along with his party preference. This fight and the factional struggle (of which it is a part) increased with the stability of voting by lists. Indeed, one can say that there is a sort of inverse relationship between the intensity of the battle for the list vote and that for the preference vote. The importance of the preference vote lies in its effect on the internal balance of power within a party; it raises or lowers the strength of the various factional leaders within the party machine, and thereby influences the kind of alliances and orientations the party will engage in. One of the paradoxes of Italian voting behaviour is that preference voting increases with illiteracy, i.e. it is greater in the backward south than in the more developed north. Hence, it indicates that the greater part of the northern electorate is uninterested in this aspect of Italian elections. The reason for the higher preference vote in the south is the 'southern clientèle system': the fact that patronage is the fundamental link between the voter-clients and the politician-patron. For example, Aldo Moro and Giulio Andreotti won the highest number of preference votes, 290,000 and 350,000 respectively, the former in 1968 and the latter in 1972, when each was prime minister. In 1972 Moro's personal tally dropped by 100,000 votes: he was only foreign minister. On the other hand, in 1976 the proportion of preference votes, above all of the historical Christian Democrat leaders, dropped dramatically in face of the increased polarisation of the electorate.[11]

Fourthly, the parties' electorates reflect organisational strength. This led Galli and Prandi to conclude in 1970 that the 'Catholic world since 1946 has had a form and structure capable of influencing moderate and conservative as well as Catholic opinion at a time when Italy had no tradition or activating force on which to build an influential secular party to represent moderate and conservative points of view'.[12] More recently, Galli[13] has estimated that Catholics represent about two-thirds of the DC vote while the remaining third, which enables it to remain the leading Italian party, comes from lay conservative opinion and its organisations (i.e. industrialists, managers and others). On the other hand, Galli and Prandi claimed that it was 'a combination of organisation and ideology which enabled the Communist Party rather than the divided and much more poorly organised Socialist Parties to mould left-wing opinion and to translate into votes a variety of tendencies and tensions'.[14]

The socio-demographic composition of the parties' voters is set out in Table 7.3. The Communist Party is strong in the 'red' provinces and weak in the 'white' provinces; its electorate is predominantly lower class, male, under 40 years of age, and non-church-going. Tarrow[15] has argued that it tends to attract workers in the north and peasants in the south, to which must be added the share-croppers and the small businessmen of the 'red' provinces, while Sani[16] has correctly stressed the importance

Table 7.3  *Socio-Demographic Characteristics of Party Voters, 1976*

| | PCI % | PSI % | PSDI % | PRI % | DC % | MSI % | OTHERS % | ITALY % |
|---|---|---|---|---|---|---|---|---|
| **1 Sex** | | | | | | | | |
| Men | 55 | 52 | 43 | 43 | 40 | 58 | 47 | 48 |
| Women | 45 | 48 | 57 | 57 | 60 | 42 | 53 | 52 |
| **2 Age** | | | | | | | | |
| 18/24 | 18 | 14 | 10 | 10 | 11 | 16 | 23 | 15 |
| 25/44 | 41 | 45 | 40 | 36 | 34 | 37 | 43 | 38 |
| 45/64 | 30 | 31 | 29 | 40 | 33 | 26 | 27 | 31 |
| Over 65 | 11 | 11 | 21 | 14 | 22 | 19 | 7 | 16 |
| **3 Class** | | | | | | | | |
| I Bourgeoisie | 1 | 2 | 1 | 3 | 2 | 2 | 1 | 2 |
| II Middle classes | 23 | 26 | 30 | 31 | 25 | 32 | 36 | 26 |
| IIa New middle classes | 11 | 12 | 11 | 16 | 9 | 17 | 20 | 12 |
| IIb Old middle classes | 12 | 14 | 19 | 15 | 16 | 15 | 16 | 14 |
| III Working class | 38 | 27 | 14 | 7 | 13 | 7 | 6 | 22 |
| IV Inactive population | 38 | 45 | 55 | 59 | 60 | 59 | 57 | 60 |
| IVa Housewives | 21 | 28 | 34 | 34 | 32 | 28 | 36 | 28 |
| N | (688) | (194) | (70) | (61) | (774) | (123) | (90) | (2,000) |
| **4 Religion** | | | | | | | PLI | |
| Catholic | 52 | 74 | 83 | 81 | 96 | 82 | 79 | |
| Other religion | 1 | 2 | 2 | 3 | 1 | 1 | 4 | |
| Not religious | 47 | 24 | 15 | 16 | 3 | 17 | 17 | |
| Practising Catholic | 18 | 37 | 49 | 41 | 83 | 50 | 47 | |
| Went to Mass Sunday | 11 | 26 | 44 | 24 | 70 | 32 | 15 | |

*Source:* Elaborated from *Sondaggio Demoskopea*, May 1976.

of middle-class support for the party. The vote of the Socialist parties, on the other hand, was formerly greater in the north, where more of the membership was found, than in the south, where its greatest gains have been made in the postwar period, so that it is now stronger in the south. These parties are now stronger in the south and the shift of gravity is confirmed by the social composition of the voters, who are now more middle class and less working class than in the immediate postwar period. They have remained, moreover, predominantly male, although more church-going than previously.

Galli and Prandi have indicated that the Christian Democrat electorate has a double nature. It is strong in the 'white' provinces, and to a lesser extent in the south; but relatively weaker in the 'red' provinces and the industrial triangle. Thus it taps two sources of support: (i) organised Catholicism; and (ii) unorganised conservatives looking for state protection. Its social composition is composite, as the party proudly claims, but with a bias towards women and the rural population. Church-going, the rural and female electorate, all emphasise the importance of the role of the church in its electoral success. Indeed, one of the party's deputies is reported to have remarked some years ago that 'it takes 50 million lira and fifty priests to elect a Christian Democrat MP'.[17] It must not be thought, however, that the church is alone; the strength of the small farmers' organisation, the *Coldiretti,* which controls many aspects of the farmers' lives through its domination of the *Federconsorzi,* in addition to control of the state machinery, local government agencies, social security institutions, banks and credit houses must not be overlooked. Finally, the Liberal Party vote is located in the fashionable residential districts of the big cities; and its support comes from the well-to-do urban bourgeoisie and professional men. On the other hand, the Neofascists and National Right win the support of the southern petty bourgeoisie as well as some small and medium entrepreneurs, and occasionally the urban poor of big southern cities like that of Reggio Calabria in 1970–1.

Class, region, age and sex are of great importance in Italian politics, but if we want to understand the underlying stability of the Italian electorate in the quarter of a century between 1948 and 1973, we need to look elsewhere. Barnes[18] carried out a tree analysis on 1968 survey data which confirmed dramatically that organisational and subcultural ties (in the shape of church attendance and union membership) were more important in explaining electoral cleavage than the more obvious variables of social class, region and sex. The analysis identified three blocs of electors: the largest single bloc was the active Catholic non-working class population which comprised a third of those identifying with a party; it became still larger when active Catholic working-class women (about 10 per cent) were added. Thus, sex is an important variable, but only within the subcultural network. These two groups are both strongly anti-Left. The second bloc which is somewhat smaller is a hard core of CGIL-affiliated respondents who are strongly anti-Right. There is a third bloc, comprising the remaining third of the population that is not caught up in these organisational and subcultural networks and which holds the balance in the system. It is within this bloc that substantial differences between north and south emerge; a majority of those who are non-practising Catholics support left-wing parties in the north where only a minority do in the south. Finally, social class emerges as an important variable, but only within any particular socioeconomic category. Among those people who are not at all tied up in the structures of the two major subcultures, the difference between the proportion from middle-class backgrounds (51 per cent) and those from worker-peasant backgrounds (75 per cent) is substantial. It seems, as Barnes notes,[19] that interest measured by class background emerges as a separate important explanatory variable of electoral behaviour only when organisational and subcultural ties are minimised.

It remains to add a few words of explanation of the realignment that has been taking place in the last three years and which has provoked a rupture in the continuity of the postwar order. Sani[20] in a recent paper has shown that the increase in level of support for the Left, and the Communist Party, is a function of age. He argues that it is a reflection of a generational change and not the life-cycle. Indeed, he goes on to show that political mobility is higher among the urban, better-educated and more secularised young, thus corroborating the notion that it has been facilitated by social change, and pin points the decline of the family, as a mechanism of political socialisation, as being the critical factor.[21] This he links to the erosion of one of the organisational networks (i.e. the Catholic) to harness popular support for the moderate parties. In view of the context of the social struggles in Italy in the 1970s we can only agree with him, noting additionally that it required an event like the divorce referendum of 1974 to provoke the realignment.

PARTY FINANCE

Italian parties keep their financial affairs pretty secret and until 1974 there was no obligation to publish balance sheets, so any analysis is largely conjectural. None the less, all observers agree that they spend large sums on their multiple activities. Passigli,[22] author of the few serious studies, estimated that the Communist Party's annual expenses in 1963 were of the order of 12 billion lire rising to 18–20 billion in 1970, and 27 billion in 1975. Respective figures for Christian Democrats are a little less, say 10 billion in 1973, 15–20 billion in 1970 and about 25 billion in 1975. The Socialists spent around 10 billion in 1975 whilst for the minor parties, figures of 5 billion lire have been mentioned for the Neofascist MSI; between a billion and a billion and a half for Social Democrats and Republicans; and the Liberal Party claims to get by on a billion lire. On top of this have to be added election campaign expenses which have been conservatively estimated at about half a billion lire for the major parties in 1963 (i.e. 2–3 billion lire in 1975). Thus these represent less than 10 per cent of the expenditure of the major parties, but for smaller parties it can represent as much as half their normal annual expenditure.

As regards party income, one thing is clear: membership dues and other fees do not cover expenditure. Passigli calculated that in 1970 the proportion of the party budget covered by membership dues was highest for the Communist Party.[23] The Christian Democrats and the other parties were thus more dependent than the Communist Party on clandestine sources of finance. In this connection, there were, and are, a number of significant differences between the financing of the Communist Party and the other parties. The Communist Party[24] enjoys the advantage of several sources of finance that include the operation of a number of industrial and commercial enterprises (including a large garment concern which maintains retail stores in most Italian towns), the control of import-export transactions with the Soviet Union and Eastern bloc by Communist-controlled enterprises which turn over most of the profits to the party (but apparently much diminished since the Czechoslovak events of 1968), the contributions of the League of Co-operatives, the indirect contribution of control of local government (such as officials and members put on the payroll of local organisations, etc., within local government patronage) and commissions on contracts where government money is spent.[25] The Christian Democrats and the other parties seem to have a smaller range of financial sources, and depend above all on the control of the state apparatus and para-state agencies[26] with all the complex operations that such control permits, especially for the Christian Democrats (from commissions on public contracts, percentages on building licences, to contributions from groups interested in obtaining special favours, to the direct use of the so-called 'secret funds'). Passigli concluded his 1970 study with these words: 'while the Communist Party added a sort of community levy (destined probably to grow with control of the regional governments) to a notable effort at self-financing (co-operative movement, direct exploitation of certain enterprises) the Christian Democrats were mainly financed out of public funds'.[27]

He also stressed another difference in the models of party finance of the two major Italian parties: the Communist Party model is monocentric while the Christian Democrats' is polycentric: 'Inside the Christian Democrats, in contrast to the rigid monolithism of the Communist Party, one finds, in fact, that the factions and not the party are the recipients of financial contributions. Similarly, it is through the factions, and not the party secretariat, that the whole mechanism of appointment to patronage positions (*sottogoverno*) is managed.'[28]

In January 1974, the scandal of the clandestine financing of political parties by the oil companies and the 'secret funds' of the state-controlled Montedison Chemical Company exploded, thanks to the investigative zeal of some young Genoese magistrates, and six ministers were implicated. In view of the gravity of the accusations, Parliament set up a Committee of Inquiry which immediately proceeded to take the investigation out of the hands of the magistrates. At the same time, Parliament passed in record time a law providing for the public funding of political parties: only ten hours' debate in the Chamber of Deputies on 9 April 1974 and six hours' in the Senate a week later.[29] Subsequently the Committee of Inquiry has made no progress at all in ascertaining responsibilities as a result of the thousand obstacles placed in its path by Christian Democrat MPs.

The 1974 law provides for two types of funding: one specifically to cover the electoral expenses of the parties; and the other to cover their general expenses. A sum of 15 billion lire was made available for the electoral fund, 15 per cent of which is shared equally among all the parties that have presented candidates for election in at least two-thirds of the constituencies and which have received at least 2 per cent of the suffrage. The remaining 85 per cent is shared among all political parties, including those of linguistic minorities (such as the *Sudtiroler Volkspartei, Union valdotaine*, etc.) and the group of Independent MPs, on the basis of the number of votes obtained.

The second fund, which is for the organisational life of the parties, amounts to 45 billion lire, 2 per cent of which is shared equally among the national parties; another 23 per cent is also shared out equally, but in this case there is a provision for a certain amount to be given to ethnic and linguistic minority parties and Independents; and the remaining 75 per cent is divided proportionally among all parties according to the number of votes obtained in the previous general election. The funds for 1975 were divided between parties as follows:[30]

Christian Democrats: 15 billion 700 million lire
Communist Party: 10 billion 780 million lire
Socialist Party: 4 billion 780 million lire
Neofascist Party: 4 billion 450 million lire
Social Democrat Party: 2 billion 850 million lire
Liberal Party: 2 billion 550 million lire
Republican Party: 2 billion 300 million lire
Independents and others: 2 billion lire.

The law also established that every party must publish an annual balance-sheet specifying all revenues, both public and private, with the exception of private donations of less than 1 million lire. The balance-sheet has then to be checked by the presidents of the Chamber of Deputies and the Senate. The penalties prescribed for receiving illicit contributions are a fine equivalent to three times the sum involved and a prison sentence of between six months and four years. Finally, the law specifically forbids public companies (including those where the state holds, directly or indirectly, 20 per cent and over of the shares) from making contributions. Private companies, on the other hand, are allowed to contribute to parties provided the contributions are openly declared and are approved by the board of directors in the normal way. It is well known that ENI (State Hydrocarbons Corporation) was from its foundation under Enrico Mattei one of the principal financiers of the government parties. Eugenio Cefis, chairman of Montedison and former chairman of ENI, claimed in a statement to the Budget Standing Committee of the Chamber of Deputies on 22 September 1972 that the reason why ENI secretly bought a stake in Montedison was to fight its corrupting influence on the political system at ENI's expense:

'The operation was conceived in the light of two very simple, but serious, considerations. The first was political. The Montedison group was the leading private industrial group and was conducting a merciless war against the State Holdings in general and ENI in particular. I consider it pointless to go into the details of the situation that was created: those who were members of the last Parliament will have some knowledge . . . It is not necessary to say too much. When there was a bill that interested ENI, pressure was exerted at all levels, those of provincial secretaries, parties and other groups, etc.'[31]

For his part, Giorgio Valerio, ex-chairman of Montedison, mentioned in the course of his interrogation by the Genoese magistrates on the company's 'secret funds' in 1974 that 'after the ENI had taken a stake in Montedison in 1963 . . . we did not speak of the "secret funds" with ENI's representatives right away because, since they were themselves subsidising political parties, it was implicit that they knew . . .'[32] It is only necessary to add that the state holding in Montedison is just under 20 per cent.

Finally, the recent investigations carried out by the American Congress have confirmed the large-scale financing of anti-Communist Italian parties by the CIA and American multinational corporations. According to the Pike Report, the CIA between 1948 and 1968 contributed to 'parties favourable to the West and their affiliated organisations' the sum of 65 million dollars, to which must be added 10 million dollars for the 1972 general elections and 4 million dollars authorised by President Ford in person in December 1975 (although in view of the scandal caused by the publication of the Pike Report, it is not known whether the latter 4 million dollars were actually paid). According to the Church Report, Esso contributed almost 20 million dollars between 1967 and 1971, Lockheed Aircraft Company 2·3 million dollars, Northrop Aircraft Company 861,000 dollars, United Brands 750,000 dollars, etc., to government political parties, individual politicians and civil servants.[33]

POWER STRUCTURE

All Italian parties are leadership parties. We have already noted that they split themselves into two levels: (1) at the grass roots, where a co-operative and associative life is organised which is oriented, within a particular subsystem of values, towards recreative activities rather than political discussions; and (2) at the federal and national levels, where political discussion is the centre of activity. Pavolini's description of the Socialist Party in 1958 is a good example of all parties except the Communists:

'The rank and file . . . participate very little in political discussions in the true sense, contenting itself with affirmations about Socialism and deprecating factional struggles considered unpropitious for unity and harmony among socialists. The leaders, whether party officials or elected office-holders, are the only ones to concern themselves with politics in the true sense, which thereby becomes an encounter and clash at the summit, leaving the rank and file more or less indifferent . . . at a higher level, on the key issues of general policy, only few groups take part: Members of Parliament (not all) a few communal and provincial councillors, officials of the provincial federations, and a small nucleus of young intellectuals.'³⁴

The local sections comprise, therefore, homogeneous social and cultural groups in which educated people seem out of place. Those interested in a political career are forced to join at the federal level: a university education normally permits an individual direct entry. Galli and Prandi have succinctly described the career of a budding politician and its effect on the party:

'A political career often begins at provincial level, with entrance into the office of the provincial directorate, where clerks are mostly engaged in paper work. Yet what might be called 'the living party', that of the ordinary people of varied social backgrounds and interests, of political and cultural debate, finds expression in the party section, with which those launched on political careers in the provincial offices have little contact. The provincial executive offers political support, alliances, and opportunities to become known to the electorate.

As the party official advances in the party hierarchy an increasing amount of his time is divided between the provincial and central offices of the party or of parliament. He seldom sees the rank and file party members; he seldom engages in conversation with them; he arrives in a rush at the section to deliver a speech, and then as quickly departs for the provincial or national capital. As he becomes increasingly committed to the party apparatus, he loses contact with the party as an expression of social needs.

In this way the political leader's competence in terms of input – his capacity to sense, understand, and interpret the needs of the rank and file – tends to disappear. At the same time his competence in terms of output, that is his ability to translate social needs into action, is progressively reduced by the commitment of his time and energy. He is besieged by the things he must do to keep or improve his position.

Since the party politician increasingly represents the party machine rather than its rank and file, he is continually in the company of party and front-organisation functionaries or representatives of specific sectional and local interests. He needs them; they need him; and this reciprocal dependence is transformed into tasks and responsibilities that the leader assumes too in order to maintain this relationship.

He is beset with some overlapping of responsibilities that characterizes many activists at local level. And like the activist who is committed to too many tasks, the party official never refuses any task that offers him more and better control over the machine. In this manner he prevents others from having access to positions of leadership and since he can devote too little energy to each of his multiple commitments, the party as a whole loses its capacity for political initiative and for reacting to social needs.'[35]

The pre-eminence of the leadership within the Communist Party is secured by its Leninist structure and emphasis on party discipline. The leadership is elected, but in fact it has been able to control election and dismissal. A system of co-option has in reality been in operation. The basis of this control is 'democratic centralism' which in practical terms means bureaucratic central-ism, resting on the career patterns of party officials. The Communist Party is the only Italian party which acts as a vehicle of social promotion for the working classes. A political career for a person of modest origin means becoming a full-time official. Entry into the national leadership is possible only for those who reach office-holding positions at the provincial level; and three-quarters of provincial officials, regardless of social origin, are full-time paid career men. Since the party apparatus is in the hands of people whose livelihood depends on their party career, it is easy to see how the party leadership controls the apparatus.

The Communist Party is an apparatus party rather than a parliamentary party. While its top leaders have simultaneously been Members of Parliament, their power has always been based on their position in the party hierarchy, as is exemplified by the career of Enrico Berlinguer, the party general secretary.[36] Moreover, the party has always conceived of Parliament as only one of the arenas of political activity and so it renews about a third of its representatives at each election (see Table 7.4 – only a limited group of top MPs remain longer than three Parliaments) with the positive effect of furnishing the party with a body of expert parliamentary personnel. Finally, strict party discipline ensures full control over who is elected to Parliament and for how long. It follows that MPs have almost no freedom of action in opposition to the central committee.

All this points to the monolithic party structure Western writers have for so long associated with Communist parties, but

Table 7.4 *Length of Parliamentary Mandates (Chamber of Deputies, 1948–72)*

|  | 5 Parliaments | 4 Parliaments | 3 Parliaments | Total Number of MPs | % MPs Re-elected for 3 Parliaments |
|---|---|---|---|---|---|
| DC | 42 | 31 | 57 | 267 | 48·5 |
| PSI | 9 | 2 | 7 | 61 | 29·5 |
| PCI | 10 | 7 | 13 | 179 | 16·7 |

*Source :* G.-F. Pasquino, 'Une crise qui vient de loin', *Esprit*, November 1976, p. 15.

it would not be a completely accurate description of the Italian party today. The Italian leaders, unlike their French colleagues until very recently, have permitted a revisionist discussion and critique and encouraged a vigorous organisational renewal,[37] thanks, on the one hand, to the theoretical prestige of the former party leader, Gramsci, and on the other, the canalisation of the energy of the labour struggles of the 1970s. None the less, the leadership was frightened by some of the possible consequences, like that of the *Manifesto* group [38] in 1969, and so has endeavoured to keep it within narrower grounds than were probably intended originally. It is difficult to assess the limits today, except to say that if debate is wide-ranging and open, once a decision is reached, often indicated from above rather than below, unanimous obedience to it is still expected.

According to Galli[39] the party's three strong points are: (i) the inheritance of the power positions and traditions of the key organisations in the labour movement; (ii) the control of local government (much expanded since June 1975); and (iii) the time MPs (without governmental responsibilities) have been able to devote to following and defending the causes of various groups of the population. To this can be added the prestige of its intellectual activity and its acquisition of national positions. The limits on the party leadership in imposing a strategy are likely to emerge when the contradictions between the reality of the 'historic compromise' and that of its client groups (workers and others) become, as they are bound to in the present crisis, too painfully apparent.

Control of the different Socialist parties by the leadership is much less secure than that of the Communist Party. In the fifties and sixties, Nenni and Saragat maintained control of the Socialist and Social Democratic parties respectively by a combination of caution in policy and personal appeal. It has been claimed that it was Nenni's charisma which enabled him to prevail over a hostile apparatus in the struggle over socialist autonomy and reunification. It was insufficient, however, to prevent party splits. The multiplication of factions, as Hine has noted, which began on the reunification of PSI and PSDI in 1966, and which continued unabated after the split again in 1969, was a new and less wholesome type of internal division; 'it was largely an expression of the struggles between various personal power groups: party leaders have changed factions, created new ones, in a quite unashamed manner'.[40] This new type of factional struggle in which parliamentary leaders play a central role was indicative of a shift in the nature of the Socialist parties from the apparatus party, founded at the time of the liberation, to the parliamentary parties which now exist.

The power structure of the Christian Democrat Party is complex. In essence, it is a confessional party whose vocation is government, but continued dominance can only be won at the cost of attracting the support of groups critical, if not hostile, towards its confessional ideology. The need to reconcile contradictions underlies its power structure which is difficult to characterise with any certainty. In the De Gasperi era (1945–53) the party was a parliamentary party. As party leader, De Gasperi attempted to take more account of the electorate's reaction than that of party militants; and also more account of certain economic groups than either because he believed that continued electoral success depended on successful economic reconstruction. His position in the party was reinforced by his prestige as pre-Fascist leader of the party, as well as his position as prime minister in the politically dramatic period of the Cold War. Although De Gasperi's position as party leader was rarely in doubt, this did not free him from difficult battles with party groups at various times. He succumbed increasingly after April 1948 to the temptations of a leadership founded on brokerage, and in consequence on immobilism, in place of one of initiative and decision.

De Gasperi's death and Fanfani's attempt to strengthen the party organisation complicated rather than simplified the internal party power-structure, because it increased the contesting elements at the very moment that the lynch-pin of party unity disappeared. Baget-Bozzo[41] has explained that the party, in an attempt at retrenchment after the electoral defeat of 1953, adopted a double government strategy. On the one hand, it played down Parliament as a decision-making centre, while, on the other, it reinforced its control, and the role, of the para-state agencies. The result was the rapid extension of a clientèlistic, not to say corporative system of politics, which, as Di Palma[42] has noted, triggered off and institutionalised extreme factionalism. It remains to be noted that the Christian Democrat Party has never, at any time, controlled, much less led, its electorate. Initially, this was controlled by the Catholic organisations; latterly, by the individual party bosses through their clientèlistic network. The militancy in the same party of politicians of divergent social views created an incipient basis for factionalism. It was encouraged, even exacerbated, by the party strategy of clientèlism and corporativism consciously pursued under Fanfani's secretaryship in the fifties, and which led quite logically to the formation of the *doroteo* faction in the sixties, i.e. a kind of alliance of semi-autonomous regional and provincial bosses.

Among the factors which encouraged this development was the stability of partisan representation, which meant that there was no electoral alternative to DC-dominated government coalitions. Although interest groups fed factionalism with a 'polycentric' flow of funds to factions and leaders, the latter were prevented from perpetrating splits by realisation that the only result would be the loss of the party's dominant position and their own share of power.

In these circumstances, it was natural that the aspiring Christian Democrat politician's objective was election and re-election to Parliament because it was the key to a political career in the party. As Pasquino has observed, 'the power of each DC MP depends essentially on his capacity to serve as an intermediary between the government and his constituency by distributing favours. The loss of his seat means the end of his political career.'[43] This explains the crystallisation of the Christian Democrat political class documented in Table 7.4. For a top leadership position, the Christian Democrat MP must dominate an existing faction, or failing that create his own (see Table 7.5). This requires either the conquest of a large provincial federation or the office of under-secretary (or preferably, both combined). Either way, the faction leader gains control over the distribution of the resources of public agencies (banks, co-operatives, chambers of commerce, local government agencies, etc.) in his constituency, and even nationally if he is big enough, which expand the factional network and ensure the fidelity of a class of public and private mediators.[44] The examples of the successful use of this strategy over the last twenty years are legion: Andreotti, Colombo, Rumor, Fanfani, Taviani, Moro, De Mita, Bisaglia, etc. It would seem, however, that the electoral defeat in the regional elections of 15 June 1975, which led to the overthrow of Fanfani as party secretary and his replacement by Zaccagnini, and the final split of the largest faction (the

Table 7.5  *Christian Democrat Factions, 1974*

| Factions | Leaders | Congress Vote % | Nat. Counc. | Nat. Exec. | MPs | Ministers | Under-Secs. | Seat | Press |
|---|---|---|---|---|---|---|---|---|---|
| Iniziativa popolare | Rumor Piccoli | 34·2 | 42 | 13 | 96 | 5 | 11 | Piazza Cardelli | Notizie Parlt. |
| Impegno demoratico | Colombo Andreotti | 16·5 | 20 | 3 | 30 | 3 | 6 | via del Caravita | Imp. democ. Concretez |
| Nuove cronache | Fanfani Forlani | 19·8 | 24 | 6 | 56 | 2 | 5 | via delle Convertite | Nuove Cronache |
| Morotei | Moro Zaccagnini | 8·7 | 10 | 4 | 50 | 1 | 4 | via Po | Progetto |
| Base | De Mita Misasi | 10·8 | 12 | 4 | 41 | 2 | 3 | via Uffici Vicario | Radar |
| Forze nuove | Donat-Cattin Brodato | 10·0 | 12 | 5 | 36 | 2 | 3 | Piazza Pietra | Forze nuove |

*Source*: A. Padellaro, 'Una bussola per orientarsi nel labirinto democristiano', *Corriere della sera*, 18 July 1974, p. 7.

*dorotei*), followed by the partial success of the general election of 20 June 1976, with its limited renewal of Christian Democrat MPs, marks the opening of a new period in the internal power-structure of the party. Unfortunately, it is too early to distinguish the contingent elements from the structural. All the indications are that the party is being transformed, albeit slowly and in spite of itself, into a lay conservative party on the north European model.[45]

In any event, if a seat in Parliament is an essential requirement for ministerial office and party leadership, this does not mean that Christian Democracy is a parliamentary party in the British sense, since party decisions can be, and are, taken independently of a Christian Democrat prime minister. None the less Parliament plays a more important role in the Christian Democrat power-structure than in that of its greatest rival, the Communist Party. All in all, the Christian Democrat Party in this respect has more in common with the Socialist Party; it exhibits a power-structure, third-parliamentary, third-state and third-party, which is common to the majority of Italian parties.

CONCLUSIONS

The various aspects of Italian parties that have been outlined attest to their striking similarity. They all claim to represent an exclusive ideological point of view; they all have a similar articulated branch-like structure; they all sponsor permanent satellite organisations and a party press. Two have been more successful than the rest: the Communists and Christian Democrats. Despite local differences, control of all parties lies with party leaders through paid party officials who control local sectional meetings and provincial congresses which elect delegates to national congresses. Factionalism exists in all parties, except the Communist Party (although it is likely that state financing of parties has strengthened national secretaries at the expense of the factions). Thus, while policy is decided and debated at the top, the consequences of factionalism are the same every-where: the leaders are so absorbed in the tactics of survival that they have little time and energy left for the strategy of achievement.

If the general election of June 1976 opened a new phase in postwar Italian politics by placing the Communist Party on a par with the Christian Democrats for the first time, it has not indicated a ready-made solution to the country's economic and social crises. The Republic, now in its thirty-second year, is already the longest surviving political regime that United Italy

# APPENDIX

*Election Results of National Parties, 1968–1976, Chamber of Deputies*

| | 1968 | | | 1972 | | | 1976 | | |
|---|---|---|---|---|---|---|---|---|---|
| | *votes (million)* | *%* | *seats* | *votes (million)* | *%* | *seats* | *votes (million)* | *%* | *seats* |
| DP | — | — | — | — | — | — | 0·5 | 1·5 | 6 |
| PCI | 8·6 | 26·9 | 177 | 9·1 | 27·2 | 179 | 12·6 | 34·4 | 227 |
| PSIUP | 1·4 | 4·5 | 23 | 0·6 | 1·9 | — | — | — | — |
| PSI | } 4·6 | 14·5 | } 91 | 3·2 | 9·6 | 61 | 3·5 | 9·6 | 57 |
| PSDI | } — | — | | 1·7 | 5·1 | 29 | 1·2 | 3·4 | 15 |
| PR | — | — | — | — | — | — | 0·3 | 1·1 | 4 |
| PRI | 0·6 | 2·0 | 9 | 1·0 | 2·9 | 14 | 1·1 | 3·1 | 14 |
| DC | 12·4 | 39·1 | 266 | 12·9 | 38·8 | 267 | 14·2 | 38·7 | 263 |
| PLI | 1·9 | 5·8 | 31 | 1·3 | 3·9 | 21 | 0·5 | 1·3 | 5 |
| Mon | 0·4 | 1·3 | 6 | — | — | — | — | — | — |
| MSI | 1·4 | 4·4 | } 24 | 2·9 | 8·7 | 56 | 2·2 | 6·1 | 35 |
| Others | 0·5 | 1·5 | 3 | 0·8 | 1·5 | 3 | 0·2 | 0·8 | 4 |

*Glossary of initials :* DP = left wing Communists; PCI = Italian Communist Party; PSIUP = Italian Socialist Party of Proletarian Unity; PSI = Italian Socialist Party; PSDI = Italian Social Democrat Party; PR = Radical Party; PRI = Italian Republican Party; DC = Christian Democrats; PLI = Italian Liberal Party; Mon = Monarchists; MSI = Neofascists.

has known. Unfortunately, surviving has to date been its greatest achievement and it is clear today that, in view of the worsening economic, social and political situations, this is no longer enough. Time is running out. Any solution would appear to require the accession of the Communist Party to government, i.e. the consummation of the 'historical compromise'. Is it possible? No one can be sure. However, what is beyond dispute is that the way that it is, or is not, achieved will determine not only the future of the party system, but also the political system, and, indeed, the survival of the Republic itself.

## NOTES

This chapter makes extensive use of material used in the first edition and subsequently re-elaborated in my book *Italy: Republic without Government?* (London, Weidenfeld & Nicolson, 1973).

1 G. Galli, *Il bipartitismo imperfetto* (Bologna, Il Mulino, 1966).
2 R. Orefeo, *L'occupazione del potere, I democristiani 1945–75* (Milan, Longanesi, 1975).
3 *Panorama*, 31 August 1972.
4 For a general overview in English, see D. Hine, 'Labour movement and communism in France and Italy', in M. Kolinsky and W. E. Paterson (eds), *Social and Political Movements in Western Europe* (London, Croom Helm, 1976).
5 Membership figures are taken from G. Galli, *Dal bipartitismo imperfetto alla possibile alternativa* (Bologna, Il Mulino, 1975), p. 89.
6 See figures given in G. Tamburrano, *L'iceberg democristiano* (Milan, Sugar, 1974), p. 74; for the DC they were: 1947, 33,920 (4·2 per cent); 1951, 37,772 (4 per cent); 1954, 46,240 (4·2 per cent); 1956, 101,940 (9·5 per cent); 1958, 187,131 (13·6 per cent).
7 Galli, *Il bipartitismo imperfetto*.
8 G. Sani, 'Profilo dei dirigenti di partito', *Rassegna italiana di sociologia*, vol. XIII, no. 1, January 1972, p. 145.
9 G. Galli and A. Prandi, *Patterns of Political Participation in Italy* (New Haven, Yale University Press, 1970), p. 54.
10 On preference voting, see L. D'Amato, *Il voto di preferenze (1946–63)* (Milan, Giuffré, 1964); and F. Cazzola, 'Partiti, correnti e voto di preferenza', *Rivista italiana di scienza politica*, vol. II, no. 4, December 1972, pp. 569–88, now in M. Cacciagli and A. Spreafico (eds), *Un sistema politico alla prova* (Bologna, Il Mulino, 1975).
11 G.-F. Pasquino, 'Trasformazioni nel sistema di potere della Democrazia Cristiana', paper presented to the Seminario sulla crisi italiana, Einaudi Foundation, Turin, 1977, p. 14.
12 Galli and Prandi, op. cit., p. 55.
13 Galli, *Il bipartitismo . . .*, p. 112.
14 op. cit.
15 S. G. Tarrow, *Peasant Communism in Southern Italy* (New Haven, Yale University Press, 1967).

16 G. Sani, 'Ricambio elettorale e identificazioni partitiche: verso una egemonia delle sinistre?' *Rivista italiana di scienza politica*, vol. v, no. 4, December 1975, pp. 516–44.

17 Remark quoted by J. Nobécourt, *L'Italie à vif* (Paris, Seuil, 1970).

18 S. H. Barnes, 'Italy: religion and class in electoral behaviour', in R. Rose (ed.), *Electoral Behaviour, A Comparative Handbook* (New York, The Free Press, 1974), p. 213.

19 ibid., p. 216.

20 G. Sani, 'Generations and politics in Italy', paper presented to the Seminario sulla crisi italiana, Einaudi Foundation, Turin, 1977, pp. 18–19.

21 ibid., p. 48.

22 S. Passigli, 'Italy', *Comparative Political Finance*, special number of *Journal of Politics*, vol. xxv, no. 3, August 1963, pp. 718–36; 'Quanto costa il PCI', *Il Mondo*, vol. xxii, no. 19, 3 May 1970, p. 4; and 'Quanto costa la DC', *Il Mondo*, vol. xxii, no. 21, 17 May 1970, p. 3.

23 M. Padovani, in *Le Longue marche di parti Communiste italien* (Paris, Flammarion, 1977), gives the following figures for state aid and membership dues, quoting *L'Unita* of 17 January 1976 (all figures are percentages):

|  | 1974 | | of which | 1975 | | of which |
|  | State aid | Party sources | Memb. dues | State aid | Party sources | Memb. dues |
|---|---|---|---|---|---|---|
| PCI | 44·8 | 55·2 | 27·3 | 39·9 | 60·1 | 29·3 |
| PSI | 58·2 | 41·8 | 17·7 | 56·7 | 43·3 | 21·0 |
| DC | 75.7 | 24·3 | 13·1 | 60·6 | 39·4 | 9·9 |

24 The Communist Party 1975 budget (*L'Unita* of 16 January 1976) contains the following headings:

| Revenue | | Expenditure | |
|---|---|---|---|
| 1 Membership dues | 29·3 | 1 Personnel | 4·5 |
| 2 State aid | 39·9 | 2 General expenses | 11·2 |
| 3 Rents, parliamentary groups | 3·9 | 3 Contributions to local organisations | 63·3 |
| 4 Press, manufacturing | 26·4 | | |
| 5 Donations | 0·1 | 4 Propaganda | 17·2 |
| | | 5 Extraordinary expenses, election campaign | 3·8 |
| (26·8 billion lire) | 100·0 | (27·03 billion lire) | 100·0 |

25 When they are the majority party in local government coalitions, the PCI and DC keep control of the financially important departments, like public works and welfare, etc.; see S. Passigli, 'Gli Enti locali', in *Annuario Politico Italiano 1963* (Milan, Communità, 1964).

26 A Christian Democrat minister stated publically some years ago that it was right and proper for ENEL (State Electrical Agency) to finance government parties.

27 op. cit., p. 3.

28 ibid.

29 For details, see D. Sassoon, 'The public funding of political parties in Italy', *Political Quarterly*, vol. xxxxvi, no. 1, January 1975, pp. 94–8.

30 ibid., p. 95.

31 Quoted in E. Scalfari and G. Turani, *Razza padrona* (Milan, Feltrinelli, 1974), p. 155.

32 Quoted in ibid., p. 183.

33 For the Pike Report, see CIA, *The Pike Report* (London, Spokesmen Books, 1977); for the Church Report, see the supplement to *L'Europeo* of 27 February 1976; *The Times* of 13 February 1976 contains a table of recent corrupt transactions.
34 P. Pavolini, 'I sette socialismi', *Il Mondo,* 26 August 1958, p. 3.
35 op. cit., p. 283.
36 Career: 1943 joined PCI; secretary of youth section of Sassari; 1944 member of national secretariat of Communist Youth Federation; 1945 member of central committee; 1948 member of party direction; 1949 national secretary of Communist Youth Federation; 1950 president of World Federation of Democratic Youth; 1957 director of party central school and regional deputy secretary for Sardinia; 1958 elected MP; 1969 deputy general secretary; 1972 general secretary.
37 Seen above all in tripling of student *quadri* and halving of worker-peasant *quadri* since 1969; for details, see F. Lanchester, 'La dirigenza di partito: il caso del PCI', *Politico,* XLI, no. 4, December 1976, pp. 713–18.
38 The *Manifesto* group was a group of Communist Party members who became increasingly concerned at what they considered to be the right-wing or social democratic drift of the party in the late sixties. In 1969, they began to publish a monthly theoretical review *Il Manifesto,* critical of the party line. After several months of internal debate the party leadership indicated that if they continued they would be guilty of factional activity. They continued and the leaders (including five MPs) were expelled (the party preferred to use the term 'struck off') in December 1969. In 1970 the group launched a daily with the same name and founded a Proletarian Communist Party (PDUP). They unsuccessfully presented candidates in the 1972 general election, but in 1976 two of their candidates were successful in the left-wing alliance (*Democrazia proletaria*) made with two other minor left-wing parties, *Lotta continua* and *Avvantguardia operaia*. Many of the group's rank and file supporters who left the PCI in 1970 appear to have returned to fold in 1975–6.
39 Galli, *Il bipartitismo imperfetto,* p. 248.
40 D. Hine, 'Italian socialism and the Centre-Left coalition: strategy or tactics?', *Journal of Common Market Studies,* vol. XIII, no. 3, June 1975, p. 448.
41 G. Baget Bozzo, 'Dibattito sulla grande coalizione', *Il Mulino,* vol. XX, September–October 1971, pp. 20–4.
42 G. Di Palma, *Surviving without Governing* (Berkeley, Calif., University of California Press, 1977), p. 268; see also G. Sartori (ed.), *Correnti, frazioni e fazioni nei partiti politici italiani* (Bologna, Il Mulino, 1973).
43 G.-F. Pasquino, 'Une crise qui vient de loin', *Esprit,* November 1976, p. 15.
44 Cf. G. Tumbarrano, '*L'iceberg democristiano*' (Milan, Sugar, 1976); F. Cazzola, 'I pilastri del regime. Gli enti pubblici di sicurezza sociale', *Rassegna italiana di sociologia,* vol. XVII, no. 3, July 1976, pp. 421–47; and a local example, G. Pansa, *Bisaglia, una carriera democristiana* (Milan, Sugar, 1975).
45 G.-F. Pasquino, 'Trasformazioni . . .', p. 8.

# BIBLIOGRAPHY

## THE POLITICAL SYSTEM

Alberoni, F. (1975) *Italia in trasformazione* (Bologna, Il Mulino).
Allum, P. A. (1973) *Italy: Republic without Government?* (London, Weidenfeld & Nicolson).

Allum, P. A. (1976) 'La crisi italiana', *Rassegna italiana di Sociologia*, vol. XVII, no. 2, June.

Armato, G. (1976) *Economia, politica e istituzioni in Italia* (Bologna, Il Mulino).

Bibes, G. (1974) *Le système politique italien* (Paris, PUF).

Cavazza F. L., and Graubard, S. R. (eds) (1974) *Il caso italiano* (Milan, Garzanti).

Farneti, P. (ed.) (1972) *Il sistema politico italiano* (Bologna, Il Mulino).

Galli, G. (1975) *Dal bipartitismo imperfetto alla possibile alternativa* (Bologna, Il Mulino).

Graziano, L. (1977) 'La crise d'un régime liberal democratique: le cas de L'Italie', *Revue française de science politique*, vol. XXVIII, no. 2, April.

Pasquino, G.-F. (1976) 'Une crise qui vient de loin', *Esprit*, November.

Pizzorno, A. (1971) 'Il sistema politico italiano', *Politica del diritto*, vol. II, no. 2, April.

Zariski, R. (1971) *The Politics of Uneven Development* (New York, Holt, Rinehart & Winston).

PARTIES

AAVV (1975) *Tutto il potere della DC* (Rome, Coines).

Aghina, G., and Jaconino, C. (1977) *Storia del partito radicale* (Milan, Gemmalibri).

Barrese, O., and Caprona, M. (1977) *L'Anatomia DC* (Milan, Feltrinelli).

Beccheloni, G. (ed.) (1974) *Cultura e ideologia della nuova sinistra* (Milan, Comunità).

Berlinquer, E. (1975) *La questione comunista* (Rome, Editori Riuniti).

Blackmer, D. L. M. (1972) 'Italian Communist strategy for the 1970s', *Problems of Communism*, vol. XXI, no. 3, June.

Blackmer, D. L. M., and Kriegel, A. J. (eds) (1975) *The International Role of the Communist Parties of Italy and France* (Cambridge, Mass., Harvard University Press).

Blackmer, D. L. M., and Tarrow, S. G. (eds) (1975) *Communism in Italy and France* (Princeton, NJ, Princeton University Press).

Di Palma, G. (1977) 'Eurocommunism?', *Comparative Politics*, vol. IX, no. 2, April.

Cazzola, F. (1970) *Il partito socialista come organizzazione, Studio di un caso: il PSI* (Rome, Tritone).

Fondation Nationale des sciences politiques (1974) *Sociologie du communisme en Italie* (Paris, Colin).

Galli, G. (1974) *La crisi italiana e la destra internazionale* (Milan, Mondadori).

Galli, G. (1974) *Storia dei partiti italiani* (Milan, UTET).

Hellman, S. (1976) 'The "New Left" in Italy', in M. Kolinsky and W. E. Paterson (eds), *Social and Political Movements in Western Europe* (London, Croom Helm).

Hine, D. (1975) 'Italian socialism and the centre-left coalition: strategy or tactics?', *Journal of Common Market Studies*, vol. XIII, no. 3, June.

Irving, R. E. M. (1976) 'Italy's Christian Democrats and European integration', *International Affairs*, vol. LII, no. 3, July.

Irving, R. E. M. (1979) *The Christian Democratic Parties of Western Europe* (London, George Allen & Unwin/RIIA).
Mammarella, G. (1976) *Il partito comunista italiano 1945–75* (Florence, Valecchi).
Menapace, L. (1974) *La Democrazia cristiana* (Milan, Mazzotta).
Orfeo, R. (1975) *L'occupazione del potere, I democristiani, 1945–75* (Milan, Longanesi).
Pansa, G. (1975) *Bisaglia, una carriera democristiana* (Milan, Sugar).
Paterson, W. E., and Campbell, I. (1974) *Social Democracy in Post-War Europe* (London, Croom Helm).
Rosenbaum, P. (1975) *Il nuovo fascismo* (Milan, Feltrinelli).
Sassoon, D. (1976) 'The Italian Communist Party's European strategy', *Political Quarterly*, vol. XXXVII, no. 3, July.
Tamburrano, G. (1974) *L'Iceberg democristiano* (Milan, Sugar).
Timmermann, H. (1974) *I communisti italiani* (Bari, De Donato).
Valenzi, P. (ed.) (1976) *Il compromesso storico* (Rome, Newton Compton).
Vettori, G. (ed.) (1973) *La sinistra extraparlamentare in Italia* (Rome, Newton Compton).
Weber, H. (ed.) (1977) *Parti communiste italien: aux sources de l'euro-communisme* (Paris, C. Bourgois).

POLITICAL SOCIOLOGY

Cazzola, F. (1972) 'Consenso e opposizione nel parlamento italiano. Il ruolo del PCI dalla Ia alla IVa legislatura', *Rivista italiana di scienza politica*, vol. II, no. 1, January.
Cazzola, F. (1976) 'I pilastri del regime. Gli enti pubblici di sicurezza sociale', *Rassegna italiana di sociologia*, vol. XVII, no. 3, July.
Dalton, R. (1977) 'Generational change within the Italian Christian Democratic Party elite', *European Journal of Political Research*, vol. V, no. 2, June.
Di Palma, G. (1977) *Surviving without Governing* (Berkeley, Calif., University of California Press).
Ferrarcsi, F., and Kemeny, P. (1977) *Classi sociali e politica urbana* (Rome, Officina ed.).
Fried, R. C. (1971) 'Communism, urban budgets and the two Italies', *Journal of Politics*, vol. XXXIII, no. 3, November.
Graziano, L. (1973) 'Patron–client relationships in southern Italy', *European Journal of Political Research*, vol. I, no. 1, April.
Lanchester, F. (1976) 'La dirigenza di partito: il caso del PCI', *Il Politico*, vol. XLI, no. 4, December.
Parise, A. (1974) 'Questione cattolica e referendum: L'inizio di una fine', *Il Mulino*, vol. XXIII, May.
Putnam, R. (1973) *The Beliefs of Politicians* (New Haven, Conn., Princeton University Press).
Sani, G. (1972) 'Profilo dei dirigenti di partito', *Rassegna italiana di sociologia*, vol. XIII, no. 1, January.
Sani, G. (1972) 'La professionalizzazione dei dirigenti di partito italiani', *Rivista italiana di scienza politica*, vol. II, no. 2, June.

Sani, G. (1974) 'Canali di informazione e atteggiamenti politici', *Rivista italiana di scienza politica*, vol. IV, no. 2, August.

Sani, G. (1976) 'Mass constraints on political realignments: perceptions of anti-system parties in Italy', *British Journal of Political Science*, vol. VI, no. 1, January.

Sartori, G. (1973) *Correnti, frazioni e fazioni nei partiti politici italiani* (Bologna, Il Mulino).

Sassoon, D. (1975) 'The funding of political parties in Italy', *Political Quarterly*, vol. XXXXVI, no. 1, January.

Tarrow, S. G. (1969) 'Economic development and the transformation of the Italian party system', *Comparative Politics*, vol. II, no. 1, January.

Tarrow, S. G. (1972) 'The political economy of stagnation: communism in southern Italy, 1960–70', *Journal of Politics*, vol. XXXIV, no. 1, February.

Tarrow, S. G. (1974) *Partisanship and Political Exchange in French and Italian Local Politics: A Contribution to the Typology of Party Systems* (London and Beverly Hills, Sage).

Wiatr, J. J., and Cazzola, F. (eds) (1974) *Partecipazione e sviluppo nella politica locale* (Rome, Officina ed.).

Zuckerman, A. (1976) *Political Clienteles in Power: Party Factions and Cabinet Coalitions in Italy* (London and Beverly Hills, Sage).

ELECTORAL STUDIES

Barnes, S. H. (1974) 'Italy: religion and class in electoral behaviour', in R. Rose (ed.), *Electoral Behaviour: A Comparative Handbook* (New York, Free Press).

Cacciagli, M., and Spreafico, A. (eds) (1975) *Un sistema politico alla prova* (Bologna, Il Mulino).

Clark, M., and Irving, R. E. M. (1972) 'The Italian political crisis and the general election of May 1972', *Parliamentary Affairs*, vol. XXV, no. 3, Summer.

Clark, M., Hine, D., and Irving, R. E. M. (1974) 'Divorce – Italian style', *Parliamentary Affairs*, vol. XXVII, no. 4, Autumn.

Clark, M., and Irving, R. E. M. (1977) 'The Italian general elections of June 1976', *Parliamentary Affairs*, vol. XXX, no. 1, Winter.

Fabris, G.-P. (1977) *Il comportamento politico degli italiani* (Milan, F. Angeli).

Galli, G. (1972) 'L'influenza della organizzazione partitica sul voto', *Rassegna italiana di sociologia*, vol. XIII, no. 1, January.

Ghini, C. (1975) *Il voto degli italiani* (Rome, Editori Riuniti).

Ghini, C. (1976) *Il terremoto del 15 giugno* (Milan, Feltrinelli).

Hazelrigg, L. E. (1970) 'Religious and class bases of political conflict in Italy', *American Journal of Sociology*, vol. LXXV, no. 1, January.

Parise, A., and Pasquino, G.-F. (1976) '20 Giugno: struttura politica e comportamenti elettorali', *Il Mulino*, vol. XXV, May.

Pennington, H. (ed.) (1977) *Italy at the Polls* (Washington, DC, American Enterprise Institute).

Sani, G. (1974) 'Determinants of party preference in Italy', *American Journal of Political Science*, vol. XVIII, no. 2.

Sani, G. (1975) 'Ricambio elettorale e identificazioni partitiche: verso un'egemonia delle sinistre?', *Rivista italiana di scienza politica*, vol. V, no. 3.

Sani, G. (1976) 'Le elezioni degli anni settanta: terremoto o evoluzione', *Rivista italiana di scienza politica*, vol. VI, no. 2.

# 8
# Luxembourg

## MARIO HIRSCH

Luxembourg constitutes a political system in its own right. Along with Switzerland, it employs a rather unusual electoral system, which may be called ordinal proportional representation. The distinguishing feature is the ordinal ballot. Party-list ballots are used, but both cumulation and panachage are permitted.[1] The fact that the voter is allowed to rank parties has major consequences on the party system, helping small parties and permitting a highly personalised vote. The country has four electoral districts and there are considerable regional variations in party strength.

The traditionally predominant role of political parties has recently been limited by the necessities of crisis management leading to the institutionalised participation of organised interest groups in decision making (*comité de conjoncture, conference tripartite gouvernement – patronat – syndicats*). Some political parties have labelled this institutional evolution by the rather derogatory phrase 'corporate state'. The political climate in Luxembourg, based on a remarkable stability and to a large extent on consensus politics, explains and facilitates these developments.

### THE CHRISTIAN SOCIAL PARTY

In 1944, the old party of the Right (Partei der Rechten),[2] founded in 1914, gave itself a new name – Chreschtlech sozial Vollekspartei, csv (Christian Social Party). Popular party *par excellence*, the csv has been able to maintain its strong confessional orientation in a predominantly Catholic country and thus become an excellent example of a 'catch-all party'. Its long involvement with governmental responsibilities (the csv has been in charge of governing the country alone or in coalition from 1919 up to 1974) accounts for most of its distinguishing features: it is the only party which is fairly evenly represented in all four electoral districts, with however its strongest implantation in the rural north; high membership (over 7,000 compared to the Socialist Party's 5,000); close links with the leading newspaper (the *Luxemburger Wort* with an approximate circulation of 80,000); and a dense network of para-party organisations. Two doctrinal tendencies cohabit inside the party: a conservative, strongly confessional group and a Christian-social orientation represented mainly by party members who are organised in the Christian trade union movement (LCGB).

As far as its electoral strength is concerned, the CSV has been on the decline since the late fifties. The party has never really recovered from its defeat in 1959 (from 45 per cent in 1954, its share of the vote dropped to 38·9 per cent in 1959). The 1974 election (though the CSV still remained the strongest party, its electoral result dropped slightly below 30 per cent of the votes) made possible an alternative coalition formula (Socialist–Liberal), without, for the first time in over fifty years, the CSV.

### THE SOCIALIST PARTY

Founded in 1902, the Letzeburger Sozialistisch Arbechterpartei (Luxembourg Socialist Worker Party) is the second largest party in the country and the leading party in the coalition government formed in 1974. Strongly established in the industrial southern part of the country with intimate links to the major Luxembourg trade union (LAV), the LSAP has been for most of its history a class-oriented party (it is still the party for which list-voting is the most normal and panachage relatively negligible).

Participation in coalition governments with the Christian Socialists from 1951 up to 1959 enabled the LSAP to enlarge its electoral basis (33 per cent of the votes in 1954 and 1959, 36 per cent in 1964, compared with figures well below 30 per cent in the first postwar elections) and to diversify regionally. Participation in coalition governments created strong internal tensions and in 1969 the trade union wing successfully opposed the renewal of the great coalition formed in 1964. The return to opposition only intensified these tensions and in 1971 a split occurred on the issue of collaboration between Socialists and Communists on the municipal level. One third of the party's members, including six MPs and most of the former leadership, left the LSAP to found the Social Democratic Party. This rightist deviation survived fairly successfully its first electoral test in 1974 with 10 per cent of the votes.

The LSAP has emerged electorally weaker (1974 elections 27

per cent of the vote), but ideologically reinforced. Strong enough to form a coalition with the Liberals, the LSAP has been the main agent of the successful crisis-management that has characterised governmental policy since 1974.

### THE DEMOCRATIC PARTY

The Demokratesch Partei (Democratic Party) emerged after 1945 from some of the resistance movements. It progressively gave up its anti-clerical orientation to become a credible representative of modern liberalism. The DP is the main beneficiary of the floating vote and especially of the panachage, which may help to explain its erratic progression up to 1968. Since that date its electoral performance has become more regular (1968: 18 per cent; 1974: 23·3 per cent of the votes). The party's electoral fate is to a large extent dependent on the magnetism of its leaders (among them Gaston Thorn, prime minister since 1974). Its electoral stronghold is traditionally the Centre District with Luxembourg City.

### THE COMMUNIST PARTY

The Communist Party came into existence after a split inside the Socialist Party in 1921. After a difficult existence in the prewar years, being the victim of all kinds of administrative persecution, the KPL achieved an impressive performance in the 1945 elections (11 per cent of the vote) and became a part of the government of national union. It left the government in 1947 and has played ever since the role of a permanent opposition.

There is an inverse ratio between the Communist Party's electoral results and those of the Socialist Party. The Communist Party has its stronghold in the industrial south district (up to 20 per cent of the votes); elsewhere it is much weaker. Overall electoral performance is erratic and determined by external events (1959: 7·2 per cent; 1968: 13·1 per cent; 1974: 8·7 per cent). The KPL has repeatedly propagated the idea of a union of the Left.

## STATISTICAL APPENDIX

Table 8.1   *Occupational Breakdown of Luxembourg's Active Population (%)*

|  | Peasants | Workers | Public and private employees | Independent professions |
|---|---|---|---|---|
| 1960 | 21·9 | 46·4 | 26·1 | 5·6 |
| 1970 | 19·6 | 45·0 | 33·8 | 5·6 |

Table 8.2  *Electoral Results per Party (gross votes and percentage of vote) for the last Four Elections*

| Election Year | CSV | LSAP | DP | KPL |
|---|---|---|---|---|
| 1959 | 896,000 | 848,000 | 448,000 | 220,000 |
| | 38·9% | 33·0% | 20·3% | 7·2% |
| 1964 | 883,000 | 999,000 | 280,000 | 330,000 |
| | 35·6% | 35·9% | 12·2% | 10·4% |
| 1968 | 915,000 | 837,000 | 430,000 | 402,000 |
| | 37·4% | 30·9% | 18·0% | 13·1% |
| 1974 | 836,000 | 875,000 | 668,000 | 313,000 |
| | 29·8% | 26·9% | 23·3% | 8·7% |
| | (Christian Social Party) | (Socialist Party) | (Liberal Party) | (Communist Party) |

*Notes:*
Gross votes equal total of votes given to each party. Each elector has several votes. The discrepancy between gross vote and percentage of vote is due to the variable weight of an elector's vote from one electoral district to the other. Thus, in the north each elector could express in 1974 nine electoral votes, in the east six, in the centre twenty, in the south twenty-four – corresponding to the number of seats in each district.

For the sake of completeness 1974 should include the SDP (Social Democratic Party): 276,000 votes and 10·1 per cent of the vote.

Table 8.3  *Regional Breakdown of Electoral Results (Luxembourg has four electoral districts)*

| | | South District (%) | East District (%) | Centre District (%) | North District (%) |
|---|---|---|---|---|---|
| 1959 elections | KPL | 15·3 | no candidate | 4·0 | no candidate |
| | CSV | 33·0 | 19·6 | 37·5 | 47·4 |
| | LSAP | 40·2 | 21·6 | 30·8 | 28·8 |
| | DP | 10·2 | 28·8 | 27·7 | 23·8 |
| 1964 elections | KPL | 17·0 | 3·0 | 9·0 | 2·5 |
| | CSV | 29·8 | 46·4 | 34·1 | 45·6 |
| | LSAP | 41·8 | 25·1 | 33·7 | 33·1 |
| | DP | 5·3 | 19·4 | 16·5 | 15·6 |
| 1968 elections | KPL | 22·0 | 5·1 | 9·4 | 4·1 |
| | CSV | 31·8 | 47·6 | 36·6 | 46·4 |
| | LSAP | 35·8 | 22·7 | 28·3 | 30·1 |
| | DP | 10·1 | 23·9 | 25·2 | 19·1 |
| 1974 elections | KPL | 15·8 | 2·8 | 5·1 | 2·8 |
| | CSV | 25·5 | 36·6 | 27·6 | 40·7 |
| | LSAP | 35·2 | 17·4 | 23·5 | 20·6 |
| | DP | 13·5 | 26·3 | 34·5 | 22·7 |
| | SDP | 9·5 | 16·9 | 7·1 | 12·8 |

## NOTES

1 See notes to Table 8.2. Electors have as many votes as there are seats. They may give all their votes to one list (cumulation) or some of their votes may be transferred to one or more named candidates on another list (panachage).
2 All party names are in the Luxembourg dialect. For European purposes they are usually cited by the French titles as in chart on pp. 276–7 below.

## BIBLIOGRAPHY

For election results consult the *Bulletin du Statec,* nos 7–8, 1974. For a general description of the Luxembourg political system, see Michel Delvaux, *Structures socio-politiques du Luxembourg* (Luxembourg, Institut Universitaire International Luxembourg, 1977); Gilbert Trausch, *Le Luxembourg a l'epoque contemporaine* (Luxembourg, Editions Bourg-Bourger, 1975). For an analysis of political parties in their environment, cf. Mario Hirsch, 'Remarques sur les clivages politiques et sociaux au Luxembourg', *d'Letzeburger Land,* 30 August, 6 September and 13 September 1974.

# 9
# The Netherlands

## HANS DAALDER

### THE TRADITIONAL PARTY SYSTEM

For half a century after the arrival of universal suffrage in 1917, five parties dominated the Dutch political system. Three of these were religious parties: the Calvinist Anti-Revolutionary Party (ARP, founded in 1879), the equally orthodox Protestant Christian Historical Union (CHU, established in 1908) and the Roman Catholic Party (called since 1946 the Katholieke Volkspartij or KVP). The two others: the Liberals (since 1948 under the name Volkspartij voor Vrijheid en Democratie or VVD) and the Socialists (organised since 1946 in the Partij van de Arbeid, PvdA = Labour Party) represented the more secular strata of the population. Of these parties, the ARP and the PvdA were typical mass parties. So to a lesser extent was the Roman Catholic Party, although the presence of a church hierarchy provided alternative organisational structures for Catholic life. These mass parties had developed during the beginning of democratisation in the late nineteenth and early twentieth centuries as part of wider emancipationist movements of fundamentalist Calvinists, Catholics and the secularised part of the working class respectively. The other two movements of Liberals and Christian Historicals had historically been closer to the dominant secular and orthodox Dutch Reformed elites of the nineteenth century; they had organised mainly in reaction to the effective challenge of the other political movements and they did so too little and too late to weather fully what La Palombara, Weiner and others have called 'the crisis of participation' (La Palombara and Weiner, 1966). For descriptions in English of Dutch political developments, see Daalder, 1955 and 1966; Lijphart, 1968 and 1975; Baehr, 1971; and Irwin, 1977. For more detailed if schematic historical surveys in Dutch see Daalder, 1958, and Lipschits, 1977.)

In the interwar and post-1945 periods the Dutch party system showed certain peculiar traits. Each main system party had its own, relatively stable electoral clientèle. The Catholic Party was supported by almost all Catholics in the country. As the Catholics numbered some 35–40 per cent of the population in this period, this made their party the largest single Dutch party, generally comprising close to one-third of the Dutch electorate and the Lower House seats. The Anti-Revolutionaries mobilised almost all adherents of the smaller Gereformeerde Kerken (some 7 per cent of the population), and a sizeable section of the orthodox members of the Dutch Reformed Church (which declined, however, from 41 per cent in 1920 to 28 per cent in 1960). Most other orthodox believers in that church supported the Christian Historical Union. Anti-Revolutionaries and Christian Historicals jointly tended to obtain from one-fifth to one-quarter of the national vote. Non-fundamentalist Protestants organised in the Dutch Reformed Church and in some minor nonconformist church communities, as well as a rapidly growing number of agnostics (7·8 per cent in 1920, 18·4 per cent in 1960) supported the Liberals and the Socialists. The Liberals had fallen from the dominant position they had occupied before the advent of universal suffrage; since the 1930s they have attracted less than 10 per cent of the national vote. The Socialists had close to a quarter of the vote in the interwar period. They edged upwards in the 1950s, and during two elections in 1952 and 1956 they wrested the front position from the Catholics, but subsequently fell back again, to a nadir of 23·5 per cent in 1967.

The religious parties (who from the late nineteenth century onwards had struggled jointly for the full recognition and equitable financial support for religious schools) always had a majority in Parliament between 1918 and 1967. Provided they did not fall out with one another, they could determine the composition of cabinets. In these circumstances Liberals and Socialists inevitably became 'junior partners' in cabinet coalitions. Unless they chose to stay in a voluntary or imposed ghetto position (as the Socialists perforce had to do on the national level until as late as 1939), they had to beg favour from the religious parties. The majority position of the religious parties did much to minimise whatever anti-clerical proclivities Liberals or Socialists might have had earlier. After 1952 they came to rival one another as alternative – and to some degree also as alternating – suitors of the religious parties.

The very stable relations among the main system parties tended to lead to relatively centrist and depoliticised policy-making processes in the Netherlands (Daalder, 1955 and 1964; Lijphart, 1968). Ideological conflict was defused as much as possible by leaving divisive issues to highly autonomous decisions within each of the separate ideological subcultures of Catholics, Calvinists and Socialists (the Liberals occupying a secure position in Dutch society without the need for separate large-scale autonomous social organisations). Between the various groups careful compromises were elaborated on the basis of expert advice, in a rapidly growing number of collegial advisory bodies, in which all groups tended to be proportionally represented.

The policy of leaving decisions to each *famille spirituelle* reinforced their organisational structures. Parties were therefore largely the visible sentinels of complex social systems. It was their task to defend a variety of organised subcultural interests, to see to it that these obtained equitable subventions and for the rest to make sure that the autonomy of subcultural interests was safeguarded. Given the stability of the system, elections tended to be incidents, rather than decisive moments. They offered an opportunity for marginal adjustments of the balance of forces in the cabinet and in other pinnacles of power. But they did not affect the underlying checks and guarantees of the system, which was characterised by constant bargaining on the basis of recognised positions rather than by mutually exclusive choices, alternate electoral mandates or drastic governmental upsets (for an excellent analysis, see *The Politics of Accommodation*, Lijphart, 1968).

## THE DISARRAY OF THE RELIGIOUS SUBCULTURES

In the 1960s fundamental cracks appeared in the Catholic and Calvinist subcultures, which drastically affected their once seemingly impregnable position. One factor was the undoubted success of the process of subcultural emancipation and segmentation itself. Claims that had once been obtained only as a result of bitter fights of principle, now tended to be honoured by routinised procedures. This dampened the strong sense of ideological fervour and solidarity which had characterised the earlier period. In addition, considerable changes occurred in the outlook of many religious leaders, whether clergy or laity. A strong concentration on transcendental values – and on the need of all the faithful to observe commands that themselves went unquestioned – gave way to a new concern with the problems of the contemporary world. Inevitably this created controversy, both on the merit of particular political issues and on the specific role the various churches should play in political matters. Dissension replaced erstwhile absolutes, and religious unity and social control weakened. As leaders became locked in conflict, masses began to waver between fundamentalist reaction, intellectual disorientation and a growing indifference in religious matters. These developments were reinforced by large-scale changes in the means of social communication. The new electronic mass media broke the information control which the churches, the schools and the printed press had tended to exercise. Increased social and physical mobility did likewise. This in turn had a far-reaching effect on the family; once the basis of the process of ideological insulation, the family became increasingly less effective as an agency of political socialisation. At the same time, the organisational structures of the religious subcultures tended to fall into disarray. Notably in the Catholic fold, many institutions (including mass media and interest organisations) broke away to a new 'independence' which consciously de-emphasised former religious bonds. Some organisations broke down. Others eventually federated or fused with non-religious organisations (as did the Catholic Trade Union Federation which federated with the Socialist Unions in 1975), or sought solace in a federation with Protestant interests.

As a net result, Catholic and Calvinist voters spread their sympathies increasingly among different parties. The combined strength of the three major religious parties (KVP, ARP and CHU) fell in four successive elections, from 49·2 per cent in 1963 to 44·5 per cent in 1967, to 36·7 per cent in 1971 and 31·3 per cent in 1972 (see also Table 9.2). Survey data for the 1960s and early 1970s reveal a massive drop in church attendance and a great decline in voting for religious parties not only among the non-observant or less-observant Catholics and Protestants, but also among those who continued to attend church (figures in Wolinetz, 1973 and 1975; Miller and Stouthard, 1975). This drop was particularly characteristic of the new age cohorts which in a period of ten years changed from a 60 per cent preference for the religious parties to 20 per cent or less (Daalder, 1974). Some voters bolted from the main religious system parties to religious-inspired splinter movements on the Left (notably the Politieke Partij Radicalen or PPR, which originated from a left split from the KVP in 1968). Others moved to the fundamentalist Right, where by 1977 as many as three Calvinist and one integralist Catholic Party splinter parties divided less than 5 per cent of the national vote. Others again began to vote for parties not tied to any specific religious creed. A study of the religious floating vote suggests that rather than voting for the established non-religious parties, many of these voters found it easier in the beginning to vote for new parties in the political market, notably for the Poujadist-oriented Peasant Party (Boerenpartij or BP) which obtained three of the one hundred and fifty seats of Parliament in 1963 and seven in 1967 and for Democrats '66 (D'66) which first contested a national election in 1967. But by 1972 the older Socialist PvdA and Liberal VVD had also become legitimate alternatives (Dittrich, 1975).

## ANTI-SYSTEM REBELLIONS

Concurrently, new groups began to rebel against the traditional operative ideals of the Dutch political system. Some of these were emphatically anti-system in orientation. Thus, the Boerenpartij voiced strong *antidirigiste* feelings, which appealed in particular to peasants and shopkeepers squeezed by the effects of economic rationalisation. After 1965 a new anarchist intelligentsia also appeared on the scene. It achieved worldwide fame in the Provo movement, which flourished in the wake of nervous elite reactions in 1966 at the time of the controversial marriage of the Crown Princess Beatrix to Claus von Amsberg, a German diplomat who had been a member of the Hitler Jugend and the German Wehrmacht in his youth. The Provo movement itself soon passed: a late spluttering in the Amsterdam municipal elections of ·1970 when its *Kabouterpartij* obtained five out of forty-five council seats proved ephemeral and suicidal. But ideological beliefs about the innate evil of authority and the need to substitute direct decision making for institutionalised representative rule spread to many circles, including notably the universities and the mass media.

Within the parties' arena, the establishment of Democrats '66 exercised a more immediate effect. Launched in Amsterdam in 1966, not long after Provo, by a group of young intellectuals, it campaigned in 1967 on a simple programme of institutional reform: direct election of the prime minister, the replacement of proportional representation by a district system with one or only few members, and the severance of the nexus of cabinet and Parliament which should secure 'open politics' and provide clear checks and controls. At its first try D'66 in 1967 won seven seats. Polls showed a massive further bandwagon effect. At first the new party proclaimed a non-ideological, pragmatic stance, aiming at the break-up of the traditional party system, but in practice, it found itself drawn increasingly to the Socialists with whom it shared the opposition benches during the Parliaments of 1967–71 and 1971–2. Once the Socialists had accepted a number of their programme points, D'66 agreed in 1971 to enter into a formal pact with the PvdA. Its ready acceptance of the Socialist embrace proved almost fatal for the new party; although the party gained four

Table 9.1  *The Political Composition and Parliamentary Support of Dutch Cabinets, 1963–1977*

| Prime Minister | Period | Seat Number of Parties Who Had Ministers in the Cabinet | | | | | | | | Total Seats |
|---|---|---|---|---|---|---|---|---|---|---|
| | | PPR | PvdA | D'66 | DS'70 | KVP | ARP | CHU | VVD | |
| V. G. Marijnen (KVP) | 24 June 1963 to 14 April 1965 | | | | | 50 | 13 | 13 | 16 | 92 |
| J. M. L. Th. Cals (KVP) | 14 April 1965 to 22 November 1966 | | 43 | | | 50 | 13 | | | 106 |
| J. Zijlstra (ARP)[1] | 22 November 1966 to 5 April 1967 | | | | | 50 | 13 | | | 63 |
| P. J. S. de Jong (KVP) | 5 April 1967 to 6 July 1971 | | | | | 42 | 15 | 10 | 17 | 84 |
| B. W. Biesheuvel (ARP)[2] | 6 July 1971 to 11 May 1973 | | | | 8 | 35 | 13 | 10 | 16 | 82 |
| J. M. den Uyl (PvdA)[3] | 11 May 1973 to 19 December 1977 | 7 | 43 | 6 | | 27 | 14 | | | 97 |
| A. A. M. van Agt (CDA) | 19 December 1977– | | | | | 49[4] | | | 28 | 77 |

*Notes:*

[1] Caretaker government pending new elections held on 15 February 1967.

[2] The two DS'70 ministers resigned on 18 July 1972; the rest of the cabinet remained in office until after new elections the Den Uyl Cabinet had been formed.

[3] The Den Uyl Cabinet fell on 22 March 1977 due to internal disagreements. It served as caretaker government until new elections on 25 May 1977 and then throughout the long period of coalition bargaining which followed, before the entry of the Van Agt Cabinet.

[4] In November–December 1977 seven deputies voted against accepting a formal parliamentary tie to the cabinet.

seats in 1971 climbing to eleven in all, it did less well than earlier polls had led them to expect, and in the following election year, D'66 lost almost half its strength. In 1973, some of its members joined a new Left-oriented government (for a list of government coalitions between 1963 and 1977 see Table 9.1). The party seemed to have lost all electoral support in the provincial elections of 1974, and was only revived before the 1977 elections through a combination of grass-roots action, a new leader and a conscious de-emphasis of special links with the Socialists.

Possibly of more lasting importance than the challenges represented by the Peasant Party, the anarchist intelligentsia and Democrats '66 respectively, was the New Left movement within the Socialist PvdA. In the *annus mirabilis* of 1966, a number of intellectuals in the universities and the mass media joined in a loosely structured but effectively organised group called Nieuw Links (Wolinetz, 1975; Wolters 1977; see also Van den Berg and Molleman, 1974). They held a series of meetings and published some radical pamphlets, calling for a change in the policies, the strategies and the leadership of the PvdA. Profiting from a climate of malaise within the PvdA, which suffered heavy electoral losses in 1966 and 1967, the group mobilised strong support. With the aid of often newly recruited party activists it scored a number of important successes in party congresses, and in a few years it captured a majority in the party executive, including the party chairmanship. Many older leaders and party stalwarts met the challenge with diffidence. While some sought to oppose Nieuw Links, others chose to go along whether grudgingly or enthusiastically. Some showed an unmistakable fear for attack in the mass media. Many argued that one should keep in touch with the 'young'. Some former leaders chose to withdraw silently. But in 1970 conflicts about nominations and electoral and coalition strategies to be followed in municipal elections led to a split-off of right-wing Socialists who formed a new party Democratic-Socialists '70 (DS'70). The new party received a boost when Willem Drees Jr – former director of the budget, the son and namesake of the popular elder statesman of the Socialist Party, Willem Drees Sr, who had been prime minister of four cabinets between 1948 and 1958 – agreed to become its leader. The DS'70 party ran against Nieuw Links, and in favour of a policy of strong retrenchment of public expenditures in the Lower House elections of 1971. At its first try, it obtained over 5 per cent of the vote and eight seats. It entered the cabinet almost immediately afterwards as an ally of the three religious parties and the Liberals (see Table 9.1). But an internal conflict in that cabinet resulted in its ousting in 1972 and in new elections at which DS'70 lost two of its eight seats. Squeezed in an uneasy position of opposition with the Liberals, its visibility declined. Conflict within its parliamentary group in 1975 dealt it a further blow from which it would not revive: returned as a single representative in the 1977 elections, its leader Drees soon resigned his parliamentary seat.

Radical forces were active not only in the Socialist PvdA, but also in parties to the left of it. They became prominent in the Pacifist-Socialist Party which since its establishment in 1957 had wavered between revolutionary socialism and old-time pacifism, finding a ready target in NATO, the atomic bomb and American policy in Vietnam. The party scored some heavy electoral gains in local elections in 1966 when it voted against parliamentary approval of the marriage of the Crown Princess and embraced the principle of republicanism. But it did not succeed in consolidating these gains for long against the competition from Socialists and Communists, joined after 1967 by Democrats '66 and by the left-Catholics and left-Protestants of the Radicals (PPR). The Communist Party edged upwards in each successive election between 1963 and 1972, seeking to exploit proletarian sentiment against the other left parties which were increasingly dominated by intellectuals. But the Communist Party remained weak and isolated. After turmoil broke out in the Dutch universities in 1969, the party recruited new members among radical academic staff and students. But this did not prevent a dramatic electoral reversal in 1977, when the Communists lost five of their seven seats.

New Left activities within the Socialist PvdA, as well as in minor parties including the PPR and the Pacifist-Socialists as well as non-party groups, made for a new, radical ideological tone in Dutch politics. A strong distrust of existing institutions went together with a great belief in the need and promises of 'direct action' tactics. Within the Socialist Party, a new emphasis was given to the party 'base', as represented by the local party activists. A need was proclaimed to control representatives, by new rules on nomination, by tying elected politicians to party programmes and congress decisions, and if need be, by instituting the possibility of intraparty recall. In their relation to other parties, New Left activists tended to have a strong distrust of the existing system parties. If numerical relations made coalitions imperative, these should be tied to the strictest possible conditions lest they impair ideological principles. In general, there was a strong inclination to prefer coalitions with parties to the left of the Socialists: if such coalitions did not have a majority at the national level, they could muster sufficient strength in provincial and local councils (see Wolters, 1977). And even at the national level, it was argued, a seemingly intransigent stance could make for clear electoral positions which might eventually result in an independent electoral mandate.

## SYSTEM PARTIES AND MINOR PARTIES

In 1963 the number of parties represented in the Dutch Lower House rose from eight to ten. This figure rose to eleven in 1967, and to fourteen in 1971 and 1972. Various conclusions can be drawn from Table 9.2.

(1) There was a strong decline in the aggregate strength of the five main system parties between 1963 and 1971. Although this was mainly due to the sharp losses of the Catholics and the Christian Historicals, the Socialists also suffered in the beginning of the period, while the Liberals remained stationary. In 1972 the latter trend was reversed: Socialists and Liberals won more than the religious system parties lost.
(2) Although the Communist Party increased its strength somewhat at every election between 1963 and 1972, the Pacifists tended to lose, making for little variation in the 5–6 per cent vote to the left of the PvdA.
(3) Between 1967 and 1972 the fundamentalist religious parties increased their strength somewhat, until they reached close to 5 per cent in 1972.
(4) The Peasant Party and other right-wing movements and interest parties reached their high point in 1967, but declined ever since.
(5) The major initial beneficiaries from the decline of the religious parties tended to be the three new parties: D'66, the Radicals (PPR) and DS'70. Of these only D'66 was to maintain itself successfully over three elections

In interpreting Table 9.2, at least three external factors must be taken into account. First, the Dutch electoral system sets an exceedingly low electoral threshold for new parties: since the increase of the number of the Lower House from 100 to 150 seats in 1956 the minimum requirement to qualify for a seat has been as little as $\frac{1}{150}$ of the national vote (Daalder, 1975). Hence, fragmentation in the electorate was immediately translated into fragmentation in the legislature. Secondly, the traditional requirement to appear at the ballot box was dropped in 1970 (Irwin, 1974). This probably adversely affected the strength of certain parties (in particular the Catholics, the left parties, and the Boerenpartij). Thirdly, the voting age was lowered in 1967 from 23 to 21, and again in 1972 to 18. Thus, a sizeable number

Table 9.2  *Percentage Strength of Dutch Political Parties, Lower House Elections, 1963–1977*

| | 1963 | 1967 | 1971 | 1972 | 1977 |
|---|---|---|---|---|---|
| **I  System Parties** | | | | | |
| **(a) Religious parties** | | | | | |
| KVP (Catholics) | 31·9 | 26·5 | 21·8 | 17·7 | — |
| ARP (Protestant) | 8·7 | 9·9 | 8·6 | 8·8 | — |
| CHU (Protestant) | 8·6 | 8·1 | 6·3 | 4·8 | — |
| Total religious system parties (in 1977 = CDA) | 49·2 | 44·5 | 36·8 | 31·3 | 31·9 |
| **(b) Non-religious parties** | | | | | |
| PvdA (Socialists) | 28·0 | 23·6 | 24·6 | 27·3 | 33·8 |
| VVD (Liberals) | 10·3 | 10·7 | 10·3 | 14·6 | 18·0 |
| Total non-religious system parties | 38·3 | 34·3 | 34·9 | 41·9 | 51·8 |
| **Total System Parties** | 87·5 | 78·7 | 71·6 | 73·2 | 83·7 |
| **II  Minor Parties** | | | | | |
| **(a) Old Left parties** | | | | | |
| CPN (Communists) | 2·8 | 3·6 | 3·9 | 4·5 | 1·7 |
| PSP (Pacifist-Socialists) | 3·0 | 2·9 | 1·4 | 1·5 | 0·9 |
| Total | 5·8 | 6·5 | 5·3 | 6·0 | 2·7 |
| **(b) Dissident religious parties** | | | | | |
| SGP (Calvinists) | 2·3 | 2·0 | 2·4 | 2·2 | 2·1 |
| GPV (Calvinists) | 0·7 | 0·9 | 1·6 | 1·8 | 1·0 |
| RKPN (Catholics) | | | | 0·9 | 0·4 |
| Total[1] | 3·0 | 2·9 | 4·0 | 4·9 | 4·1 |
| **(c) Non-religious right-wing parties** | | | | | |
| BP (Peasants) | 2·1 | 4·8 | 1·1 | 1·9 | 0·8 |
| Total[1] | 3·6 | 7·4 | 4·3 | 3·0 | 1·2 |
| **(d) New parties, gaining a place in the system** | | | | | |
| D'66 (Democrats '66) | | | 6·8 | 4·1 | 5·4 |
| PPR (Radicals) | | | 1·8 | 4·8 | 1·7 |
| DS'70 (Democratic Socialists '70) | | | 5·3 | 4·1 | 0·7 |
| Total | | 4·5 | 13·9 | 13·1 | 7·7 |

Note:

of young age cohorts were added to the electorate. Judging from survey data, they showed a disproportionate preference for the smaller parties, notably those on the Left.

## THE LOSS OF POSSIBLE MAJORITY POSITIONS AND THE NEW COMPLEXITIES OF COALITION BUILDING

Figure 9.1 shows how the three major religious parties lost their traditional parliamentary majority in 1967. In the following election of 1971, the coalition of the three religious system parties and the liberal vvd also lost its majority; they declined further in 1972. Although the combined Left parties increased their total strength in 1971 and again in 1972, they remained far short of an independent majority. Since 1967 the Socialists have ogled the possibility of an exclusive coalition with the Anti-Revolutionary Party, or have hoped for a sufficiently sizeable split in the Catholic Party. But when a split came in 1968 through the walk-out of the Radicals (PPR), this new ally proved too weak and too fickle to muster the required parliamentary strength.

Complicated political arithmetic ensued, in which the minor parties were increasingly taken into account. Thus, the support of DS'70 offered a temporary respite for the main religious parties and the Liberals in 1971. The Socialists entered into formal coalition compacts with Radicals and D'66 in 1971 and 1972. Some Left militants began to think in terms of a popular front with Communists and Pacifists even though such a support would not help the progressive parties to a majority either. Mirroring this hope for an exclusive coalition, a few leaders of the Liberals and the religious parties began to speculate in turn on support from the fundamentalist splinters on their Right.

Strategic reasoning was further complicated by a possible conflict between electoral and government coalition politics. The electoral losses of the religious parties changed the position of Socialists and Liberals towards them. If the former rock-like position of the main religious parties had forced Socialists and Liberals into moderate stances, the latter now saw opportunities for electoral gains in a new militancy. Socialists and Liberals thus became tacit allies in a non-zero sum electoral game at the expense of the religious parties. Although they remained dependent on a post-election coalition with the religious parties for the formation of cabinets, they had every incentive to polarise the vote at election time. Notably, the Socialist PvdA therefore adopted a series of new political stratagems in the late 1960s.

These new stances had their origin in certain traumatic events during the Parliament of 1963–7. During that Parliament two

Figure 9.1    *The composition of the Dutch Lower House, 1963–1977 (number of seats 150)*

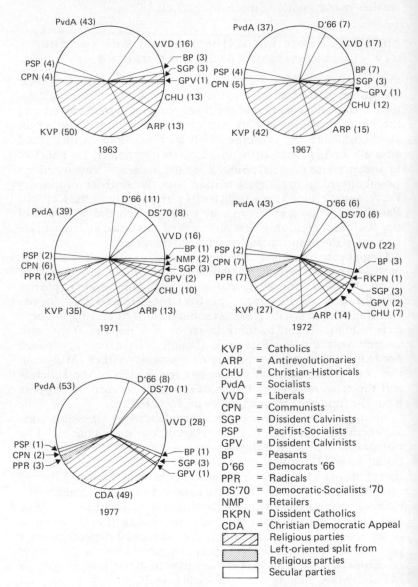

*renversements des alliances* took place. First, in 1965 a coalition of the religious parties and the Liberals gave way to a coalition of Socialists, Catholics and Anti-Revolutionaries (see Table 9.1). This coalition was broken up in turn by a Catholic parliamentary vote in 1966 against a tax proposal of the Socialist minister of finance. The latter caused great resentment among the Socialists who henceforth came to insist that in future no intermediate cabinet change should be allowed without an appeal to the electorate, and that democratic doctrine required that the electorate be allowed to vote on a coalition and cabinet programme presented before an election rather than afterwards.

Under New Left pressure, the Socialist Party Congress passed a resolution in 1969 declaring that the PvdA would not join in a future coalition with the Catholic Party, unless that party changed its leadership and opted for a Left-oriented coalition before election time. The Catholics and the two orthodox Protestant parties were not willing to meet such demands, not least through fear of losing votes to the Liberals on their right. The Left parties then mounted a strong attack on the cabinet of Liberals and religious parties, culminating in the presentation at the elections of 1971 of a rival slate of ministers and an elaborate cabinet programme of their own. Although this Left coalition gained votes, they could not prevent the return of a cabinet composed of the religious parties, the Liberals and DS'70. But when this new coalition fell over internal conflicts after little more than a year, new elections took place in 1972. Again the three Left parties presented a rival ministerial team and a cabinet programme entitled *Keerpunt '72* (Turning Point 1972). Both the Left and the Liberals gained ground at the expense of the religious parties, but the fifty-six seats of the Left coalition still fell far short of the majority point of the Lower House.

The Left parties had declared *Keerpunt* unalterable, and had formally rejected the idea of post-election negotiations, given the continued refusal of the religious parties to embrace them before election time. Interparty relations thus led to a complete deadlock. After an unprecedented 164 days of interparty negotiations a cabinet was formed in 1973 under the prime ministership of the Socialist leader J. M. den Uyl, comprising ten ministers of the Left parties, four Catholics and two Anti-Revolutionaries. It had a hybrid character: while the Left parties declared that they regarded the cabinet as a normal parliamentary formation, Catholics and Anti-Revolutionaries only agreed to 'suffer' it for lack of a real alternative. The cabinet programme was based both on the Left *Keerpunt*-manifesto *and* on the election plank of the joint religious parties, with an elaborate protocol to harmonise points of conflict between these rival programmes.

The Den Uyl Cabinet was to last almost its full parliamentary period, but fell shortly before the May 1977 elections on internal disagreement between the Left ministers and ministers of the religious parties. The cabinet negotiations of 1972–3 had resulted in a severance of Catholics and Anti-Revolutionaries who went along with the Den Uyl Cabinet, and the Christian Historicals who opposed it. The Socialists had hoped to push their advantage further by forcing also a split between Left-oriented Catholics and Calvinists and their more conservative brethren. Instead, resentment at their second-rate status *vis-à-vis* the Den Uyl Cabinet became a powerful impetus in the decision of the three chief religious parties to join forces for the 1977 elections, and to enter these with one common list, labelled the *Christen-Democratisch Appèl (CDA)*. The list was headed by the outgoing Catholic minister of justice, A. A. M. van Agt. The ARP, KVP and CHU continued to exist as separate parties, and controlled their own nominations for the joint list, but with the intention of forming one parliamentary group after the election.

The new formation showed considerable strength in public opinion polls in the winter of 1976–7 (de Hond, 1977), producing jittery reactions from the Left parties. Militant elements in the Socialist PvdA and the Radical Party (PPR) attempted to impose new pre-election conditions, but their tactics were deflated by the premier Den Uyl. In the end, the Socialists committed themselves before the elections took place to the idea of a normal parliamentary coalition with the CDA, provided Den Uyl could remain prime minister in a cabinet in which Left ministers had at least half the seats, and provided the Socialists and the PPR jointly would retain at least the same number of parliamentary seats as they had had in 1972. D'66 had already decided to go it alone, and the PPR congress eventually refused the idea of a post-election government responsibility with the CDA altogether. The May 1977 elections were thus fought by the Socialists on their own, under the slogan 'Elect the Prime Minister'. The results looked a massive personal triumph for Den Uyl. The PvdA climbed from forty-three to fifty-three seats, largely at the expense of the Communists, the Radicals (PPR) and the Pacifist-Socialists.

## THE ELECTIONS OF 1977; THE NEW FOUR-PARTY SYSTEM

The elections of May 1977 thus brought a drastic reversal of the earlier trend towards fragmentation of the Dutch party system. The three religious parties had joined in one list, and for the first time since 1963 they won votes (even though their gains were slight: one seat for a rise in votes from 31·3 to 31·9 per cent). Both Socialists and Liberals increased their vote strongly: the PvdA went up from 27·3 to 33·8 per cent (a gain of ten seats), and the Liberals from 14·6 to almost 18 per cent (a gain of six seats). Of the other parties, only D'66 did well, increasing from 4·2 to 5·3 per cent (a gain of two seats). The great losers were the Communists (a loss of five seats), the Radicals (a loss of four seats; they would have lost one more seat but for a new possibility of *apparentement* in the Dutch election system, see Lijphart, 1977), DS'70 (a loss of five seats), the Pacifist-Socialists (a loss of one of its two seats), the Peasant Party (BP, a loss of two seats), and two of the three fundamentalist religious parties (a loss of one seat each by a Catholic and a Calvinist splinter party). Even so eleven parties were returned to the Dutch Lower House, due to the very low electoral threshold. In fact, only four parties (CDA, PvdA, VVD and D'66) crossed the 5 per cent threshold valid in West Germany. One other party (the Calvinist SGP) barely crossed the 2 per cent threshold which an abortive Catholic parliamentary initiative in 1971 and again in 1976 would have imposed. If a 1 per cent threshold had existed (as a large majority at Parliament had demanded in the 1950s when the number of the Lower House was increased from 100 to 150 seats), only two more parties would have secured representation (the PPR and the Communists). As it was, no fewer than four parties (the BP, the Calvinist GPV, DS'70 and the Pacifist-Socialists) obtained one seat with less than 1 per cent of the national vote. Even so, a concentration of votes, together with the combination of the KVP, ARP and CHU in one list, meant a decrease in fractionalisation.

Various factors account for this dramatic reversal of earlier tendencies. The 1977 election was visibly about rival claims for power: a continuation of Socialist dominance in the cabinet exemplified by the premiership of Den Uyl, the challenge by the new CDA-combination for the position of largest party in a more equal cabinet coalition, an appeal by the Liberal VVD for a fundamental change in the composition of the cabinet. None of the smaller parties could rival such appeals. Only D'66 was successful in portraying itself as 'the reasonable alternative' for those who wanted to vote for a moderate Left without voting Socialist.

There were certain plebiscitary overtones in the 1977 campaign: the media gave extensive attention to the rival personalities heading the different lists (Den Uyl for the Socialists, Van Agt for the CDA, the young populist Hans Wiegel for the Liberal opposition, and the 'reasonable' new leader of the D'66 party, Jan Terlouw).

The other smaller parties had lost the freshness of their initial appeal, and did therefore not attract the same media exposure as they had done at earlier elections. Moreover, an incident in the last few days before the election reinforced the importance of Den Uyl and Van Agt in the mind of the voters: South Moluccan terrorists captured a train and a school to publicise their unpopular campaign for an independent Republic of the South Moluccas. Immediately all electioneering was stopped, freeing premier Den Uyl and minister of justice Van Agt for their momentous responsibilities in this terrifying affair.

The combination of the religious parties in one CDA list gave them a new credibility, their self-esteem was buttressed by the pre-election polls. As a new phenomenon in the parties arena, they were no longer tarred by the brush of doom. At the same time, Van Agt chose a style of campaigning (singling out the abortion issue and calling for a new Ethisch Reveil) which allowed the CDA to fight off the potential challenge of more fundamentalist religious splinter parties. Precinct poll data, collected on election day for NOS-Television by Intomart, made it clear that the CDA lost votes to D'66, won votes from both the Socialists and the Liberals, lost a few votes to the dissident fundamentalist parties, but did not do too well among either younger voters and newly mobilised former non-voters (*NOS-Intomart*, 1977; *De Nederlandse Kiezer* '77).

The deliberate mutual polarisation between the Socialists and the Liberals (as the alternative poles on the Left and the Right of the political spectrum) helped these parties to collect votes, which had once been dispersed among the smaller Left and Right parties. On balance, the Liberals also won votes from the Left parties, but this was more than compensated by the ability of Den Uyl to mobilise non-voters, and to increase the strength of the PvdA among young voters who had earlier tended to vote for more radical Left alternatives. As a result of these developments the Liberal VVD has become much more of a mass party. The VVD has sought to shed its former elitist image by posturing as the champion *par excellence* of the 'active working population' who do not wish to see their hard-earned income go in excessive public expenditures or social security payments.

While factors such as these made for a new image for the four larger parties, the smaller parties met with a turn of the tide. Some of them represented extreme ideological principles which were less attractive when the electorate was faced simultaneously with substantive fights between the larger parties. It was not only the 'fundamentalist' parties on the Left and the religious Right which declined, but also some of the new parties which appeared on the

Dutch party scene in the 1960s. As we saw, former voters of the religious parties originally tended to opt for new parties (like the BP, D'66, the PPR and DS'70), in preference to voting directly for the old Liberal and Socialist rival parties. However, once voters had begun to break away from traditional allegiances, the latter choice also became increasingly legitimate, and in the end visibly more effective. Ease of direct electoral traffic between the religious parties and Socialists and Liberals thus destroyed the special transit-function which some of the new parties had exercised at the beginning of the break-up of the religious sub-cultures.

## THE PERSISTENT DIFFICULTIES OF THE 'SIMPLIFIED' PARTY SYSTEM: THE CABINET NEGOTIATIONS OF 1977

After the elections of May 1977 a cabinet between Den Uyl's successful PvdA and a consolidated CDA seemed to be in the nature of things. However even five months of PvdA–CDA negotiations failed to bring this about. Instead, more than 200 days after the election, a cabinet was formed consisting of CDA and VVD, leaving Den Uyl on the opposition benches. The extraordinary coalition negotiations of 1977 revealed the importance of persistent strains between parties and within parties. They may be schematically explained as follows.

(1) *The position of parties on major issues.* Data drawn from a Leiden University survey among members of the Dutch Lower House (see Figure 9.2) present the average self-chosen position of the main parties on a number of important issues before the arrival of the Den Uyl Cabinet of 1973–7. Figure 9.2 shows that on all issues except abortion, members of the Lower House tended to arrange themselves in 1972 in a similar rank order, with the Socialists on one side, followed by D'66, then the three parties which were later to merge in the CDA, and finally the VVD on the other. On three issues (development aid, co-determination in industry and income differences) the members of the religious parties tended to see themselves as closer to the Socialists than to the Liberals; on one issue (the overall level of public expenditures and taxation) they chose a half-way position; and on two issues (defence and public order) they were on average closer to the Liberals. The seventh issue (abortion), on the other hand, ranged all secular parties against the religious parties, with the Catholics taking the most militant stand against freeing abortion.

Later developments were to substantiate these 1972 findings. The formation of the Den Uyl Cabinet in 1973 had represented

Figure 9.2 *Average Issue Positions of the Main Parties in the Dutch Lower House, 1972*

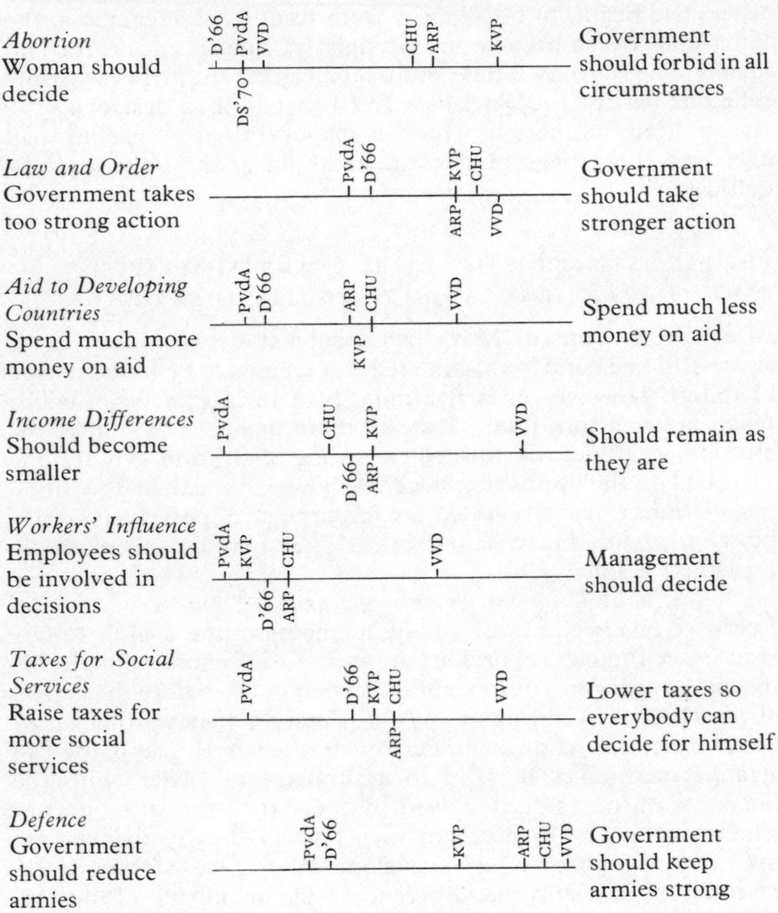
Abortion
Woman should decide
D'66
DS'70
PvdA
VVD
CHU
ARP
KVP
Government should forbid in all circumstances
Law and Order
Government takes too strong action
PvdA
D'66
KVP
ARP
CHU
VVD
Government should take stronger action
Aid to Developing Countries
Spend much more money on aid
PvdA
D'66
ARP
KVP
CHU
VVD
Spend much less money on aid
Income Differences
Should become smaller
PvdA
CHU
D'66
KVP
ARP
VVD
Should remain as they are
Workers' Influence
Employees should be involved in decisions
PvdA
KVP
D'66
CHU
ARP
VVD
Management should decide
Taxes for Social Services
Raise taxes for more social services
PvdA
D'66
KVP
ARP
CHU
VVD
Lower taxes so everybody can decide for himself
Defence
Government should reduce armies
PvdA
D'66
KVP
ARP
CHU
VVD
Government should keep armies strong

*Source:* Leiden University Survey among Members of Dutch Parliament, as reported in J. J. A. Thomassen, *Kiezers en Gekozenen in een Representatieve Democratie* (Samsom, Alphen, 1976), pp. 66*ff*., and in Galen A. Irwin and Jacques Thomassen, 'Issue consensus in a multi-party system: voters and leaders in The Netherlands', *Acta Politica*, no. 10, 1975, pp. 389–420. Members were asked to place themselves on nine-point scales, the scales on abortion, income differences and workers' influence being presented in reverse order. Individual positions were then averaged by party.

a clear victory for the progressive parties in the manning of ministerial posts but it did not solve divisions between the parties in Parliament and the ministers in the cabinet. Although the KVP and the ARP continued to maintain the Den Uyl Cabinet in office, important issues were resolved.

Removing the abortion issue from the political arena was in the common interest of Socialists and Liberals, as the issue adversely affected the future coalition possibilities of either party with the religious parties. A joint Socialist–Liberal parliamentary initiative foundered, however, on an Upper House vote in 1976 (in which the majority of the Liberal senators joined the senators of the religious parties in rejecting the Bill that had earlier been passed by the secular parties in the Lower House). However, even if it had passed the Upper House, the Bill would probably not have obtained the necessary *contraseign* from the Catholic minister of justice Van Agt – making his occupancy of that ministry a strong bone of contention in the later 1977 cabinet negotiations between PvdA and CDA.

On socioeconomic matters, four issues were to acquire explosive symbolic significance in the Den Uyl Cabinet: (a) the extension of the power of workers' councils in the running of industrial enterprises, (b) the allocation of profits (following a policy of wage restraint) to a national fund which would be mainly controlled by union representatives, (c) control over investments which in the view of the Socialists should be made subordinate to considerations of employment, the environment, the careful use of raw materials, and the interests of the Third World, and (d) control over land acquisition prices for urban development. As the years of the Den Uyl Cabinet passed by, Socialists inside and outside Parliament came to demand the passage of pertinent bills in these areas as proof that KVP and ARP were in fact willing to commit themselves in the eyes of the electorate to a progressive cabinet. Before the elections took place, the Den Uyl Cabinet fell. The new CDA entered tle elections without any formal commitment to any particular coalition.

(2) *Conflicting strategies in the 1977 cabinet negotiations.* Cabinet-making has traditionally been a period of clearance of sensitive issues in Dutch politics (requiring since 1946 an average fifty-five days of interparty bargaining before a new cabinet could be formed). In the exhilaration of their gain of the new seats in the election of 25 May 1977, the Socialists posed strong demands on the CDA: binding agreements should be reached on all four issues mentioned earlier before other points should be negotiated; the cabinet should be manifestly of a progressive character; to buttress this fact the Socialists should have at least one more cabinet seat

than the CDA, in addition to the premiership with its casting vote in case of ties. The CDA countered with the demand that the abortion issue should again be put on the cabinet agenda; this time a true parliamentary coalition of equal partners should be formed; and there should be absolute parity of the number of ministers of PvdA and CDA in the cabinet. In the struggle between PvdA and the CDA, D'66 was accepted as a third partner, although with some reluctance from the CDA. Coalition bargaining became an exceedingly long process. Three times Den Uyl asked the Queen to relieve him from a commission to investigate the possibility of forming a cabinet, when compromises could not be reached: first, on the union-controlled national profit-sharing fund, then on abortion, and finally on the division of cabinet posts amongst the three parties. Three times, successive *informateurs* cleared the way for a resumption of negotiations. Months went by with arduous nocturnal meetings. The tempers of the leading personalities became increasingly frayed. Finally, in October 1977 agreement was reached by the party leaders and the parliamentary parties both on a cabinet programme and on the division of cabinet seats. But by that time other actors had become increasingly involved.

(3) *The role of extra-parliamentary organs.* Both the national executive of the PvdA, and its Partijraad (a body of some hundred members empowered to take important decisions in the absence of a full party congress) became increasingly involved in the cabinet negotiations. On 25 October 1977 the parliamentary party voted thirty-five to fourteen to accept a proposal by a team of a Socialist and a CDA *informateur* to allocate ministerial portfolios as follows: seven seats including the premiership for the PvdA, seven for the CDA and two for D'66. The same evening the Partijraad rejected this compromise with fifty-three to thirty-five votes, demanding that the leader of the Socialist parliamentary group reopen negotiations. He refused and the next day the parliamentary party voted forty-three to five to persist in its agreement to the earlier formula subject to a final decision by a special party congress. After this vote, Den Uyl accepted for the fourth time a commission by the queen to form a cabinet. Yet, the possible threat of a negative decision by the party congress (made more likely by the ambiguous stand of a highly divided PvdA national executive) led Den Uyl to choose a very tough stand against the CDA. This became apparent in two ways: an attempt to regain exclusive control for the Socialists in important policy domains by a demand that Socialist under-secretaries be given extensive powers in departments allotted in principle to CDA ministers; and a refusal to accept the nomination of the former

leader of the Catholic group to the Ministry of Economic Affairs. These stratagems led to extensive counter-manoeuvres by the CDA parliamentary leaders, who consulted the chairmen of the three parties (KVP, ARP and CHU) which made up the CDA-federation. Finally, the CDA parliamentary group refused to accept Den Uyl's ultimative demands, one day before the special congress of the Socialist Party was to meet on 5 November 1977. Whilst this made the special PvdA congress a forlorn affair, it also implied an absolute *impasse* in the cabinet negotiations.

(4) *The search for alternative formulae.* A new Catholic *informateur* then successively checked out possibilities for any of the theoretical cabinet coalitions listed in Table 9.3.

Table 9.3 *The Attitudes of Dutch Parties towards possible Coalitions in November 1977, after five months of abortive negotiations for a cabinet of PvdA, D'66 and CDA*

|  | PvdA (53 Seats) | D'66 (8 Seats) | CDA (49 Seats) | VVD (28 Seats) | Theoretical Number of Seats in the Lower House of 150 Seats |
|---|---|---|---|---|---|
| 'National Cabinet' | No | No | Yes | Yes | 138 |
| Cabinet of the main secular parties | No | No |  | No | 89 |
| Cabinet of D'66, CDA and VVD |  | No | Yes | Yes | 85 |
| Cabinet of CDA and VVD |  |  | Possibly | Yes | 77 |

Only when all other options proved impossible, did the CDA parliamentary party agree to enter into cabinet negotiations with the VVD. Their two leaders (Van Agt and Wiegel) agreed on the outlines of a new cabinet programme within five days. But the CDA group in Parliament insisted on a large number of amendments. The Liberals went along with most changes. Even then, seven members of the CDA (six of ARP origin including the former ARP leader and now deputy-leader of the CDA, W. Aantjes) voted against accepting a formal parliamentary commitment to the new cabinet coalition which could therefore formally rely only on 70 out of 150 seats. The seven dissidents made it clear however that they would not oppose the coming about of a CDA–VVD Cabinet by voting for a motion of non-confidence which might be introduced by the new Left Opposition. The *informateur* also secured support in principle from the six deputies which the SGP, GPV, DS'70 and BP could muster. On this fragile parliamentary basis, Van Agt formed a new cabinet which entered into office on 19 December 1977 – almost seven months after the 'simplifying' elections had taken place.

These developments underline once more the vital place of the religious parties in the Dutch political spectrum as well as the importance of their internal divisions. The religious parties traditionally shunned clear choices, preferring to perform a balancing act between the Socialists on their left and the Liberals on their right. If the establishment of one CDA parliamentary group has restored their decisive role, it has also added the new difficulty, that the CDA had to accommodate the ambitions of three parties, not to speak of their party leaders who had earlier been used to wield independent authority. The immediate advantages of a minimum-size coalition were obvious for the CDA: in the new coalition with the Liberals, the CDA had the upper hand in numbers and apparently in weight, which was in strong contrast with the secondary status Den Uyl had seemed to grant them. But on the other hand, certain CDA politicians were not sanguine about the life chances of the narrowly-based CDA–VVD Cabinet. They argued that a coalition with the Socialists would have given the cabinet not only a stronger basis in Parliament, but also in the country at large at a time of foul economic weather. Their refusal to accept office in the new cabinet could also be interpreted by a desire to consider cabinet coalition games in a longer time-perspective.

PARTY MEMBERS AND PARTY FINANCES

In the most recent Dutch election study *(De Nederlandse Kiezer '77)* some 10 per cent of the population indicated that they were members of political parties. Table 9.4 – based on more precise data provided by the main parties directly – shows that this is a clear case of over-reporting, the actual number of party members being less than 5 per cent of those voting. Comparison with earlier figures (Baehr, 1969) reveals that there has been a sharp decline in the membership figures for all parties except the Liberal VVD which more than doubled its membership after becoming the main opposition party in 1973, and D'66 which was resuscitated from near-death in 1976. The decline in membership is partly due to better accounting by parties which introduced a more exact system of central registration of members in recent years and thereby enforced more precise and uniform membership criteria. But there has also been a very real exodus of members from most parties. In a 1971 Leiden University survey on political participation some 12 per cent of the population stated being presently a member of a political party; only a slightly lower percentage (8 per cent) said that they had once been member of a party but now were members no longer. There has been a relative decline in working-class party membership. Clearly, there was heightened political action – within and outside parties – in the wave of 'democratisation' movements in the 1960s, but it did not become any less elitist. It is noticeable that the older system parties have a higher percentage of working-class members than the new parties or the direct action groups.

The great number of parties, and the complexity of decision-making processes within each of them, make it impossible to analyse differences of structure in detail in this chapter (the general picture given in Baehr, 1969, is still valid, however). The most 'open' party in the past decade was D'66 which until 1977 allowed all registered party members to vote at its congresses. In contrast the CDA is as yet chiefly an 'indirect' party: it has one parliamentary group, but a federal executive and a federal assembly to which the three participating parties and only a few 'direct' members send representatives; but a full merger into one unified party is foreseen for 1980. Of the old parties the PvdA and the ARP continue to have the more active organisational life. Even in these parties only a small minority within the small minority of the voters who are party members tend to participate in all but the most unusual decisions. (However, the PvdA reported particularly active attendance at branch meetings shortly before the special party congress of November 1977; there was also a mass movement among members of the religious parties in favour of a common electoral list, when some leaders stalled the process of CDA-formation in 1975.) The KVP, CHU and VVD have traditionally been less active, although regional and sectional interests have tended to be prominent in nomination processes within the KVP; also within the CHU regional forces have been of importance.

Table 9.4 gives details about regular party finances, both for the parties' normal operating expenditure and their 1977 election funds. In a comparative perspective Dutch party politics are a very low-cost affair, the sum total of election expenses of all parties combined running below £1,000,000 in 1977, and their combined operating budgets not yet being £2,500,000 per annum. In judging these figures, it should be realised, however, that parties receive substantial support from the public purse, through subsidies for regular television and radio broadcasts, through special subsidies for their research institutes, and through considerable support for staff aid to their parliamentary groups on the budget of the Lower House.

Table 9.4    *Membership and Finances of Dutch Parties in 1977*

| | *Members* | | *Members as a % of Party Vote in May 1977* | *Size of Annual Budget in Thousand Guilders* | *Election Expenditures in 1977 in Thousand Guilders* |
|---|---|---|---|---|---|
| PvdA | 109,365 | | 3·9 | 4,200 | 1,552 |
| VVD | 92,263 | | 6·2 | 1,700 | ± 700 |
| KVP | ± 55,000 | ⎫ | | no data provided | ± 400 |
| ARP | ± 60,000 | ⎬ CDA | 5·4 | 1,900 | ± 500 |
| CHU | ± 28,000 | ⎭ | | 437 | ± 200 |
| D'66 | ± 7,600 | | 1·7 | 300 | ± 100 |

*Source :* Data provided in August–September 1977 by secretariats of the parliamentary party concerned.

### SOCIAL DIVISIONS AND PARTY CHOICE

Tables 9.5–9.11 contain information about social divisions in the Dutch electorate, and the way they translate into party choice. In the first six tables the total voting population is put at 100; these tables show how differences in sex, age, religion, religious practice, social class and rural–urban divisions affect political preferences. Table 9.11, on the other hand, is a summary table which presents the composition of the electorates of the main parties resulting from the earlier patterns of voter preference. Data have been drawn from a variety of sources: the actual vote, a massive precinct survey held for NOS-Television by Intomart on the day of the election, and the most recent Dutch National Election Survey undertaken by an Inter-University Working Group of political scientists *(De Nederlandse Kiezer '77)*. The latter study has many more variables, but many fewer respondents; it also substantially under-represents the vote for the Liberal VVD. Data on age and religion have therefore been taken from the Intomart study which permits a detailed breakdown also for the smaller parties. Data on sex, religious practice and social class, on the other hand, are from the National Election Study.

### Differences in sex

Table 9.5 shows a very substantial difference in the vote of men and women. Whereas both sexes gave their choice about proportionally to the PvdA, the religious parties and also D'66 attracted substantially more women. In contrast, many more men voted for the VVD than did women. Some observers have attributed this fact to the ambiguous stand of the VVD on the abortion issue (which might also help to explain the very substantial over-representation of women – presumably wishing to see abortion liberalised – in the D'66 electorate). The strong preference of women in comparison to men for the religious parties is in agreement with earlier and international findings.

Table 9.5    *Electoral Choice in 1977 by Sex (%)*

|  | PvdA | D'66 | CDA | VVD | Other | N |
|---|---|---|---|---|---|---|
| Men | 35·9 | 5·8 | 32·5 | 17·3 | 8·5 | (554) |
| Women | 35·6 | 7·6 | 38·0 | 11·0 | 7·8 | (607) |
| All | 35·8 | 6·7 | 35·5 | 14·0 | 6·7 | (1,161) |

*Source:  De Nederlandse Kiezer '77.*

### Differences in age

In Table 9.6, a breakdown is given of party preferences by age cohorts. It shows a clear break between the generations under and over 35: while a majority of those under 35 voted Left, less than 40 per cent of the older age cohorts did so. The combined column of votes for the religious parties shows the expected increase in voting for the religious parties as one moves up from younger to older age cohorts; but only the over 65s still gave a majority vote for the religious parties which as recently as 1963 had been characteristic for the whole electorate. The column for the VVD shows particular strength among those of middle age, with older and younger voters being less numerous. The smaller parties (notably those on the Left, but also BP and DS'70) had more strength among the youngest part of the electorate than among older voters who had been socialised into the traditional party system before the arrival of new contestants.

### Religion

Table 9.7 shows how the main religious groups are divided over the parties. The new CDA held one out of every two voters who considered themselves Catholics, about one out of three who considered themselves members of the Dutch Reformed Church, and almost two out of three of the more homogeneously orthodox Gereformeerden. The relative preference of the remaining voters from these church communities for the combined Left parties (including D'66) and the VVD tended to divide in a ratio of two to one. Of those not belonging to any church, a large majority had a Left preference.

Table 9.6  Reported Vote by Age Cohorts, 1977 (%)

| Age | CPN | PSP | PPR | PvdA | D'66 | Total Left Parties | CDA | SGP | GPV | Total Religious Parties | VVD | DS'70 | BP | Others | |
|---|---|---|---|---|---|---|---|---|---|---|---|---|---|---|---|
| 18–24 | 1·9 | 3·8 | 5·4 | 35·2 | 8·5 | 54·8 | 23·1 | 1·1 | 0·8 | 25·1 | 16·5 | 1·1 | 0·7 | 1·6 | 100·0 |
| 25–34 | 1·5 | 2·3 | 3·2 | 35·3 | 9·3 | 51·6 | 24·1 | 1·2 | 0·9 | 26·3 | 20·3 | 0·6 | 0·3 | 1·0 | 100·0 |
| 35–49 | 1·5 | 0·5 | 1·4 | 30·8 | 5·1 | 39·3 | 35·5 | 1·4 | 0·7 | 37·8 | 20·4 | 0·9 | 0·5 | 1·2 | 100·0 |
| 50–64 | 1·5 | 0·4 | 0·5 | 34·1 | 3·4 | 39·9 | 38·3 | 1·8 | 0·9 | 41·4 | 16·1 | 1·0 | 0·6 | 0·9 | 100·0 |
| 65 and over | 1·2 | 0·1 | 0·5 | 31·3 | 1·7 | 34·8 | 47·7 | 2·5 | 0·9 | 51·8 | 11·7 | 0·5 | 0·6 | 0·5 | 100·0 |
| Total sample | 1·6 | 1·4 | 2·2 | 33·5 | 5·8 | 44·5 | 32·9 | 1·5 | 0·8 | 35·5 | 17·5 | 0·8 | 0·5 | 1·0 | 100·0 |

*Note:*
N = 32,516.

*Source:* NOS-Intomart Precinct Survey, 25 May 1977.

Table 9.7 Percentage Reported Vote of Main Church and Non-Church Groups by Party, 1977 (%)

| Religious Group | CPN | PSP | PPR | PvdA | D'66 | Total Left Parties | CDA | SGP | GPV | Total Religious Parties | VVD | DS'70 | BP | Other | Total |
|---|---|---|---|---|---|---|---|---|---|---|---|---|---|---|---|
| Roman Catholic | 0·5 | 0·8 | 2·1 | 22·4 | 4·5 | 30·3 | 50·9 | 0·1 | 0·0 | 51·7 | 16·8 | 0·4 | 0·6 | 0·3 | 100·0 |
| Dutch Reformed | 0·6 | 0·4 | 1·8 | 34·4 | 5·8 | 43·3 | 30·3 | 2·3 | 0·6 | 33·7 | 20·7 | 1·1 | 0·8 | 0·8 | 100·0 |
| Gereformeerde kerken | 0·2 | 0·3 | 2·5 | 9·3 | 2·1 | 14·4 | 63·9 | 4·4 | 6·5 | 75·0 | 7·3 | 0·3 | 0·4 | 2·8 | 100·0 |
| Other | 1·2 | 1·2 | 2·3 | 30·3 | 7·8 | 42·8 | 16·3 | 11·9 | 2·3 | 30·6 | 19·0 | 1·4 | 0·7 | 5·5 | 100·0 |
| No church | 4·0 | 3·6 | 2·8 | 53·3 | 9·1 | 72·8 | 4·1 | 0·1 | 0·0 | 4·2 | 20·0 | 1·3 | 0·3 | 1·3 | 100·0 |
| Total | 1·6 | 1·4 | 2·2 | 33·5 | 5·8 | 44·5 | 32·9 | 1·5 | 0·8 | 35·5 | 17·5 | 0·8 | 0·3 | 1·0 | 100·0 |

*Note:*
N = 31,988.

*Source:* NOS-Intomart Precinct Survey, 25 May 1977.

Table 9.8 (drawn from the National Election Study which suggested a stronger attraction of the CDA for the Gereformeerden than the Intomart Survey revealed) controls the data on religious affiliation for church attendance: of those going to church at least once a month, two out of three Catholics, three out of four Gereformeerden and more than half of the Dutch Reformed voted CDA in 1977; the very substantial hold of the combined religious parties on observant religious voters is further shown by the fact that the relatively high percentages of preferences for 'other parties' in Table 9.8 masks in fact a very strong vote of observant Protestants for minor religious parties. Two factors should be borne in mind. First, church attendance has been slipping considerably in recent years: only 38 per cent of the respondents in the Dutch National Election Study reported going to church at least once a month in 1977 (against 51 per cent in 1968). Secondly, Table 9.8 shows that a substantial number of practising Catholics and Dutch Reformed voters had begun to

Table 9.8   *Reported Vote of Main Church Groups by Church Attendance, 1977 (%)*

|  | PvdA | D'66 | VVD | CDA | Other | N |
|---|---|---|---|---|---|---|
| All Catholics | 24 | 6 | 12 | 54 | 4 | (444) |
| Practising Catholics | 17 | 5 | 10 | 66 | 2 | (285) |
| All Dutch Reformed | 35 | 6 | 20 | 31 | 8 | (257) |
| Practising Dutch Reformed | 17 | 4 | 15 | 52 | 12 | (108) |
| All Gereformeerden | — | | 7 | 70 | 17 | (121) |
| Practising Gereformeerden | 5 | — | 3 | 75 | 17 | (108) |

*Source: De Nederlandse Kiezer '77*, unpublished data. 'Practising' are all those who report going to church at least once a month.

vote for the Socialist PvdA and the Liberal VVD. In contrast, very few non-church voters voted for the CDA, even though this new party formation sought to stress its openness and its particular merit as a party in the centre of Dutch politics. Given the relatively weak hold of the CDA on younger age cohorts (see Table 9.6), this implies an uphill fight for the CDA for the future.

The summary Table 9.11 illustrates these developments in yet another way: a quarter of both VVD and PvdA votes now regard themselves as Dutch Reformed; the VVD attracts as many as one-third, the PvdA a quarter of its voters from Catholic milieux. The same table also reveals the very clear interconfessional character of the CDA: fully 56 per cent of CDA voters were Catholics, and almost 40 per cent belonged to the two main Protestant parties.

*Social class*

The distribution of political preferences by social class in 1977 is presented in Table 9.9. The Dutch National Election Study used

Table 9.9   *Electoral Choice in 1977 by Self-Reported Social Class (%)*

| | PvdA | D'66 | CDA | VVD | Other | N |
|---|---|---|---|---|---|---|
| Upper, upper-middle and middle class | 23·8 | 8·3 | 37·3 | 23·1 | 7·2 | (568) |
| Upper-working class and working class | 48·9 | 4·9 | 33·7 | 4·4 | 7·8 | (525) |
| All | 35·9 | 6·7 | 35·7 | 14·2 | 7·5 | (1,093) |

*Source:  De Nederlandse Kiezer '77, p. 160, and unpublished data.*

a self-rating measure, containing five categories (upper class, upper-middle class, middle class, upper-working and working class) which have been dichotomised in Table 9.9 into two almost equal groups of 'upper and middle class' and 'all working class'. The strong showing of CDA amongst self-styled working-class voters reminds one of the deep roots which the parties composing the CDA have in Dutch history. The fact that five times as many Liberal voters describe themselves as middle class than as working class, shows that it has not succeeded in its deliberate attempt to woo working-class voters (see also Andreweg, 1977). D'66 also is much more strongly represented in the highest social echelons. The PvdA attracted almost half the self-styled working-class voters; if one adds the votes for other Left parties, about 52 per cent of the working class can be described as voting for one of the parties to the left of D'66 and CDA.

*Urban–rural divisions*

Table 9.10 gives a breakdown of the actual 1977 vote by various categories of residence. The pattern is familiar: a stronger share of the vote by the religious parties in rural communes than in larger cities, a reverse pattern for the PvdA and a strong showing of both D'66 and the VVD in the more well-to-do suburbs serving as dormitory towns. Inspection of Table 9.10 leads one to the conclusion, however, that all parties successfully compete for votes in all types of communities. Although time-series data (De Hond, 1977) reveal that the CDA parties have lost relatively more votes in the cities than in rural areas, they continue to obtain considerable support from city electorates. Conversely, VVD and PvdA combined outpoll the CDA parties in all types of communities,

Table 9.10    *Electoral Choice in 1977 by Rural–Urban Divisions ( " ₀)*

|  | PvdA | D'66 | CDA | VVD | Other | Total |
|---|---|---|---|---|---|---|
| **Rural communes** |  |  |  |  |  |  |
| (11·5"₀ of total vote) | 26·5 | 4·0 | 41·9 | 17·1 | 10·5 | 100·0 |
| **Rural-urbanising communes** |  |  |  |  |  |  |
| (21·2"₀ of total vote) | 28·4 | 4·0 | 41·9 | 15·1 | 11·6 | 100·0 |
| **Suburban communes** |  |  |  |  |  |  |
| (14·7"₀ of total vote) | 26·8 | 7·2 | 30·7 | 26·0 | 9·3 | 100·0 |
| **Cities below 100,000** |  |  |  |  |  |  |
| (25·9"₀ of total vote) | 36·6 | 5·5 | 30·2 | 17·1 | 10·6 | 100·0 |
| **Cities above 100,000** |  |  |  |  |  |  |
| (26.8"₀ of total vote) | 42·3 | 6·1 | 22·0 | 17·0 | 12·6 | 100·0 |
| Total | 33·8 | 5·4 | 31·9 | 18·0 | 10·9 | 100·0 |

*Source:* Actual vote on 25 May 1977, as calculated by *Algemeen Nederlands Persbureau,* The Hague.

including the aggregated rural ones. Although the VVD scores a relatively heavy vote in the suburbs, its strength there is not greater than that of the PvdA.

*Conclusion*

Table 9.11 brings together data on the composition of party electorates which result from the distribution of votes within the various social division categories discussed. The table shows definite differences in the social background of the different parties. These mirror historical differences in the way each party emerged. But over time, some differences have become less marked, notably religion which was at one time clearly the most important single factor in Dutch political life (Lijphart, 1974). Parties can rely less on traditional clienteles than they once did. They struggle nationwide, for all manner of strategic groups in the electorate: the young and the middle aged, the observant and the less religious, the working class and the middle class, town as well as country. There is thus a growing concern among party elites about voters' choice. At the same time no party has yet been able to claim an undiluted electoral mandate. Once the voting is over, coalition bargaining still decides on government and policies.

Table 9.11 *The Composition of the Electorate of the main Dutch Political Parties, 1977 (%)*

|  | PvdA | D'66 | CDA | VVD | Total Sample |
|---|---|---|---|---|---|
| *Sex* | | | | | |
| Men | 47·8 | 41·0 | 43·7 | 58·9 | 47·7 |
| Women | 51·9 | 59·0 | 56·1 | 41·1 | 52·1 |
| N | (416) | (78) | (412) | (163) | (1,282) |
| *Age* | | | | | |
| 18–24 | 19·0 | 25·9 | 12·8 | 16·8 | 18·1 |
| 25–34 | 25·3 | 37·2 | 17·7 | 27·4 | 23·9 |
| 35–49 | 23·5 | 21·7 | 27·8 | 29·3 | 25·5 |
| 50–64 | 20·9 | 11·8 | 24·2 | 18·6 | 20·5 |
| 65+ | 11·3 | 3·5 | 17·6 | 7·9 | 12·0 |
| N | (10,862) | (1,936) | (10,591) | (5,773) | (32,516) |
| *Religion* | | | | | |
| Roman Catholic | 24·7 | 27·3 | 55·9 | 34·2 | 36·3 |
| Dutch Reformed | 24·4 | 22·5 | 21·4 | 27·0 | 23·3 |
| Gereformeerde kerken | 2·6 | 3·1 | 17·5 | 3·7 | 9·0 |
| Other | 3·3 | 4·7 | 1·8 | 3·8 | 3·6 |
| No church | 45·1 | 42·4 | 3·5 | 31·2 | 27·8 |
| N | (10,530) | (1,909) | (10,560) | (5,699) | (31,988) |
| *Self-reported social class* | | | | | |
| Upper class | 1·5 | 2·9 | 1·3 | 5·1 | 2·0 |
| Upper-middle class | 2·5 | 10·0 | 4·4 | 18·6 | 5·9 |
| Middle class | 30·7 | 52·9 | 48·7 | 60·3 | 42·7 |
| Upper-working class | 16·2 | 15·7 | 14·1 | 8·3 | 13·8 |
| Working class | 48·7 | 18·6 | 31·3 | 7·7 | 35·3 |
| N | (394) | (70) | (390) | (156) | (1,211) |
| *Rural–urban division* | | | | | |
| Rural | 9·1 | 8·4 | 15·1 | 10·9 | 11·5 |
| Rural urbanising | 17·8 | 15·4 | 27·8 | 17·8 | 21·2 |
| Suburban | 11·6 | 19·5 | 14·1 | 21·3 | 14·7 |
| Cities under 100,000 | 28·1 | 26·4 | 24·6 | 24·6 | 25·9 |
| Cities over 100,000 | 33·5 | 30·3 | 18·5 | 25·4 | 26·8 |
| Actual vote in 1,000 | (2,811) | (452) | (2,653) | (1,492) | (8,314) |

*Sources:* Data on sex and self-reported social class are taken from Dutch National Election Study, 1977.
Data on age and religion are from NOS-Intomart Precinct Survey, 1977.
Data on rural–urban divisions are from *Algemeen Nederlands Persbureau* (actual vote).

APPENDIX

Table 9.12    *The Netherlands, Elections Lower House, 1963–1977 (number of votes in nearest thousands)*

|  | 1963 | 1967 | 1971 | 1972 | 1977 |
|---|---|---|---|---|---|
| KVP | 1,997 | 1,823 | 1,380 | 1,305 | — |
| ARP | 545 | 681 | 543 | 654 | — |
| CHU | 537 | 560 | 399 | 354 | — |
| PvdA | 1,751 | 1,620 | 1,554 | 2,021 | 2,810 |
| VVD | 643 | 738 | 653 | 1,068 | 1,492 |
| CPN | 173 | 248 | 247 | 330 | 143 |
| SGP | 144 | 138 | 148 | 163 | 177 |
| PSP | 189 | 197 | 91 | 111 | 78 |
| BP | 133 | 328 | 70 | 143 | 70 |
| GPV | 46 | 59 | 102 | 131 | 79 |
| D'66 | — | 308 | 428 | 307 | 452 |
| PPR | — | — | 116 | 355 | 141 |
| DS'70 | — | — | 337 | 305 | 60 |
| NMP | — | — | 96 | — | — |
| RKPN | — | — | — | 68 | — |
| CDA | — | — | — | — | 2,653 |
| Total | 6,258 | 6,878 | 6,318 | 7,394 | 8,314 |
| Turnout[1] | 95·1% | 94·9% | 97·1% | 83·5% | 87·5% |

*Note:*
[1] Compulsory attendance at the ballot-box was abolished in 1970.

BIBLIOGRAPHY

The following bibliography only lists publications on Dutch politics which are referred to in the text. For a recent, very elaborate survey on sources for the study of the history of Dutch political parties, see I. Lipschits, 'Geschiedschrijving over de Nederlandse Politieke Partijen', *Bijdragen en Mededelingen betreffende de Geschiedenis der Nederlanden,* vol. 91, 1976, pp. 212–40. Professor Lipschits also edited a publication on the election programmes of the Dutch Parties in 1977, *Verkiezingsprogramma's* (The Hague, Staatsuitgeverij, 1977).

Andeweg, R. B. (1977) 'The middle classes and electoral change in the Netherlands: some preliminary findings', paper presented to the Workshop on Political Attitudes and Behavior of the Middle Classes in Western Europe, European Consortium for Political Research, 27 March–2 April, Berlin.

Baehr, P. R. (1969) 'The Netherlands', in S. Henig and J. Pinder (eds), *European Political Parties* (London, PEP/Allen & Unwin), pp. 256–81.

Berg, J. Th. J. van den, and Molleman, H. A. A. (1974) *Crisis in de Nederlandse Politiek* (Alphen, Samsom).

Daalder, H. (1955). 'Parties and politics in the Netherlands', *Political Studies*, vol. 3, pp. 1–16.

Daalder, H. (1958) 'Nederland: Het Politieke Stelsel', in *Repertorium voor Sociale Wetenschappen: Politiek* (Amsterdam, Elsevier), pp. 213–38.

Daalder, H. (1964) *Leiding en Lijdelijkheid in de Nederlandse Politiek*, Leiden Inaugural Address, 2 March 1964, reprinted in Daalder (1974).

Daalder, H. (1966) 'The Netherlands opposition in a segmented society', in Robert A. Dahl (ed.), *Political Oppositions in Western Democracy* (New Haven, Yale University Press), pp. 196–236.

Daalder, H. (1974) *Politisering en Lijdelijkheid in de Nederlandse Politiek* (Assen, Van Gorcum).

Daalder, H. (1975) 'Extreme proportional representation: the Dutch experience', in S. E. Finer (ed.), *Adversary Politics and Electoral Reform* (London, Anthony Wigram), pp. 223–48.

Dittrich, K. L. L. M. (1975) 'De Gevolgen van de Veranderingen in Partijvoorkeur van de Nederlandse Kiezers sinds 1966 voor KVP en PvdA', unpublished Master's thesis, Department of Political Science, Leiden University.

Hond, Maurice de (1977) *25 Mei 1977: Uitslagen en Analyse van de Tweede Kamer Verkiezingen van 25 Mei 1977 en Wat Aan Vooraf Ging* (Hilversum, VARA).

Irwin, G. A. (1974) 'Compulsory voting legislation: impact on voter turnout in the Netherlands', *Comparative Political Studies*, vol. 7, pp. 292–315.

Irwin, G. A. (1977) 'From order to chaos (and a new order?): trends in the Dutch party system, paper prepared for the American Political Science Association, Washington, 1–4 September.

Lipschits, I. (1977) *Politieke Stromingen in Nederland: Inleiding tot de Geschiedenis van de Nederlandse Politieke Partijen* (Deventer, Kluwer).

Lijphart, A. (1968) *The Politics of Accommodation: Pluralism and Democracy in the Netherlands* (Berkeley, Calif., University of California Press).

Lijphart, A. (1974) 'The Netherlands: continuity and changes in voting behavior'), in Richard Rose (ed.), *Electoral Behavior: A Comparative Handbook* (New York: The Free Press), pp. 227–68.

Lijphart, A. (1975) *The Politics of Accommodation: Pluralism and Democracy in the Netherlands*, 2nd edn (Berkeley, Calif., University of California Press).

Lijphart, A. (1977) 'Extreme proportional representation, multipartism, and electoral reform', report prepared for *Journées d'études sur les Modes de Scrutin Européens*, University of Paris II, 7–8 January.

Miller, W. E., and Stouthard, Ph. C. (1975) 'Confessional attachment and electoral behavior in the Netherlands', *European Journal of Political Research*, vol. 3, pp. 219–58.

*De Nederlandse Kiezer '77*, first report of National Election Study (1977) G. A. Irwin, J. Verhoef and C. J. Wiebrens (eds) (Voorschoten, VAM).

NOS-Intomart (1977) *Verkiezingsonderzoek Tweede Kamer, 25 May 1977* (Hilversum, Intomart).

Rae, D. (1968) 'A note on the fractionalisation of European party systems', *Comparative Political Studies,* vol. 1, pp. 413–18.

Wolinetz, S. B. (1973) 'Party re-alignment in the Netherlands', unpublished PhD. dissertation, Yale University.

Wolinetz, S. B. (1975) 'New Left and the transformation of the Dutch Socialist Party system', paper prepared for the American Political Science Association, San Francisco, 2–5 September.

Wolters, M. (1977) 'Dutch social-democracy in the era of polarisation', paper presented to the Workshop *Trends and Tensions in European Social Democracy*, European Consortium for Political Research, Berlin, 27 March–2 April.

# 10

# The United Kingdom

## STANLEY HENIG

### INTRODUCTION

An undercurrent of change has accompanied developments in the
party system of the United Kingdom since the late 1960s. Writing
in the first edition of this book it was easy and accurate to
speak of two parties – Labour and Conservative – enjoying 'a
virtual stranglehold on British political life at all levels'. At six
general elections between 1950 and 1966 these two parties between
them never won less than 87·5 per cent of votes cast, whilst on
two occasions the figure exceeded 96 per cent. Through the
electoral system – first-past-the-post in single-member constituencies – the two parties gained complete dominance in the
House of Commons, always holding at least 98 per cent of the seats
between them and with one or other able to control an overall
majority and form a government unaided by any other group.
The two major parties delineated the political battleground and
determined the course of the major political arguments. At local
government level the same clash between Labour and Conservative dominated almost all the large authorities and there was no
great variation between the four countries making up the United
Kingdom. In 1964 Labour and Conservative between them gained
87·5 per cent of the vote in England, 87·2 per cent in Wales,
89·3 per cent in Scotland and 79·1 per cent in Northern Ireland.
Two years later the respective figures were 90·5, 89·5, 87·5 and
74. Arguments at the time about a gradual corrosion in support
for the two major parties had to be based more on speculation
about future trends than on hard factual evidence. In 1964 other
groups and parties did win 12·5 per cent of the vote, the highest
figure since the pattern of two-party dominance was established
in 1935, but by 1966 the figure was down to 10·2 per cent and it
showed little improvement in 1970. If electoral turn-out is taken
as a yardstick of satisfaction with the political system – clearly a

two-party one during the fifties and sixties – then the evidence is hardly more conclusive. At two elections in 1950 and 1951 when the two parties were running neck and neck at a time of relatively high ideological passion, electoral turn out exceeded 80 per cent, but Table 10.1 suggests that this is an aberration from the long-term pattern. Isolating these two general elections there is no real evidence of a long-term drop in electoral participation. Up to 1970 the pattern is clear: between 72 per cent and 79 per cent of those eligible vote at elections and of these nearly nine-tenths support one or other of the major parties. This is the basis for arguing that the two elections of 1974 mark the really sharp change in fortune for the major parties who are able to win only 75 per cent of the vote on average turn-outs. This crude figure covers over the fact that Northern Ireland had broken away completely from the party system of the rest of the United Kingdom, whilst by October 1974 the two major parties could only win 61 per cent of the vote in Scotland – a fall of practically one-third in a decade. If the patterns of voting evinced in the 1974 elections persist then a radical restructuring of the British party political system is inevitable. However, whilst it is reasonable to seek explanations of the reversal suffered by the major parties in political and sociological developments during the previous twenty years, attempts to project backwards a forward trend are highly questionable.[1]

Table 10.1 brings together some of the relevant statistics.[2] Taking the academic view which relates the share of the vote gained by the two major parties to electoral turn-out, column 3 gives their share of votes out of the total electorate. This suggests a gradual but steady corrosion of support for the two major parties at every election since 1951 apart from a momentary pause in 1966.[3] The apparent trend seems so linear that perhaps suspicions are in order! Any ready assumption that non-voters are a consistent group who identify with opponents rather than supporters of the major parties needs verification. Column 4 shows the votes given to other parties and groups in relation to the total electorate and reinforces the argument that 1974 was a break in, rather than a continuation of, the old pattern. The figures in column 4 cluster in an interesting way for at five of the postwar elections the share of votes taken by candidates from other than the major parties fluctuates narrowly between 7·6 per cent and 9·6 per cent, with a sharp drop during the 1950s and an equally dramatic rise in 1974. This sharp increase in support for other parties and groups clearly indicates a clear weakening of allegiances to the two large parties, although the vagaries of the electoral system may also be relevant as will be shown.

Table 10.1   *Performance of Major and Minor Parties in British General Elections, 1935–1974*

| Year | (all columns give figures in percentages) | | | |
|------|------------------------------------------|---------|------------------|------------------|
| | Share of Votes Cast Gained by Labour and Conservatives | Turn-out | Share of Total Electorate Gained by Labour and Conservative | Share of Total Electorate Gained by Other Parties and Groups |
| 1935 | 91·6 | 71·2 | 65·2 | 6·0 |
| 1945 | 87·6 | 72·7 | 63·7 | 9·0 |
| 1950 | 89·6 | 84·0 | 75·3 | 8·7 |
| 1951 | 96·8 | 82·5 | 79·9 | 2·6 |
| 1955 | 96·1 | 76·7 | 73·7 | 3·0 |
| 1959 | 93·2 | 78·8 | 73·4 | 5·4 |
| 1964 | 87·5 | 77·1 | 67·5 | 9·6 |
| 1966 | 89·8 | 75·8 | 68·0 | 7·8 |
| 1970 | 89·4 | 72·0 | 64·4 | 7·6 |
| 1974 (Feb.) | 75·0 | 78·7 | 59·0 | 19·7 |
| 1974 (Oct.) | 75·0 | 72·8 | 54·6 | 18·2 |

*Source:* see note 2.

The British electoral system has historically given a massive premium to large, well-organised national parties. Throughout long periods of political history there has been domination by two large *majoritaire* parties. Any third party seeking to compete on a national basis is discriminated against by the system. Since 1922 the Liberals have been such a third party and they have consistently received less than their 'fair share' of seats. In that year they won 17·5 per cent of the votes but only 8·8 per cent of the seats or half their entitlement on a strictly proportional basis. In October 1974 their share of the poll was very similar – 18·3 per cent – but support was so evenly spread across the entire country that they only gained 0·2 per cent of the seats. It can easily be argued that the improbability of actually being able to elect a Liberal MP induces voters to desert their party. The sheer cost involved in fighting so many hopeless electoral contests led the Liberals to reduce very sharply their number of candidates after the 1950 election and this rather than any further loss of support in seats fought was a principal reason for the apparently calamitous drop in their total vote in 1951. Equally it must be remembered that in 1974 the Liberals fought more seats than ever before: this in turn must be one reason for the sharp rise in their vote. Table 10.2 illustrates some of these features. It is tempting to assume that those seats fought during the lean years of the 1950s represent the party's real strongholds, so that other

Table 10.2    *Liberal Votes in British Elections, 1935–1974*

| Year | Liberal Share of Vote (%) | Number of Liberal Candidates | Average Share of Votes in Seats Contested (%) |
|------|------|------|------|
| 1935 | 6·4 | 161 | 23·9 |
| 1945 | 9·0 | 306 | 18·6 |
| 1950 | 9·1 | 475 | 11·8 |
| 1951 | 2·5 | 109 | 14·7 |
| 1955 | 2·7 | 110 | 15·1 |
| 1959 | 5·9 | 216 | 16·9 |
| 1964 | 11·2 | 365 | 18·5 |
| 1966 | 8·5 | 311 | 16·1 |
| 1970 | 7·5 | 332 | 13·5 |
| 1974 (Feb.) | 19·3 | 517 | 23·6 |
| 1974 (Oct.) | 18·3 | 619 | 18·9 |

*Source :* see note 2.

things being equal the party's average share of votes in seats contested will vary inversely with the number of seats contested. The 1974 experience may seem to confirm this for the Liberals did strikingly less well in October in those seats not fought in February.[4] However, this evidence is not conclusive and may be quite misleading where the earlier period is concerned: so weak was the Liberal Party throughout much of the fifties and the sixties that decisions on whether and when to fight particular parliamentary seats depended on a whole range of factors of which the likely relative success was only one.

The Liberal disadvantage in having their votes spread fairly evenly is not necessarily shared by other small parties whose appeal is specifically local or regional. Although the first-past-the-post system may inhibit their early growth, it may also help them to do disproportionately[5] well in terms of seats once they have become entrenched as a major party within their own area. This is one factor accounting for the rapid growth in the nineteenth century of the Irish Nationalists and in the 1970s it may be beginning to work in favour of the Scottish and Welsh Nationalists. In October 1974 they took 3·5 per cent of the vote and 2·2 per cent of the seats which was far better relative representation than that received by the Liberals. Separate analysis of the different countries is interesting. In Scotland the Nationalists were the second largest party in terms of votes, winning 30 per cent, but only gaining 15 per cent of the seats. The smaller but more concentrated Welsh Nationalists took 11 per cent of the vote in Wales and 8·5 per cent of the seats. At present the relatively even spread of the Scottish Nationalist vote may have a slightly inhibiting effect on their prospects. According to one calculation[6] the party would need to take 6 per cent more of the Scottish vote than Labour to win the same number of seats. However, with 40 per cent of the vote the party would take an absolute majority of the Scottish seats and with a relatively small advance thereafter it would almost sweep the board. Leaving aside Northern Ireland as a very special case, it may be worth an academic look at the notion of the Liberals, the Scottish Nationalists and the Welsh Nationalists as alternative vehicles of protest against the two-party system. Table 10.3 shows the gradual growth in the 'three-party vote' and also relates it to the number of constituencies contested. Once again the elections of 1974, especially February, stand out as exceptions to the general pattern, not simply explained away by reference to long-term trends or the mechanics of the electoral system. Before, though, examining in detail the events of 1974, it is worth considering the argument that British electoral behaviour is steadily growing more volatile. During the 1966 and 1970 Parliaments there were a total of 69 by-elections, with 25 changes of party control and 20 government losses. The contrast with the 1955 and 1959 Parliaments is striking: 114 by-elections; 15 changes of party control; 11 government losses. Earlier still between 1945 and 1955 there were only four changes in 116 by-elections with not a single government loss. During those ten years only one seat changed hands between the major parties. At first sight this evidence seems clear confirmation of a long-term trend, but the figures should be treated with caution.

Table 10.3  *Electoral performance by Liberals, Scottish and Welsh Nationalists (combined figures) at British general elections, 1959–1974*

| Year | Share of Poll Gained by Three Smaller Parties (%) | Number of Candidates | Constituencies Contested | Index of Support in Constituencies Contested (1959 = 100) |
|---|---|---|---|---|
| 1959 | 6·3 | 241 | 234 | 100 |
| 1964 | 11·6 | 403 | 386 | 112 |
| 1966 | 9·1 | 351 | 339 | 100 |
| 1970 | 9·4 | 433 | 391 | 89 |
| 1974 (Feb.) | 21·9 | 623 | 558 | 154 |
| 1974 (Oct.) | 21·8 | 726 | 623 | 130 |

*Source :* for first three columns see note 2.

There have been other periods this century when the electorate showed great volatility as measured at by-elections. In the 1900 and 1906 Parliaments there were 214 by-elections with 50 changes of which 44 were government losses, whilst in the 1924 Parliament the respective figures were 63, 20 and 16. On average three seats have changed political hands at by-elections every year this century – usually to the disadvantage of the government of the day. The real exception to the general pattern is the period from 1945 to 1955. If recent statistics can be interpreted as showing an increasing volatility – since then, it is equally legitimate to argue that they also demonstrate a return to normality!

Evidence from by-elections, local government elections and public opinion polls all show that a sharp shift of opinion against any government of the day is usual. This explains the traditional belief that at general elections governments will lose ground, although once again the 1950s are an obvious exception. At general elections oscillations in opinion are always considerably muted by comparison with these other yardsticks. Table 10.4 gives the crude national swing between the two major parties at general elections since 1950 and reveals no trends at all.

Table 10.4    *Crude National Swing between the Two Major Parties at General Elections, 1950–1974*

| Year | Swing to Labour | Swing to Conservative |
|---|---|---|
| 1950 | | 2·7 |
| 1951 | | 0·9 |
| 1955 | | 2·15 |
| 1959 | | 1·15 |
| 1964 | 3·15 | |
| 1966 | 2·65 | |
| 1970 | | 4·7 |
| 1974 (Feb.) | 1·3 | |
| 1974 (Oct.) | 2·1 | |

*Sources :* see note 2.

THE ELECTIONS OF 1974

The election of February 1974 which struck at the roots of so many assumptions about British politics was precipitated under unusual circumstances. By autumn 1973 the Conservative government, elected three years previously on a normal swing from Labour, seemed reasonably secure. It had succeeded in taking Britain into the European Communities and had actually made some progress on Northern Ireland. Prior to the outbreak of the Middle East War the economy also seemed reasonably healthy with industrial production rising rapidly, unemployment at its lowest level for some years and inflation just about under control. Even if the seeds of future economic difficulties were present, the government's record seemed good enough in conventional, materialist terms to suggest that they might win a further term of office at the next election. Inevitably the public opinion polls showed Labour ahead of the Conservatives, but the lead was narrow enough to be wiped out in an election campaign. There seemed little doubt that 1974 would be an economic boom year, suitable for the government to call a general election.

Economic prognostications were sharply upset by the enormous increases in the price of oil during the last part of 1973 and this made the government all the more determined to stick to certain guidelines with regard to pay increases. When the miners took strike action in pursuit of their claim, a large group in the cabinet felt this was a direct confrontation which could be taken for its resolution to the people. It was an added incentive that the economic advantages of delaying a general election might now be slipping away. To call an election a full eighteen months before the expiry of Parliament's maximum five-year term required some public reason – on this analysis conveniently supplied by the miners. Government uncertainty and public speculation as to the possibility of a 'who governs' election removed any element of surprise, whilst the introduction of the three-day working week to meet the coal shortage and appeals to the 'Dunkirk spirit' had little appeal in the Britain of the 1970s. The small national swing to Labour, itself masking a variety of differential movements with much bigger swings in the large industrial cities, was completely overshadowed by a general reaction against both major parties. Through the vagaries of the electoral system and aided by the break between the Conservatives and dominant Protestant opinion in Ulster, Labour emerged as the largest party but on its lowest share of the poll since 1931 and without even a plurality of votes. None the less the Conservative government, which had precipitated the election, determined the issue and asked for a mandate to deal with it, had clearly lost.

During the campaign there was much speculation as to what would happen if neither major party gained an overall majority. The refusal of party leaders to discuss the hypothesis would hardly have been credible in any other Community country. The Liberal Party – presumably in business to bring about such a situation – actually issued a directive to candidates that any questions on coalition be referred to the major parties as being their responsibility.[7] Immediately after the results were known the Conservative prime minister, Edward Heath, suggested an arrangement whereby the Liberals give parliamentary support to the government but without any formal coalition. In the absence of any policy decision the Liberal leader was only able to suggest that matters take their course whilst offering a vague hope that a national coalition of all parties might emerge. Inevitably this gave Labour the chance to form a new government, their own minority status momentarily obscured by what looked like Conservative manoeuvring to avoid the electoral verdict. In addition the Liberals had effectively limited their political options: having apparently publicly turned the Conservatives out of office, they could hardly do the same to Labour too quickly if they wished to appear as a responsible party. As a result the new Labour government was able to act as if it had the usual parliamentary majority whilst devoting a good deal of the next few months to seeking a fresh election which might bring this about.

At the October general election there was a further direct swing from Conservative to Labour, but without any general reversal for the minor parties this produced only a small overall majority. For two years thereafter Labour faced no real difficulties in the House of Commons: with general agreement that the public would not want a third election, the government could usually rely on the tacit support or neutrality of one or other of the smaller opposition parties. Divisions inside the Labour Party over membership of the European Community were finally overcome by resort to a referendum to confirm the so-called 'renegotiation' of the terms of entry. This gave the government a relatively free hand to try to tackle the rate of inflation which had been soaring since autumn 1973. Through the 'social contract' with the trade union movement the government was able for the two years immediately after the referendum to control the rate of wage increases in a way which their predecessors might have envied. Problems began to mount, however, during the 1976–7 session of Parliament. Defections and lost by-elections removed the overall majority at the same time as initial failure to pass measures of devolution for Scotland and Wales ensured that henceforth the Nationalists would be in constant opposition. Massive economic problems – balance-of-payments deficits, the highest level of unemployment since the war, falling living standards and a still high rate of inflation – contributed to government unpopularity, demonstrated through local government and by-elections as well as in the public opinion polls, and ruled out any government initiative to call an early general election. Immediately after the collapse of the first Devolution Bill, the

Conservatives launched a major onslaught which the government, led since mid-1976 by James Callaghan, could only survive through a semi-formal parliamentary pact with the Liberals. This traded Liberal votes in the House of Commons for certain rights of consultation at the pre-policy-making stage and in effect gave the Labour government what had been refused to their predecessors in March 1974.

The pact has been bitterly resented by sections of both the parliamentary and the wider Labour Party, unwilling to accept the implications of any kind of arrangement with any other party. It is interesting to reflect on the analysis made by Hugh Dalton[8] on the record of Labour's minority government of 1929. He considered that the leadership had three reasonable courses of action open – to refuse office and leave responsibility with non-Socialist parties who might in due course be decisively defeated at a subsequent general election; to accept office, introduce bold Socialist measures and fight an election on them after the inevitable parliamentary defeat; or to have an open arrangement with the Liberals geared to a limited but definite programme. Dalton comments bleakly:

'We took none of these courses. We took a fourth which combined the disadvantages of them all, and none of the advantages of any. We accepted office, we brought in no bold measures, and we cold-shouldered and irritated the Liberals. This fatal combination . . . gradually imposed itself for lack of positive decisions to the contrary.'[9]

The 'fatal combination' also led directly to the electoral disaster of 1931. British politics over the last thirty years have been characterised by considerable consensus in many policy areas between successive governments of different parties: the phrase 'coalition policies' may not be entirely inappropriate. None the less political tradition, inertia and the partisanship of activists have at the same time combined to resist any implication that the accepted norm of single party majority government might require modification. In the event of the election results of 1974 being repeated, the pact between the Labour government and the Liberals might well acquire a historic significance. There is a scenario for British politics which visualises the Nationalist parties sweeping the board in Scotland and Wales and then playing off the major parties in the same way as did their Irish predecessors in the last century. To avoid continually changing, unstable multi-party coalitions, the major parties might conceivably find themselves faced with the alternatives of granting independence to Scotland and Wales thus breaking up the United Kingdom, or introducing proportional representation to ensure that the Liberals and not the Nationalists hold the balance and thus bringing to an end the traditional two-party system. For Labour, which has only twice won an absolute majority of seats in England and which has a deeply inbred suspicion of coalitions or arrangements with other parties, the agony of such a dilemma would be considerable and this may help to explain the bitterness of debate in 1977 over both devolution and the pact with the Liberals.

BASES OF THE PARTY SYSTEM

Labour/Conservative domination of British politics has been based on the existence of only one party-forming issue – class. Analysis of supporters of the two major parties is striking. In 1963 the middle class divided in a ratio of 75:25 between Conservatives and Labour with the figures for the working class almost the exact obverse – 28:72.[10] The first major study of the British electorate by Butler and Stokes[11] appeared while the first edition of this book was going to press. It demonstrated the salience of class in determining political preference and showed the gradual gain to Labour from generational change – differential death rates and the greater likelihood than hitherto that new cohorts of voters would be from Labour families. During the 1960s a good deal of attention was paid to the phenomenon of the working-class Conservative,[12] but by the time the second edition of Butler and Stokes appeared[13] there was even greater interest in evidence as to the gradual decline of class voting. This trend has been further confirmed by the British Election Study team at the University of Essex whose analyses extend to the October 1974 election.[14] On the same two-party basis as before they find the middle class dividing at that election 65:35 for the Conservatives and the working class 67:33 for Labour. The decline in class voting since 1963 is not enormous on this basis, although the trend has been persistent, despite a marked surge in Labour support from the working class at the time of the February 1974 election. The study team make the point that, with so many electors supporting other parties or not voting, there are analytical weaknesses to the Labour/Conservative dichotomy. If the distinctions are changed to Conservative or non-Conservative for the middle classes and Labour or non-Labour for the working classes, then the index of class voting falls to 51 per cent so that, 'by the last election knowledge of a voter's manual or non-manual status was no better than tossing a coin as a predictor of his partisanship; it would only have served to predict which of the major parties the voter did not support'.[15] Perhaps this is slightly disingenuous for class remains the central dividing line in the Labour/Conservative dichotomy and is reflected in supporters, members, activists and programmes. However, in three of the four constituent parts of the United Kingdom the class issue now coexists with other issues – religious and constitutional – which are party forming in their own right. Voters from all occupational classes are attracted to the indigenous parties of Scotland, Wales and Northern Ireland, none of which any longer operates a two-party system.

The working-class/middle-class dichotomy persists in the membership and activists of the Labour and Conservative parties although there is a great shortage of survey material. Information is more readily available on the backgrounds of members of Parliament. Since the war fewer than half of Labour's parliamentary party have had working class backgrounds and by October 1974 the figure had fallen to 28 per cent, but this remains in stark contrast to the situation in the Conservative camp where not a single parliamentarian was of manual working-class origin although four had backgrounds in engineering, clerical or technical work. A further contrast is that whilst a third of the Conservatives were company directors, farmers or landowners the figure for these categories combined on the Labour side was less than 1 per cent. Professional groups have come to predominate on both sides: for the Conservatives the spread is fairly even with law as the biggest group, whilst for Labour no less than 24 per cent are teachers or lecturers.[16]

Regional factors have always had some effect on Conservative/ Labour voting. Butler and Stokes found that for the period 1963–6 4 per cent more of the middle class and 7·5 per cent more of the working class voted Conservative in the south of England than was the case in the north of England, Scotland and Wales. In October 1974 Labour only won 30 per cent of the vote in the south outside London, whilst the Conservatives took nearly 45 per cent. During the years of their greatest weakness the Liberals sometimes looked almost like a regional party based on the west of England, rural Wales and the Scottish Highlands. After 1974 this is much less obviously the case. In October the Liberals failed to reach 10 per cent of the poll only in industrial Scotland. Taking the eight regions into which England is normally divided the Liberal vote ranged from 17 to 21 per cent in seven of them; only in their old stronghold of the south-west did the figure go up to 27 per cent. Clearly the development of the Liberals into a would be national third party has to an extent left behind the old regional bases, for they took fewer votes in Scotland or Wales than in any of the English regions.[17]

Finally, religion is also relevant to voting. In all classes Roman Catholics and nonconformists are more likely to vote Labour than the average population whilst Anglicans are more likely to vote Conservative. The City of Liverpool offers a neat illustration of the interaction of regional and religious factors. Situated well in the north it has a large working-class population split between Anglicans and Roman Catholics – many in both religious camps of Irish origin. In 1945 Labour took 47 per cent of the vote in Liverpool – more or less the same as its national share. In October 1974 Labour won nearly 55 per cent of the vote in Liverpool – some fifteen points higher than its national share. By way of contrast and over the same period Labour's share of the vote was identical in Manchester and 3 per cent down in Birmingham. Even on this limited basis the evidence suggests that increasingly class and regional factors exert a greater pull than the religious.

The foregoing sections have analysed the structure of the British party system as it operates in the mid-1970s. The remainder of the chapter will examine the philosophy, aims and structure of the major and minor parties as well as giving some comparative material on party membership and finance.

THE LABOUR PARTY

The Labour Party today acts as a fairly typical European Social Democratic party in pursuing policies of state intervention and welfare promotion through the mixed economy whilst owing a vague allegiance to Socialism as a long-term goal. Historically there is one major difference: organised trade unions played an equal role with Socialist intellectuals in founding a party to which they have always been directly affiliated. Throughout the European Community Socialist parties have special relations with trade unions, but in no other case is there this particular kind of organic link.[18] According to Tawney, 'the trade union base . . . has ensured that Socialism in this country rests on broad popular foundations; has averted the deadly disease of dogmatic petrification which afflicted the pre-1914 German Social Democrats; and has saved British Socialism from the sterility which condemns to impotence a party, like the French, severed from working class roots'.[19] Owing little to Marxism and following a tradition of native thinkers such as Morris, Shaw, the Webbs and other early Fabians, the fundamental impulse of Labour Party Socialism has tended to be ethical rather than economic. Richard Crossman's claim that 'the Labour Party was founded as a movement of moral protest'[20] is echoed in the writings of its first prime ministers. Ramsay MacDonald argued that 'Socialism can only move men by education and moral idealism; its sound economic criticisms of the classes must be used as logs by which the fires of moral enthusiasm are kept blazing',[21] while Clement Attlee simply asserted that the first aim of Socialism is 'to give greater freedom to the individual'.[22] The idiosyncratic natures of the origins and development of the Labour Party in comparison with Continental Social Democratic parties may not seem to make an enormous difference when one examines government policy, but it is strongly reflected in the party's self-perception. There is an underlying tendency – epitomised by the statement of Tawney quoted above – to disclaim any affinity with the other parties who at different times are criticised as being both doctrinaire and revisionist!

It has sometimes been suggested that the Labour Party formally adopted Socialism in 1918 when establishing its present constitution,[23] but this is vastly exaggerated. On the brink of becoming one of the two major parties Labour needed a programme which would demonstrate its separateness from the Liberals, who until then had been frequent parliamentary, and occasional electoral, allies. Ringing declarations of Socialism distanced Labour from the Liberal/Conservative establishment, whilst the rhetoric of a commitment 'to secure for workers by hand or by brain the full fruits of their industry . . . on the basis of the common ownership of the means of production, distribution and exchange' (Clause 4 of the party constitution) gave to party members a distinctive credo, although one hardly reflected in the actual policies of Labour governments save in the period between 1945 and 1951. There is some truth to the savagely ironic words penned by John Strachey during his Marxist phase – 'Social Democratic parties satisfy the workers' need to dream of Socialism whilst remaining tied to capitalism'.[24]

None the less the stress on nationalisation has been central in the Labour tradition with widespread acceptance that it is a crucial element in, or the key to gaining, a Socialist society. Dichotomy between means and ends has been important in intra-party controversy. To a guild Socialist like G. D. H. Cole the aim was 'a classless society in which economic activities are directly conducted under public auspices, on a basis of public ownership of the means of production'.[25] Attlee simply took it for granted that as part of Labour's long-term programme land and all major industries should be owned by the community. An early revisionist, E. M. Durbin, was even more keen on widespread nationalisation, but as a strategic weapon, arguing that future Labour governments must give it priority before further measures of amelioration lest it otherwise find itself starved of the financial resources needed both for investment and for welfare programmes.[26]

Following the party's third successive electoral defeat in 1959 Hugh Gaitskell sought to refurbish its image by repealing or amending Clause 4 of the constitution. He argued that no Labour government would in practice seek such widespread public ownership: since nationalisation had a bad electoral image, prospects could only be improved by a change which gave formal recognition to reality. Strands of thought from the ensuing 'revisionist' controversy have lingered. Tony Crosland, the leading political philosopher of the reformers, attempted to define areas within which a Labour government could promote progressive, welfare-oriented measures without involvement in any Socialist dogma, dismissing class war concepts as irrelevant.[27] The intellectual reply came from Richard Crossman who claimed to detect an impending crisis in capitalism. In his view genuinely radical governments would only come to power every thirty years or so, and there could be no advantage in compromising deeply held beliefs. British Socialism would reap the rewards for intellectual purity in the 1970s.[28] The outcome of the controversy was inconclusive: Gaitskell failed to change Clause 4, his critics failed to unseat him as leader and the party continued on its traditional, pragmatic course.

Throughout these arguments Harold Wilson, who succeeded on Gaitskell's death in 1963, remained on the sidelines. For tactical reasons he often chose to veer towards the Crossman position, but his subsequent contribution as party leader for over thirteen years and prime minister for eight was to make Labour as natural a party of government and administration as the Conservatives. Pragmatism itself became a dogma. During the first period of office from 1964 to 1970 there was major expansion and reorganisation in education and the social services, but only a few industries were taken into public ownership and those on an *ad hoc* basis. The government may well be most remembered for the large number of liberal, humanitarian reforms implemented – the abolition of capital punishment and changes in the laws on abortion, divorce and homosexuality. Government since 1974 has been even more completely overshadowed by economic crisis, but it has also been characterised by an extremely close working relationship with the trade union movement through the so-called 'social contract'. From 1975 to 1977 this enabled the government to intervene centrally in wage fixing without recourse to legislation.[29]

There is always a danger that concentration on Labour as a party of government will give a misleading impression as to the degree of unity on aims or methods. True to its origins, Labour has always been a heterogeneous coalition, and the mechanics of the British electoral system ensure that it remains the home of virtually the entire Left. The major thrust of the party in office has been towards welfare and ameliorative measures as advocated by Crosland, and the consequent high levels of taxation have caused some redistribution of income and wealth. However, state involvement in industry has been piecemeal. The left wing in the party has opposed many of the Labour government's financially orthodox measures for dealing with Britain's economic problems and attempted to define alternative economic strategies. These involve systematic state control over the economy, including direct government investment and resistance to international financial pressures. The flavour of the left critique is well given by Eric Heffer, one of its most articulate spokesmen. His Socialism is democratic and revolutionary, and he roundly condemns pragmatism: 'In the future, the Labour Party must completely reject the concept of the mixed economy . . . it does not work . . . it does not bing about a redistribution of wealth, nor does it bring about growth in the economy.'[30] The Left is usually much more successful in influencing the party's programme in opposition. Europe is a good example, for the Left has in general been bitterly hostile to British membership of the Community.

In seeking to rally opposition to the European Community, the Left has been assisted by the strong reservations traditionally held throughout the movement about the credentials and political prospects of European Social Democrats. Labour's negative sentiments towards Europe are also bolstered by a feeling of paternity towards the multi-racial Commonwealth – created out of the Conservative Empire when a Labour government granted independence to the countries of the Indian sub-continent. Around 1950 the Left itself actually toyed with the 'European' idea in association with the notion of the third force: since then it has acted as a rallying point for opposition to British involvement and has been able to appeal to widespread sentiment across the party.

Harold Wilson's government sought British membership in the late 1960s in the face of disappointments with both the USA and the Commonwealth as prime alignments in British foreign policy. Acceptance of Britain's diminished world role, economic and political logic all combined to push every British government since 1960 towards acceptance of the desirability of Community membership. Had Labour won the election of 1970, the government would unquestionably have accepted terms similar to those which were actually negotiated by the Conservatives. Whilst there would have been internal party problems, critical resolutions at party conference and possibly even some ministerial resignations, the government would have been no more deflected from its chosen course than it had been on most other issues between 1964 and 1970. However, party dialectics in opposition were quite different. Inevitably the immediate response to loss of office was a shift to the left, but this was undoubtedly exacerbated by the growing confrontation between the Conservative government and the trade union movement. This in turn stimulated the gut reaction of hostility to entry into the European Community which was clearly a major Conservative priority. As usual Harold Wilson sought to unite the party and this could only be done through the adoption of a broad anti-European stance, although accompanied by small print to indicate to those who wished to read and understand that Labour's prime objections were to the Conservative terms and the fact that the question of entry had never been put to the British people. Back in office after February 1974 Labour were once again subject to the pressures of international politics and major economic problems: there was simply no prospect of withdrawal from the Community. The government's prime need was to legitimate membership for the party rather than for the British people and to outflank those who would still be opposed. Renegotiation of some of the details of British membership fell well short of fundamental change in the structure of the Community or its disliked agricultural policy, but they gave a majority in the cabinet a basis for appeal to the people through a first national referendum. The party itself officially advocated a 'No' vote, but members at all levels, including the cabinet, were left free to act as they pleased. In the event Labour voters divided almost equally for and against Britain's continued membership but the overall result was a decisive two to one victory for continued membership and thus for the government. On an issue where the Left had the instinctive backing of a majority of the party and where they were able to gain a majority at both conference and the national executive, they were still unable to control the policy of a Labour government in office. The degree of legitimation given to membership by the referendum even within the Labour movement has been demonstrated by developments within the Trades Union Congress. At its annual conference in September 1977 a motion for withdrawal was overwhelmingly defeated. In the long run this is likely to close the issue as far as Labour is concerned.

Analysis of the structure of the Labour Party[31] involves an examination of the relationships between five crucial elements – the constituency Labour party (CLP); annual conference; the national executive committee (NEC); the party machine – Transport House and the regional organisation; and the parliamentary Labour party (PLP). CLPs consist of members' branches which correspond with local government electoral boundaries and the local branches of nationally affiliated trade unions. Whilst their influence over national party policy is extremely limited, they have virtually complete autonomy in the selection of parliamentary candidates. CLPs, nationally affiliated trade unions and the few Socialist societies all send delegates to the annual conference with one vote for every thousand members represented. Conference thus represents some $6\frac{1}{2}$ million members of whom nearly 90 per cent are from trade unions: the three largest trade unions cast 40 per cent of the total votes between them. Theoretically conference is the supreme policy-making organ and it can place any item in the party programme by a two-thirds majority vote. However, this does not guarantee the inclusion of that same item in the party's election manifesto, let alone in the legislative programme of a Labour government. In practice no institution with more than 1,000 delegates and meeting normally for less than five days per year can hope to control the destiny of a governmental party. However, conference should not be dismissed as an annual jamboree or circus with no influence: it is manipulated and stage-managed by the major contenders for power inside the party – NEC, leader, trade unions, Right and Left factions – but in the long run its attitudes are important in the gradual evolution of policy. Outflanked it may have been over the European issue, but it was the Labour conference which ensured both renegotiation and the referendum.

Each year conference elects the NEC to administer the party and undertake the work of policy preparation. Twenty-six of its twenty-eight members – the others being the leader and deputy leader – are elected at the conference with the trade unions effectively controlling eighteen places. There has always been some tendency for the large trade unions to carve out the places between them, but intraparty and especially the broad Left/Right battles are very relevant in determining NEC composition. In recent years a majority of trade union representatives on the NEC have been on the Left of the party: with their virtual stranglehold on the CLP representation, the left wing have thus been in control of the most important single organ in the party. The NEC not only controls the party machine – even a Labour government has virtually no influence in this – it also directs the nature of debates at the conference. Where in the past Labour governments have been able to control conference, this has come about through a close working relationship or even alliance between the party leadership, leading trade unionists and the majority of the NEC. Over the last ten years this alliance has tended to break down, making it far more difficult for the party leaders to rely on conference support.

The PLP has traditionally asserted its autonomy *vis-à-vis* both conference and the NEC. So far it alone elects the leader and deputy leader and also, theoretically, determines tactics to be pursued in the House of Commons. When an election is called the PLP through its elected parliamentary committee joins the NEC as an equal partner in choosing those items from the party programme which will go in the manifesto. However, the PLP is not a caucus in the same way as the *Fraktion* of the German SPD or the parliamentary group of the Australian Labour Party. When Labour is in office, the PLP has no formal influence over the distribution of posts and no organic control over the formation of policy. In so far as it is one forum for the discussion of policy, it is itself subject to government control, for all ministers – and they may be one quarter of the PLP – and expected to abide by the traditional conventions of collective responsibility. In opposition the PLP does have greater influence for it elects the shadow cabinet and may determine policy. None the less it may be argued that the greatest beneficiary of the autonomy of the PLP is a Labour leader and especially a prime minister. Classically, he may resort to 'divide and rule': the PLP is an essential power-base for a leader being pressurised by conference and the NEC.

The party machine, controlled by the NEC, is extremely small for the task of servicing such a large, nationwide party. At the apex it is directed by the party secretary, but Transport House – the headquarters – only employs a few dozen people. It is particularly weak on the research side, although some of the gap is filled by bodies like the Fabian Society, and supplies few services to the PLP. Small regional offices operate as arms of the NEC in giving procedural and organisational advice and assistance to the CLPs and also in servicing regional conferences and executives. Most CLPs are organisationally and financially weak. Less than one in six employs a full-time agent (and many of these are in effect paid for by direct contributions from affiliated trade unions and Labour's sister Co-operative Party) and in most cases activities are concentrated on fighting elections and raising funds. Most of Labour's large traditional support in the country has virtually no involvement with its political activities. 'Less a party, more a way of life' may be a description of the social role of some

Continental parties – it is certainly not appropriate in Labour's case.

## THE CONSERVATIVE PARTY

'[The Tory party's] whole purpose is to make it possible for a governing class to get on with the job of governing, within the context of universal franchise; to relate the practical requirements of good government to the contemporary circumstances of majority rule; to translate the idea of aristocratic rule into terms which make sense in a democracy, which means organising mass support for what is basically an elitist or paternalist system of government.'[32]

The characteristic common to Europe's centre-right parties is their close identification with established groups and interests in society – land, business, church. These are an inadequate basis for *majoritaire* status and there is a consequent need to seek support from historic enemies – Liberals and Radicals – and above all from the working class which is the major source of electoral support of the Left. In Britain the Conservative Party combines the intellectual legacies and traditions of nineteenth-century Tories who were inimical to neither a loose, regulatory role for government nor the use of benevolent policies to win support for the *status quo* and their contemporary Liberal opponents with their characteristic belief in *laissez-faire*. The leadership and membership of the Conservative Party are overwhelmingly middle class,[33] but around two-fifths of those actually voting Conservative are from the ranks of unskilled and semi-skilled working class.[34]

After 1945 the Conservative Party underwent a revolution in structure and programme without parallel in modern British politics and with little of the internal upheaval which might have accompanied similar change in more doctrinaire parties. By 1950 the Conservatives could be presented to the electorate as a moderate party, strong on economic management and willing to accept an important role for central government in housing and the social services. There have always been different views within the party as to the appropriate reaction to radical changes introduced by other governments, but the dominant stream has normally been to accept reforms once they have been initiated and not to seek to turn the clock back. The norm for a period of Conservative government has historically been consolidation and administration rather than radical change in any direction. Thus after 1951 Conservative governments did not question the bases of the welfare state, although there were changes of emphasis. Having given housing a 'priority second only to national defence' the party's proudest boast was to be that it had built the 300,000 as promised, whilst on the social services Conservatives were anxious to claim that they could offer higher standards for the same outlay. The veritable bonfire of wartime controls gave private enterprise and *laissez-faire* an Indian summer during the 1950s and the Conservatives under Macmillan won the 1959 election on the cry 'You've never had it so good'. Thereafter the Conservatives seemed to lose some intellectual steam as Britain's economic problems mounted and Labour returned to office in 1964 on the claim that they could best harness modern technology to the national purpose. Characteristically the Conservative Party responded through selecting as new leader Edward Heath who seemed at the time very much in the Wilson image. However, by 1970 British politics were dominated by the question of inflation and the new Conservative government resolved on a more radical approach aimed at limiting central involvement in industry and finance, but seeking indirectly to regulate wage change as a weapon of economic control. During the very first phase of this policy the government sought to curb the power of the trade unions through legal means: this effectively ruled out co-operation with both sides of industry and caused even greater problems when the government changed tactics and sought directly to control wages. Ultimately confronted by the miners' strike, the government appealed to the people and lost.

In contrast to the periods after 1945 and 1964 the reaction to this much more slender, but psychologically much more unexpected, defeat was for the party to turn in on itself, to seek to define its Conservatism and, therefore, almost inevitably to move to the right. The inherent flexibility of the Conservative Party was shown by its choice as new leader of Margaret Thatcher – the first woman to hold such a post in British politics and in a party which has never had more than fifteen women MPs. Of equal significance is the fact that she is the first Conservative leader since the war to be overtly leading the party from the Right. Whilst the policies of a future Conservative government under Thatcher might not be very different from those followed in the past, defeat at the next general election is likely to bring into the open strife between the right wing of the party which has accepted many of the economic theories of Milton Freedman and the traditional, more pragmatic moderates.

The very nature of the Conservative Party makes it more difficult to analyse characteristic attitudes and policies than is the case with Labour. The only doctrine which seems in statements of Conservative policy is to be found in the regular incantations that Labour is a Marxist party. Thus it is argued that 'all attempts to find a "third force" which is neither Marxist nor Tory have proved equally unrealistic', whilst 'the only people in the Labour Party who have a coherent prescription for the long-term problems of Britain are those who would substitute an authoritarian, near-Communist regime for the free democratic society in which we have so far chosen to live'.[35] There is an interesting contrast between this language and that of the October 1974 election manifesto when Heath was leader and Labour were attacked for being unwilling to 'put aside their political differences and unite Britain to deal with the crisis'.[36] It is a recurrent theme in Conservative thought that they are a national party seeking to serve all rather than a purely sectional interest. Conservative programmes and actions alike have shown the party quite willing to maintain and even improve social services, to give the same priority to education and even on occasion to intervene directly in industry, but the motivation is different. Whilst the Labour image of a better Britain implies the full range of social services and state involvement for their own sake, Conservatives see these as no more than means which may have to be employed to deal with peculiarly recalcitrant problems. Where a balance needs to be struck between social and economic considerations, the latter tend to loom relatively larger for Conservatives.

The most positive and characteristic Conservative policy of the 1960s and early 1970s was espousal of British entry into the European Communities. Whatever later claims may have been made, there were no influential voices in Whitehall, Westminster or elsewhere urging British entry when the Communities were first created. The gradual disappearance of the British Empire and the delayed trauma induced by the failure of the 1956 Suez expedition ultimately played a major role in determining the first British application by Macmillan's government in 1961. There was perhaps also just a tiny streak of opportunism for the Conservatives were beginning to need a new rallying cry for the elections of the 1960s. Lack of popularity of the European cause certainly precluded this, but for many Conservatives it did fill the emotional void left by the loss of Empire and it may also have fed on the resentment held by some in the traditionally imperial party towards the United States. Entry into the Community was the major achievement of the 1970–4 government, but loss of office so soon thereafter diverted attention from this. Perhaps because of the inability of the Community to offer any immediate succour to the ailing British economy or possibly from a psychological need to distance herself from Heath, the present leader Margaret

Thatcher has actually shown markedly less enthusiasm for Europe than any other since the war with the exception of Eden. Although there is no argument in the Conservative Party over possible withdrawal from the Community, it is unclear that the substance as distinct from the style of British policy towards Europe would be much changed if a Thatcher-led government were to emerge from the next general election.

The predominant organisational characteristics of the Conservative Party reflect its origins as a parliamentary caucus needing mass support and, therefore, mass organisation as the electoral franchise was gradually widened in the nineteenth and early twentieth centuries. The party has never aspired to the creation of one single, unified structure: its national and parliamentary wings and the central organisation coexist as a tryptich, each autonomously from the others, whilst 'the pivot of the Party, holding these various elements together, is its Leader'.[37] Since 1965 the leader has been elected by Conservative members of the House of Commons using an exhaustive voting procedure. Previously the traditional method of choosing a leader had involved 'taking soundings' of Conservative opinion in both Houses of Parliament and in the party in general. Often this was occasioned by a monarch's need to find a prime minister when the party was in office and Edward Heath in 1965 was the first to be named as leader with the party in opposition at the time. A decade later he was the first British political leader to be pushed out of office directly as a result of a formal party election. It can be argued that under the old system Heath might never have become leader and there is very little evidence that in 1975 rank-and-file Conservatives preferred Thatcher to Heath. The changes in effect mean that the parliamentary party is now much more obviously the power-base for leadership than used to be the case. However, it is the figures of the Conservative establishment – peers, landowners and leading non-House of Commons members – who have lost influence, rather than constituency associations whose views have historically been of little importance in determining the leadership.

The leader is given full control over the entire Conservative central organisation which is better financed and accordingly larger and more effective than its Labour counterpart. The leader chooses personally the directors and the heads of the major departments at the Conservative Central Office and they are in turn responsible to him or her. A change of leadership as when Thatcher succeeded Heath is likely to mean a good many changes in the top personnel. The wider Conservative Party is organised through the so-called national union which groups together all the constituency associations. The national union is theoretically autonomous in running its own affairs, but there is no pretence that it makes policy for the whole party, this being clearly the preserve of the leader. Indeed it is formally stated that amongst the powers of the large and unwieldy executive committee is 'to consider such aspects of the policy of the Party *as may be selected from time to time*'.[38] The composition of all the important committees of the national union is laid down in detail and the central leadership of the party is strongly represented, but in policy matters none of them has more than an advisory role. The national union has the responsibility of organising the annual conference which is for the entire party and which theoretically may discuss anything. However, annual conference has no power to take any binding decisions – policy, organisation or the personnel of the leadership – and it tends to resemble a rally of the faithful.

Whilst Conservatives have never been unduly concerned with trying to create internal party democracy, individual members of the party may exert influence in one important respect. As with their Labour counterparts it is the Conservative constituency associations which select parliamentary candidates and despite advice on procedures and the existence of central lists of recommended individuals, they have virtually complete autonomy in this respect. Conservative associations tend to be better off than Labour constituency parties and a majority of them are able to employ a full-time agent.

The power-structure of Britain's two major parties differs markedly. In one there is a tradition that policy should be strongly influenced if not controlled by rank-and-file members. Labour leaders have constantly to maintain a balance between the different sections and factions within the party and formally speaking there is no deference to the notion of leadership. A Conservative leader by contrast is given those luxuries denied to his or her Labour counterpart – complete control over the machine and unchallenged influence over policy. At the same time, though, Conservative leaders seem to be expected to assume total responsibility for the performance of the party. Traditionally the party is one of government and it is willing to sacrifice a leader who jeopardises or has lost that position. Its caucus origins also imply that there are others in the party of a stature almost equivalent to the leader who may be required to act in the event of the latter not fulfilling his or her responsibilities. Thus in practice the position of Conservative leader has been much less secure than that of the Labour leader. Modern British politics may be said to have begun in 1923 with the first confrontation of Baldwin and MacDonald as leaders of the major parties. Of six Labour leaders since then, one died in office, two clearly chose their own time to go and one more or less left the party whilst still in office. Only one Labour leader clearly lost his position as a result of internal party pressure. During the same period the Conservatives have had eight leaders of whom no less than three – Chamberlain, Home and Heath – were pushed out through loss of support inside the party. Only two of the eight clearly selected their own moment of departure and one of these – Churchill – was originally foisted on the party as leader by the exigencies of war, including the refusal of Labour to enter a coalition under any other Conservative. It is perhaps a ruthless instinct for survival which has made the Conservative Party one of the most enduring and successful in Europe.

OTHER PARTIES

The evolution of the Liberal Party has paralleled that of many centre parties. Its characteristic nineteenth-century philosophy – economic *laissez-faire* and free trade – reflected powerful economic interests, and as the traditional vehicle for radical pressure it was able early in the twentieth century to add a certain amount of government social intervention. Decline was occasioned by the growth of Labour as the normal vehicle for working-class interests and a gradual transfer of allegiances by the Liberals' own traditional middle-class supporters to their old Conservative rivals. The increasing salience of class as the dominant issue in the British political alignment seemed to ensure the ir-reversibility of the Liberals' decline, and with the catastrophic election results of the early 1950s the party seemed doomed to final extinction. The retention of both a national organisation and a chord in the folk memory were, however, to be crucial determinants of the Liberals' ability to offer themselves as the 'new' national alternative when the stranglehold of the two major parties began to decline. Benefiting from the gradual erosion of the class alignment, the Liberals have offered middle-of-the-road policies, steering a balance between the programmes of their major rivals, although 'the intellectual policy revival of the party may be slippery to trace'.[39] Several times during the 1960s the party seemed about to enter a new era of electoral success and political influence, but the breakthrough in popular political consciousness did not occur until 1974 when Jeremy Thorpe as leader was suddenly elevated to the same rank as his two major party rivals – a position enjoyed by no liberal since Lloyd George. At the 1974 elections the Liberals emerged with about half the share of the popular vote given to each of the major parties, but lost out heavily through an electoral system which had itself helped determine a strategy of seeking to become a major party and 'to form a Liberal government'[40] rather than simply aim for the presence in Parliament of an effective third force. In the immediate aftermath of the February 1974 election the Liberal Party's considerable popular support enabled it to wield a political influence out of proportion to its tiny number of MPs. After the October election Labour could carry on for a time in the traditional majority party manner, but by 1976 when the government was at the nadir of its popularity and apparently facing parliamentary and electoral defeat the Liberals at last had the opportunity to exert some political brokerage. The Lib–Lab pact was a conscious decision to sustain a Labour government and thus delay or possibly avoid a new Conservative government. However, the continued erosion of Liberal support in both by-elections and public opinion polls (not uninfluenced by the circumstances surrounding Thorpe's removal from the leadership) coupled with Labour's relative revival have subsequently reduced the party's parliamentary influence.

The major weakness of the Liberal Party is the scattered and transient nature of its support. According to one survey less than 1 per cent of those entitled to vote in both 1959 and 1970 voted Liberal on both occasions.[41] The ephemeral nature of the party's support was even more clearly shown in 1974: 'nearly half those who voted Liberal in February 1974 failed to do so again in October'.[42] Lacking the permanent allegiance of an identifiable class or other group interest and with no really strong regional base outside the sparsely populated south-west, the Liberals seem unlikely to enjoy the political power and influence wielded by electorally smaller centre parties in many Continental countries. In the circumstances the party's major achievements are to act as a catalyst in the formation of political ideas which are ultimately acted upon by the major parties, as in the case of British entry into the European Communities and – possibly in the future – industrial co-determination and profit sharing.

In general the Liberal Party is well to the left of most Continental equivalents and may be considered as a radical, but non-Socialist party. Distancing itself from both big business and the trade unions, the party's major concerns are with individual liberty; institutional reform, particularly for regional government as well as, inevitably, changes in the electoral system; and more effective social services, possibly involving greater selectivity in public expenditure. The party has been rather more consistent than either of the others in supporting the notion of incomes policy and it is generally critical of the extension of public owner-ship.

As with the Conservatives, the Liberal Party grew out of a parliamentary caucus, but today the influence of the latter is circumscribed by its small size. Most of the major problems con-fronting the leadership in recent years have been tactical rather than substantive and both Jeremy Thorpe and his successor, David Steel, have required a certain dexterity in handling the wider party organs. The change of leadership itself involved a shift in internal party authority with a new electoral system. Candidates for the post must be MPs and nominated by a group of colleagues, but voting is by constituency parties. Each has ten votes plus another ten if they were also affiliated the previous year and an additional one for each 500 votes received by a Liberal candidate at the general election. Constituency associations are required to organise a ballot of their members and to distri-bute their votes proportionately between the candidates.[43] Curiously, this new system emerged almost as a by-product of the bizarre circumstances surrounding Thorpe's enforced resigna-tion. Suggestions about his possible involvement in personal scandal occasioned considerable criticism in the parliamentary group. The new method of election resulted from twin pressures by those anxious anyway to produce a system more democratic than those of the other parties and by Thorpe's supporters anxious to find a way by which he might retain the leadership should he wish to contest the election which ultimately he did not.

The Scottish Nationalists (SNP) and Welsh Nationalists (Plaid Cymru) have existed since the 1920s mainly as non-parliamentary pressure groups for self-government. Apart from a solitary success in a by-election early in 1945 in a straight fight with Labour who in turn easily regained the seat in a three-way contest at the general election, the SNP's first electoral success was to be at another by-election in 1967, a year after Plaid Cymru had won its first seat. The spectacular breakthrough was in 1974 when in February the two parties returned a total of nine MPs increasing to fourteen in October. Since then SNP has been the close rival of both Labour and Conservative in Scotland. By contrast Plaid Cymru is much weaker in terms of popular support which is concentrated in particular parts of Wales. Both parties aim at self-government, regarding devolution proposals as half-way houses and federalism as inadequate.[44] The general flavour of the SNP's programme tends to be populist, seeking support from both Left and Right. Future Scottish prosperity would, however, be based on a considerable amount of government direction of the economy exploiting *her oil resources*. Plaid Cymru's programme has a more overtly left-wing flavour, especially on economic and industrial questions. Given that until recently neither party had significant representation in Parliament it is not surprising to find that a much greater degree of control is exercised in both the making of policy and the determination of tactics by the wider party than is the case with Labour, Conservatives or Liberals. Westminster MPs of the SNP and Plaid Cymru have the prestige of having won electoral victory but they are no more than spokesmen for political movements which do not accept the legitimacy of a single UK Parliament.

Much analysis of the present political scene in Britain treats Welsh and Scottish Nationalism as identical phenomena. There are, though, interesting differences. Plaid Cymru's cultural background in a country administratively integrated with England for centuries is essentially a separate language, whilst the SNP may point to a different legal system, a considerable amount of administrative if not legislative devolution and a particular educational tradition. Generally both Scotland and Wales have been economically poorer than England and historically played important roles in the evolution of the Labour Party. SNP and Plaid Cymru propaganda lays considerable stress on 'economic exploitation', but a traditional weakness of the Nationalist position has been the fear that independence would simply end all redistribution of resources from England without any compensating gain. Whilst this may still be the case for Wales, the discovery of large amounts of oil off the Scottish coast has been an enormous boost for the SNP and may explain their much greater political success.

Up to the 1960s Northern Ireland enjoyed legislative, executive and administrative devolution with politics revolving around an interaction of the religious split between Protestants and Catholics and the attempted importation of the British parties. The Stormont Assembly and Northern Ireland's representation at Westminster were both totally dominated by the Ulster Unionists, exclusively Protestant and linked to the Conservative Party. Traditional opposition based on the Catholic community was divided between Labour and Republican groupings of various kinds, some of which simply boycotted the political system. Terrorism by, and virtual civil war between, groups reflecting extremist Protestant and Catholic positions necessitated the ending of devolution and direct rule by British governments anxious to pacify and normalise the province. For the moment the major political implications have been the break-up of the old Ulster Unionist Party and its replacement by a collection of 'loyalist' political groups who reject any automatic link with the Conservatives. These groups can expect to win nine or ten of Northern Ireland's twelve Westminster seats. One important development has been the emergence of the Northern Ireland Social Democratic Labour Party as an opposition force with the support of most Catholics and willing to accept that Irish partition cannot and should not be ended by force. None the less the future of Northern Ireland's parties will obviously depend on the outcome of the struggle against terrorism.

In addition to the Liberals and the purely sectional or national parties, the UK has a considerable number of minor parties. For the moment only one, the National Front, has any real political significance. Based on a merging of a variety of extreme right-wing groups, the Front has been fuelled by, and has sought to exploit, racial tensions aroused by new Commonwealth immigrants. The party has a strong neo-Nazi strain[45] and has sought publicity and influence through marches and demonstrations – where it has often clashed with left-wing groups – as well as through contesting elections at national and local level. In October 1974 the Front put up ninety candidates and won over 100,000 votes. In 1975 it scored further advances in local elections in a number of conurbations with large immigrant communities, but subsequently much of the impetus has faded. The National Front may well field over 300 candidates at the next general election – if only in order to obtain free time on radio and television. Assuming that the average candidate wins 1,000 votes, the party will take about 1·5 per cent of the overall national vote.

The political impact of the cluster of issues surrounding immigration and race relations has not been limited to the growth of parties on the extreme Right: they have also had a considerable effect on the major parties.[46] When a Conservative government introduced the first immigration controls in 1962, Labour – traditional champions of the multi-racial Commonwealth – found it easy to unite in opposition. Little more than five years later a Labour government, conscious of the political unpopularity of more immigration, further tightened the controls. Even so it was the Conservative Party which remained most positively identified with restricted entry. Its most effective populist politician, Enoch Powell, gained support for the party by his crusades against further immigration and his introduction of the notion of repatriation, even though he was formally disowned by Edward Heath and dismissed from the shadow cabinet. Immigration may well have been one factor contributing to Labour's defeat in 1970.[47] Before the 1974 elections Powell had broken with the

Conservative Party over the European issue: his advocacy of a Labour vote had a significant impact in his west midlands base – an area noted for its sensitivity on the immigration question.

It is characteristic of the two-party system that issues with potentiality for creating rival groups are likely to be adopted by one or other major party. Margaret Thatcher's reopening of the immigration issue in 1977 was a clear attempt to gain political support by distancing Conservative from Labour and by offering voters a respectable and responsible alternative to the National Front. The electoral impact of this fresh appeal to the 'Powell constituency' is hard to gauge. At the October 1974 election there were fifty-nine seats in which the majority was less than the number of voters of New Commonwealth origin. Of these fifty-nine only sixteen were won by the Conservatives as against twenty-nine in February.[48] It is difficult to assess the importance to Labour of the immigrant vote in winning these thirteen seats which were mostly in downtown areas with enormous social problems but also with potentially disaffected white voters. It remains an open question as to whether the Conservatives will gain more from white 'backlash' than will Labour from closer identification with the aspirations of ethnic minorities.

PARTY MEMBERSHIP AND FINANCE

There is a shortage of accurate information about the membership and finance of British parties. Only Labour publishes annual membership figures, but these are recognised as inaccurate. Parties are required by law to publish annual income and expenditure accounts, but these only apply to the national level and ignore constituency parties which are responsible for about half of total income and expenditure. The report of the Houghton Committee on the question of possible state financial aid for political parties[49] is now much the best source of detailed information about finance and, indirectly, membership, but the material is sometimes presented in a confusing manner.

Labour claims a total membership of just over 6,600,000 of whom 5,900,000 are affiliated through trade unions. Once a trade union decides to establish a separate political fund, members wishing to avoid the extra levy must take the positive step of contracting out. Inevitably some who are not sympathetic to the objects of the political fund, which is almost invariably used in the interests of the Labour Party, none the less continue to pay. Although affiliation fees will be drawn from the political fund, the number paying the levy and the number for whom the union affiliates are not always identical. Individual membership of the Labour Party has been in excess of 1 million, but the present figure of 660,000 is now accepted as wildly optimistic for it is based on the assumption that every constituency party has a minimum of 1,000. Since the average constituency membership is little over half this, total individual membership seems unlikely to be much above 350,000. Given the Conservative Party's rather different structure, less constitutional importance is attached to the act of joining and the whole notion of membership tends to be rather vague. The party has never issued detailed membership figures, although at one time it claimed a total of more than 2 million. The present total is certainly lower than that – probably in the range 1,000,000 to 1,250,000. Labour and Conservatives both peaked – as far as individual members are concerned – in the 1950s, while the Liberals' high point came in 1964/5 when a figure of 250,000 was claimed. Since then it, too, has fallen – probably to about 150,000. No figures are available for SNP and Plaid Cymru, but their combined membership is probably between 100,000 and 150,000. Allowing for other minor groups, it follows that some 2 million people – 5 per cent of the electorate – are individual members of British political parties. Including Labour's affiliated trade unionists and making an appropriate deduction for possible double membership, the figure rises to around 7,500,000 or nearly 19 per cent of the electorate.

In analysing party finance it must be remembered that whilst three parties seek to cover the whole of Britain, SNP and Plaid Cymru operate respectively in Scotland and Wales alone. The Conservatives are easily the best off at both central and constituency level. Annual income at the centre is now about £2,000,000 of which about one-quarter comes from the constituency associations and the bulk of the rest from individual and business donations. A large slice of expenditure is on both regional and constituency activities, although fully 20 per cent is devoted to research. At general elections the party is able to to raise and spend an additional £1,000,000. In non-election years the combined central income of Labour and the associated Co-operative Party is about 70 per cent of that of the Conservatives. Almost all of this is from subscriptions and affiliation fees, so that constituency parties produce barely 10 per cent of the total. The exigencies of running the headquarters of a major political party on limited finance means that proportionately less goes on regional and constituency activities and on research than is the case with the Conservatives. When it comes to general elections the discrepancy is even more marked, for Labour centrally can expect to raise no more than £500,000 – mostly from trade unions – and much of this has to be used to supplement constituency resources. It is also worth noting that a semi-autonomous organisation British United Industrialists[50] raises considerable sums of money for Conservative political causes and spends a good deal of this directly itself. The amount spent directly by trade unions in the Labour interest is much smaller, although the party may conceivably gain some feeling of security from the knowledge that sums of money are held in reserve in the political funds.

The Liberals have far fewer financial resources than either of their major rivals: at the centre their regular income is barely 10 per cent that of Labour. Little is available to give help outside headquarters which are themselves run on literally a shoe-string. The two nationalist parties are proportionately much better off than the Liberals: Plaid Cymru's annual income of about £80,000 suggests that at central level it is proportionately actually better off than Labour.

Few hard data were available on the financing of constituency parties before the publication of the Houghton Report. Its findings suggested rather higher levels of income in absolute terms for Labour and Liberal constituency parties than had sometimes been supposed. None the less the national rank order was maintained with the average Conservative association having something like two and a half times the income of its Labour rival and five times that of the Liberals. These gaps widen still further in absolute – though not in proportional – terms at general elections when a fair slice of the income of Labour constituency parties comes from the centre. As far as expenditure is concerned the major variable for constituency parties is the employment of a full-time agent or organiser which is the norm for a majority of Conservative parties. In contrast there are less than eighty full time Labour constituency agents, whilst the Liberals have virtually none. Even though part of an agent's time is inevitably devoted to ensuring his next week's salary, the result of this difference between the parties is to give the Conservatives a very considerable advantage in organisational terms – particularly demonstrated in the organisation of the postal vote.

Taking election and non-election years together Britain's parties have an average annual income of about £13,000,000, 60% of which goes to the Conservatives. About one third of the total is raised centrally. A general election is likely to cost an additional £3,500,000. Despite the recommendations of the Houghton Report it seems unlikely that any direct state financial aid will be given in the near future. The state does, however, undertake the entire process of electoral registration and at election times offers all candidates limited free postage and meeting-hall facilities as well as radio and television time given to the parties nationally. The only precedent for direct financial payments was during the referendum on the European Community when small grants of £125,000 each were made to umbrella organisations representing the pro and anti groups.

CONCLUSION

The British political system has received its share of criticism in recent years. The electoral system and the notion of alternating majority governments – for so long complacently assumed to be exportable to other democracies – lays enormous salience on the government/opposition syndrome. While the policies and programmes of parties *in office* tend to be interest-aggregative rather than sectional, political behaviour is strongly influenced by hopes of total victory and fears of total defeat which are not so omnipresent in systems where coalitions are more normal. So long as the attitudes of the major parties exclude coalitions from the realm of practical politics in Britain, the tendency for oppositions simply to oppose must be strong. Given Britain's major economic and political problems, some have doubted whether the country can any longer afford this kind of confrontation politics – possibly seen at its worst in the harassment by oppositions of both parties as governments of both parties have sought over the last decade to curb inflation through regulation of prices and incomes. Labour's changes of heart on the European Communities and the Conservatives on government/industry relations are other examples which may be cited. It is on this analysis conceivable that without the bonus of North Sea oil and the possibility of some kind of British economic miracle the presssure for institutional change would have been overwhelming. During the early 1970s many organs of the liberal intelligentsia argued that Britain was becoming ungovernable and that some kind of revolution from within or without the political system was becoming inevitable. By 1974 and 1975 this same analysis involved a comparative assessment that no other country had ever suffered Britain's rate of inflation and yet remained democratic.[51] Perhaps in retrospect this argument may be reversed: the British system of government has been strong enough to survive economic problems of a kind which would have caused the overthrow of most others. It could be argued that faced with the loss of Empire and other associated problems, no conceivable political system could have delivered the economic goods over the last two decades. It may be a tribute to the durability, resilience and capability of inspiring loyalty of Britain's recognised political parties that the political system has emerged relatively unscathed through massive economic problems, civil strife in Northern Ireland and the problems of integrating well over a million new Commonwealth immigrants.

The notion that the British public have by and large accepted the more critical argument and that this is borne out by electoral statistics requires elaboration. Many analysts of British politics, including in the past this author,[52] have made the mistake of taking the 1945/50 period as a beginning and, therefore, the norm for postwar British politics. In fact the years of Labour's first majority government brought about a domination by two parties which is practically unparalleled in British political history. Gradual erosion of that domination leading to the 1974 elections may seem to presage the gradual emergence of a new kind of political system. However, future projections based on extrapolating trends are often misleading. Four years after the February 1974 election the Liberals seemed to have fallen back to the level of national support normal during the 1960s, whilst neither the National Front nor any of the fringe parties seem to have made significant headway. The biggest question mark in British politics lies over Scotland where there is every indication that the SNP now has as a base the permanent allegiance of between 20 and 30 per cent of the voters. With the fate and implications of continued attempts to produce legislative devolution for Scotland and Wales still unclear, particularist nationalism in Britain could go in either direction. In the last analysis, though, this author's assessment is influenced by the near certainty that during the next decade Britain's economic performance is going to improve sufficiently sharply to remove for the moment much of the talk of an impending crisis of political and civil institutions. Against this background the probability is that Britain will continue to be dominated by two relatively heterogeneous and fairly opportunistic political parties with scope in the system for smaller groups to play many roles – as has indeed been the case for much of this century.

# APPENDIX

Table 10.5   *General Election Results, 1966–1974 (votes in '000s;*
*% of those voting)*

| | 1966 | 1970 | 1974 (Feb.) | 1974 (Oct.) |
|---|---|---|---|---|
| **Labour** | | | | |
| Votes | 13,065 | 12,179 | 11,639 | 11,457 |
| % | 47·9 | 43·0 | 37·1 | 39·2 |
| Seats | 363 | 287 | 301 | 319 |
| **Conservative** | | | | |
| Votes | 11,418 | 13,145 | 11,869 | 10,465 |
| % | 41·9 | 46·4 | 37·9 | 35·8 |
| Seats | 253 | 330 | 297 | 277 |
| **Liberal** | | | | |
| Votes | 2,328 | 2,117 | 6,063 | 5,347 |
| % | 8·5 | 7·5 | 19·3 | 18·3 |
| Seats | 12 | 6 | 14 | 13 |
| **SNP** | | | | |
| Votes | 128 | 307 | 632 | 840 |
| % | 0·5 | 1·1 | 2·0 | 2·9 |
| Seats | 0 | 1 | 7 | 11 |
| **Plaid Cymru** | | | | |
| Votes | 61 | 175 | 171 | 166 |
| % | 0·2 | 0·6 | 0·6 | 0·6 |
| Seats | 0 | 0 | 2 | 3 |
| **N. Ireland[1]** | | | | |
| Votes | | | 718 | 702 |
| % | | | 2·3 | 2·4 |
| Seats | | | 12 | 12 |
| **Others[2]** | | | | |
| Votes | 233 | 421 | 241 | 212 |
| % | 0·9 | 1·5 | 0·8 | 0·7 |
| Seats | 2 | 6 | 2 | 0 |

*Notes:*
All votes are to nearest thousand.
[1] 1974 elections only. For 1966 and 1970 Northern Ireland votes divided between major parties and others.
[2] Whole of UK for 1966 and 1970; excludes Northern Ireland for 1974 elections.

*Source: British Political Facts;* D. Butler and A. Sloman, London, Macmillan, 1975.

# NOTES

1 The British Election Study at the University of Essex has produced an enormous amount of valuable survey material, much of which seems to imply that the reversal of the major parties is part of an ongoing long-term trend; see I. Crewe, B. Särlvik and J. Alt, 'Partisan dealignment in Britain 1964–74', *British Journal of Political Science,* 1977; also I. Budge, I. Crewe and D. Fairlie, *Party Identification and Beyond* (London, Wiley, 1976).

2 In the absence of official electoral statistics for the United Kingdom, I have throughout relied upon the copious and detailed material gathered in D. Butler and A. Sloman, *British Political Facts 1900–75* (London, Macmillan, 1975), and the appendices to the Nuffield General Election studies, also mainly written by David Butler.

3 See also Crewe, Särlvik and Alt, op. cit. Their figures are very slightly different, but the trend is identical.

4 See the appendix by Michael Steed analysing the results in *The British General Election of October 1974,* D. Butler and M. Kavanagh (London, Macmillan, 1975).

5 Disproportionately well, in comparison with nationwide minor parties. Comparison of Labour and Irish Nationalists election results in 1910 offers an historic example.

6 Steed op. cit.

7 See introduction by Michael Steed to A. Cyr, *Liberal Party Politics in Britain* (London, Calder and Boyars, 1977).

8 A leading Labour figure in the 1920s and 1930s, he became Chancellor of the Exchequer in 1945.

9 H. Dalton, *Practical Socialism for Britain* (London, Routledge, 1935).

10 For convenience I have equated the 'middle class' with occupation classes 1 to 4 and the 'working class' with occupation classes 5 and 6. The figures are drawn from *Political Change in Britain,* D. Butler and D. Stokes (London, Macmillan, 2nd edn, 1974).

11 ibid., 1st edn, 1969.

12 See the writings of Goldthorpe, Guttsman and McKenzie (cited in detail in bibliography to first edition).

13 Butler and Stokes, op. cit.

14 Crewe, Särlvik and Alt, op. cit.

15 ibid.

16 See R. Rose, *The Problem of Party Government* (Harmondsworth, Penguin, 1976) and *The Times Guide to the House of Commons, October 1974* (London, Times Books, 1974).

17 Cf. Table 10.3, p. 213. The decline of the Liberal vote in Scotland and Wales as a percentage of the total Liberal vote helps justify the approach taken in that table.

18 Outside the Community it does, of course, exist in Norway and Sweden; see S. Henig and J. Pinder, *European Political Parties* (London, Allen & Unwin, 1969).

19 Article in *Socialist Commentary,* June 1952; reprinted in R. Tawney, *The Radical Tradition* (London, Allen & Unwin, 1964).

20 Article in *Encounter,* April 1960; reprinted in R. H. S. Crossman, *Planning for Freedom* (London, Hamish Hamilton, 1965).

21 R. MacDonald, *Socialism: Critical and Constructive* (London, Cassell, rev. edn, 1924).

22 C. Attlee, *The Labour Party in Perspective* (London, Gollancz, 1937).

23 See, for example, S. Beer, *Modern British Politics* (London, Faber, 1965).
24 J. Strachey, *The Coming Struggle for Power* (London, Gollancz, 1932).
25 G. D. H. Cole, *Socialism in Evolution* (Harmondsworth, Penguin, 1938).
26 E. Durbin, *The Politics of Democratic Socialism* (London, Routledge & Kegan Paul, 1940).
27 See, for example, C. A. R. Crosland, *The Conservative Enemy* (London, Jonathan Cape, 1962).
28 R. H. S. Crossman, *Labour in an Affluent Society*, Fabian Tract No. 325, reprinted in *Planning for Freedom*, op. cit.
29 In effect the TUC negotiated norms for increases with the government and then enforced them on a voluntary basis. Trade unions seemed to have been brought into the government policy making process when the chancellor of the exchequer twice made budgetary tax cuts conditional on trade union agreement to continuation of the social contract. This was denounced as 'unconstitutional' by many Conservatives.
30 E. Heffer, *The Class Struggle in Parliament* (London, Gollancz, 1973).
31 For information on the formally separate but closely allied Co-operative Party and also the Fabian Society, the last survivor of the nineteenth-century Socialist societies, see Henig and Pinder, op. cit.
32 Peregrine Worsthorne in A. Gamble (ed.), *The Conservative Nation* (London, Routledge & Kegan Paul, 1974). Worsthorne may be considered an idiosyncratic exponent of the philosophy of Toryism in the modern Conservative Party.
33 Rose, op. cit.
34 Crewe, Särlvik and Alt, op. cit.
35 *The Right Approach*, Conservative Central Office, 1976.
36 Election manifesto of the Conservative Party, October 1976.
37 *Campaign Guide*, Conservative Central Office, 1977.
38 *Rules and Standing Orders of the National Union of Conservative and Unionist Associations*, revised 1975.
39 Cyr, op. cit.
40 *Pathways to Power*, Liberal Research Department, 1974.
41 Butler and Stokes, op. cit.
42 J. Alt, I. Crewe and B. Särlvik, 'Angels in plastic: the Liberal surge in 1974', *Political Studies*, vol. XXV, no. 3, September 1977.
43 *The Constitution of the Liberal Party*, revised 1976.
44 See *Scotland's Future*, SNP, 1975; *Power for Wales*, Plaid Cymru, 1974; and *The Peaceful Road to Self-Government*, Plaid Cymru, 1969.
45 See M. Walker, *The National Front* (London, Fontana, 1977).
46 See Zig Layton-Henry, 'Race, electoral strategy and party organisation', paper presented to Political Studies Association, 1978; also Nuffield Election Studies, op. cit.
47 There is an interesting attempt to quantify the effect in W. L. Miller, 'What was the profit in following the crowd? Aspects of Labour and Conservative strategy since 1970', Centre for the Study of Public Policy, University of Strathclyde, 1978, mimeo.
48 Layton-Henry, op. cit.
49 D. Houghton *et al.*, *Report of the Committee on Financial Aid to Political Parties* Cmd 6601 (London, HMSO, 1976).
50 See R. Rose, *Influencing Voters* (London, Faber, 1967); also R. Rose, *The Problem of Party Government*, op. cit.
51 This was a continuing theme in *The Economist* during this period.
52 See, for example, Henig and Pinder, op. cit.

# 11

# Transnational Parties in the European Community I: The Party Groups in the European Parliament

## GEOFFREY PRIDHAM AND PIPPA PRIDHAM

The role of political parties within the process of European integration is increasingly being recognised as an important aspect of the development of the Community in the 1970s, particularly as this gradually assumes a more overtly political form. The increasing scope of political activity in the EEC, notably in its external relations, has together with its enlargement in 1973 and an international recognition of its importance, produced a new momentum in integration after the stagnation of the late 1960s, in spite of the inhibiting effects of the world economic situation and the failure of the most ambitious of the 'second-generation' policies, economic and monetary union. At the institutional level, this developing 'politicisation' of activity in the EEC has been reflected in the widening range of debates in the European Parliament and in successive efforts to upgrade its role.

The recent growth of party political activity within the Community is a response to these developments, although it can trace its history back to the early years of European integration. So far, studies of the party political aspects of integration have tended to treat three dimensions separately and somewhat in isolation: the activities of the transnational party groups in the European Parliament, whose own isolated role has encouraged this partial approach; the positions of parties on European policy within the contexts of their own national political systems; and the elaboration of transnational (extra-parliamentary) organisational links between political parties of the same ideology or tendency. It is the third and most recent of these dimensions, developing primarily though not exclusively in response to the prospect of direct elections, which is beginning to draw together the other two. The result is a growing inclination to express party political differences at the European level. This has always existed within the national context since the integration process began, especially in countries where domestic debate over European policy has been polarised (such as West Germany in the early 1950s, and Britain in the 1960s and 1970s), although interest in this subject has concentrated more on the government/ opposition perspective than on the intrinsic position of individual parties on European integration.[1]

Similarly, the relatively new phenomenon of transnational party activity at Strasbourg/Luxembourg has attracted attention from a few scholars,[2] but the possibilities for party competition here have hitherto been substantially limited by the obvious weaknesses of the European Parliament as an institution.

The recognition that political activity at the European level can no longer be largely confined to sessions of national ministers and heads of government (i.e. interstate) has derived not only from the less exclusively economic scope of Community policy, but also from the growing weight of executive power-centres (specifically the Council of Ministers), which has strengthened arguments for trying to rectify the 'democratic deficit' in the EC, through increasing control by the Parliament. Most party group leaders at Strasbourg view direct elections as making this development inevitable. The debate over policy making in the Community and initiatives to strengthen its institutional structure have enhanced the tendency to express, not only different national viewpoints, but also conflicting outlooks between political parties and even within them. Such a development has been further encouraged by the growth in the number of party groups in the European Parliament and in the complexity of their composition, especially since enlargement.

While much potential significance may be attached to the developing party-political dimension to Community activity, many questions arise as to the overall motivation behind this process and the form it takes. First, since the national focus of activity continues to claim prior attention in the thinking of individual political parties, one must suppose there is a basic limitation on their willingness to merge their sovereignty within the framework of party co-operation at the European level. Secondly, ideological fraternity does not presuppose a strictly common viewpoint on a range of individual policies: a special feature of this problem of cohesion in the Community, as demonstrated by the experience of the party groups, is the existence of cross-pressures between national differences and differences of ideological interpretation (which may also exist within national parties). Thirdly, will the relationship of the party groups in the European Parliament to the party federations be a dominant one, on the model of many member countries where the parliamentary group overshadows the party organisation in policy matters? Fourthly, some attention will also be paid to the 'fall-out' effect either way of party activity at both the European and national levels. This question touches in particular on the domestic interests which affect individual parties in their seeking transnational co-operation within the EC. Finally the catalytic impact of direct elections on transnational party co-operation will be discussed.

For the purposes of this study, it is useful to divide the evolution of the European party groups into four historical phases. First, the period of the Common Assembly of the European Coal and Steel Community (1953–8) saw the beginnings of intergroup conflict, even though the scope of integration policy was limited. Secondly, the birth of the Common Market led in its early years (1958–62) to an optimistic view of the future of European integration, which in turn affected the prospects for European party co-operation and even aroused discussion of direct elections. Thirdly, the period of stagnation in integration (1962–9) impeded the development of the party groups and discouraged initiatives to strengthen transnational party co-operation at the organisational level. The end of this period of stagnation was marked by the Hague summit conference (December 1969), following de Gaulle's retirement, which led to enlargement negotiations. The period since then may be regarded as an important fourth phase in the development of the party groups.

The present chapter concentrates on the operation of the various groups in the European Parliament. The succeeding chapter will examine the emergent transnational links outside the Parliament, at the same time endeavouring to relate the two sets of developments.

THE EUROPEAN PARLIAMENTARY GROUPS

This study of the party groups in the European Parliament attempts to answer three principal questions. First, how politically important are the party groups within the European Parliament? Secondly to what extent may the groups be regarded as supranational? Thirdly, are traditional criteria applicable to the analysis and evaluation of the 'party system' in the European Parliament?

Party groups clearly dominate the organisation and procedures of the European Parliament. The ultimate aim of the groups individually, and of the Parliament as a whole, is to influence Community legislation emanating from the Council of Ministers and Commission. Within the Parliament, the main aim of a group is to present a common political view on all matters arising in the committees and the Parliament. Among their other functions, the groups nominate and elect the president of the Parliament and the twelve vice-presidents, who with the president comprise the parliamentary bureau. This, with the aid of the parliamentary secretariat and the secretary general, directs all the activities of the Parliament, and is responsible for liaison with Brussels. The bureau and the group chairman form the enlarged bureau, which with the twelve standing committee chairmen (also appointed on a group basis) draws up the agenda of the plenary sessions. In the debates, the group spokesmen have priority and longer speaking time for the presentation of group viewpoints than do individual members. Groups also influence the appointment of parliamentary staff.

However, this transnational party activity has to be seen in relation to the basic deficiencies of the Parliament as an institution and the limitations imposed on the political influence of the groups by its methods of procedure. The Parliament suffers from a general lack of authority and legitimacy, for it is a consultative assembly not a legislature; it does not appoint the Commission and has no control at all over the Council. Although some of Parliament's debates have become more political, there is still much technical discussion (as in national parliaments), which together with a highly structured agenda, the problems imposed by the necessity of interpretation, and the non-confrontational atmosphere tend to reduce its political impact. Partly as a result of this, the Parliament still suffers from a lack of publicity and interest in the member countries. The internal organisation of the parliamentary system, in one specific way, also limits group domination of its activities, for proposed Community legislation is channelled into the relevant committee so that groups as a whole are excluded at this initial stage. Although the groups may discuss a report immediately before it is raised in the plenary session, votes have often been agreed between the secretariats before the debate. A final weakness is that the groups meet rarely outside plenary sessions.

This discussion of the role of the party groups in the institution of the Parliament relates to the second question of their supranational character. There are three major indicators of supranationality: how far group policies and views transcend national boundaries and interests to promote European interests; how far a group is able to present a meaningful common viewpoint; and how genuinely transnational is the composition of the group.

The political activity of each group is directed by its bureau, led by the chairman, which is an executive committee of MEPs chosen from the group according to national and political representation. The chairman plays a particularly important part in the decision making of the group, partly because the Parliament sits and the whole group meets relatively infrequently. In the larger and more heterogeneous groups he must make strenuous efforts to reconcile ideological and national differences in order to achieve group consensus and be able to present a group viewpoint in the plenary session. To aid the bureau and chairman in the formulation of group policies, some of the groups have working parties or committees, which draw up policy positions for discussion by the group. Each group has a permanent and politically committed secretariat which gives continuity to its work and is responsible for everyday administration. Its size and financial allowances accorded it by the Parliament are directly proportional to the size, and number of the nationalities incorporated in the group. In the larger groups, the secretariat plays an important political role of co-ordinating and resolving ideological and national differences and implementing and executing any decisions taken. The groups usually meet early each day of the plenary session to discuss the day's agenda and to determine their position on the issues arising. The week prior to each plenary is kept free of official parliamentary business to enable groups to meet, and the European Parliament funds study days to discuss longer-term policy twice a year.

Despite an organisational structure which aids the promotion of group activity on a supranational basis, there are limits imposed on this by their composition. The larger groups have the problem of negotiating in several languages, exacerbated by the sometimes slow and spasmodic translation of documents, and although the smaller groups have fewer problems of geographical spread and language, they have a major disadvantage in that they have proportionally smaller secretariats and fewer allowances. Finally, the method of selecting MEPs may inhibit the functioning of groups supranationally. Individuals are designated from their national parties and governments (except the Labour Party, who for the first time in 1977 elected their MEPs in the parliamentary party on a regional list system), generally taking into account regional, political and economic representation. However, the choice may be limited by the safety of a member's seat in certain countries, and by his desire to attend. There are few career prospects in the European Parliament and European work may detract from efficacy at home and jeopardise marginal seats as well as imposing extra strain under the present dual mandate system and isolation from national career structure.

## THE SOCIALIST GROUP

The Socialist group, together with the Christian Democrats and the Liberals, is one of the original party groups of the Common Assembly of the ECSC. Since the 1960s and up to enlargement of the Community in January 1973, the Socialist group was regarded generally as 'the most cohesive . . . group'.[3] The Socialists had a certain common ideological background accompanied by a tradition of international fraternity and co-operation, as well as an acceptance of fairly strict internal party discipline, despite an open attitude to policy debate. Up to that time, the group was almost unanimous in its support of rapid progress towards a federalist Europe with strengthened supranational institutional structures and greater 'democratisation' of the Community, increased control of the institutions and legitimation of community action, and was active in fully exploiting the powers of the Parliament, asking questions and applying pressure for furthering their demands.

Since then, the group has become more heterogeneous with the arrival of the four Danish members on enlargement, and the eighteen British Labour Party members, after the British pro-European referendum result in 1975 terminated Labour's boycott of the Parliament (which had been much regretted by European Socialists). The Danish members have tended to reflect the Danish Folketing's restrictive view on institutional developments and have dissociated themselves from group policy on institutional matters of community development, such as budgetary powers and policy co-operation.[4] On all other matters, however, they have been involved fully in the formulation of group policy and are generally considered to have presented a more positive attitude towards Europe than the British Labour Party. Despite some ideological reservations, Labour joined the Socialists who became the largest group in the Parliament – to the chagrin of the Christian Democrats. The Labour delegation made it clear that it could not always accept majority decisions although it would endeavour to do so.

As the largest group, and the only one with members from all Community countries, the Socialist group has gained in political weight and status within the Parliament and increased its prestige and influence in the administrative organs. But the arrival of the Labour MEPs, comprising just under half anti-marketeers, posed a political challenge to the traditional cohesion of the group, and a numerical threat to dominance and influence of the SPD. However, although some of the Labour members have tended to follow a somewhat individualistic and 'nationalistic' line, even former anti-marketeers have become actively involved in the work of the Parliament.[5] Despite earlier fears, the SPD continues as in the past to have a powerful and cohesive influence on the group (for example, the chairman, the secretary general and the press officer are West German), which may be attributed to their general assiduousness, as well as to their geographical proximity and individual abilities.

Although recently it has been more difficult to achieve, the Socialist group has tried to formulate a view on every issue. The group meeting is the sovereign body, which takes policy decisions. It usually meets each day of the plenary session to discuss the day's proceedings, has study days twice a year and meets regularly in the week before the plenary sessions in the national capitals in turn. Until the group was enlarged, it 'had accepted the much stricter rule of observing majority decisions'.[6] Since that time, the group has had under a formal provision to relax that practice, although it continues to endeavour to reach agreement or obtain consensus in private, preferring to avoid a vote or direction on how to vote in the plenary session. However, if the group is unable to reach agreement on an issue, differing MEPs may take a different line in the plenary session[7] from that of the group spokesman, or the group may be allowed a free vote.[8] The necessity of relaxing previous disciplinary rules in order primarily to accommodate two groups of 'reluctant Europeans' has increased the difficulties of the chairman in acting as integrator of the various national and ideological interests. His role has developed into that of a conciliator of various political interests,[9] thus necessitating close liaison, negotiation and co-operation with the leaders of national delegations, who are automatically group vice-chairmen and members of the group bureau. The assiduousness with which Ludwig Fellermaier (chairman since .1975) has approached this task has reflected the general desire of the group to maintain its traditional cohesion and its determination to present a united European position in the face of rival groups, particularly the Christian Democrats.

To facilitate the achievement of a common viewpoint, the group has several working parties, including one on economic and social affairs and one on agriculture, which follow the work of the standing committees in Parliament, co-ordinate the work of the Socialist members on them and prepare policy positions for discussions by the group. In addition the Socialist members of each of the twelve standing committees in the Parliament form a special committee, which meets before the relevant standing committee to prepare positions.[10] This range of activities, as well as the work of the bureau and the chairman, is documented and co-ordinated by the secretariat, so that while the size and the complexity of the group may make it unwieldy to manage, the secretariat plays an important unifying as well as administrative role, giving expert assistance and continuity to the work of the group.[11] Its work is not purely administrative[12] for according to the group's rules of procedure (point 15) the secretariat is given the function of 'directing' the attention of the group to particular policy problems and preparing reports on these. The secretariat and the secretary general work in close contact with the chairman and the bureau, and play a useful part in resolving the national and ideological differences within the group as a whole.

Despite these efforts at co-ordination, there are limitations to the ability and success of the group in presenting a united position. Ideologically, the group incorporates strands of Socialist ideology which range from the near-Marxist and statist approach of the Italians (PSI), through the relatively 'left-wing' standpoint of the British Labour Party and the French (PS) to the 'right-wing', more pragmatic social-engineering approach of the SPD. These generalised ideological divisions do not, however, always fall neatly along national frontiers.

National differences emerge more clearly over the approach to and the degree of interest in certain issues, the interests of individual MEPs, the view of the general role of the group in the Parliament and the relationships with home parliaments and constituencies. The most obvious point of tension has been the British Labour Party's continued hostility towards the progress of the Community and, in particular, to direct elections. Although the Labour members have regarded themselves as being responsible to the PLP, they have not considered themselves as subject to direction from Transport House or the NEC.[13] But the divisions in the national party over Europe have caused the MEPs to vacillate on institutional questions. The Danish MEPs have a similar problem in their parliamentary party, but not in such an extreme form, for care has been taken in their national parliament to avoid open conflict[14] in view of the severe consequences that such divisions had for the Norwegian Labour Party.

More generally, national concerns emerge over particular interests in certain policy areas. The German MEPs have a special interest in economic affairs, concentrating on planning, control of inflation and competition policy, for their country funds much of the Community activity; the Dutch are interested in institutional issues, regional policy and transport, because of its importance for their economy;[15] the Belgians are particularly interested in social policy and agriculture.[16] More specifically an individual's interest may be influenced by an awareness of constituency requirements, such as John Prescott's interest in fishing policy, being an ex-seaman and MP for the port-city of Hull.

Despite the limitations imposed by national and particular attitudes on the 'supranational' functioning of the group in the European Parliament, it is united on the fundamental political principle that 'the goals of European socialism are freedom, justice and solidarity',[17] and on representing the interests of the working man and the consumer. The group believes in the protection of the basic rights of the consumer, including health, safety and economic interests, by means of a coherent action programme and increased budgetary expenditure.[18] The group regards social justice as being of paramount importance, and views as essential the aim of overcoming the structural differences between rich and poor in the various regions of the community. On the other hand, the Common Agricultural Policy 'has caused the most political and technical difficulty and dispute'.[19] Problems arise between members from those parties with almost no votes among farmers, such as the SPD and the British Labour Party, and those from the French Socialist and Irish Labour parties, seeking support for their farmers. Despite these difficulties, the group managed to produce a statement concerning the reform of the CAP, which approved its aims and recognised certain advantages in it. They also believed that agricultural policies 'must be more outward looking, more efficient, fairer to the consumer and defensible in both international political and economic terms',[20] and called for a structural reappraisal and a review of the pricing policy. The formulation of positions on regional policy must overcome similar problems of differences over national interest, but the group would like to have more concentrated effort on 'practical policies to reduce unemployment and regional differences in living standards and opportunities for development',[21] desiring that remedies have long-term effects and not be merely short-term palliatives. These examples illustrate the strenuous efforts made in the Socialist group to reach a compromise over important European policies and to produce as detailed and specific a Socialist viewpoint as possible.

Up to enlargement, the Socialists were considered to be the most cohesive of the party groups, but their expansion to include Danish and British members has required flexibility of discipline and a decrease in cohesion, although political and organisational advantages have accrued from being the largest group in the Parliament. As the British 'anti-marketeers' have become more involved in the work of the Parliament they have become less 'negative', and there remains a general desire in the group to promote the 'co-operation of progressive political forces on a transnational basis'.[22]

## THE CHRISTIAN DEMOCRATIC GROUP

Unlike other party groups, which have undergone a significant change in their composition and size since enlargement of the Community in 1973, the Christian Democrats have remained largely consistent in both respects save for the inclusion in that year of three Irish Fine Gail members who with their party's Catholic rural background have presented no special problems of absorption (there are no Christian Democratic parties in Britain and Denmark). The size of the group has varied between fifty-one and fifty-three during 1969–78, changes occurring mainly as a result of national election trends. The possibility of the British Conservatives joining the group discussed at the time of enlargement did not materialise, so that once the British Labour delegation formed part of the Socialist group in 1975 the Christian Democrats lost their status as the largest group in the European Parliament, which they had enjoyed since the beginning of the Common Assembly in the 1950s.

While the Christian Democrats dominate the proceedings of the Parliament less than before – not only in the face of the increased weight of the Socialists, but also owing to the active role of British members generally in parliamentary work – their consistency of composition and their tradition of working in the Parliament have allowed them to function as a group with relative ease, in spite of the internal differences inevitable in this form of transnational activity. It is important, however, to examine the special characteristics of the group which both promote and inhibit its performance.

The over-riding common denominator among the Christian Democrats, applicable also to their national political parties in general, is their unquestionably strong ideological attachment to the process of European integration, featured both in their historical role as 'pioneers' of European unity after the Second World War and in their persistent advocacy of political union, looking towards a federal Europe. The general conceptual tone of their approach to this subject has distinguished the Christian Democrats from the other groups' more specific definition of certain goals within integration, and it has provided the group's point of reference for its position on many issues. Predictably, this has been most apparent in the group's support for moves towards a federal structure in Europe, notably with the report of Tindemans (himself a Christian Democrat) on European Union. In opening the debate in the Parliament on this subject in July 1975, Alfred Bertrand (Belgian CVP), chairman of the group until 1977, expressed the stand of his group as follows:

'European union must be conceived as a pluralist democratic Community, whose priority aims should be to ensure increasingly strict respect for liberty and human dignity, to promote social justice based on solidarity between member states and Community citizens . . . The union must be based on an institutional structure, on a single decision-making centre in the nature of a European government.'[23]

This statement encompassed many of the particular aims which have motivated the group's activity, as well as 'values' which have typified Christian Democratic parties generally. In the institutional field, for instance, the group has been in the forefront of pressures for greater budgetary control by the Parliament (though not alone in this respect) and also assertive in its claims that the Commission show 'the obstinacy and the courage needed to force a Community solution' concerning the operation of the EC as a whole.[24] At the same time, the group has shown a 'protective' attitude towards the 'supranational' institutions of the Community:

'The thing that matters for the Community is that the Commission should fully exploit the possibilities the Treaties offer it. In this, the Commission has always been able to look upon the European Parliament as a trustworthy partner – the Christian Democratic group has largely contributed to this situation.'[25]

Hence the group's refusal to support the Conservative censure motion against the Commission in June 1976 (on milk surpluses) on the grounds, among others, that the criticism 'was not aimed at the right people' for it 'mainly concerned the Council of Ministers'.[26] The general approach, described above by Bertrand, has also featured in a strong advocacy of greater legitimacy for Community institutions, notably in the resolution moved by Giovanni Giraudo (chairman of the political affairs committee) in December 1974 for 'action that would win support for Community ideals',[27] and the response to the agreement on direct elections in 1976 that this would bring the EC closer to the

European citizen and offer an important way of furthering political union.[28]

Although this framework of pronounced pro-integration ideology combined with other Christian Democratic 'values' has provided the basis for individual standpoints within the group (e.g. Heinrich Aigner's activity on behalf of budgetary control, Bertrand's interest in human rights), the weakness of this common bond is that it focuses on a long-term view whereas active politics, as in the sessions of the European Parliament, is more concerned with immediate and concrete everyday events. The vague character of Christian Democratic ideology is not sufficient to ensure group cohesion over policy, although this problem is not critical owing to the political weakness of the European Parliament and the absence of government/opposition conflict. The problem of cohesion stems particularly from the fact that the group 'consists of parties which are ideologically related, but which have their own national history and national structure.'[29]

In any consideration of transnational party. co-operation, the importance of differences of policy interest and ideological emphasis both between national parties and within them must be estimated. The question of policy interest is usually attached to the domestic situation, such as the particular concern in the group of the Italians and the Irish in agricultural and regional issues, and on the other hand of the Germans in budgetary matters,[30] so that while there is a general support for CAP (not surprising in view of the large rural vote for Christian Democratic parties), differences of emphasis have arisen over specific aspects.[31] Similarly, van Oudenhove's conclusion that the Christian Democrats 'usually reach agreement on the purely political level, but are liable to suffer internal stresses as soon as economic and social issues arise'[32] still holds true. Although the group as a whole pronounces allegiance to the ideas of the social market economy, there are divergences between the Italians in the economic sphere with their postwar experience of partial state control and the Germans' preference for the freedom of market forces. The Benelux parties tend to place a priority on social questions, as evidenced by the activities of Bertrand, a Belgian ex-miner, an interest explained by these parties' close links with the Christian trade unions in their countries. Divergences over socio-economic issues also reflect of course the progressive and conservative ideological strands within Christian Democratic parties, notably within the Italian Democrazia Cristiana (DC). A special feature of Christian Democratic parties is the confessional aspect, for although in most cases they have a strong Catholic background a few also attract Protestant electorates, notably the West

Germans and the Dutch. However, in party group activity in the European Parliament such particular differences should not be overemphasised.

The Christian Democratic group is also characterised by a 'spirit of compromise',[33] which has been elevated to the status of a value in itself. Compared with the Socialists, there is less doctrinal dispute, perhaps because of the generally pragmatic character of the two dominant parties within the group – the CDU/CSU and the Italian DC – which have both had long-term experience in government. Indeed, the dominance of these two parties (they have together usually accounted for more than three-fifths of the MEPs) has facilitated group solidarity.

Finally, the organisation of the group itself must be considered as a factor influencing the performance of the group. Here, the Christian Democrats differ little from the other main groups in that they view their task as a group at Strasbourg as being to 'filter' different viewpoints, in which they are assisted by the secretariat (whose staff has risen by 20 per cent to about forty-five in recent years) playing a co-ordinating as well as administrative role.[34] There are no formal rules of discipline on voting as a group, 'but we expect from those members of the group, who do not agree to the compromise found, that they inform the group leadership beforehand'.[35] Usually there is an attempt to iron out differences so that 'at least on 90 per cent of the matters there is a group position',[36] though somewhat at the cost of precision. According to Egon Klepsch, an important contribution to the integration of the group over policy matters has been made by committee chairmen and experts in different fields, for 'like national groups, the European Parliament is very dependent on its experts and their ability to communicate'.[37] Institutional arrangements aim to encourage the integration of different nationalities, notably in the composition of the group executive (bureau), which includes representatives of the national delegations. The burden of work faced by the group chairman has increased over the years with more frequent sessions of the Parliament, so that in 1975 the group's rules of procedure were revised to provide for a 'presidium' of three to relieve the chairman of some of his work.[38] Of course, the Christian Democrats suffer as much as any other group from the generally recognised impossible conditions imposed by the dual mandate, though this could depend also on whether or not MEPs (as with the West Germans) were elected by the party list system or by constituencies.

It should be noted in conclusion that the Christian Democrats have, like the other groups, been inhibited in functioning as a 'supranational' entity by the European Parliament's lack of political authority (of which they have been particularly conscious) and by the absence of a viable extra-parliamentary organisational base, though in the latter respect they have been assiduous in promoting the development of one for direct elections. At the same time, they have shown a new interest in informal *ad hoc* coalitional arrangements (with the Conservatives – see below) as a way of overcoming some disadvantages of their loss of position as the largest party, in the context of the development in the 1970s of a more multi-party situation in the European Parliament.

### THE LIBERAL GROUP

The Liberal group is the third largest of the party groups and, although numerically only half the size of the Christian Democrats, it contains representatives from as many parties. From 1959, the Liberal group was larger than the Socialists, until the Gaullists left in late 1962. During the 1960s, its twenty-five or so members represented approximately thirteen Liberal parties of all six member states, but usually with not more than one or two members from each party, so that ideologically and organisationally, it was the least cohesive of the groups. It possessed a progressive element, a traditional liberal element, a conservative element and to some extent a right-wing element,[39] for the Continental Liberals ranged from 'progressive social reformers to die-hard free traders'.[40] After the 1972 Italian elections, the extreme right-wing Italian members (of the neo-Fascist – MSI and Monarchist – PDIUM – parties) left the group to become independent members. On enlargement, two Danish parties joined (Venstre and Radicale Venstre) as well as two British Liberals (later reduced to one when the Labour delegation arrived), but no Irish members. As a result the Liberal group actually became more cohesive than it had been in the 1960s.

The Continental Liberal parties have, like the Christian Democrats and the Socialists, long been concerned about the development of European institutions. This is reflected in the group's generally united approach to the furtherance of European integration on institutional and constitutional questions (with the exceptions of the Danish Radicale Venstre member and the French Independent Republicans, now renamed French Republicans, who have been hesitant about the furtherance of European institutions),[41] its support of a 'federal system at European level' and its readiness to accept 'a fair measure of supranational authority'.[42] More specifically, the group accepts that the Council of Ministers must remain as the most important institution, but it would like to see the introduction of majority voting. Although the group would like to see the powers of the Commission extended and the legislative responsibilities of the Parliament increased as well as the introduction of direct elections, it also feels that the existing powers and opportunities of the Parliament and the Commission should be more fully exploited.[43]

The major unifying concern of the Liberal group in the European Parliament is the respect for the traditional Liberal value of human rights: the protection, promotion and freedom of the individual, equal opportunities for all and free competition of ideas and parties. However, since Western European political structures have absorbed such liberal designs over time, Liberalism with its inherent recognition of compromise and diversity does not easily translate into an alternative dynamic political programme. Nevertheless the Liberal group has called for a guarantee of human, civil (including specifically minority) and political rights;[44] it seeks to ensure that at Community level workers participate in the management and control of undertakings and have a share in any profits; and it advocates a reduction in social disparities between individuals by means of the Social Fund and 'a better use of the Regional Fund . . . to limit the imbalance between the regions'.[45]

Although the group is broadly united on the importance of European policy for the promotion of human rights, other policy areas raise problems of reconciling the multiplicity of national and ideological outlooks contained in the group. The parties which label themselves 'liberal' spring from many different traditions, and have been associated with a variety of movements and philosophies dedicated to liberation. The difficulties this presents for reaching consensus is exacerbated by the liberal tradition of individualistic behaviour. In the European Parliament, the group encompasses a wide range of political attitudes, from the progressive Left (Danish Liberals) through the British Liberals and FDP to the conservative Right (Italian Liberals). Since 1969, the group has become more oriented to the left of the political spectrum, for the German Liberals, who form one of the core parties of the group (partly because they have consistently been in government at the national level, and partly because of the quality of the individual members), have become more associated with the left of centre in Germany, owing to the FDP's change of coalition partners from the CDU/CSU to SPD in the 1960s. This reorientation of the group was encouraged by the departure of the Italian right-wing parties in 1972, while the membership of Britain and Denmark in January 1973 introduced a new element of liberalism, which inclined to the Centre or Centre-Left. As well as differences in ideological outlook between nationalities, there are differences between the parties which represent Liberalism at the national level, e.g. the Italian Republicans and Italian Liberals are both represented, as are the Danish Venstre and Danish Radicale Venstre, while France has nine MEPs representing four parties in the Liberal group.

There are profound differences of outlook in the group, which emerge over CAP, economic issues, fishing and energy. The most important divisions in the Liberal group are noticeably over CAP.[46] The group has had members from the rural areas of France and Germany, and many have represented constituencies with agricultural and regional problems. The French are reluctant to promote any major structural changes, tending to prefer assistance and the assurance of good prices for the French farmers, while the German, British and Dutch Liberals tend to favour a pricing policy which is of benefit to the consumer. The group has managed to agree on a rather vague compromise 'on the development of the Common Agricultural Policy in ways which both benefit consumers and encourage efficient farming'.[47] In spite of these basic differences members of the group have managed to take a lead over agricultural policy; for example a Liberal has always held the important chairmanship of the agricultural committee in the European Parliament.

Although there are predictable national differences over economic policy, with the Benelux Liberals identifying with big business and the French, British and the Danes being somewhat suspicious of it,[48] there are also important ideological differences within each party so that in the Dutch Liberal party the young are less pro big business than the older members, and the British Liberal party contains those who are pro and anti big business. Thus, there tend to be two strands of economic thought present in the Liberal group: those who take a more negative approach to big business, 'concerned with the danger that large, overmighty companies with monopolistic tendencies present for freedom and democracy . . . political liberty and individualism';[49] and others who consider it vital to create a European-scale industry, which can compete with the United States and Japan. However, the group has declared that it believes 'in free enterprise and free competition, in the right of ownership and . . . in the market economy', so that 'the role of the central authority should be to complement but never to replace private enterprise'.[50] The Liberals are also agreed on the need for economic growth and the need for progress towards economic and monetary union.

As with all other groups, fishing policy has divided the group nationally, and resulted in acrimonious debates in the European

Parliament. There are also national divisions in the Liberal group over atomic energy policy, with the French, Dutch and Belgium Liberals being more pro atomic energy, while the Danish, British, Germans and Italians express scepticism and concern at the development of atomic power. The compromise has been to agree that there is a need for new sources of power, including nuclear energy under certain conditions, such as scarcity of traditional resources.[51]

The difficulties of reaching a common group viewpoint are reflected in the content of the policy statements of the Liberal group which tend, particularly in the more controversial policy areas, to be rather vaguely phrased and not too specific, and therefore open to wide interpretation. This indicates the problems, not only of translating Liberal values into concrete policies, but those of reaching a meaningful compromise in a group which encompasses such a broad range of ideological and national representation.

These differences are reflected in the group's minimal and fluid organisation. Much of the work is carried out informally, for the bureau does not play a major role in the group, much of the organisation and administration being carried out by the chairman in conjunction with the secretariat,[52] which plays an important political role in attempting to co-ordinate and reconcile the multiplicity and diversity of the views incorporated in the group. The group meeting officially takes the decisions, but tends to meet less frequently than the other groups 'and often adopts the compromise of appointing more than one spokesman to represent the Liberals in plenary sessions'.[53]

Although the Liberal group is small, it represents eight countries and fourteen parties of the European Community. The wide range of ideological viewpoints contained in the group makes it difficult to formulate concrete policy alternatives rather than statements of principle, or to achieve a forceful common viewpoint for presentation in the debates. For this reason, and that of the stress on individuality in 'liberal' ideology, the group as a whole has had less of a major impact in the Parliament than provided a backdrop for the activity of individual members.

## THE COMMUNIST AND ALLIES GROUP

The Communist and allies group was formally constituted in October 1973, when three French Communists joined nine Italians and a member of the Danish Socialist People's Party.[54] Previously the French Communists had not been represented in the European Parliament, though Communists had been present since March

1969, when the Italian Parliament extended representation to the PCI. Too few for recognition as an official group, they were excluded from participation in the administration of the Parliament and committees, although because they chose to function as a group rather than as individual members they were granted some 'facilities' such as one representative per committee, the same speaking time as other groups and a small secretariat. Since that early time, when no formal organisation was needed as the group was uni-national (but not entirely Communist since it included members from the PSIUP and Independenti di Sinistra, small and dominated by the PCI) it has developed a more formal structure, with a small elected bureau. The expansion of the group to include the French has led to a decline in its ability to present a common viewpoint in the Parliament, particularly on institutional matters such as direct elections. This has derived from differences at national level between the Italian Communist Party's flexible approach to European affairs and the French Communist Party's more restrictive view.

In the late 1950s, both the Italian and French Communist parties had refused to recognise the establishment and existence of the European Community since they regarded it as representing a higher stage of capitalism. However, the Italian Communists soon began to appreciate that the Community offered benefits for Italian interests. Thus they began to press for representation in the European Parliament which they achieved in 1969. Meanwhile the French Communist Party remained adamantly opposed to the Community and did not want representation within the European Parliament.

In 1969, the aim of the PCI members was to reform and democratise the Community from within: they wanted to end discrimination against Communists, taking it upon themselves to represent the interests of other European Communist parties; they aimed at establishing relationships with other forces of the European Left; and they undertook the defence of Italian workers and small farmers.[55] The group was cohesive and comprised active members of high calibre, who conscientiously pursued those objectives, taking an effective part in committee and plenary work. But the arrival of the Danish member of the Socialist People's party on enlargement, the French members later in 1973 and a Dutch member has changed the character of the group in many essential respects. Although the Danish member has had his own preoccupations and 'has rarely spoken for the group, but often in his own name',[56] it was the arrival of the French that posed the greatest threat to the cohesion of the group and united backing for its policies.

The differences in attitude towards the European Community of the Italian and French Communist parties were clarified in the opening speeches of the Brussels conference of West European Communist parties in January 1974[57] when Enrico Berlinguer indicated 'that the Italians are much more flexible and positive than the French about the possibility of using the Community to further the workers' interests'.[58] Although French Communist participation in the European Parliament has reflected the evolution of Soviet policy and the PCF's tentative steps towards Italian-style Communism, the French party have still tended to regard the European Community with deep suspicion, and Georges Marchais called for a 'real European Community of countries liberated from the domination of large-scale capitalism, a Community which can expand into socialism'.[59] The French Communists' opposition to supranationality has remained for they are 'against Community Europe as it is at the moment, because they believe that this Europe, even more so than Member States, will be an accomplice to policies which are evil for the workers'.[60] There have been such deep and fundamental differences between the French and Italian Communists in this respect that a press conference held in November 1976 'developed into a lively and passionate debate between the various viewpoints within the group, on European elections'.[61]

These divisions may have reduced the Communists' credibility, particularly as they are often now represented in the Parliament by two spokesmen, but the group itself does not view them so seriously, since they regard group organisation as a vehicle for achieving financial and administrative privileges in the Parliament, while not committing them to defending common standpoints. Giorgio Amendola, the leader of the group, has said: 'each Communist party follows an independent line, depending on how it views the interests of its own country'.[62]

The Communist group is united on the broad objective of achieving a 'Europe of the working man' with workers and trade unionists playing a leading role, 'so that those who represent the working man can confront national governments and multinational companies with the working man's view of economic, social and political issues that affect him'.[63] The group agrees on the need for the 'autonomy' of European policy, in particular on energy and foreign affairs, but one which is neither anti-American nor anti-Soviet. The Italian Communists in particular believe that economic unity is a basis for political unity: 'divided, the countries in the European Community are subject to heavy [external political and economic] pressures',[64] since sovereign states cannot individually 'solve problems such as the battle against inflation, multinational blackmail and the sources of energy'.[65] They believe that, for example, multinational companies can only be fought with multinational powers which have a democratic basis, and that multinationals have contributed to inflation (together with American influence on the European economy), to unemployment and to social inbalances in the Community. The group feels that European integration generally has been negative, that regional and social policy have been inadequate, and that the CAP has favoured large-scale producers, has been a heavy penalty on consumers and has been indifferent to the needs of the small farmer. The French and Italian Communists also favour an agricultural policy which takes into account their particular national problems.

Since the PCI has been involved in informal support of the Christian Democratic government at the national level from 1976, the PCI MEPs have been less assiduous in attending both plenaries and committees. Although the French Communists in the European Parliament tend to be more 'European' than those in the National Assembly,[66] they are inclined to avoid sensitive and controversial issues by not attending the relevant sessions. Both parties are open about their over-riding concern with the defence of national interests and those of the 'working classes' in their respective countries. They are therefore no longer opposed to the existence of the European Community or predicting its collapse. Rather, their representatives in the Communist group in the European Parliament are more sceptical and questioning than the other groups in their distrust of the social and economic content of the Community and its lack of democratic control.[67]

## THE EUROPEAN CONSERVATIVE GROUP

The European Conservative group was formed in January 1973, when the eighteen British Conservative MEPs and one member each of the Danish Conservative People's Party and the Danish Centre-Democrats joined the European Parliament. The decision to form a separate Conservative group rather than ally with the closest group in the political spectrum – the Christian Democrats – was taken for ideological and organisational reasons. These included a reluctance on the part of the Christian Democrats to be linked with a Conservative Party, as the term 'conservative' can often have reactionary connotations in a European context. In addition, the Christian Democrats have taken the 'Christian' element of their ideology seriously, in that they feel that a party must have a moral basis and take a stand on moral issues, such as abortion; whereas the British political parties tend to leave such matters up to the conscience of the individual. In view of the different politico-religious history and background of the two parties, the Conservative group felt it would be appropriate to avoid institutional links with so many parties which have predominantly Catholic associations.

Organisationally, the Christian Democrats would have gained by embracing the new Conservative members, for it would have ensured their role in the long term as the largest party in the European Parliament, with its accompanying status and financial advantages. For the Conservatives, however, the position of a separate group gave them proportionally more influence in the Parliament than they would have had as part of a larger group, a greater freedom of manoeuvre and all the organisational advantages of separate facilities, staff and sources of income, as well as ease of communication in a fundamentally mono-linguistic group.

On arrival in the European Parliament in 1973, the group's impact was immediate and had some important long-term consequences concerning the procedural developments of the Parliament. Peter Kirk (leader of the Conservative group until his death in April 1977) was given his brief by Edward Heath, then prime minister, to 'shake up the European Parliament as the leaders of the party groups already there expect'.[68] Peter Kirk's maiden speech was, as he later put it, 'a declaration of faith in the European Parliament, coupled with some practical suggestions as to how its workings might be improved',[69] and he at once 'enlivened the Assembly with a stirring call for procedural innovations along Westminster lines'.[70] These practical proposals were reiterated in a twenty-two-page memorandum presented to the European Parliament, and thus the group provided the dynamism for achieving an extension of the parliamentary budgetary powers, increased control of accounting, including the conciliation procedure over budgetary matters and for the increasing number of foreign policy debates. The group has also been largely responsible for the introduction of a Westminster-style question-time of the president of the Council of Ministers and Commissioners as well as of 'emergency' and short adjournment-type debates. The question-time has however tended to be dominated by the British MEPs, partly because the 'Continental' members of the Parliament tend to regard anything less than a structured ten-minute speech as 'beneath the dignity of such an institution'.[71] The parliamentary chamber has become more lively than it was before enlargement, although some of this is attributable also to the exchange of domestic grievances between the Conservative and Labour and the CDU/CSU and SPD delegations, in whose national parliaments the government/ opposition role is most clearly delineated.

As its activity on arrival in the European Parliament indicated, the group, while essentially national in composition, has presented a fundamentally European outlook. The British Conservative MEPs have been chosen on the basis of political and regional representation and the professional and specialist requirements of the group in the work of the Parliament. Although the group has comprised mainly convinced Europeans, notably Peter Kirk with his preceding experience in the Council of Europe's consultative assembly, anti-Europeans have not been excluded.

Although it was decided to form a separate group in the European Parliament initially, the Conservative Party now openly favours the idea of a large European-based centre party,[72] and to avoid the appearance of isolation at the European level has attempted to establish informal links with the Christian Democrats, Gaullists and Liberals. During the first eighteen months, the Conservative and Christian Democratic groups arranged joint bureau meetings, joint group meeetings and a joint working party on agriculture,[73] and occasionally employed the same group spokesman. However with the change in Christian Democratic group leadership from H. A. Lücker (CSU) to Alfred Bertrand (Belgian CVP), there was a decline in the close links between the two groups. These may revive under the chairmanship of Egon Klepsch, appointed in May 1977, who as chairman of the CDU/CSU Junge Union 1963–9 promoted closer international co-operation between Conservative and Christian Democratic youth movements.[74] Links with the Christian Democrats have generally been closer than those with the Gaullists, while the Liberals are prepared to have discussions, but 'not to enter any formal agreements'.[75]

The group's internal organisation at the parliamentary level is informal compared with that of the larger groups. Although the group meeting is the official decision-making body, the group chairman and the four-member bureau have had a central and determining role in the formulation and application of policies as well as the organisation of the group.[76] The number of Danes in the group has ranged from one to three, and there is provision for taking into account the Danish point of view in the group meeting so that this may allow them proportionately more influence. There has been the minimum of formal internal organisation with individuals responsible for policy areas, while long-term policy is agreed during the study days,[77] such as that held in Copenhagen in May 1974 on 'European Problems and Policies', the results of which were embodied in the publication

*The European Community: Our Common Cause* in September of
that year.

Three major events at the national level affected the role and
influence of the Conservative group in the European Parliament:
the Conservative Party's change of role in Britain from government to opposition in February 1974, the Common Market
referendum in June 1975 and the change in party leadership in
February 1975.

Up to June 1975 and despite loss of office at national level,
the Conservatives were to some extent able to claim to be Britain's
representatives, 'standing-in' for the Labour Party. Although
this gave them increased political weight – as for example on
Fridays, when 'firm whipping has kept the entire delegation in
the chamber and in line, when rival factions have already
dispersed to their various constituencies'[78] – it had the practical
disadvantage that Conservative MEPs commonly found themselves
*en route* between Westminster and Strasbourg some four to six
times a week, in the attempt to maintain their voting strength in
both parliaments. After the referendum the group could no longer
claim to be the only major representative of Britain's interests, and
the Labour delegation remained in Strasbourg on Fridays too! In
addition, the success of the referendum produced an increased
interest in European affairs at the national level of the Conservative
Party, which to a certain extent created conflict with the group
over who should define policy, for previously the group had been
used to a fairly considerable degree of autonomy.[79] The group
has at times formulated its own policy; indeed it was ahead of
the Conservative Party on industrial democracy supporting
worker participation in the context of EEC company law initiatives,
and it formed a view on atomic energy somewhat different from
that of the party at home. The change of national leadership to
Margaret Thatcher has also affected the group, as she has shown
a more reserved attitude towards the European Community than
Edward Heath. The group has indeed been generally concerned
by the lack of interest shown by the Conservative Party in the
activities of the Parliament as well as the Labour government's
organisation of the Westminster timetable, whereby European
debates take place during the European parliamentary sessions.

Although the change from government and the change of leadership had a profound effect on the party at the national level, they
have not greatly affected the general policy position of the group.
The group has tended to direct its concern to the defence of British
national interests, for example over the Common Agricultural
Policy, of which they defend the basic principles and existing
mechanisms, but call for consumer interests to be taken more

effectively into account by attacking excessive price increase proposals.[80] It is also greatly concerned about the protection of individual rights, and is 'opposed to any tendency to place the citizens of the Community in the straitjacket of laws and regulations, which result in an unnecessary degree of harmonisation, in effect standardisation, of the conditions in which they live and work'.[81] The group has furthermore placed great emphasis on external relations, believing that member states must progress towards a common foreign policy, and has been active in the Parliament in this respect.

The Conservative group is a predominantly national group, with a pragmatic approach to questions' like the development of democratic control of the institutions of Europe. The group brought to the European Parliament some of the tried and tested Westminster procedural devices, and had an enormous and stimulating impact when it arrived. As much of this was due to the personality and industriousness of Peter Kirk, it remains to be seen what sort of role the group will play under its, new leader – Geoffrey Rippon, also a strongly committed European, and former negotiator of British entry to the European Community.

EUROPEAN PROGRESSIVE DEMOCRATS GROUP

The group of European Progressive Democrats was formed when the twelve Gaullist members of the European Parliament joined with the five Irish Fianna Fáil members in July 1973. The French national elections in March of that year had reduced the number of Gaullist delegates from nineteen to two short of the fourteen needed to continue as an established group. The Irish members had been sitting in the Parliament as Independents, since Ireland joined the Community in January 1973. A Danish member has since joined the group.

The Gaullist deputies first entered the Parliament as members of the Liberal group, in early 1959. However, as a consequence of their unanimous pursuit of Gaullist policy, irrespective of and often opposed to that of the rest of the Liberal group, they formed their own group in January 1965, when the minimum number required was reduced to fourteen. During the 1960s and early 1970s the Gaullist members maintained close links with the mother party in France, and they have been united and vociferous in their opposition to progress towards a 'United States of Europe', favouring instead the alternative concept of a 'Europe des Patries'. Nevertheless they 'have made a distinctive contribution to the discussions of the Parliament', while acting as 'a consistent opposition to supranationalism as a practice or as an aim, to the attempted extension of the powers of the Parliament, [and] to the "political" use of the powers that it has'.[82] For example, the Gaullists opposed the censure motion of George Spenále in December 1972 (later withdrawn), because they considered that the Parliament had no right to adopt a 'political' censure motion, and 'because they did not want any increase in the Parliament's powers nor any acceptance of new responsibilities by the Commission'. During the 1970s, the conflict over institutional matters has generally been reduced, and the violent confrontations between the Gaullists and European federalists, such as those which occurred between the Gaullists and Socialists during the 1965 crisis, have disappeared. This is not so much due to a change in Gaullist policy as the fact that other groups have come to terms with the realities of the slow progress towards European Union, and lowered their expectations accordingly.

After the French national elections in March 1973, when the Gaullists lost support, their number of MEPs was reduced proportionately. However, the Gaullists were anxious to preserve the various procedural and financial advantages deriving from official group status which they were therefore liable to lose. They first approached the Conservatives and then the Christian Democrats but were rejected, so they made overtures to the Fianna Fáil members. Although some of the latter were in favour of an alliance, others argued that they had little in common with the main French ruling party. However, they left the decision to the party leaders in Dublin, who approved the alliance. Despite the opportunistic reason for forming the group, the two parties have managed to work in reasonable harmony.

Both parties have claimed to be pragmatic, taking stands on issues as they arise. Both have been anxious to preserve and defend their respective national and economic interests. They believed that the development towards a united Europe should be based on the 'reality of its member states coming together'.[83] Although the group's attitude towards European Union is predictably cautious, it regards as a major long-term objective: 'building a European Union . . . so that in due course a European Confederal Government can be established'.[84] In the shorter term, however, the group was unanimous in its rejection of the report of the parliamentary political affairs committee on the need for closer European union, debated in July 1975, considering it 'totally unacceptable'.[85]

Apart from a common outlook on the direction of European union, these two 'nationalistic' parties are supported by a similar electorate which is predominantly Catholic and agricultural; both parties claim they have the same type of approach to 'life

and tradition';[86] they have been united in their belief that the
nation state is the basic unit of international affairs;[87] and both
the French Gaullists and the Irish Fianna Fáil share a devotion
to the 'father' figures of de Gaulle and De Valera respectively.
At the European level, both have gained from the organisational,
administrative and financial advantages of being an official group.
However, their main common bond at this level is their dedica-
tion to the Common Agricultural Policy while they are in broad
agreement on other European policies, in particular over regional
policy and social policy. On certain controversial policies, such as
fishing, they have agreed to differ and to vote different ways.
In those policy areas where one nationality is particularly
interested, and the other's interests are not affected or it is of no
special concern, mutual passive support may be offered.

The group approved an agricultural charter in June 1975, which
stated that 'it is not basic modifications which are needed for the
CAP, but a consolidation of its foundation'.[88] They called also for
a Europeanwide agricultural economy, involving stronger market
organisations and a structural policy aimed at maintaining a
balanced agricultural population.[89] The group believes that the
'Regional Fund can, and should, play a key role by improving
economic conditions in certain backward and peripheral regions'.[90]
This is of particular interest to the Irish Fianna Fáil, since there
are 'tremendous differences between the West of Ireland and the
generality of the Community'.[91] In view of the widening gap
between the rich and poor regions of the Community, the group
agrees that there is a need for a more effective and far-reaching
social policy, of which 'employment is the foundation'[92] – to be
achieved with a minimum of institutional development.

Among the issues over which the Irish and the Gaullist members
have accepted their inability to agree is that of direct elections.
The Gaullists were explicitly instructed to abstain on direct
elections for, as de la Malène said, 'we will not get far with
mere parliamentarianism; without a prior definition of common
action, even direct elections have no meaning'.[93] The Fianna Fáil
members voted for them, for they believe that direct elections are
fundamental to ensure the participation of the people of Europe, a
basic principle of the group. On issues which are of particular
interest to either one party or the other, they tend to give each
other support, notably over NATO and defence,[94] where the
Irish are not particularly concerned and have somewhat reservedly
supported France over nuclear tests.

The Gaullists remain largely dominant in the group of European Progressive Democrats. However, on those issues in which
they have a lesser interest than the Irish Fianna Fáil members,

they support the latter's stance, such as over regional policy. For this reason, as well as diligence, facilitated by being in opposition at the national level up to 1977, the Fianna Fáil members have proportionately more influence than their numbers. Therefore although the group is small, the Irish members have more influence within it than the Fine Gael and Irish Labour members of the much larger Christian Democratic and Socialist Groups.

The DEP is one of the smallest groups in the European Parliament, and has opposed the development of Europe towards a federal system, regarding the Treaty of Rome as a limit rather than a take-off point. The group's major policy concern is the maintenance of the CAP to the benefit of their farmers. Because of its small size and minimal organisation, and its obvious concern with the defence of its respective national interests, the DEP group does not play such a forceful part in the work of the Parliament as some of the other groups.

UNAFFILIATED MEMBERS

There are currently (1978) three MEPs who are not members of or affiliated to any of the party groups discussed above: two Italian members of the MSI–DN.

Since party groups dominate the procedures of the European Parliament, independent members are subject to major disadvantages. They have not been represented on the bureau, although an Independent (Winifred Ewing) stood for the first time in 1977 and obtained an appreciable number of votes, or on the enlarged bureau. Although the independent members each sit on two committees, they have not been appointed to the bureaux of these. They also have less speaking time in debates than the groups, and are not granted financial allowances for research assistance as given to the groups by their secretariats. In general, the advantage of being an independent member is that there is no submission of particular interests to those of the rest of the group.

However, not being a member of a group is no bar to activism. Lord (Charles) O'Hagan, a British cross-bench peer (MEP, 1973–5), became renowned for his assiduousness in questioning the Commission and the Council. He was also active in the social affairs committee and spoke in a wide range of debates. Winifred Ewing, SNP member, has also participated actively in the parliamentary debates, is on the regional and legal committees, and takes a particular interest in the opening-up of European decision making as well as Scotland's interests and industries, notably fish, textiles and energy.

## CONCLUSION

Two specific approaches formed the basis for the analysis of the party groups: the question of policy interest and ideological emphasis; and the degree of organisational articulation. The problems of defining policy positions by the groups have illustrated the persistence of national differences as well as differences of ideological interpretation in their influence on the 'European' content of policy positions. Ideological fraternity provides the necessary pre-condition for transnational co-operation, but it is not sufficient alone as a basis for the regular functioning of a group. There are two reasons why in the 1970s group activity has become more complex: the increasing scope of European integration itself places a greater burden on the groups with their involvement in policy discussion; and the enlargement of the European Community in 1973 produced an influx of more national parties into the Parliament which has accordingly made policy cohesion for the groups more difficult.

Direct elections will throw an important new light on the development of the party groups. Given a direct mandate there is likely to be increased pressure for power and influence of the Parliament, and an increased independence for its component groups from the party lines at home, because they will be less responsible than before to their national party groups. On the other hand, the increased number of European parliamentarians and consequent increased size of groups may make them even more unwieldy and less capable of producing a meaningful policy approach.

## NOTES AND REFERENCES

1 For examples of the latter, see Byron Criddle, *Socialists and European Integration: A Study of the French Socialist Party* (London, Routledge & Kegan Paul, 1969); and W. E. Paterson, *The SPD and European Integration* (1974).

2 See Guy van Oudenhove, *The Political Parties in the European Parliament* (Leiden, Sijthoff, 1965); John Fitzmaurice, *The Party Groups in the European Parliament* (Farnborough, Saxon House, 1975).

3 S. Henig and J. Pinder (eds), *European Political Parties* (London, Allen & Unwin, 1969), ch. 12, esp. p. 487.

4 Fitzmaurice, op. cit., p. 88.

5 Interview with Michael Stewart, former leader of the British Labour delegation, in London, May 1977.

6 Ibid. See also Fitzmaurice, op. cit., pp. 165, 166.

7 Gwyneth Dunwoody voted against, and some British colleagues abstained over, too low a minimum fat content in milk, March 1976. The entire Labour delegation abstained on the vote on political and economic union, 10 July 1975.
8 See Fitzmaurice, op. cit., pp. 88–9 and 165.
9 Interview with Michael Stewart, May 1977.
10 Fitzmaurice, op. cit., p. 90.
11 Ibid., p. 91.
12 Ibid.
13 Interview with Michael Stewart, May 1977.
14 Interview with Bent Wigotski, deputy secretary general, Socialist Confederation, in Brussels, April 1977.
15 Fitzmaurice, op. cit., pp. 165 and 96.
16 Interview with Bent Wigotski, April 1977.
17 Publicity brochure of the Socialist group, March 1976.
18 Draft policy document on consumer policy, discussed by the group in June 1977.
19 Fitzmaurice, op. cit., p. 102.
20 Document on the *Reform of the Common Agricultural Policy*, adopted October 1976.
21 Draft policy document on regional policy discussed by the group in June 1977.
22 Fitzmaurice, op. cit., p. 98.
23 *The Times*, 10 July 1975.
24 Statement by Bertrand, quoted in the *Guardian*, 15 May 1974
25 Alfred Bertrand in CD-*Europe Bulletin*, monthly publication of the Christian Democratic group, February 1977, p. 4.
26 See explanation by Jan de Koning, Dutch member of the group, in ibid., June 1976, p. 3.
27 *The Times*, 10 December 1974.
28 See statement on direct elections by Bertrand in CD-*Europe Bulletin*, October 1976, p. 1 and *Das Parlament*, 4 December 1976, p. 8.
29 Egon Klepsch, vice-chairman of the Christian Democratic group, in interview, Strasbourg, April 1977.
30 Interview with Vivion Mulcahy, secretariat of the group, in Brussels, April 1977.
31 Fitzmaurice, op. cit., pp. 82–3.
32 G. van Oudenhove, op. cit.
33 A phrase used in interviews by members of the Christian Democratic group to describe its workings.
34 Fitzmaurice, op. cit., pp. 71–2.
35 Interview with Egon Klepsch, April 1977.
36 Interview with Vivion Mulcahy, April 1977.
37 Interview with Egon Klepsch, April 1977.
38 *Zusammenarbeit der Parteien in Westeuropa* (Bonn, Schriftenreihe der Bundeszentrale für politische Bildung, 1976), p. 311.
39 Fitzmaurice, op. cit., p. 109.
40 *The Times*, 11 January 1973.
41 Interview with Martin Bangemann, vice-chairman of Liberal group, in Strasbourg, April 1977.
42 Publicity brochure of the Liberal group, November 1975.
43 See statement by Jean Durieux, chairman of Liberal group, in *Das Parlament*, 4 December 1976.
44 Stuttgart Declaration adopted in March 1976.
45 Address given by Jean Durieux in January 1977 at the Epiphany meeting of the FDP.
46 Interview with Martin Bangemann, April 1977.

47 Stuttgart Declaration, March 1976.
48 Interview with Richard Moore, secretariat of Liberal group, in Strasbourg, April 1977.
49 Fitzmaurice, op. cit., p. 112.
50 Publicity brochure of Liberal group, November 1975.
51 Interview with Martin Bangemann, April 1977.
52 Fitzmaurice, op. cit., p. 109.
53 Geoffrey Pridham, 'Transnational party groups in the European Parliament', *Journal of Common Market Studies*, March 1975.
54 The Socialist People's Party was strongly opposed to EEC membership in the 1972 referendum campaign. It is a non-Stalinist Marxist party, independent of Moscow. Fitzmaurice, op. cit., p. 143. See also above, p. 34.
55 *L'Unità*, 22 March 1969, statement by Giorgio Amendola.
56 Fitzmaurice, op. cit., p. 168.
57 Brussels, January 1974, theme – 'The Present Crisis of Capitalism'.
58 *The Times*, 28 January 1974.
59 Opening speech at Brussels Conference.
60 European Report, June 1976.
61 European Parliament Report, December 1976.
62 Interview in *The Times*, 1 February 1977.
63 Publicity brochure of the Communist group, November 1975.
64 Giorgio Amendola, *The Times*, 1 February 1977.
65 Ibid.
66 In 1973 the PCF members of the European Parliament were in favour of the ratification of budgetary powers. But in 1976 the PCF in the National Assembly voted against them.
67 John Fitzmaurice, 'The European Parliament and the concept of opposition', paper presented to UACES annual conference in January 1976, mimeo.
68 *The Times*, 27 November 1972.
69 Peter Kirk, 'Britain's imprint on Europe', *The Spectator*, 4 September 1976.
70 *The Times*, obituary, 18 April 1977. See also *The Times*, 17 January 1973.
71 Interview with Timothy Bainbridge, secretariat of the European Conservative group, in Strasbourg, April 1977.
72 See section on transnational links under 'Other Groups' in this chapter.
73 Interview with Timothy Bainbridge, April 1977.
74 See *European Parliament Report* (European Parliament, June 1977).
75 Interview with Richard Moore, April 1977.
76 See rules of procedure of European Conservative group.
77 Fitzmaurice, *The Party Groups in the European Parliament*, p. 146.
78 *The Times*, 17 March 1973.
79 Interview with Timothy Bainbridge, April 1977.
80 Fitzmaurice, *The Party Groups in the European Parliament*, p. 149.
81 Publicity brochure of the European Conservative group, November 1975.
82 Fitzmaurice, *The European Parliament and the Concept of Opposition*.
83 Publicity brochure of the group of European Progressive Democrats, November 1975.
84 ibid.
85 Report in *The Times*, 7 July 1975.
86 Interview with Senator Michael Yeats, vice-president of the European Parliament in Strasbourg, April 1977. Member of the Irish Fianna Fáil Party.
87 Fitzmaurice, *The Party Groups in the European Parliament*, p. 121.
88 *Towards a European Agricultural Economy*, p. 47, Agricultural Charter of the group of European Progressive Democrats, June 1975.
89 *Towards a European Full Employment Policy*, p. 19, memorandum of the group of European Progressive Democrats, September 1975.

90 ibid., p. 18.
91 Interview with Michael Yeats, April 1977.
92 Towards a European Full Employment Policy, op. cit., p. 56.
93 *The Times*, 1 June 1976.
94 Interview with Michael Yeats, April 1977.

# APPENDIX

Party Groups in the European Parliament (as of October 1978)

| Group | Socialists | Christian Democrats | Liberals | European Conservatives | European Progressive Democrats | Communists | Independents |
|---|---|---|---|---|---|---|---|
| Total number | 66 | 52 | 23 | 18 | 17 | 18 | 3 |
| Belgium | (5) Parti socialiste belge (PSB), 3; Belgische Socialistische Partij (BSP), 2 | (7) Christelijke Volkspartij (CVP), 5; Parti social-chrétien (PSC), 2 | (2) Partij voor vrijheid en vooruitgang (PVV), 1; Parti des réformes et de la liberté de Wallonie (PRLW) 1 | — | — | — | — |
| Denmark | (4) Socialdemokratiet (S) | — | (1) Venstre (V) | (2) Centrum-Demokraterne (CD), 1; Det konservative folkeparti (KF), 1 | (2) Fremskridtspartiet (FRP) | (1) Socialistik folkeparti (SF) | — |
| West Germany | (15) Sozialdemokratische Partei Deutschlands (SPD) | (18) Christlich-Demokratische Union (CDU), 14; Christlich-Sozial Union (CSU), 4 | (3) Freie Demokratische Partei (FDP) | — | — | — | |
| France | (10) Party socialiste (PS), 8; Mouvement des radicaux de gauche (MRG), 2 | (2) Réformateurs et démocrates sociaux (RDS), 1; Union centriste des démocrates de progrès (UCDP), 1 | (9) Parti républicain (PR), 5; Républicains indépendants d'action sociale (RIAS), 1; Union pour la Démocratie… | | (9) Rassemblement pour la République (RPR) | (5) Parti communiste français (PCF) | |

| Country | | | Réformateurs et démocrates sociaux (RDS), 1; Mouvement des radicaux de gauche (MRG), 1 | | | | |
|---|---|---|---|---|---|---|---|
| Ireland | (1) Labour Party (Lab) | (3) Fine Gael (FG) | — | — | (6) Fianna Fail (FF) | — | — |
| Italy | (5) Partito socialista italiano (PSI), 4; Partito socialista democratico italiano (PSDI), 1 | (15) Democrazia Christiana (DC), 13; Südtiro er Volkspartei (SVP), 2 | (2) Partito liberale italiano (PLI), 1; Partito repubblicano (PRI), 1 | — | — | (12) Partito comunista italiano (PCI), 10; Indipendente di Sinistra (Ind Sin), 2 | (2) Movimento Sociale Italiano–Destra Nazionale (MSI–DN) |
| Luxembourg | (2) Parti ouvrier socialiste luxembourgeois (POSL) | (2) Parti chretien social (FCS) | (2) Parti démocratique (PD) | — | — | — | — |
| Netherlands | (6) Partij van de Arbeid (PvdA) | (5) Christen Democratisch Appél (CDA), 3; Katholieke Volkspartij (KVP), 2 | (3) Volkspartij voor Vrijheid en Democratie (VVD) | — | — | — | — |
| United Kingdom | (18) Labour Party | — | (1) Liberal Party | (16) Conservative Party | — | — | (1) Scottish National Party (SNP) |

*Note:*
Names given in language of country, but in the case of Luxembourg cf p. 174 above.

# 12

# Transnational Parties in the European Community II: The Development of European Party Federations

## GEOFFREY PRIDHAM AND PIPPA PRIDHAM

Institutionalised co-operation of any importance at the level of (extra-parliamentary) party organisation in the European Community was not seriously initiated until the mid-1970s. Although the Internationalists of the different political tendencies offered an earlier forum for activity and were to be among the progenitors of EEC party federations, their own membership included parties from outside the Community, their activity was confined largely to policy discussion and their structures were extremely loose.[1]

The most significant new development in party political integration in the European Community in the 1970s has been the inauguration of European party federations, involving a departure from all the earlier organisational links which were little more than discussion forums for the exchange of ideas rather than the promotion of political activity. These federations, which are confined to the three political tendencies of Christian Democracy, Socialism and Liberalism, differ in that they have initiated a basic institutional structure and some commitment to common action, and are also generally viewed as a first step towards the creation of European party organisations. The judgement on the party groups at Strasbourg that they were essentially parliamentary organs with no political base consequently no longer holds true.

The stimulus behind this change is directly attributable to the agreement on direct elections to the European Parliament following discussion of this matter in the Community during 1974–6, though it must also be viewed in the wider context of events in the EC since the decade began. Primarily, European integration received a new opportunity for development following The Hague summit of 1969, and the negotiation of enlargement of the Community encouraged new ideas among several of the political tendencies. The widening scope of integration activity itself helped to intensify this process. Finally, the prospect of direct elections stimulated party political competition at the European level, and generally acted as a catalyst.

The authors are fully aware of the difficulties of analysing the importance of the European party federations at such an early stage in their development, if only because information can easily be outdated. It is expected that the preparations for direct elections as well as the European campaign itself will have an important effect in intensifying party political activity at the extra-parliamentary level.[2] Certain features are, however, already apparent. First, the main purpose of these federations (at least until direct elections take place) is to formulate common programmes, and agree on a limited form of co-ordination for the European campaign. Secondly, it is clear from developments so far that the main party groups in the European Parliament have an established relationship with these incipient federations. This is illustrated, for instance, by the co-initiating role played by these groups in setting up the federations, the interflow of personnel involved in both parliamentary work and the organisation of the federations, notably through the important position of the group secretariats in the administration of the latter, and the function allotted to the groups in arranging the allocation of the funds to the parties from the European Parliament (2 million units of account) for the conduct of the European campaign. Thirdly, several problems evident over time in the operation of the party groups in the Parliament are repeating themselves with the federations. These include the diversified approach to particular policy areas within ideological 'schools', the element of national outlook expressed by different individual parties according to their general stand on European integration and the effects of domestic political situations on their willingness to engage in this new form of European party co-operation.

## THE EUROPEAN PEOPLE'S PARTY (EPP): FEDERATION OF CHRISTIAN DEMOCRATIC PARTIES OF THE EUROPEAN COMMUNITY

The European People's Party, founded in April 1976, illustrates clearly the stimulus provided by direct elections for the intensification of party co-operation within the European Community.

For its president, Leo Tindemans, the Belgian prime minister, it represented a conscious decision to strengthen the political base of the EC, for 'only European political parties can bridge the gap between the hopes of public opinion and the powerlessness of governments to turn these expectations into proposals for concrete policies'.[3] Similar though more specific reasons for its founding were outlined by Josef Müller, executive secretary of the Christian Democratic umbrella organisation, the European Christian Democratic Union (UEDC): such co-ordination was necessary as it was 'unthinkable' that the different Christian Democratic parties in the member states should announce diverse aims for the European election; the principle of federalism, to which the European Christian Democrats strongly adhere, should also be applied to the structure of Communitywide political parties; and the politicisation of the European Parliament following direct elections was essential for the democratic character of European Union.[4]

The extent to which preparations for prospective direct elections marked a new departure in the form of co-operation between Christian Democratic parties in member countries of the EC is indicated by referring briefly to the organisational links which had existed before. The main distinguishing features of these earlier links were a membership not strictly confined to parties in EC countries and a largely noncommittal and passive approach in their policy discussion, both of which applied to the first such organisation, the Nouvelles Equipes Internationales (NEI) established in 1947, and its present successor the European Union of Christian Democrats (UEDC), formed in 1965. The latter, which includes parties from non-EC states like Austria, Spain, Portugal and Switzerland, has however acted as the umbrella under which early efforts were made to knit together more closely the activities of parties in Community countries. Following the Hague summit of 1969, the UEDC set up a standing conference of party chairmen of the EC parties in April 1970 to meet thrice yearly at the initiative of the UEDC chairman and the chairman of the group in the European Parliament to 'give the necessary orientation for the great political questions of the Community',[5] thus formalising a procedure which had occurred sporadically since 1958. This was followed in 1972 by the formation of the political committee of the EC parties, a body intended to institutionalise co-operation between the national parties and the European parliamentary group. A number of working groups were set up under its auspices, and the committee was itself conceived as the first stage of a European Party organisation.

Although these moves in the early 1970s towards closer co-operation within an EC framework involved discussion of a common programme and even a European Party organisation, they lacked the necessary political impulse to carry such ideas into practice. This problem was spotlighted by Westerterp of the Dutch member party who proposed in June 1970 a European Christian Democratic Party with a common programme and collective discipline as an answer to the inadequate 'interstate' structure of the UEDC. His proposal attracted at this stage little more than academic interest, and no new initiative was taken until the congress of the UEDC at Bonn (November 1973), which led to the formation of a working group on a common programme and witnessed a stirring speech by the CDU theoretician Richard von Weizsäcker, claiming that the integration of EC institutions had no meaning unless one began with the political parties as the determining factors.[6] When in September 1975 a group was entrusted to draft statutes for a European Party, the question of direct elections was already becoming a concrete possibility. During 1976 various initiatives were taken culminating in the formal launching of the EPP: a meeting of the Political Committee (Paris, February) adopted a manifesto and approved the statutes for such a party; a further meeting (Brussels, April) agreed to establish a common party; and in July (Luxembourg) the EPP was formally constituted. It consisted of twelve national parties from seven member countries.[7] Since then, further plans for the elaboration of this incipient organisational network have been developed, including the announcement of a Robert Schuman Foundation for political education (January 1977), while steps have been taken to initiate special groups for employees (similar to the social committees of the CDU/CSU) and women and a youth branch.[8]

While the EPP can trace its lineage back through its precursor organisations of a pan-West European kind, it differs from them in two essential respects: it projects itself as an organisation aiming in the long-term at the integration of its national components in the field of European policy (e.g. its conscious use of the term 'party', which has not been adopted by its Socialist and Liberal equivalents); its activities are specifically geared to the political 'deadline' of the European elections, with all the stimulation that comes from rivalry with other political forces during the campaign. If these early moves associated with the EPP give some appearance of a 'take-off' in party co-operation in the EC, one may justifiably ask to what extent further such transnational development will lead to a reorientation of national parties towards the European level.

In the case of the Christian Democrats, various signs already exist as to the possibilities as well as limitations of this process.

The federal element is defined as follows by the EPP statutes: 'the member parties and équipes shall retain their name, their identity and their freedom of action within the framework of their national responsibilities' (art. 2), while the party ensures 'close and permanent collaboration between its member parties and équipes in order to implement their common policy in the construction of a federal Europe' (art. 3).[9] The political bureau of the EPP has relatively wide powers for it may take decisions by majority, regulates finance and will organise and co-ordinate the European election campaign.[10] In May 1977, a meeting between Tindemans and the general secretaries of the member parties together with their election specialists was held to discuss initial ideas for the campaign, but the importance of this co-ordination should not be exaggerated as the EPP will not have the machine to carry this activity far and it is likely to confine itself to the production of common posters and the agreement on central themes for the campaign.[11] The other main organisational provision, apart from a congress to be held at least once every two years, concerns the relationship between the EPP and the Christian Democratic group in the European Parliament. The close co-operation between leaders of the latter and the EUDC from the 1960s was carried into the preparatory work in establishing the EPP, and is acknowledged by the rule that the group chairman is an *ex officio* vice-president of the EPP.[12]

It is in the area of policy that the complexities of transnational party co-operation are really evident. Although Christian Democratic ideology is conveniently loose in its terminology, so there is little difficulty in expressing a common adherence to traditional concepts like the dignity of man and a pluralist community[13] and there is no disagreement over the development of federalism in the EC, differences emerge when attention is focused on specifics. The first conflict arose over the very name of the new party and whether to adopt the term 'Christian' in line with the group in the Parliament (favoured by the Dutch and Italian parties) or omit it (advocated by the German CDU/CSU, which looked to a wider Centre-Right grouping to include the British and Danish Conservatives). Behind this argument lay differences between the progressive and conservative tendencies of the respective parties.[14] A compromise was eventually worked out whereby the name 'European People's Party', preferred by the CDU/CSU, was adopted (with the subtitle 'Federation of Christian Democratic Parties of the EC'), but the question of further membership and indeed coalition alliances was left open until after the European election. Such varied ideological tendencies in member parties, conditioned in particular by coalition alliances in

domestic politics, also have affected the drafting of a common programme for the election. A programme commission under
Wilfried Martens commenced work in July 1976, its draft was
considered at meetings of the political bureau in the late spring of
1977 and it was finally approved at the congress of the EPP in the
spring of 1978. While general agreement was reached on the last
section which proposed a federal institutional structure for the
EC, differences of emphasis were apparent between the parties
over certain policies, notably the degree of planning suggested
for economic policy.[15] The Christian Democratic programme
will therefore be suitably vague, with an emphasis on traditional
concepts like 'Man and Society' and 'Justice and Solidarity'.

The degree to which the EPP will become a political factor in
the Community will depend initially on the catalysing effect of
direct elections in politicising European issues. Some element
of partisan feeling was already visible early with the tendency of
many noted politicians, seeking a European platform, to warn
against the dangers of a European popular front[16] and the concern expressed about the need to emerge from the European
elections as the strongest political force, even though there was
no prospect of any European government being formed as a
result of them.

THE CONFEDERATION OF THE SOCIALIST PARTIES OF THE
EUROPEAN COMMUNITY

The overall process of both establishing this confederation –
created in April 1974 on the basis of previous (loose) organisational links between parties of the EC member countries –
and of its activities, leading to direct elections with the formulation of a common programme and a subsequent congress early
in 1978, is remarkably similar to that of the Christian Democrats,
especially as the relevant group in the European Parliament
has in both cases played an important role in the whole of this
process. With the Socialists, there is much overlap of administration and personnel between the parliamentary group and the confederation – the former's secretariat services the latter, and the
secretary general and the press officer are the same for both – and
members of the group take an active part in the four working
groups for a common programme.[17] A distinction is made
between the functions of the parliamentary group, 'which looks
after the day-to-day work for Europe's interests and must concern
itself with problems that are frequently of a technical nature' and
those of the Confederation, whose 'problems . . . are of a more
long-term nature'.[18]

While the outline of developments concerning the Socialist Confederation has revealed many parallel features with the Christian Democrats, thus confirming the impact of the agreement on direct elections on efforts to integrate European parties, some important differences emerge. These differences between the Socialists and Christian Democrats appear most clearly in looking first at the motivation behind the process and secondly at the problems encountered in harmonising programmes. Both these differences reflect on the divergent character of Socialist and Christian Democratic movements in Western Europe.

The Socialist parties can point to a long history of transnational contact through the Socialist International, an association with a wide membership (by 1971, twenty years after its founding, it comprised fifty-four parties) whose main purpose has been that of a discussion forum.[19] The sense of belonging to a 'family' of political parties began to assume a Community orientation with the establishment in 1958, the year of the birth of the EEC, of a liaison bureau of the Socialist parties of the Six, whose main purpose was to facilitate communication between the European parliamentary group and the national parties. Its activities consisted chiefly of trying to stimulate the formulation of common programmes for European policy between member parties through the organisation of conferences and meetings. The stagnation of European integration in the later 1960s affected its work, for no such conference was called between 1966 and 1971. In 1971, the liaison bureau was renamed the office of the Social Democratic parties in the EC with a view to reorganising their transnational co-operation, now that the prospects for integration were brighter since The Hague summit of 1969.[20]

Since 1971, such co-operation has become intensified, while at the same time, in acquiring a more concrete form, it has exposed the complexities of integrating the European positions of different national parties. Predictably, the main concern behind efforts at institutionalising their co-operation as with the other political tendencies is the desire to determine the future course of the EC: in the words of Willy Brandt, the SPD chairman, himself a candidate in direct elections, 'the Social Democratic parties and the trade unions are together concerned decisively that the European Community develops and proves itself to be a socially progressive large association'.[21] On the other hand, attempts to launch a European Socialist Party have met with a strong reluctance, especially on the part of the major parties (at first the SPD, and at a later date the British Labour Party). This problem, which has limited the degree of integration possible between member parties, was clearly illustrated by the lack of positive response to the proposal initiated by the Dutch Labour Party in 1971 for creating a Progressive European Party with a federative character. This idea, which was based on the belief that the existing (nationally oriented) party structures were no longer sufficient for effective action at the European level, was intended to have 'shock effect' in stimulating member parties to closer co-operation, but it failed to engender enthusiasm largely because at that time the SPD held that any transnational organisation must exist alongside (i.e. leave untouched) the national party structures.[22]

The establishment in 1974 of the Socialist Confederation was proclaimed, more modestly than in the case of the Christian Democrats, as a reform of the pre-existing office of the Social Democratic parties than as a consciously new departure. New statutes were introduced, providing for more regular congresses (every two years) and containing a compromise whereby binding resolutions could be passed by the congress on a two-thirds majority, but only after the unanimous recommendation of the bureau.[23] According to its first president, Wilhelm Dröscher (SPD), the Confederation conceives of itself as 'an instrument for supporting co-operation' between the parties, who formed it on the basis of their own 'freedom of decision'.[24] The basic reason for this insistence on the autonomy of member parties is that the Socialists do not have the same clear attachment to the principle of federalism as the Christian Democrats, even though their various national parties have since the 1950s evolved a positive approach to European integration (with the important exception of the British Labour Party). This underlying attitude is expressed in the choice of the loose term 'confederation', for Dröscher himself has stated:

'It must be quite clearly noted that the development of a 'European Socialist Party' is not a realistic possibility in the near future. This would create insoluble problems for the national parties. But it is essential that in this transition stage the member parties of the Confederation should be united in a 'family of parties', which in a spirit of mutual understanding, constant dialogue and common resolve sees to it that the policy of democratic socialism does not remain a dead letter in the European Community, but in a common spirit of valiant endeavour points the way to transnational progress on important questions.[25]

This statement indicated recognition of the essential fact that member parties are anchored in their respective national political systems and that they are conditioned in their formulation of

European positions by the domestic political environment. The same applies to the Christian Democrats in spite of their strong conceptual adherence to the values of European integration. This may appear less obvious because of the second main difference between the Socialists and the Christian Democrats, for unlike the latter the Socialists have an established tradition of programmatic involvement and discussion conducted in a relatively open manner. The Christian Democrats tend to be more discreet about their current policy differences, although the essential divergences of standpoint between their national parties are of course known. Hence, much attention has been focused on the process of formulating a common programme by the Socialist Confederation for direct elections, which is of course its main activity until the European campaign begins.

While the Confederation was founded less exclusively in response to prospective direct elections in 1974 (when such elections were still a distant possibility) than was the Christian Democratic EPP, the progress towards such elections has nevertheless provided an important stimulus to working out programmatic differences. In so far as any political development affected the establishment of the Confederation, it was the expectation that enlargement of the EC in 1973 would create a new momentum for co-operation between parties,[26] even though the much-deplored boycott of the European Parliament by the British Labour Party still operated. Late in 1975, the procedure for elaborating a common programme was laid down by a meeting of the Confederation bureau, following which a meeting at Elsinore (January 1976) instituted four working groups on economic policy, social policy, democracy and institutions and external relations, under a general working group which had been functioning since early 1975.[27] Based on the work of these groups, a draft programme was ready in the spring of 1977,[28] and was then sent to the individual national parties for further discussion but differences arose on its common acceptance. The congress of the Confederation was planned for early 1979 and it was envisaged that at least a common declaration would be issued.[29] According to Schelto Patijn, the Dutch Socialist, the first programme might 'be a little vague, but it will be a short clear statement for the Socialists of Europe'.[30]

One question of particular interest in studying these incipient European Party organisations is to what extent their policy formulation will confine itself strictly or not to matters of EC policy concern. One noted feature of the Socialist Confederation's activities in this respect has been its tendency to compartmentalise its discussion of policy matters as in the form of conferences on areas of common concern. This 'partial' approach to policy formulation has been necessary, for any blanket treatment of European integration would occasion sharp differences between national parties, notably over integration strategy itself (e.g. the Dutch Socialists are pro-supranationality, the British Labour Party is largely against it), and also general ideological cleavages between Social Democrats and Socialists as well as differences over specific issues like co-determination. Too strict a concentration on EC policy matters is not possible, since some parties have insisted on certain points which are outside the scope of the Community.[31] All the same, the work on a common programme represents an important first step in harmonising the activities of Socialist parties at the European level,[32] for which reason the British Labour Party chose not to participate in the working groups even though it officially joined the Confederation early in 1976.

Impending direct elections have as with the Christian Democrats produced a new level of mild politicisation on the part of the Socialist parties in the EC, even though the first campaign will be '90 per cent national' with some European dimension,[33] such as with internationally known speakers addressing audiences in different member countries. Apart from the platform, there will not be much cross-national co-ordination. Nevertheless, a common purpose is evident in the desire that the Socialists should become the largest single group in the directly elected Parliament, and a long-term perspective has led to the Confederation establishing close links with the Spanish and Portuguese Socialist parties (the former already has observer status) with a view to further enlargement of the Community.

## FEDERATION OF LIBERAL AND DEMOCRATIC PARTIES OF THE EUROPEAN COMMUNITY

In the case of the Liberal parties, there has been a process of intensification of their European organisational links parallel to that of the Socialists and Christian Democrats, leading in March 1976 to the founding of a Liberal Federation and plans to formulate a common programme for direct elections. As with the other two political tendencies, there has been a similar though somewhat weaker background of 'fraternal' links through the Liberal International, established in 1947, and the Liberal Movement for a United Europe, formed in 1952.

Specific attention has been given to EC policy matters by the yearly congresses of the Liberal International since 1969. In 1972, the congress in Paris passed a resolution proposing the setting up of a Liberal Federation for the parties in Community countries. The stages culminating in the establishment of the Federation were as follows: the Florence congress in 1974 adopted draft statutes produced by a working group; since 1974 there have been twice yearly informal meetings of Liberal party chairmen together with the Liberal members of the European Commission and (from 1975) the chairman of the Liberal group in the European Parliament; and finally, the founding congress took place in Stuttgart in March 1976, with the election of Gaston Thorn, the prime minister of Luxembourg, as president of the Federation and the adoption of the Stuttgart Declaration, a broad definition of programmatic aims which covered the multiplicity of Liberal viewpoints represented by the member parties.[34]

The Liberal Federation has presented itself as an important initiative in the construction of party political forces with a European character. Its statutes (art. 2)[35] define the purpose of the Federation as threefold: seeking a common position on all important problems affecting the Community; supporting direct elections to the Parliament; and, involving the public in building a 'united and liberal Europe'. The organs of the Federation consist of a congress, which may take binding decisions by a two-thirds majority on 'all matters within the competence of the treaties establishing the European Communities and on matters regarding political co-operation of the EC' (art. 26), and an executive committee, which among others includes twelve members elected by the congress and twelve appointed by the national parties as well as Liberal members of the Commission. Of particular interest is the organic link established with the parliamentary group, for as Article 10 states specifically: 'The Federation is represented in the European Parliament by the Liberal Group.' It is made clear that the congress receives reports from the group and makes recommendations to it (art. 26). The question of the relationship between the group and the Federation had been discussed at the FDP congress in October 1975. Martin Bangemann, a vice-chairman of the group and a leading figure in the establishment of the Federation, had argued that, although the group without a political basis had a considerable freedom of manoeuvre in formulating policy, such an initiative in establishing a Federation was in principle an 'act of democratisation', for 'we will give it the competence, which it will exercise *vis-à-vis* the group in the European Parliament and can use as an instrument of control over practical policy carried out in this group'.[36] In the course of implementing these aims, some sense of rivalry has been evident in the group, particularly following the speed with which the Federation was created.[37]

The Liberal Federation therefore provides the basis for a federal party structure in the Community, an aim in some ways more explicitly defined than in the case of the two other party federations. There is one major difference however relating to the compelling motivation behind the Liberals' initiative, which is that unlike many of the Socialist and Christian Democratic parties the Liberal parties are all small forces in their national political contexts. The European stage consequently offers them an attractive opportunity to gain new prestige and publicity. In no case is this so evident as with the British Liberals, who are seeking to use support from their European connections to increase pressure for electoral reform in Britain. In arguing for multinational parties in 1973, Jeremy Thorpe commented in reference to possible direct elections that 'some form of proportional representation will be needed and eventually the electoral system adopted for Strasbourg will become hard to resist at Westminster'.[38] Indeed, the leaders of the Federation have frequently stressed the priority they attach to 'winning the battle' over the principle of PR.[39] Equally, the sense of European solidarity acquired by member parties is regarded by them as important in strengthening their domestic political bases, for they are generally not highly organised parties and cannot count on solid electorates, a problem faced even by governing parties like the West German FDP and the French Independent Republicans.

The main problem in building the Federation is similar to that faced by the Liberal group in the European Parliament, which is the heterogeneity of Liberal forces in the Community with an ideological range spreading from Left-Liberal (e.g. the British party) to strongly Conservative Liberal (e.g. the Italian PLI, the French FNRI) and the variety of specific electorates encompassed by the different member parties. Some difficulty arose over the fact that not all parties concerned call themselves 'liberal' so that the term 'democratic' was incorporated in the title of the Federation. A dispute also absorbed the Federation during 1976 as to whether certain parties, notably the FNRI (because of its Gaullist associations), should become members, a matter only finally settled at The Hague congress (November 1976). The FNRI was eventually admitted – its exclusion would have been difficult since it was already in the parliamentary group, and the latter's chairman was from the FNRI – but the real test of its membership would be its acceptance of the common programme of the Federation.[40]

As with the other two party federations, the main activity has centred on the formulation of a common programme for European elections. Seven working groups (e.g. on the rights of man and

the citizen, European institutions, food and agriculture and other
EC policy areas) were set up to prepare drafts for a European
programme. Their work was examined at The Hague congress,
which created three further groups (on small businesses, social
policy and energy). The draft programme, produced by a commission chaired by Bangemann, was presented in the spring of
1977 and approved at the congress of the Federation at Brussels
in November 1977. In spite of the specialism involved in its
preparation, the final programme presented for the European
campaign will as with the other two federations inevitably be
vague.[41]

The Liberal Federation will play a limited co-ordinating role in
the organisation of the Liberals' European campaign. As already
specified by the statutes (art. 17), 'the list of approved candidates
from each country will be drawn up by the national member
parties after consultation with the [Executive] Committee', and
there will be some co-ordination of electoral themes. This of
course allows a considerable freedom to the national parties in
their own conduct of the campaign. A general attachment to the
promotion of Liberal ideas in the construction of a united Europe
provides the common denominator between the various parties
contained in the Federation, although a foretaste of the complexities involved in institutionalising party activity at the
European level is indicated by Bangemann's assertion that the
solution of the (long-term) 'coalition question' in the Community
is only possible if one accepts the principle that European coalitions between parties do not have to accord with those at the
national level.[42] Although this distinction is illustrated by looking
at the wide variety of coalitions which Liberals have formed in
national capitals, the same principle of flexibility will probably
also have to be adopted by the other political forces attempting to
integrate their activities in the European Community.

THE COMMUNISTS

Unlike the Christian Democrats, Socialists and Liberals, the
Communists have made no special efforts to institutionalise co-
ordination procedures outside their group in the European
Parliament. On several occasions, leaders of the PCF and PCI have
been explicit in stating that no organisational machinery is en-
visaged in developing their common approach towards the
European Community. At the 1974 conference in Brussels of
West European Communist parties, the PCF chairman Georges
Marchais emphasised: 'We exclude the idea of a single decision-
centre for the European or world Communist movement; the

conference has created no secretariat nor any other common organisation at the European level.'[43] More recently, the leader of the Communist group in the European Parliament, Giorgio Amendola (PCI), expressed his sceptical viewpoint about the integration of parties in relation to direct elections:

'The time is still not ripe for the creation of European parties. Anyway, you have only to look at the differences between the British Labour Party and the German Social Democrats, between Strauss's Christian Democrats and the Italian Christian Democrats in order to understand the artificial character of certain alignments, that have purely an electioneering value.'[44]

Co-ordination between the Communists over their policy towards the EC has taken rather a conceptual form, involving the common analysis of general problems or the formulation of broad guidelines. This process, pursued particularly by the two dominant Communist parties from Italy and France, has by no means been geared specifically to European elections.

There are two main reasons for this difference between the European Communists and the other political tendencies. First, their elaboration of a common regional strategy towards Europe, a process generally labelled 'Eurocommunism', has a broader scope than strictly EC policy matters, with a strong relevance on the one hand to domestic political positions (in the PCI's case, the 'historic compromise') and on the other hand wider international factors, in particular the redefinition of the respective parties' relationship with the Soviet Union. For instance, the regional conferences of West European Communist parties – on multinational companies in 1971, and the 1974 Brussels conference on 'capitalist Europe' – were not confined to parties from EC member states. The regional strategy does however have a strong EC slant, especially as the two most important parties – the PCI and the PCF – are in Community states, and have worked within the same group in the European Parliament since 1973. A series of bilateral PCI/PCF 'summits' have taken place between Berlinguer and Marchais to define their stand on European affairs, notably that in November 1975 in Rome which issued a joint declaration pledging the two parties to the plurality of political parties, the development of democratic institutions and stronger action than the EC had so far been prepared to mount against multinational companies.[45] The PCI and PCF have also been developing closer links with Communist parties in prospective member states of the EC, and in March 1977 a 'summit' was held in Madrid between them and Santiago Carrillo, leader of the

Spanish PCE.[46] While the Communist parties have shown an increasing tendency in the 1970s to focus more on the EC within the framework of a wider Europe, they have at the same time given the impression of 'looking beyond' the present stage of integration with their emphasis on the need to develop its social structural aspects and their as yet undefined discussion of an alliance with other political forces representing the interests of workers.

Secondly, the co-operation between Communist parties has not been institutionalised on an EC basis because of some fundamental differences, specifically between the PCI and PCF, over European integration itself. These differences, acknowledged by both parties, have been apparent especially over supranational institutions and direct elections. The Italian party, whose strategy towards Europe has evolved over a long period since the early 1960s,[47] has taken a positive position on both questions. While the PCI sees supranationality as 'a condition for the independence of European states',[48] Giorgio Amendola, the party's active 'European', has repeatedly confirmed the PCI's support for direct elections. PCI leaders view direct elections, in spite of a reservation about the absence of a uniform PR system, as a first step towards the construction of a more democratic Europe and as a way of overcoming 'immobilism' in the Community.[49] On the other hand, the PCF has taken a negative line on both issues. As Madame Goutmann, a PCF member of the group in the European Parliament, commented at a press conference in November 1976: 'The French Communists oppose any supranationality and also direct elections, though when they take place the Communists will participate in them.'[50] In April 1977, however, Marchais changed his party's position on direct elections, saying that the PCF 'might contemplate' supporting them if the Bill ratifying them in the French Parliament included a 'solemn and binding' undertaking that such elections would not entail any strengthening of the powers of the European Parliament.[51] It was understood this change of approach had more to do with the PCF's desire at that time for a fuller agreement with the French Socialists for domestic political reasons than with 'Eurocommunist' relationships.

The position therefore of the Communist parties is that no common organised action is planned for the European campaign, although certain common policy statements will be published to give their individual national campaigns some European 'coloration'. This approach will be in line with the conceptual rather than institutional character of 'Eurocommunist' co-ordination, as it has so far developed. It cannot therefore be said that the prospect of direct elections has stimulated any form of integration between these parties.

OTHER PARTIES

The position of the remaining parties represented in the European Parliament is that no institutional links of a European form are being developed with regard to direct elections, because they are strictly 'national' parties, having no recognised ideological relationships of a transnational kind. Their campaign for the European Parliament will be strictly national with no special European flavour. This approach is all the more likely because certain of these parties take a nationalist stance in European affairs, notably the Gaullists (RPR), who have been predictably cool about direct elections. The Irish Fianna Fáil, with whom the Gaullists form a group in the European Parliament, will also conduct their own separate campaign,[52] and they in any case differ from the Gaullists in that they take a positive line over both supranational institutions and direct elections. With the regional nationalist parties, the prospect of European elections has had a mildly stimulating effect and a charter for co-operation was signed in March 1977 by the Welsh Plaid Cymru and the Belgian Volksunie. No important outcome is likely especially as the SNP did not sign this charter on the grounds that it was already represented in the European Parliament. It sees itself as different from these parties in having a promising political future, and it consequently takes a less 'generous' line than the Plaid Cymru towards other parties from the 'unrepresented nations'.[53]

There is a European Union of Conservatives, a loose grouping, which includes the Gaullists and the CDU/CSU as well as the Scandinavian Conservative parties, but this has produced no intensification of transnational relationships mainly because of its diverse composition. The Conservatives, specifically the British party, are confining discussion of a European programme to the group in the European Parliament.[54] A mild form of institutional arrangement is however presented by the European Democratic Union (EDU), a loose grouping conceived of as an 'alliance of parties' which includes the Gaullists and the CDU/CSU as well as Scandinavian Conservatives, but this is unlikely to produce much intensification of transnational relationships mainly because of its diverse composition including non-EC political parties (e.g. from Norway, Finland and Austria). The Conservatives, specifically the British party, are confining discussion of a European programme to the group in the European Parliament,[55] although an EDU declaration of policy is envisaged in time for direct elections. The European Democratic Union has been the main result of the British Conservatives' contacts with other like-minded parties, notably the West German Christian Democrats, and was formed at a meeting in Salzburg in April 1978.[56] A month later, the annual conference of the British Conservatives paid special attention to the need for a European link as a defence against Socialism. The Conservatives' concern at their isolation within the context of European party organisational links was further provoked by the shock effect, also felt by the Christian Democrats, when the Socialists became the largest group at Strasbourg (after the admission of British Labour members) in the summer of 1975. The idea of a Centre-Right alliance had also been promoted by such figures as Sir Christopher Soames (European Commissioner, 1973–7) and leaders in the CDU/CSU. There are nevertheless several obstacles to the prospects of such a plan before the first European elections in spite of the establishment of the EDU expressing a solidarity between the parties concerned. Such solidarity will not acquire a party-political character similar to the European party federations mainly because of the CDU/CSU's own membership of the European People's Party (EPP) and the objections of other Christian Democratic parties to close links with the Conservatives. The question of 'coalition-building' on the centre-right is therefore postponed until after direct elections.

CONCLUSION

Even the projection of such coalitional arrangements, although somewhat academic at this stage, is an indication of the extent to which the party-political dimension of European integration has progressed by the later 1970s and in particular of the catalytic effect produced by the plans for direct elections to the European Parliament. The prospect of direct elections clearly emerges from this survey of the European-level activities of the different political tendencies as the most important single factor conditioning this process. Their impact in this respect must however be measured against other pressures which have promoted the intensification of transnational party co-operation – notably, the widening scope of integration policy activity and its more overtly political orientation. At the same time, the possible consequences following European elections for the further integration of political parties must be related to the intrinsic character of such transnational co-operation as it has evolved during the course of the last decade, especially at the European parliamentary level, witnessing in particular the emergence of a multi-party situation with a diversification of ideological patterns.

The developments since the end of the 1960s therefore amount to a new historical phase in the growth of European transnational co-operation. It is even viable to claim that this phase is more significant than any of those preceding it, as unlike in the 1950s and 1960s party-political integration has for the first time been motivated by a potential power factor – in the form of the strengthened, albeit modest, powers of the European Parliament, and the prospect that after direct elections this institution will be enhanced in status, if not authority. It is becoming less possible to discuss an individual (national) party's position on European policy without some reference to its role and participation in the growing organisational transnational links, where these exist. Equally, this survey of the incipient European party federations has shown how much national party-political considerations enter into their prospects for committed action, a problem already encountered in the experience of the party groups; just as it is expected that national political trends will affect party preferences in the first and later European elections. Ultimately, party-political integration has to operate against the background of differently structured electorates in each of the member countries of the European Community.

Perhaps the most useful lessons to be drawn at this stage are from the longer-term development of party groups in the European Parliament as pointers for the new development of European party federations. Indeed, the problems of national differences of outlook as well as differences of ideological interpretation, groups present in the work of these groups, have already emerged in the work of the party federations, notably in their efforts to formulate common programmes. On the organisational level, differences must emerge between the groups and the federations if only because of their distinct roles as parliamentary and organisational entities, with the former engaged more in everyday politics at least so far. The party federations are of course in a very early stage of organisational development, although the question already discussed by them of the sovereignty of their component national parties does highlight a basic problem of their future structural development.

Finally, all these various aspects of party-political integration in the 1970s reflect on the broader matter of supranationality within the context of the European Community. If supranationality is understood as a method of modifying national positions and interests for the sake of the European cause, then the activity of both party groups and federations offers an interesting and increasingly important example of this process. In so far as European integration is accepted as a process which is *sui generis*, then it becomes difficult to measure transnational party co-operation by the traditional yardsticks applied to the evaluation of national party systems. However, it can also be said that the very existence of European parliamentary groups, and now also of European party federations, does itself provide a 'motor' for further integration, although one very much limited by the present deficiencies of the European Parliament as an institution.

## NOTES

1 See S. Henig and J. Pinder (eds), *European Political Parties* (London, Allen & Unwin, 1969), pp. 529–34.

2 The authors have attempted to limit this problem of research by using interviews conducted in Brussels and Strasbourg in April 1977 both to establish the main stages of arrangements for the European campaign and to investigate the 'thinking' behind the party federations. This chapter was subsequently updated to the summer of 1978.

3 CD–*Europe Bulletin*, publication of the Christian Democratic group, June 1976, p. 1.

4 Josef Müller, Vorgeschichte und Gründung der europäischen Volkspartei (mimeo, 1977), pp. 4–5.

5 ibid., p. 2.

6 ibid., p. 3.

7 Belgium: Christian People's Party (CVP) and Social Christian Party (PSC); West Germany: CDU and CSU; France: Centrists (UCDP); Ireland: Fine Gael; Italy: Democrazia Cristiana (DC) and South Tyrol People's Party (SVP); Luxembourg: Christian Social Party (PCS); Holland: Anti-Revolutionary Party (ARP), Christian Historical Union (CHU) and Catholic People's Party (KVP).

8 Interview with Josef Müller, executive secretary of the European Union of Christian Democrats (UEDC), in Brussels, April 1977.

9 Statutes of the EPP, 8 July 1976, p. 1.

10 ibid., p. 4.

11 Interview with Josef Müller, April 1977.

12 Rules of procedure of the EPP, 8 July 1976, p. 2.

13 For example, see the manifesto of European Christian Democrats, 21 February 1976.

14 *Frankfurter Allgemeine*, 24 February 1976; *Europa Union*, April 1976.

15 Based on interview with Josef Müller, April 1977.

16 Notably, Kurt Biedenkopf, general secretary of the CDU, see 'CDU–Perspektiven für das gewählte EG–Parlament', *Neue Zürcher Zeitung*, 26 February 1976.

17 Interview with Bent Wigotski, deputy secretary general of the Socialist Confederation, in Brussels, April 1977.

18 Helga Köhnen, *Co-operation between the Socialist Parties of the European Community*, publication of the Socialist Confederation (reprint of article in *Die Neue Gesellschaft*, June 1976), October 1976, p. 10.

19 *Zusammenarbeit der Parteien in Westeuropa* (Bonn, Schriftenreihe der Bundeszentrale für politische Bildung), Band 108, pp. 169–74.

20 Helga Köhnen, op. cit., pp. 7–8.

21 Quoted in *Die Neue Gesellschaft*, October 1971, p. 704.

22 For an explanation of this proposal of the Dutch Labour Party, as well as the text of its resolution, see H. Vredeling, 'The common market of political parties', *Government and Opposition*, Autumn 1971, pp. 448–61.

23 See Rudolf Hrbek, 'Parteibünde: Unterbau der EP-Fraktionen und unverzichtbares Element einer funktionsfähigen Infrastruktur der EG', *Zeitschrift für Parlamentsfragen*, June 1976, pp. 187–8.

24 Wilhelm Dröscher, speech of November 1974, reprinted in *Europa-Union*, March 1975.

25 Quoted in Helga Köhnen, op. cit., p. 11.

26 Interview with Bent Wigotski, April 1977.

27 Bent Wigotski, 'Sozialdemokratische Plattform für die europäischen Wahlen – zum Stand der Diskussion', *Die Neue Gesellschaft*, April 1977, p. 335.

28 See interim outline of this programme in ibid., pp. 335–8.

29 Press conference statement by Dröscher in Strasbourg, 21 April 1977.

30 European Commentary, broadcast on BBC Radio 4, 23 March 1977.

31 Interview with Bent Wigotski, April 1977.

32 The member parties of the Socialist Confederation are: the West German Social Democratic Party (SPD); the Belgian Socialist Party (PSB); the French Socialist Party (PS); the Italian Socialist Party and Social Democratic Party (PSI and PSDI); the Luxembourg Socialist Workers' Party (POSL); the Dutch Labour Party (PvdA); and the British Labour Party. The Confederation therefore is represented in all the member countries of the European Community.

33 Interview with Bent Wigotski, April 1977.

34 The member parties of the Liberal Federation are as follows. Belgium: the Party of Freedom and Progress (PVV and PLP) and the Party for Reforms and Liberty in Wallonia (PRLW); Denmark: the Left Land Organisation (V) and the Radical Left Land Association (RV)*; West Germany: the Free Democratic Party (FDP); France: Independent Republicans (FNRI) (renamed Republicans); Movement of the Radical Left* and the Radical Socialist Party; Britain: Liberal Party; Italy: Liberal Party (PLI) and Republican Party (PRI); Luxembourg: Democratic Party (PD); Holland: Party of Freedom and Democracy (VVD). However, two parties marked with * have temporarily withdrawn.

35 Constitution of the Liberal Federation, March 1976.

36 FDP, *Leitlinien liberaler Europa-Politik* (Bonn, 1975), p. 11.

37 Interview with Martin Bangemann, vice-chairman of the Liberal group, in Strasbourg, April 1977.

38 Jeremy Thorpe, 'The case for multinational parties', *The Times*, 2 January 1973. See also David Steel's address to the Liberal group of the European Parliament, February 1977, published in *Présence Libérale*, publication of the group, August 1977, pp. 3–4.

39 For example, the speech by Jean Durieux, chairman of the Liberal group, to FDP conference, January 1977, published in ibid., pp. 7–10.

40 Interview with Martin Bangemann, April 1977.

41 For an outline of some of the policy ideas supported by the Liberal Federation, see statement by Gaston Thorn in *Das Parlament*, 4 December 1976, p. 10.

42 Interview with Martin Bangemann in *Europa-Union*, August 1975.

43 *Le Monde*, 27 January 1974.

44 Interview with *The Times*, 1 February 1977.

45 Details of communiqué in *The Times*, 18 November 1975 and 19 November 1975.

46 See article in *The Times* (Europa), 1 March 1977.

47 On this, see Donald Sassoon, 'The Italian Communist Party's European strategy', *Political Quarterly*, July 1976.

48 Statement by Sergio Segre, foreign affairs spokesman of the PCI, in *Le Monde*, 25 January 1974.

49 See the reprint of statements by PCI leaders on direct elections in *Les Communistes Italiens,* February 1977, published by PCI headquarters in Rome.
50 *Europa-Union,* December 1976.
51 *The Times,* 19 April 1977.
52 Interview with Senator Michael Yeats, member of the DEP group, in Strasbourg, April 1977.
53 Interview with Winifred Ewing, Independent (SNP) MEP, in Strasbourg, April 1977.
54 *European Report,* 5 June 1976.
55 See *The Economist,* 29 April 1977.
56 See text of resolution of Salzburg meeting in *Europa-Union,* November 1975.

## FURTHER READING

Bonvicini, Gianni (1973) 'The future role of Parliament in the EEC: interaction between the European Parliament and political forces', *Lo Spettatore Internazionale,* October/December, pp. 229–40.

Cocks, Barnett (1973) *The European Parliament : Structure, Procedure and Practice* (London, HMSO).

Coombes, David, and Wiebeke, Ilka (1972) *The Power of the Purse : the budgetary powers of the European Parliament* (London, Chatham House/ PEP).

Fitzmaurice, John (1975) *The Party Groups in the European Parliament* (Farnborough, Saxon House).

Hrbek, Rudolf (1976) 'Parteibünde: Unterbau der EP-Fraktionen und unverzichtbares Element einer funktionsfähigen Infrastruktur der EG', *Zeitschrift für Parlamentsfragen,* June, pp. 179–90.

Irving, R. E. M. (1977) 'The European policy of the French and Italian Communists', *International Affairs,* July.

Irving, R. E. M. (1979) *The Christian Democratic Parties of Western Europe* (London, George Allen & Unwin/RIIA).

Leich, J. F. (1971) 'The Italian Communists and the European Parliament', *Journal of Common Market Studies,* June, pp. 271–81.

van Oudenhove, G. (1965) *The Political Parties in the European Parliament* (Leiden, Sijthoff).

Pridham, Geoffrey (1975) 'Transnational party groups in the European Parliament, *Journal of Common Market Studies,* March, pp. 266–79.

Vredeling, Henk (1971) 'The common market of political parties', *Government and Opposition,* Autumn, pp. 448–61.

*Zusammenarbeit der Parteien in Westeuropa : Auf dem Weg zu einer neuen politischen Infrastruktur* (1976) (Bonn, Schriftenreihe der Bundeszentrale für politische Bildung, Band 108).

# 13
# Conclusion

## STANLEY HENIG

During the last decade major questions have been raised about both the stability of some of Western Europe's democracies and the ability of traditional governing parties and party systems to deal with a range of problems some of which had not been previously encountered in the postwar period. For nearly three decades after 1945 Western Europe enjoyed, and increasingly took for granted, a continuing sharp rise in living standards. The original six-member European Community both benefited from and helped facilitate this boom. During the decade 1958–68 GNP per head rose at an annual average rate of 4·3 per cent in the Six, holding out the prospect of doubling living standards in little more than fifteen years. A sharp change in economic prospects took place after 1973 – the year in which British membership of the Community took effect – as a result of the Middle East War and subsequent massive rises in oil prices which precipitated economic stagnation throughout the Western world. High levels of unemployment – for the first time since the thirties – have accompanied considerable rates of inflation and, in many cases, balance-of-payments problems. Britain and Italy have been worst affected, but none of the Western European countries has entirely escaped an economic mixture which has seemed to defy solution. As a result the ability of existing governments and political institutions to continue to deliver further increases in living standards has been severely limited. At the same time there have been more overtly political problems. Even in the 1970s Western Europe still faces the residue of its imperial past, particularly in the form of large non-European immigrant communities and the tensions engendered around them. In addition, a generation after the end of the last major war, groups have emerged which are willing to use force in their endeavours to overthrow existing political institutions. Apart from bringing about the suspension of traditional civil government in Northern Ireland, they have to date been unsuccessful. Urban terrorism is one of the nastier manifestations of modern life, but there is little evidence to suggest that it weakens allegiance to established political institutions.

Within the enlarged nine-member European Community only Germany and Ireland have avoided any change in the broad contours of their party system. All the others have been affected to a greater or lesser degree by the emergence of new parties or groupings, often coupled with splits in existing parties. In two countries – Belgium and Britain – there has been the emergence of federalist or nationalist parties which have sought the break up of the unitary state. New 'radical' parties have also made a considerable electoral impact in Denmark and the Netherlands. In France and Italy changes in the configuration of the separate parties have been overshadowed by the apparently relatively constant alignment which poses fundamental questions about the survival of the present regimes. In each case there is a critical political demarcation between groups permanently in office and those apparently permanently excluded. The Fifth Republic has shown an ability to survive even without the personal charisma of its founder, but half the nation votes for the 'permanent outs'. The Italian system of government amounts in effect to one-party rule through a series of unstable coalitions with various small partners, whilst the second largest party – permanently excluded from office – grows ever stronger. In each case the opposition is subject to cross-pressures – acceptance of the norms of the system in the hope of winning enough votes to come to power or equating opposition to the government in office with opposition to the regime itself.

Throughout Western Europe traditionally dominant parties or groupings or party *families* have come under pressure. In Italy the gradual growth of the Communists is bringing them closer in size to the Christian Democrats, whilst the weakening of the latter's allies on the Right and Centre is gradually eroding the basis of government. In Denmark the leading Social Democrats dropped to 25 per cent support at one election: over the last decade there has been an increase in the number of parties represented in the Folketing from six to eleven. There have been considerable changes in the Benelux countries: in the Netherlands there has been a sharp decline in support for the religious parties; in Belgium traditional combinations of the old parties are no longer always adequate as bases for government; in Luxembourg the Christian Social Party is out of office for the first time in fifty years. In the United Kingdom the two large parties continue to dominate government, but it is no longer automatically the case that one or other holds an absolute majority of parliamentary seats: their combined electoral strength was only 75 per cent in 1974 compared with 90 per cent in 1966. In France the presidential government majority still has the capacity for winning elections, but it now commands the allegiance of less than half the voters.

Dominance by one or two parties is not necessarily incompatible with multi-partism. The countries of the European Community have always been rich in the number and diversity of their political parties: independence and integrity are zealously maintained even when there are attempts at rationalisation and realignment as there have been in France, Italy and the Netherlands. The sharpest increases in the number of parties represented in Parliament has been in Britain and Denmark. The crude average for the number of parties represented in the nine parliaments is now seven – a slight increase over the last decade. Two countries, though, remain exceptions as far as all the trends so far discussed are concerned. Germany and Ireland are respectively the most and the least prosperous countries in the Community. Each has three parties represented in Parliament – two large and one small; all can aspire to hold office from time to time; and their relative size has hardly changed during the last decade.

Challenges to patterns of dominance and the emergence of new parties are indicators of the electorate's restlessness and possibly its desire for political reform, but they are imperfectly translated into changes in the composition of government. Since 1968 there have been two complete changes of government in both Britain and Ireland with the party or parties hitherto in office going into opposition and vice versa. During the previous decade there had been only one such change in Britain and none at all in Ireland. The single change in Germany was less complete in that the Social Democrats who assumed the leading role in government in 1969 had already been coalition partners, but the exclusion of the Christian Democrats from office is perhaps the most important single event in that country's postwar domestic politics. The one change in Luxembourg after the 1974 elections is equally significant in domestic terms. All these changes in the four countries so far considered were the result of elections, but the situation has been somewhat different in the other five. Changes in government are not solely a function of electoral success or failure in multi-party systems. In Denmark the mixed fortunes of the Social Democrats have occasioned four major changes in the composition of government over the last ten years.

Two of these were either side of a rather bizarre period of minority rule by the Liberals which started after a parliamentary election in which they lost more than a quarter of their seats and ended after another in which they nearly doubled their representation. In Belgium and the Netherlands party changes in government composition are hardly seminal events given the frequency with which they occur and the fact that there are very few 'permanent outs': the concept of government change does not mean the same as it does in Britain or Germany. It is, however, noticeable that in Belgium, the Netherlands and Italy there are frequent and ever lengthier crises in forming coalitions – often aimed at negating the apparent results of recent elections rather than implementing them! In Italy and France the pattern of government has scarcely been altered at all by elections or any other events – a surface stability which partially masks the regime problems discussed earlier.

The break-up of a political system or the emergence of radically new and durable alignments has often seemed imminent, but in practice this has not happened. There have been no changes of regime in any of these countries since France in 1958. Whilst traditional parties may have ebbed in political strength, they continue for the most part to play significant roles in the government of their countries. The major government figures in Western Europe in the 1970s come from the same political families as did their predecessors in the 1950s and 1960s. The older political parties have been able to command sufficient loyalty and allegiance from large sections of the electorate to give them the durability for weathering the storm. As a result many of those parties wich may loosely be termed anti-system (because they seek major changes in the rules and parameters of the party system and the nature of government) have been unable to grow beyond a certain point and in some cases have even declined. Belgian Federalist parties have made no significant electoral advance since 1971, neither have the rash of new parties in the Netherlands. The level of support for the Danish Progressives has hardly varied since they first burst on the national scene in 1973. In Britain the Liberals, although not the Nationalists, have lost much of their popular support since the apparent breakthrough in 1974.[1] Older parties have, meanwhile, shown the ability to transmute themselves into formations more likely to win support in the political climate of the 1970s – the Dutch religious groups into a single electoral grouping and the French SFIO and Centre Left into the new Socialist Party. They have also demonstrated a knowledge of traditional governmental skills in the ways in which they have sought to buy off or outflank those political pressures which have nurtured the new groups – willingness for some Federalist compromise in Belgium and Labour's espousal of devolution in the United Kingdom. At the same time some of the anti-system parties have been sucked not unwillingly into the very systems they condemn. This has clearly been the case in both Belgium and the Netherlands where no parties save the Communists are considered inherently 'untouchable'. In different ways the process is reflected in both Britain and Italy. Through the Lib-Lab pact the Liberals have ensured the survival of a Labour government after it lost its parliamentary majority. In Italy the Communists may even have lost in revolutionary *élan* more than they have gained in political respectability through their willingness to tolerate Christian Democratic governments. The inherent nature of Western European democracy seems to be such that the greater the political strength of anti-system groups, the greater their tendency to accept some features of the system in their searches for more influence and more support. As a self-defence mechanism for the system, this is not ineffectual.

Whilst the party systems of the nine have largely survived recent vicissitudes, they have not emerged unscathed: physiognomy and, therefore, classification are now rather different from what they were a decade ago.[2] Classification of party system is determined by both the total number of parties and the number who share or control government. Two types of system seem most characteristic of the countries of the European Community: two and a half party and multi-party. In addition there are two other tendencies which characterise at least some of the countries: bipolarity in political alignment and unipolarity in government domination. Germany, Ireland and Luxembourg operate two-and-a-half party systems in which both parliament and government are monopolised by three parties of which two are *majoritaire* and the other is very much smaller. There are five conceivable government combinations: either major party on its own, a combination of one or other with the minor party and a coalition of the two large parties. This system offers the possibilities of both government continuity through coalition and alternation through its approximation to the two-party system. Until the eruption of the federalist parties Belgium was also in this category.

Belgium, Denmark and the Netherlands currently operate multi-party systems where there are a large number of parties represented in Parliament and sharing government with a much less constant relationship in size than that characteristic of the two-and-a-half party system. There are a large number of alternative bases for government and there tend consequently to be frequent changes. Whereas in the two-and-a-half party system change of government tends to be a function of elections, this is much less obviously the case in the multi-party system.

The United Kingdom has always been considered as the leading example in Western Europe of a bipolar system. Domination by the two major parties of government and Parliament is facilitated by an electoral system which discriminates against small parties without a strong regional base. It is, however, conceivable that continued growth by the Nationalists might ultimately shift the UK into the two-and-a-half party category. Bipolar trends are also apparent in France, Italy and even Denmark through the alignment of bourgeois parties against the Social Democrats. France and Italy are peculiarly difficult to classify. In both cases government has been dominated by a party or regular coalition of parties. Frequently the challenge of those permanently excluded from office implies the emergence of a bipolar system in the form of a simple Left/Right demarcation. However, both countries also show tendencies towards multi-partism, tempered in the French case into four large groups and possibly distorted in the Italian by the extremely unequal size of the different parties.

What lies behind these categories and tendencies? President de Gaulle's aphorism that parties reflected the French nation as in a cracked mirror may be illustrated by the conflicting patterns of that country's politics. The electorate are visibly influenced by a variety of cross-currents, political and institutional: the unity of the nation is expressed in the presidency and in unipolar domination of government; the notion of government against opposition is demonstrated by the dominant alignment which contested the 1978 legislative election; the cleavage into four – or historically six – major groupings is a reflection of popular memory and gut feeling.

In general a party system is determined by the number of party-forming issues. Throughout Western Europe, with the single exception of Ireland, the most important such issue is that of labour against capital. The whole notion of Left and Right – central to political analysis of eight Community countries – is founded on this issue.[3] It reflects an ideological divide as well as a clash of class interests, neither of which has been resolved by the omnipresent mixed economy and welfare state. However, in all cases there are other issues superimposed across this cleavage. Regime questions have produced 'extremist' parties on right and left as well as nationalist and federalist groups. Historic issues concerned with the role of the church are significant for the party alignment in many European countries, and there is also the interplay of economic interests other than labour and capital. Indeed, underlying the formation of many of the newer groupings has been a belief that the historic basis of the Left/Right divide – the labour/capital issue – is, or ought to be, out of date.

The actual party pattern which emerges in parliament or government is determined by the degree of salience attached to these various issues; norms of political culture and particularly the acceptability of new forces; and the rules and parameters of the political system. The electoral system is a particularly important feature of the latter.

There have been no major changes in the electoral systems used in the nine countries since 1958,[4] although the minimum voting age has now been lowered to 18 in all save Belgium and Denmark. Seven countries use proportional systems (Britain and France are the exceptions) and the most normal type (Belgium, Denmark, Italy, Luxembourg and the Netherlands) is based on party lists in multi-member constituencies. Various methods are used to allocate seats between the lists and they are most favourable to smaller parties in Belgium and Denmark. In Denmark almost one-quarter of the seats are used to make the overall national result as proportional as possible with threshold rules to prevent excessive fragmentation.[5] Ireland alone uses the single transferable vote in multi-member constituencies so that the system is both proportional and preferential. In those countries using the list system the power of electors to alter the order of candidates varies considerably. Britain, France and Germany all have single-member constituencies, but in the latter half the seats are reserved to ensure that the result is also proportional, although the threshold is considerably higher than in the Danish case. The French two-ballot system is not proportional, but it does introduce a preferential element which affects parties according to their position in the political spectrum. Britain is the only country with a single member, winner-take-all system, which is neither proportional nor preferential.

Turning to the parties which actually exist in the nine countries of the European Community, only one type is omnipresent: the Social Democratic. The relative strength of this party is determined by two considerations: the salience of the labour/capital issue and the strength of anti-system feeling on the Left. In all except Ireland the labour/capital issue is the most important of those which form parties, while in France and Italy the Social Democrats are confronted by effective Communist rivals representing a left-wing anti-system tendency. It is in these three countries that Social Democracy has been weakest with electoral support below 20 per cent, although the new French Socialist

Party may be climbing away from this trough. In the other six countries Social Democrats are one of the two leading groups with popular support normally in the range 35–45 per cent. The Danish party invariably takes first position and the Belgian second, but all six parties have played major roles in government.

The major counterweight to the Social Democrats are parties of the moderate right. Traditionally based on industry, commerce and agriculture and in many cases maintaining strong links with the church, these parties have come to accept many of the norms of the welfare state and mixed economy. In four of the countries where the Social Democrats are strongest – Belgium, Germany, Luxembourg and the United Kingdom – and also in Italy, the moderate right is represented by a single large party. In all five cases these parties command electoral support in the 35–45 per cent range. Taken together the three religious parties in the Netherlands used to be as strong: gradual erosion of their vote has led them to form a joint electoral combination. In France and Ireland forces to the right of centre have permitted themselves the luxury of two large parties in each case. Only Denmark has no *majoritaire* party on the moderate right.

Before the emergence of the labour/capital issue, Liberal parties were the major representatives of those seeking to change the *status quo*. In all Community countries except Ireland there are parties operating under the broad label of liberalism. Except in Italy these parties tend in political terms to straddle the Right/Left divide, although their policies are not invariably central to the actual state of controversy between the moderate right and the social democrats. National circumstances and historic battles are, however, more important than any common dogma in determining party programmes. Liberalism is also an available label for those who wish to protest against the dominance of the labour/capital issue. No Liberal party is *majoritaire* or even leading, although in Denmark the centre has tended to be electorally stronger than the moderate right. Liberal parties command electoral support of around 15 per cent in Denmark and the Benelux countries and 8 per cent in Germany, but in all five cases their pivotal position has given them disproportionate influence in government. Polarisation of French and Italian politics has substantially weakened those parties, whilst the real electoral strength of the British party is much harder to gauge.

Western European democracies are characterised by social democratic, moderate right and liberal parties. The only other type to be found at all universally in the nine is the communist. However, they are politically significant only in France and Italy where they command the allegiance of one-fifth and one-third of the electorate respectively. The historic divide between communism and social democracy has inevitably produced splinter parties which reject both whilst seeking to act as a bridge between them. This 'leftist' philosophy has sometimes been important in France and Italy when the Communists and Social Democrats have been particularly antagonistic,[6] but only in Denmark has it been a sufficient basis for a durable party with parliamentary representation. Anti-system parties on the Right have even less political significance. Over the last three decades the most important were the Gaullists in the French Fourth Republic, but since 1958 they have been effectively accommodated inside a system they created. The Italian neo-Fascist MSI with support from some 6 per cent of the electorate is now the only effective extreme right party. Although a party of protest, the much larger Danish Progressives are more difficult to classify in traditional Left/Right terms. Finally, although Western Europe is fairly rich in small parties and splinter groups espousing the interests of regional, linguistic and ethnic groups, it is only in Belgium and the United Kingdom that they have effective parliamentary representation.

It has not proved very easy to obtain reliable statistics for party membership. Excluding indirect membership through the trade unions in the United Kingdom, Italy has easily the highest total membership of political parties – over 4½ million, more than 10 per cent of the population aged 15 and over. On the same criterion Belgium ranks as the next most politicised country with half a million party members, 7 per cent of the population aged 15 and over. On the same basis about 5 per cent are party members in the United Kingdom and the Netherlands and about 2½ per cent in France and Germany. It would, though, be unwise to base too much on these comparisons, for the notion of party membership varies from country to country. Even allowing for the fact that voting is compulsory in Belgium, Italy and Luxembourg, it would be difficult to establish any clear correlation between levels of party membership and turn-out at elections, whilst voter identification and partisanship do not seem to be strikingly less in, say, France than in countries with higher membership figures. Normally left-wing parties seem able to enrol a higher percentage of their voters as members than do those of Right and Centre. This is clearly the case in Belgium, France, Germany and Italy: the Belgian Socialist and Italian Communist parties have recruited as many as 15 per cent of their voters into membership. On the other hand, ignoring indirect membership, the British Conservative Party has far more members than Labour, while in the Netherlands the combined Christian Democrat parties have more than Labour and in percentage terms both are exceeded by the Liberal vvd.

Financial strength is only partly a function of party membership: other factors such as commercial interests and state aid also play a considerable part. *Prima facie* one might expect right-wing parties to be relatively better-off financially, but this is not automatically the case. The right is certainly considerably financially stronger in France, Italy and the United Kingdom. On the other hand the spd finds it far easier to raise a large income through membership subscription and is far less dependent than its rivals on state aid; and the Dutch Labour Party has a greater income than any of its rivals. There is clearly some correlation between financial resources and electoral success, but the nature of the cause-and-effect relationship is much less clear.

At the end of this survey of parties in the countries of the European Community, two almost mutually contradictory questions may be posed. First, do political parties in practice fulfil tasks which are socially useful and which could not be carried out in any more convenient manner? Secondly, do they have any functions in terms of the future development of the European Community and do they show any capacity for fulfilling them? In answering the first, it is initially relevant to make the point that Western democracies are not governed by parties alone: alongside bureaucrats, economic interest groups and other factors which make up pluralist society, they are only one of the factors involved in the governmental process. The major contribution of political parties is to give government a creed or doctrinal colour. Through the medium of the electoral system parties translate the vague ideas and interests of the wider public into a relatively coherent government programme. Technocracy alone cannot offer a complete answer to the problems posed by interest aggregation and the distribution of resources. The major disutility of parties springs from the nature of their competition. In the contest for votes inner qualities may seem to matter less than external packaging and marketing. Appeals to the lowest common denominator of electoral interest may make it more difficult to solve certain problems such as inflation in the United Kingdom. It can be argued that systems in which elections determine the party complexion of government are peculiarly susceptible to this disutility. In the last analysis, though, the defence of political parties rests on the nature of government in the modern pluralist society. The removal of parties (hypothetical because unreal) would void government of their most overt political force and leave it at the mercy of rational economic factors alone. A dream for some, this is the ultimate nightmare for others!

Operating within the socially and culturally homogeneous countries of Western Europe, political parties have in at least a passive sense contributed towards political stability;[7] only in Germany are their postwar achievements arguably greater. Capacity for playing a more active role in the creation of a different political order seems much more open to question. Whilst it has been possible in the preceding pages to discern common patterns in the different party constellations of the various countries, it remains the case that the basic factors moulding virtually every party in Western Europe are national. This is even the case with Communist parties, especially the larger ones. Difficulties in agreeing even a minimum common programme for the omnipresent Social Democrats offer a further illustration of this proposition.[8] Direct elections have led to a plethora of apparently transnational party activity, but any argument that this now has a life of its own, independent of Community institutions, is at best unproven. Nevertheless, direct elections do represent a watershed. For the first time the European institutions have forced the separate national parties to work together outside the limited context of the institutions themselves (in this case the European Parliament). Even if co-operation between parties remains sketchy in the first instance, dynamic factors will be at work – for example, the likelihood of a single electoral system for the second direct elections. Elections for any area foster party activity and the existing political parties are exceedingly unlikely to wish to leave a vacuum for others to fill. Indeed, the adaptability and longevity of parties in Western Europe suggest that whilst initiatives in Community development are unlikely to come from this direction, parties will fulfill roles in new institutional frameworks which are extraneously (as far as they are concerned) created. In this Europe's parties will be true to themselves, for their outstanding characteristic has been not the ability to bring about change but rather the facility for cementing society.

## NOTES

1 The Liberal Party is obviously not anti-system in the same sense as other, newer parties discussed in this section. However, many of those voting Liberal in 1974 were doing so for the first time and consciously rejecting the two-party system of government.
2 See S. Henig and J. Pinder (eds), *European Political Parties* (London, PEP/ Allen & Unwin, 1969).

3 See, for example, the chapter on France, pp. 51–89.
4 In 1958 France switched from a broadly proportional list system to the present single-member two-ballot system.
5 See European Parliament, *Electoral Laws of Parliaments of the Member States of the European Communities* (Luxembourg, 1977).
6 As used in this chapter, the term 'Social Democrat' is an accurate labelling of the Italian Socialist Party. However, the name 'Social Democrat' is given in Italian politics to a small centre party, see above p. 138. Both are members of the Socialist International.
7 Cf. their role in Belgium; see above pp. 22–4.
8 See above pp. 283–7.

# Index